REVOLUTION AT THE ROOTS

Making Our Government Smaller, Better, and Closer to Home

WILLIAM D. EGGERS

&

JOHN O'LEARY

THE FREE PRESS

NEW YORK   LONDON   TORONTO   SYDNEY   TOKYO   SINGAPORE

Portions of chapter 1 originally appeared in the Spring 1993 issue of
Policy Review and the August/Spetember issue of *Reason* magazine.
Portions of the National Performance Review profile in chapter 2
originally appeared in the Spring 1994 issue of *Public Issues*, the
magazine of the Municipal Bond Industry Association, and in the
April 1994 issue of *Reason* magazine.

Library of Congress Cataloging-in-Publication Data

Eggers, William D.
   Revolution at the roots : making our government smaller, better
and closer to home / by William D. Eggers and John O'Leary.
      p.   cm.
   Includes index.
   ISBN 0-02-874027-0
   1. Administrative agencies—United States—Management.
2. Bureaucracy—United States.   3. Government productivity—United
States.   4. Waste in government spending—United States.
I. O'Leary, John   II. Title.
JK469 1995b
353'.0009'049—dc20   95-9212
                                                                          CIP

The Free Press
A Division of Simon & Schuster Inc.
1230 Avenue of the Americas
New York, N.Y. 10020

Printed in the United States of America

printing number
2 3 4 5 6 7 8 9 10

353.009
E29

To the memory of my parents,
and for Toph.

—W.D.E

To my parents, John and Eleanor,
for all their love and support.

—J.P.O.

TABLE OF CONTENTS

PREFACE AND ACKNOWLEDGMENTS

America's government institutions are beset by problems. From public schools to the Postal Service, from a destructive welfare system to a rising national debt, our political systems are in crisis. The failures of government are mirrored in the problems of our society. Change is imperative. But what sort of change is needed?

To answer this question, we looked beyond the Beltway to America's states, cities, and neighborhoods. Over the past several years, we have had the privilege of working closely with many of the public-sector innovators profiled in this book. Many of these officials sought out the Reason Foundation for advice before embarking on their reform agendas—whether in privatization, rightsizing, education reform, or other policy areas. We sat in on strategy meetings, gave briefings to city council members, and developed a series of "How-To" guides designed to streamline government. As more officials began implementing these reform ideas, they in turn educated us on the dynamics of achieving fundamental change in government. We interviewed hundreds of public officials at all levels of government, from governors and mayors to the people filling potholes, from state education officials to classroom teachers.

This interaction was key. It gave us an insider's view into the operation of state and local governments—warts and all. Some of our most important insights about government were garnered from line employees: social workers, garbage collectors, and sign makers.

We learned two important lessons. First, public employees are rarely bumbling bureaucrats, but are more often intelligent and dedicated workers. Second, with few exceptions public bureaucracies cannot function as efficiently as private-sector organizations—an important reason why governments should do only what they *have* to do.

Most books arguing for smaller government focus only on the waste and inefficiencies of government. While we do not hesitate to expose problems, we offer a positive vision for a smaller but better government for the 21st century. Our goal was to find the good and praise it, in the hopes that other governments would follow these pathbreaking examples. We attempted to keep in our minds at all times that better government was a means to a better society.

Many people contributed to making this book a reality. We first and foremost wish to thank the Reason Foundation, especially President Robert Poole and Vice President of Research Lynn Scarlett, who believed in us enough to support us during the research and writing of this book. Bob, one of the original pioneers on the subject of privatization, helped us to understand the subject inside and out. Lynn deserves special thanks for reading (and re-reading) the draft manuscript, providing input that substantially improved the final product.

Thanks also to our other colleagues at the Reason Foundation, who provided both encouragement and support. Special thanks go to Janet Beales on the education chapter, and Virginia Postrel on issues of economic growth and voluntarism. In addition, Donna Braunstein, Noah Hochman, and Raymond Ng deserve tremendous thanks for their diligent research assistance throughout.

We also wish to extend appreciation to the generous supporters of the Reason Foundation, who made this work possible. We would especially like to thank the Lilly Endowment, which has provided substantial support to the Reason Foundation Privatization Center for several years. Thanks in particular go to Gordon St. Angelo, our program officer, and Clay Robbins, the Lilly Endowment's president. We would also like to thank The John M. Olin Foundation and the J.M. Foundation for their generous financial support for the book project.

We wish we had the space to thank each of the more than

four hundred public officials, scholars, policy experts, and private-sector community builders we interviewed for this book. We learned more than we can express from their insights into the political realities of revolutionizing government. We are indebted to all the public officials we talked to, but would like to thank especially Charlie Baker, Chris Carmody, David Cohen, David Cooke, John Donlevy, Stephen Kelman, James Kerasiotes, Norm King, Ann Spray Kinney, John Kost, Mark Liedl, Linda Morrison, Dina Reinhard, Harvey Robbins, Mitch Roob, Tom Rose, Skip Stitt, Larry Townsend, Gerald Whitburn, and Steven Wilson. In addition, we would also like to thank the many mayors and governors who took time from their busy schedules to speak with us, some on more than one occasion.

Dozens of colleagues at other research organizations and academia helped us grapple with the complex issues covered in the book. In particular, we would like to acknowledge Barbara Anderson, John Fund, Steve Hayward, Heather Higgins, John Hood, Michael Joyce, Byron Lamm, Myron Magnet, John McKnight, Terry Moe, Steve Moore, Adam Myerson, Bill Niskanen, Grover Norquist, Marvin Olasky, Steve Postrel, Larry Reed, Doug Seay, Fred Siegal, Sam Staley, Louis Winnick and our colleagues around the country from the State Policy Network. In addition, those on the front-line of community building such as Charles Ballard, Ron Cote, Sister Connie Driscoll, Reverend Lee Earl, Jackie Gelb, Bill Lucas, Jo Ann Means, Sylvia Medina, Victor Trevino and others showed us that the spirit of voluntarism and self-governance that Alexis de Tocqueville observed is still thriving in America.

Two thinkers in particular deeply influenced our thinking in a number of areas. Social scientist James Q. Wilson of UCLA taught us to be skeptical of grand claims and helped us to understand the inherent limitations on government efficiency. Indianapolis Mayor Stephen Goldsmith, skilled both as a policy theorist and a manager, pushed the boundaries of public-sector efficiency and demonstrated the possibilities of radical change.

As with any such work, the final product and all its shortcomings are entirely our own. The input of those listed above is not intended to imply agreement with the conclusions in the book.

During the many months of working long hours, we have each been supported by our friends and families. To those long neglected, we hope the finished product makes up for it. Special thanks to Kathleen Roever, who read the manuscript and helped one of us through writer's block.

We also wish to thank our agents, Lynn Chu and Glen Hartley, who believed in a pair of rookie authors and who gave us critical early advice regarding the scope of the book. Thanks also to Bruce Nichols, our superb editor at the Free Press, who understood from the beginning exactly what we were trying to do with the book and kept us on track throughout the grueling process. We consider ourselves fortunate to have worked with such a professional team.

I

FIRST PRINCIPLES

CHAPTER 1

A NEW ERA OF
REVOLUTIONARY CHANGE

Good government is not an oxymoron. But it certainly is an elusive goal. It is possible for our government to promote the well-being of its citizens—but it is far from easy. It is much easier to be cynical about government, to be scornful of politics, or to complain about what's wrong. It is much harder to change things for the better.

But change is necessary. American government has grown inimical to the interests of its citizens. Instead of working for us, government has been working against us. In previous times, it was the American people—whose task has always been to act as the stewards of the government—who steered their political leaders down the road to renewal. It is time for America's citizens to play this vital role once again.

America, after all, started with a tax revolt. When a bunch of angry colonists dressed up as Indians and dumped British tea into Boston Harbor, they established an American tradition. Americans still aren't shy about letting their leaders know when they've reached their limit.

There needs to be "a gentle revolution in this country from the voters who just say, 'We're mad as hell, we're not going to take this anymore,'" said Johanna Lockhart, a 50-year-old Houston voter a few weeks before the November 1994 elections. "It's got to come from the voters."[1]

It did. A gentle revolution is exactly what took place on November 8, 1994. More philosophical than partisan, the voters were sending an unmistakable message to Washington: we want smaller, better government. Democrats, who caught the brunt of the voters' discontent, say they got the message. "A lot has changed since yesterday," said a shell-shocked Bill Clinton the day after the election. Clinton said the public was saying, "'We don't think government can solve all the problems,'" adding, "I think they want a smaller government . . ."[2]

The 1994 elections were historic. Voters gave Republicans control of Congress (for the first time in 40 years) and put Republican governors into office in 30 states. Prior to 1994, in exactly three states Republicans held control of the governorship and both houses of the legislature. After November 8, 15 states were fully under Republican leadership.

In 1992, Democrats were given the reins of government, then headed the wagon in the wrong direction: national service, a national crime bill, national education goals, and, almost, national health care. This was not the New Democrat platform voters had backed in 1992. Winning back the voters' trust will require fundamental changes in the party's philosophy. "If we Democrats don't reduce taxes and spending, our party is going to be extinct," says Representative Rob Andrews (D-N.J.). "The issue before Democrats today is whether we change or die."[3] Republicans, for their part, know they must deliver on their promises of a smaller government closer to the people.

The vote of 1994 shocked many. Washington insiders and the media were blindsided by the limited government sentiment expressed by voters. But if they had listened less to the Sunday-morning pundits and more to the 99 percent of Americans who live *outside* the Beltway, they wouldn't have been surprised in the least. Like the Boston Tea Party and other voter revolts, the 1994 elections reflected the deep, building frustration the American people have felt with their government for several years. The 1994 election was the culmination of years of growing anger.

THE VOTERS GROW RESTLESS

Former Connecticut Governor Lowell Weicker—a Republican turned Independent—got an early taste of Americans' growing anger with "politics as usual" in October 1991. During the previous year's gubernatorial campaign, Weicker had pledged not to enact a state income tax. Once in office, Weicker abided by this pledge for almost a full month. He then proposed a 4.5 percent income tax, and after three unsuccessful attempts rammed it through the legislature. (In the spirit of the day, he was subsequently awarded the John F. Kennedy "Profiles in Courage Award.")

One night soon after the tax vote, the new governor visited the New London Opera House. Weicker was to participate in the evening's program by reciting the poem "Ode to the Working Man." When he stepped out of his limousine, he was greeted by a raucous mob of nearly 1,000 working men and women—angry tax protestors, every one.

Upon seeing Weicker, the unruly crowd burst through police barricades and chased their governor until he escaped into the Opera House.[4] The tax protestors waited for the end of the program to get another chance at Weicker, but the governor eluded the picketers by sneaking out a rear exit. As his limousine sped away, it was chased down the street by hundreds of angry taxpayers. "It was like watching a scene from the French Revolution," observed Joe Markley, executive director of the Connecticut Taxpayers Committee.[5]

The picketers at the Opera House were the diehards left over from the largest political gathering in state history, a tax protest that drew over 50,000 angry voters. Banners reading "DUMP WEICKER THE TAX HIKER," and "CUT GOVERNMENT FAT, START WITH LOWELL WEICKER" provide a hint of the crowd's mood.

After four years in office, Weicker chose not to seek reelection. This was probably a wise choice. In 1994, voters chose as

Weicker's replacement Republican John Rowland, who was elected after promising to repeal Weicker's hated income tax.

Weicker was not the only politician to pay a heavy price for breaking a tax pledge to the voters in the early 1990s.

After making a campaign pledge not to increase taxes, in 1990 New Jersey Governor Jim Florio, a Democrat, enacted the largest tax increase in state history, a $2.8 billion hike.[6] Voters never forgot Florio's broken pledge. Governor Florio once joked that reading bumper stickers would cause visitors to New Jersey to think his first name was "Dump." After seeing dozens of incumbent Democrats purged from the state legislature in 1991, Florio lost his own reelection bid in 1993. His replacement? Republican Christine Todd Whitman, who promised to cut New Jersey income taxes by 30 percent in her first term.

Voter anger with pledge-breaking, tax-raising politicians has been enthusiastically bipartisan. Campaigning in 1988, Republican George Bush told voters, "Read My Lips—No New Taxes!" In 1990, he approved one of the largest tax increases in United States history. By the end of 1992, George was spending more time with his grandchildren, defeated by a Democrat who (surprise!) had promised middle-class tax cuts.

Astute observers might have noticed a pattern developing. Astute observers might have suggested that government should tone down the spending. Astute observers might have concluded that an elite ruling class had lost touch with voters.

Astute observers were in short supply. The mainstream media concluded that *voters*, not politicians, were the problem. "Washington Really Is In Touch. We're the Problem," declared a *New York Times* headline a few weeks before the 1994 elections. On the very same day, *The Washington Post* ran a story headlined: "You Think Congress is Out-of-Touch? Look in the Mirror, Voters; The Trouble Starts With You."[7]

The source of all this "trouble" graced the cover of *Time* magazine way back in September 1992: The Angry Voter. Almost one in four Angry Voters in the 1992 presidential election rejected the political establishment and chose outsider Ross Perot. Between 1991 and 1994, Angry Voters in 22 states passed term limits, which succeeded in every state where they appeared on the ballot.

Beltway insiders were annoyed by these Angry Voters who were upsetting the apple cart. They wanted voters to stop being so unreasonable. House Speaker Tom Foley, for example, sued his own constituents in Washington state to overturn their vote for term limits. (Voters soon limited Foley's terms manually, the first time a seated speaker was defeated since 1860.)

Looking across the American landscape, we find plenty of cause for justifiable anger. The Angry Voter is not just upset about tax rates—although taxes serve as an important focus of rebellion. The Angry Voter is the assembly-line worker in Detroit whose neighborhood is racked by violence. The Angry Voter is the single mother in Milwaukee disgusted with the public schools. The Angry Voter is the entrepreneur of Silicon Valley choking on a steady diet of high taxes, lawsuits, and regulatory red tape. The Angry Voter is America's common man, disenchanted with a political system seen as swallowing up taxes and giving too little in return.

Dumping tea into the harbor is one way to express discontent, but there are others. Angry Voters in many states are using the referendum process to limit government spending. Since 1992, taxpayer-sponsored amendments have passed in Arizona, Colorado, Oklahoma, and Nevada. These states now require either a supermajority vote of the legislature or voter approval for any tax increases.

Some politicians see these measures as irresponsible. Most taxpayers see politicians as irresponsible, and compare these laws to locking up the liquor cabinet with an alcoholic in the house. Either way the practical effect is the same: tax increases will be much harder to come by in the future. "The role of legislators has changed," says Oklahoma Senate President Pro Tem Bob Cullison. "We'll meet and cut services. There will never be any more money."[8]

Politicians used to be able to scare through a tax increase by putting a much-needed service on the chopping block. Not any more. In the spring of 1993, Angry Voters in Kalkaska, Michigan, shut down their schools ten weeks early when they rejected a property tax increase. "The property-tax revolt and the school battle are part of the same basic issue—the people have lost faith in the ability of the public sector to do its job," said one Kalkaska teacher.[9]

American discontent with government is at an all-time high. In a November 1993 Harris poll, 67 percent of respondents said that they had "reached the breaking point" on taxes; a similar number told a New York Times/CBS poll that government creates more problems than it solves; two-thirds of Americans also think government is "almost always wasteful and inefficient."[10]

The League of California Cities in 1993 held a number of focus groups to get the public's view of government. *Without interviewers even asking the question*, most people volunteered within minutes that government wastes money. "There was not a single individual who believed government did not waste money, and a lot of the commentary wasn't particularly polite," reports the League.[11]

Angry Voters can be heard every day on the nation's talk-radio programs. Rush Limbaugh has become a megacelebrity by bashing government failures. Jerry Williams, Boston's top talk-show host, frequently interrupts his show to play a memorable segment from the movie "Network": "I'm mad as hell, and I'm not going to take it anymore!"

While some demagogues tap into voter discontent as an end in itself, much of the anger is justified. There is an important difference, however, between anger and hatred. Democratic Senator Barbara Boxer quotes a saying from St. Augustine: "Hope has two lovely daughters, Anger and Courage; Anger at the way things are and the courage to change them." With courage, today's anger can be put to constructive ends as a catalyst for needed change.

"To those who see this public attitude as disappointing or

dangerous, I would point out that just such a mood was at the heart of the American experiment in self-government and personal liberty," said New York Governor George Pataki in his 1995 inaugural address. "Discontent with punitive taxation and the excessive bureaucracy and an oppressive government was exactly the emotion that put the spark to our own revolution and the democratic way of life it gave us ... much good can come from the people's determination to see government as their servant and not their master."[12]

Grassroot drives for term limits, tax limits, and a balanced-budget amendment give an indication of the direction voters want government to take. But these blunt measures are only means to an end. We believe the American people want a smaller government because they think it will result in a better society.

What do Americans want? We believe most Americans want government closer to home; they want more responsibility for their own lives; they want an end to the needless intrusion of government into their private lives and businesses; they want a government that treats their tax money with respect. In short, Americans are demanding revolutionary change. The good news is that the revolution has already begun.

THE REVOLUTIONARIES

Beyond the Beltway, in the towns, cities, and states of America, vanguard politicians have been pushing for radical change. Years before Washington got the wake-up call of 1994, these leaders began putting an end to politics as usual. These revolutionaries come in all sizes. They are Democrats, Republicans, and Independents. They are building the models for 21st-century government: the changes they are undertaking are creating the most fundamental transformation of government since the Progressive Era ushered out Boss Tweed and Tammany Hall.

The man in the street must drive the transformation to better government, but all revolutions have their leaders. In government, inertia is the rule, change the exception. Even with rising voter discontent, positive change requires a strong-willed agent of change, a leader with a vision of where government needs to be in the next century and how to get there. Without such leaders, the chances of achieving dramatic innovation in the public sector are slim. In this book we will meet dozens of innovators and visionaries who are overcoming these odds.

Governors, such as John Engler of Michigan, William Weld of Massachusetts, Tommy Thompson of Wisconsin, and New Jersey's Christine Todd Whitman, have been streamlining state government. These and other leaders have started the process of doing more with less by lowering taxes, shrinking the bureaucracy, and making state government competitive. They have also stood up to entrenched interest groups to push through historic reforms in education and welfare.

In the future, America's governors will take on greater importance. In part because of technology, we are witnessing a worldwide trend toward decentralized decision-making, in business as well as in politics. In the new Era of Radical Devolution, power will shift from Washington, D.C., to state capitals. No longer will the federal government issue mandates controlling everything from water quality to classroom standards to speed limits. Increasingly, states will call the shots on welfare, transportation, environmental issues, property rights, and a host of other issues.

Even if Congress drags its feet in this process, the governors have a backup plan to force the federal government's hands. Led by federalist firebrands such as Arizona's Fife Symington and Virginia's George Allen, the nation's increasingly rebellious states have crafted strategies—including several constitutional amendments—to seize control back from Washington and restore a proper balance to our federal system of government. The 1994 election may have accelerated the process, but the shift toward radical devolution has been coming for some time. As Ronald Reagan predicted in 1988, "The 21st century will be the century of the states."

The shift of power is likely to occur at every level of American society, as individuals demand greater control of their lives and their government. Parents want control of their schools, and neighborhoods want to take back their streets. In fact, many of the revolutionaries in this book are not politicians at all. They are courageous leaders of community groups who are rebuilding broken community in some of America's most troubled neighborhoods.

The historic changes in America's political climate are driven in part by the alarming decline in national well-being. Nowhere is this decline more serious than in America's cities. Fed up with high taxes, high crime, and bad schools, urban voters are increasingly turning to a new breed of innovative, business-minded mayors to run their cities. Leaders such as Philadelphia's Edward Rendell, Cleveland's Michael White, Jersey City's Bret Schundler, San Diego's Susan Golding, and New York City's Rudolf Giuliani have rejected the "tax, spend and complain" politics of the past. No longer will every social woe bring forth a new government program and every budget shortfall a tax increase. Instead, these visionaries are "rightsizing" City Hall by privatizing services, cutting the work force, and devolving some services and decision-making back down to the neighborhood level.

For openers, let's look at just two examples of this new breed of leaders, the mayors of two very different midwestern cities. One a Republican, one a Democrat, these leaders offer a hint of America's political future.

> *Opening up city hall to competition must be the fundamental aspect of change.*
>
> *Indianapolis Mayor Stephen Goldsmith*

The Indianapolis Department of Parks and Recreation had a problem: the end of the fiscal year was fast approaching and the department still had money in its budget. The administrator didn't want to return the money to the general fund, because doing so would likely lead to next year's budget being cut by at least that amount.

Rather than risk it, the department administrator went on a shopping spree, buying *40 tons* of chalk. A few months later, the mountain of chalk—enough to line a baseball field with 101 miles between the bases—was useless, because the department had switched to spray paint for lining ball fields. The great chalk mountain stands as a testament to the perverse incentives that government officials often face.[13]

But the purchase of 1,600 50-pound bags of chalk also offers hope, for when it was brought to his attention, Indianapolis Mayor Stephen Goldsmith didn't dress down park officials for wasting taxpayer money. Instead, he issued a press release. Rather than taking the easy route and blaming a bureaucrat, Goldsmith took his own administration to task. The 47-year-old Republican mayor said, "The problem is they are trapped in a system that punishes initiative, ignores efficiency, and rewards big spenders."[14]

Changing that system is what Indianapolis's mayor is all about. To survive in the 21st century, Goldsmith believes Indianapolis and other big-city governments must become smaller and more efficient and foster an environment of "chaos." Job classifications, descriptions, and hiring forms will have to be tossed.

Since his inauguration in January 1992, the workaholic mayor has put his ideas into practice at a blistering pace that has left little time for building consensus or indulgences like sleep (though when he fell to below five hours of sleep a night he found it to be "counterproductive"). "We have only four years of our lives to make the city better for everyone in Indianapolis," says Goldsmith, who is unable to sit through an hour-long interview without sneaking impatient peeks at the e-mail messages coming across his laptop computer screen.[15]

Mayor Goldsmith's revolution involves downsizing, deregulation, measuring performance and productivity, introducing competition into service delivery, eliminating waste, and decentralizing government by devolving authority to neighborhoods. The mayor regularly assigns reading to his top staffers, including the 800-plus-page tome *Liberation Management*, by management guru Tom Peters. Staff meetings move easily from garbage collection to political philosophy. His relentless drive has led one local writer to refer to him as "Robomayor."

Goldsmith has gained a national reputation for having the most ambitious privatization program of any large city in the United States, but he claims he doesn't have a privatization program; he calls it a competition program. The distinction: his goal is not to privatize for its own sake but to break up the government monopoly. As long as there's competition, Goldsmith doesn't care whether a private firm or a city department delivers the service. "There is no great value in and of itself for privatization, as contrasted to the competitive process," says the mayor.

To identify competition opportunities and drive radical change in government, Goldsmith created a private-sector advisory group called SELTIC (Service, Efficiency, and Lower Taxes for Indianapolis Commission). SELTIC was not your typical task force that produces reports that go unread. An all-volunteer cast, SELTIC has yet to produce a single report—nor does it plan to. It is interested only in results.

SELTIC's chairman described the commission's work as "antitrust for government." It examined everything the city did and asked two questions. First, should government even be involved? If the answer was no, SELTIC recommended that the city get out of the service. "Doing things more efficiently is not the ultimate end of government," says Mayor Goldsmith. "Sometimes, government should just get out of the area."

If the answer to the first question was yes, a second question was asked: how can we make the service subject to competition from the private sector? Over 60 city services have been opened to competition, saving Indianapolis nearly $30 million a year. Mayor Goldsmith's ultimate goal is revolutionary:

expose nearly all of city government to competition—including parts of the police and fire departments—by creating markets, both internal and external, for every public service possible.

What should 21st-century city hall look like? As Mayor Goldsmith ponders the question, you can almost hear the gears turning. "You'll have obviously smaller government, more outsourcing [privatization], dramatically increased neighborhood-based service provision, and a much higher percentage of people involved in protecting and developing their own areas. Government will act more as a skilled purchasing director, rather than a service provider." In other words, Angry Voters will join with local politicians, solving their problems by themselves.

> *You can't build a city on pity.*
> Milwaukee Mayor John Norquist

Milwaukee is a city famous not only for beer, but for a welfare-state tradition rooted in the city's German, Scandinavian, and East European heritage. Its citizens have long expressed great confidence in government's ability: many of Milwaukee's mayors this century have identified themselves as socialists.

By the mid-1980s, however, Milwaukee was ready for a change. Big and generous government had come with a price tag—high taxes and a costly welfare system associated with high crime, family breakdown, and neighborhood decay. As in other cities, rising taxes, crime rates, and deteriorating schools were driving businesses and middle-income residents to the suburbs. Milwaukee could not afford to spend itself to prosperity.

In 1988, Milwaukee elected a new Democratic mayor, and ever since he has been weaning the city's citizens from the notion that government can solve all their problems. A former state senator, John Norquist was elected at the age of 38, and like many of the revolutionaries transforming the public sector,

Norquist defies easy ideological labels. He had earned a repu- tation in the state senate as a member of the left wing of the Democratic Party.

Mayor Norquist, however, has always been skeptical of big government and has grown more so in his tenure as mayor. Liberal on some issues, he likes the idea of school choice, favors a low, flat federal income tax, and wants to abolish the welfare system. "This federal welfare system—both for what it does and what it fails to do—is such a failure that we should stop trying to reform it. We should scrap it," he says.[16]

Norquist is a rarity among urban politicians: an independent thinker who comes to his policy views seemingly without regard to the political consequences. He calls money from Washington "the gift that stops giving" and says cities would be better off with zero federal involvement. "Cities are natural economic organisms," he told us. "They're like coral reefs. They create markets. They create businesses. That's been their role throughout the history of civilization. The federal govern- ment's programs—by and large—have tended to undermine the natural value of cities."[17]

With the motto "You can't build a city on pity," Norquist set about dealing with each of the city's major problems. To keep down the cost of living in the city, Mayor Norquist cut proper- ty tax rates in each of his first six years in office. He successful- ly opposed a $366 million spending referendum for schools, arguing that higher property taxes would drive people from the city—as had occurred in Detroit and Philadelphia.

Like Goldsmith, Norquist understands that most of the problems within government arise from the system, not the employees. He set about radically altering the incentives for Milwaukee city officials by introducing a new budget that does something quite remarkable for government: it rewards good management and makes officials accountable for achieving their goals. The police department is judged according to how well it reduces the crime rate, for example, not according to the size of its budget or the number of police officers.[18] The result?

Norquist has kept Milwaukee's spending growth below the rate of inflation while maintaining service.

Together with crime and taxes, poor-quality education is a major cause of the flight of people and jobs from inner-city neighborhoods. Mayor Norquist minces no words when he describes the failure of Milwaukee's public schools: "What we have is a school-finance monopoly that is not helping public school children, is suppressing quality, is not customer-oriented, and is overly bureaucratic."[19]

As with the welfare system, Mayor Norquist argues that tinkering around the edges with education reform is not enough— that the current public school system should be "scrapped." He has supported the state-funded pilot program in Milwaukee that enables low-income students to attend private schools. Norquist is a strong proponent of a plan to expand the voucher program, now serving only about 830 students, to the entire city and to allow religious schools to participate. He has also supported a private voucher program that enables more than 2,000 low-income children a year to attend private schools, including religious ones. "Government monopolies have proven not to work very well and public education is too precious, education of our young people is too important, to have a monopoly system," says the maverick mayor.[20]

REINVENTING GOVERNMENT: ADDRESSING THE SYMPTOMS, NOT THE CAUSE

Meanwhile, back inside the Beltway, Washington was attempting in its own febrile fashion to grapple with a dysfunctional federal leviathan. The time seemed right for the release of a report.

"The government is broken, and we intend to fix it," said President Clinton in September 1993, announcing the release of Vice President Al Gore's report on how to "reinvent" the federal government. "Make no mistake about this," Clinton told us. "This is one report that will not gather dust in a warehouse."

Clinton and Gore stood together on the lawn of the White House, posing for cameras in front of a forklift full of federal regulations. Clinton called it a "revolution," stressing that reinventing government would be a top priority of his administration.

To promote the report, the normally reserved Al Gore even appeared on the David Letterman show, offering charming anecdotes of bureaucratic inefficiency. The most famous of these was an elaborate specification for buying an ashtray—more accurately, an "Ash Receiver, Tobacco—Desk Type." To qualify as a federal ashtray, this ash receiver must break into no more than 35 pieces after "striking with a hammer in successive blows of increasing severity until breakage occurs." Who says government work is dull? This material was perfect for Letterman's "Stupid Government Tricks."

The federal government's well-publicized decision to reinvent itself followed in the wake of a similarly named movement at the state and local level. Prompted by fiscal pressures and inspired by the 1992 best-selling *Reinventing Government* by David Osborne (who played a key role in the federal reinvention effort) and Ted Gaebler, public officials throughout the United States were already working to make government more efficient. These efforts to improve government should be commended. Valuable improvements have taken place. But the premise of the reinventing government movement is fundamentally flawed. Like a mansion built on weak and shifting sands, the reinventing government paradigm is a beautiful edifice that lacks a sound foundation.

The Gore–Osborne–Gaebler approach is built on the assumption that the central problem of governments is "not what they do, but how they operate." They dismiss any examination of what government ought to do, deriding such debates as "secondary." But as Angry Voters know, governments have taken on many tasks they shouldn't be doing in the first place. An examination of the purpose of government should be the *primary* concern of anyone interested in better government.

Mindless pursuit of government efficiency risks repeating the quandary of "The Bridge on the River Kwai." In that movie, the epitome of British efficiency, Alec Guinness, a WWII officer in a Japanese prison camp, organizes his men to build a railroad bridge in a remote jungle, a difficult task accomplished only with great effort and intelligence. He becomes so caught up constructing the bridge, however, that he forgets it is intended to serve the purposes of his enemy. Only when American William Holden dies in an attempt to destroy the bridge does Guinness's character realize the enormity of his mistake. In the same way, governments have in certain cases worked hard to improve programs that shouldn't exist at all, streamlining programs that do more harm than good.

For example, if giving money to drug addicts with no strings attached is harmful—which it is—then the $1.4 billion a year the federal government hands out each year through its Supplemental Security Income (SSI) and Social Security Disability Insurance (SSDI) programs to a quarter-million adults, most of whom are alcoholics or drug addicts, doesn't make sense. Doing this efficiently is even worse.

This is not intended to dismiss the many valuable management strategies of *Reinventing Government*; many of the techniques it discusses are useful tools for improving government. The book also deserves praise for inspiring public officials to become more innovative in approaching their jobs. But better public management strategies are only a small part of the change needed to improve government. Efficient operation is a necessary but not sufficient attribute of good government. The Nazi war machine was a ruthlessly efficient engine of human destruction, but it was not good government.

The central problem with government today is that it attempts to do too much. In trying to be all things to all people, government has grown out of control in the past 30 years.

Striving to do everything, government winds up doing nothing well. The federal government sells helium, produces puppet shows, delivers mail, immunizes children, owns a Rural Telephone Bank, and, while $4 trillion in debt, is planning a manned mission to Mars. Al Gore's ashtray specification is just one of the ways the federal government keeps busy. Federal regulations relating to the sale of cabbage run to 26,911 words.[21]

To proceed on the path toward better government, we must rekindle the debate over the purpose of government, both among public officials and the public at large. "This is an historic time," says Ohio Governor George Voinovich. "The issue is what should government do and what level of government should do it."

UNINTENDED CONSEQUENCES

Consider the federal government's attempt to solve America's social ills. After adjusting for inflation, total social spending increased 547 percent between 1960 and 1990 (while our population grew by just 41 percent). What do we have to show for 30 years of unparalleled government generosity? A five-fold increase in violent crime; a fourfold increase in births to single mothers; a tripling in the fraction of children living in households that depend on welfare; and a doubling in the rate of teenage suicide.[22] Inefficiency isn't the problem here. Rather, the government's approach has had unforeseen consequences that frustrated its good intentions, harming the very groups that were supposed to benefit. Many of these social programs were flawed in their conception, not just their execution.

Through its vast expansion, the federal government has often displaced, and thereby weakened, the elements that make a community strong. Especially in the cities, we need to strengthen the social infrastructure of our country, including family, churches, and neighborhood and community groups.

To renew America, power must be transferred from Washington and returned to the local level. Government must demand that individuals take responsibility for their own lives.

Government everywhere exhibits the same sort of problems: too much centralization, too much bureaucracy, not enough input from the people who receive the service. The Chicago public school system—one of the worst in the nation—requires 3,300 administrators to oversee its 410,000 students. In the same city, the Catholic archdiocese educates 124,000 students for about half the per-pupil cost, and employs only 36 central administrators.

The problems of government are not unique. Any organization can become too large, take on too many missions, or neglect its customers. Similar problems cropped up at many bloated American companies in the 1980s. U.S. Steel, for example, failed in the market despite having an enormous corporate headquarters staffed by hundreds of highly paid administrators. It was outperformed by its competitor Nucor, which oversees its $1.6 billion steel empire with a central headquarters that has just 22 employees.

In the past 20 years, corporate America has undergone a revolution. In the 1970s, the common wisdom declared that bigger was better. Companies that were successful with one product often moved into different industries in the quest for profit. Abandoning their core business, these formerly successful companies had their attention diverted as they tried to make an assortment of products for an assortment of markets. With bigness came bureaucracy. These once dynamic firms lost their ability to innovate. They lost touch with their customers' needs. They lost their profitability under the weight of layers of middle management. Despite having tremendous resources at their disposal, they couldn't seem to do anything right. Company leaders faced a stark choice: change the way they do business or go out of business.

The transformation of corporate America, though painful, has produced a streamlining of operations previously believed impossible. According to one estimate, America's Fortune 500 companies have stripped away four million jobs since 1980.[23] Along with the downsizing has come a renewed profitability and vitality.

American business is now leaner and more competitive, but America's public bureaucracies remain bloated, centralized, and resistent to change. "We're in the middle of a revolution here in the way organizations work," acknowledged President Clinton in late 1994. "And government is still behind the eight ball." Government needs to concentrate on doing fewer things better. Though resistance to change is the hallmark of all large organizations, the current crisis in government means that anything short of fundamental change in the public sector is no longer a viable option.

BOTTOM-UP REVOLUTION

No matter who is in power, American renewal will not come from Washington. In fact, it is crucial to realize that the problems of government cannot be solved by putting "the right people" in charge. The problems of government are systemic. Improvements will require systemic changes.

One of the remarkable aspects of the American democratic experience is that our form of government allows us to reshape our nation. Improvement is possible, though change is never easy. The abolition of slavery, women's suffrage, and civil rights represent major steps forward. In every case, it was citizens that led the charge for change, altering our political institutions to reflect the realities of the changing times.

In like manner, our government today is in need of a dramatic, fundamental change of course. We need to reverse the centralization and expansion of government that has marked the past 60 years. As with other such changes, it must be led by citizens ready to carry out the responsibility of democracy and public leaders ready to carry out the responsibility of governing.

We have met many revolutionaries in our travels across the country. We believe they represent the future of government in America. In this book we present a portrait of the revolution, in two major parts: its principles and its applications.

CHAPTER 2

FOCUSING ON CORE FUNCTIONS

When government tries to be everything to everybody it becomes nothing to anybody.

Chicago Mayor Richard M. Daley

Betting parlors are illegal in New York City—except those that are run *by* New York City. Despite an official stance that otherwise regards gambling as villainous, in 1970 New York went into the off-track betting (OTB) business.[1]

New York's OTB was touted as a big revenue raiser. When it was first established, officials estimated it would yield profits of $200 million a year. But despite enjoying a legal monopoly, the city hasn't done very well playing the ponies.[2] By 1994, OTB's operating deficit had reached $5.3 million. During his election campaign, New York City Mayor Rudolph W. Giuliani called OTB "the only bookie operation in the world to lose money."[3]

Considering that organized crime enjoys a steady revenue stream from illegal bookmaking, one might expect a legal monopoly on gambling to be a sure bet. But OTB's management is not exactly made up of racing industry experts. A senior advisor to Giuliani calls it "a dumping ground for patronage employees."[4] Top managers at OTB ride around in chauffeur-driven cars, and some have been known to take jaunts to Monte Carlo and St. Croix at taxpayer expense.

New York's OTB treats its employees better than its customers. In Las Vegas, sports bettors enjoy large-screen TVs, comfy chairs, and free drinks. New York's OTB offices look like Soviet bus stations. Gesturing at the surroundings, one frequent customer describes the ambience: "Take a look around. No refreshments. No food. No smoking. And nowhere to sit down—unless you want to park yourself knee deep in dirt on the floor." What's more, OTB's product is second-rate compared to what gamblers can get from their bookies; it pays out only 76 percent of the handle, while bookies pay out 81 percent.[5] Where does OTB's money go? Salaries, mostly. "Our labor costs are 75 percent of our total costs," says Robert Palumbo, OTB's executive vice president. "It's absurd to be paying betting clerks nearly $30 an hour and branch managers nearly $60 an hour on Sundays."[6]

New York City is the mecca of big government. The city has one full-time employee for every 17.6 residents. By comparison, the resident/employee ratio is 53 in Philadelphia, 70 in Los Angeles, and 107 in San Diego.[7] New York City owns and operates two radio stations, one television station, several golf courses, a community-college system, uncounted parking garages, hundreds of gas stations, daycare centers, two airports, and a four-star hotel.

New York also has an unmatched municipal presence in the health care industry. The Big Apple owns and operates over a dozen hospitals. New York City's hospitals employ more city employees than the *total number of city employees* in Boston, San Diego, Seattle, and Cleveland *combined.*[8]

There is scarcely a human enterprise in which New York's government is not involved. At the Department of Consumer Affairs, 323 employees are involved in such critical efforts as monitoring delicatessens to make sure they don't charge people for the plastic trays that hold their potato salad.[9] With so many agencies, New York often finds itself working at cross purposes. The tiny City Arts Commission, with a budget of just $212,000, enjoys veto power over all city building projects. It once held up approval of 19 public minischools during a classroom space crisis because the minischools' designs "were not artistically favorable."[10]

The city does a lot of things, and it does a lot of things poorly. Despite the city's enormous staff and high spending, the streets aren't safe to walk, the roads aren't safe to drive, and the hospitals aren't a great place to get sick—at least, not according to New Yorkers. Sixty-two percent of New Yorkers rate criminal safety as poor; 53 percent believe street, road, and highway maintenance is poor; and 37 percent rate the city's health care services as poor.[11] This isn't simply coincidence. The proliferation of activities distracts attention from the basics.

The Radio Wars are a good example. Early in 1994, Mayor Giuliani casually mentioned that it wouldn't be a bad idea if Curtis Sliwa, a campaign supporter, were given a talk show on the city's radio station, WNYC. Station president Thomas B. Morgan, who depends on the city for $1.7 million each year, cancelled several popular shows including "Talk of the Nation" to give Mr. Sliwa an afternoon talk slot. *The New York Times* complained that "the Mayor is getting away with using the station to dispense patronage."[12] As with *Pravda*, government ownership of the media makes such mischief possible. *The New York Times*, however, steadfastly opposed selling the station. Why? Perhaps the *Times* staff enjoys the programming on WNYC, which leans towards classical music and National Public Radio programs. Defending the existence of WNYC, the *Times* notes that the almost $50 million such a sale could bring the city would be "nowhere near enough to make much difference in a budget gap measured in billions," and the station's annual subsidy is "a $1.7 million flyspeck in the $32 billion municipal budget."[13] That's a *$1.7 million* flyspeck.

FIRST ASK THE RIGHT QUESTION

Before asking how New York City's gambling operation can be redesigned, reengineered, or reinvented, we should ask a more fundamental question: should government be doing this at all?

This ought to be the first question asked of any government

activity. Reducing *what* government does—focusing on core tasks—is essential to improving *how* government operates. Low-priority activities drain away resources and distract public managers from their central duties. New York City's government won't radically improve as long as it tries to be everything to everybody.

Harvey Robins is a veteran of New York City government, having directed numerous social service agencies and its Office of Operations. Robins, a self-described liberal, has grown disillusioned with the giant, unwieldy bureaucracy for which he once worked. "I believe in an activist government, but a government that also says we are going to do fewer things well," says Robins. "What does this mean? It means choosing, making the hard decisions, and setting priorities."[14] We heard from countless people like Harvey Robins, people who believe in government yet know that for government to improve it must learn how to say no. John Franco, a 30-year veteran of Los Angeles city government, told us that unless the focus of reinventing government shifts, "we will all end up doing lots of inessential things very efficiently."[15]

Governments across America operate all kinds of programs far removed from their core missions. Dallas and Nashville run classical radio stations; Denver and numerous other cities manage botanical gardens; 18 states are involved in selling liquor; Rye, New York, operates an amusement park; nearby Greenburgh runs a dating service; Jacksonville, Florida, runs a do-it-yourself canning plant (it's strictly BYOF—Bring Your Own Fruit); dozens of cities operate zoos; and the State of New York owns and operates ski resorts, 64 college campuses, and a cheese museum.

It's time for a rational reassessment of whether governments need to be involved in all these activities. Unfortunately, the reinventing government movement has so far ignored what government does to focus on how it operates. The result is that many public managers are hard at work reinventing activities that government shouldn't be doing at all.

Learning from Business about the Core Concept

When governments downsize, they usually do it the easy way, by cutting staff and expenses across the board. Each department is asked to perform the same tasks but with fewer personnel. Such cutbacks are usually undone as soon as tax revenues begin flowing back into government coffers. Just as the effects of many diets disappear as soon as they are declared successful and abandoned, such short-term reductions usually have little long-term benefit. What is required is a lifestyle change. How does the private sector operate when dollars are short? By eliminating unprofitable activities. In the 1970s, there was a rash of corporate-giant "diversifications." Companies believed they could minimize risk by involving themselves in so many markets that they would be immune to cyclical downturns in any one of them.

This premise was flawed, and companies discovered themselves to be incapable of efficiently managing product lines that they didn't understand. Now, even in flush times, a competent CEO constantly reevaluates everything his or her company does, asking:

- Does the activity fit our strategic plan?
- Does the activity produce more value for the customer than it consumes in resources?
- If not, why are we doing this?

Crucial to corporate downsizing is deciding what the company does well. A smart company focuses on the value it can deliver to its business partners, including its customers, suppliers, and employees. Management expert Robert H. Waterman, Jr., tells of this self-evaluation at Rubbermaid:

The idea of making mailboxes would crop up on potential new products lists at Rubbermaid, only to be dropped like a hot potato. It wasn't clear to the company how they could bring value to

*the consumer—how it could make mailboxes clearly superior to
the next vendor's. And if Rubbermaid people don't think they can
add value to a product line, they won't pursue it.*[16]

If a firm finds itself involved in an area where it isn't adding
value for those it deals with, it abandons that area. A corporation will take nonessential units and pare them down, sell them
off, close them down, or spin them off as independent operating units.

Closing down units is never easy. But an activity that consumes more than it delivers in value is wasting precious
resources. Rational resource allocation simply means putting
scarce resources to good use. When government performs a
function in which it lacks a comparative advantage, it is wasting
scarce resources. If a government department consumes $100
but produces only $95 in value, it should be reevaluated. This is
not to say a government activity should be inherently profitable
(i.e., capture some of the value created, which is used for public
goods), but it should produce more value than it consumes.

A business has a ready tool for assessing whether or not it is
successfully delivering and capturing value: the profit and loss
statement. Unfortunately, there is no similar tool to easily quan-
tify the benefits of public activities. This difficulty in measurement, however, in no way excuses us from asking the tough
questions: is this activity worth doing? Is it producing value for
every dollar expended?

WHAT SHOULD GOVERNMENT DO?

To revolutionize government, political leaders will have to
focus on doing fewer things and doing them better. This guiding principle of government follows from this fundamental
question: what should be the core functions of government in a
free society?

This question has been debated in America since our founding.

Key to making sense of the question is an understanding that Americans don't live under a single government. Local, county, and state governments, as well as numerous special district authorities, all operate under the larger umbrella of the federal government. It doesn't make sense for a county government to purchase its own aircraft carriers, and it doesn't make sense for the federal government to build police stations. As a general rule, government activities should be handled by the smallest unit of government feasible. This not only gives individual voters a greater voice in their governance, but it also helps ensure that local taxes pay for local programs. Insofar as possible, the scope of the activity should be consistent with the level of government.

Without limits on government, every conceivable activity can become the responsibility of government. In China, the government decides how many children a couple may have. Governments have built pyramids and sent rockets to the moon. Governments have run religions, built airplanes, and designed greeting cards. Government can do virtually anything. The question is, what should it do?

When it comes to theories regarding the purpose of government, 1776 was a very good year. That year saw not one but two seminal documents of political philosophy make their appearance on either side of the Atlantic: Thomas Jefferson's *Declaration of Independence* and Adam Smith's *Wealth of Nations*. Central to both documents was a single idea: government should be limited.

Adam Smith saw the core functions of government as falling under three general headings:

First, the duty of protecting the society from the violence and invasion of other independent societies; secondly, the duty of protecting, as far as possible, every member of the society from the injustice or oppression of every other member of it, or the duty of establishing an exact administration of justice; and, thirdly, the duty of erecting and maintaining certain public works and certain public institutions, which it can never be for the interest of any individual, or small number of individuals, to erect or maintain . . .[17]

Thomas Jefferson likewise thought the central duty of government was to protect individuals:

We hold these truths to be self-evident: That all men are created equal; that they are endowed by their Creator with certain inalienable rights; that among these are life, liberty, and the pursuit of happiness; that to secure these rights governments are instituted among men . . .

Times have changed since 1776, and certainly some functions of government are now necessary that could not have been foreseen at that time (such as environmental protection). In general, however, much harm has resulted from the expansion of America's government. Government expansion has unintended harmful consequences, and the 20th century has provided tragic examples of societies based on a vision of unlimited government.

A vision of a limited government provides a framework for citizens, elected officials, and government managers to think strategically about core functions. Resources are limited, and tradeoffs must be made. Policy makers as well as public managers need to ask important questions about current and proposed government activities, such as: Is the private sector already providing this service and if not, is it capable of doing so better than government? Does this program displace voluntary community or neighborhood networks?

Just like their private-sector counterparts, public officials need to constantly reassess what they are doing. *Asking these tough questions is an essential role for public officials and government managers.* Doing so provides a check against government assuming tasks it is ill-equipped to handle. It keeps government focused on those tasks that Adam Smith called "duties of great importance."

Another way of looking at government activities is to consider whether it is just to forcibly require taxpayers to pay for a particular activity. As Massachusetts Governor William Weld puts it, "There is no such thing as government money, only taxpayer money." Rather than automatically assuming that government ought to address every issue under the sun, a case must be made for government activity that justifies taking money away from the individual who earned it.

THE NATIONAL PERFORMANCE REVIEW: AVOIDING THE TOUGH QUESTION

REINVENTION IS NOT ENOUGH

"Mark this date: President Clinton is starting a revolution in government," said Vice President Al Gore in March of 1993, as he announced the start of the National Performance Review (NPR or REGO, short for REinventing GOvernment). "It will fundamentally change the way government works." As one NPR staffer put it, "A cultural change of this scope is unequaled in the history of human endeavor."[18]

Despite Al Gore's appearance on "Late Night with David Letterman," the National Performance Review had no chance of living up to its advance billing. Why? Because the National Performance Review, by its own admission, "focused primarily on *how* government should work, not on *what* it should do . . . Today, the central issue we face is not *what* government does, but *how* it works."[19] Politically this may have been a smart move, for it avoided ruffling some well-feathered nests. But if you're out to inspire a revolution, it's a losing strategy.

Al Gore likes to tell of the British lookout station established on the coast at Dover in the 1580s to warn Londoners of the approach of the Spanish Armada. The lookout station was finally eliminated in 1946. The NPR explains:

> *Why is it so difficult to close unneeded programs? Because those who benefit from them fight to keep them alive. While the savings from killing a program may be large, they are spread over many taxpayers. In contrast, the benefits of keeping the program are concentrated in a few hands. So special interests often prevail over the general interest.*[20]

This enduring truth should be carved in stone on the Washington Monument. But while the NPR paid lip service to discontinuing unnecessary government programs, it lacked any commitment to this objective.

Consider the Federal Helium Reserve. Begun in the 1920s to supply army zeppelins, the federal government now stores 30 billion cubic feet of helium near Amarillo—enough to last 100 years. Federal agencies such as NASA are required to purchase this helium, even though an abundant market of private helium producers charge less.[21] "There is no justification for this program's existence. It is rather silly for the federal government to be in the helium business," Gore advisor Elaine Kamarck told *The Los Angeles Times*. "We identified this early on as one of those weird things that government does. We don't pretend this makes sense."[22]

But what was the recommendation of the NPR report? "Improve the federal helium program."[23] (This breaks rule number one: never improve what should be eliminated.)

The main improvement made to the facility was that it would sell helium in larger containers, meaning taxpayers' money will be wasted much more efficiently. This is like a company that is losing money on every sale but hopes to make it up on volume. Is it merely a coincidence that Rep. Bill Sarpalius (D-Tex.), whose district benefits from the helium facility's 214 federal jobs, cast a key vote in Clinton's budget battle in 1993? Or maybe this is an example of the politics described in the report:

when an unneeded program meets a special interest, that interest prevails.

The helium program is not an isolated example. The Department of Interior's Bureau of Reclamation, established to develop water resources and promote economic development in the West, acknowledged in 1987 that it no longer had a mission. The NPR's recommendation? "Create a new mission for the Bureau of Reclamation."[24] What need is there for 7,716 federal bureau employees wandering about in search of a mission?

The NPR report correctly identified the problems of politics but didn't confront them. The NPR recommended only a handful of programs for the scrap heap—amongst them the Wool and Mohair Subsidy program and the Honey Subsidy program, two programs that had long been targeted for elimination. NPR's timid recommendations failed to match its bold rhetoric. If you can't kill a program that was started to keep blimps afloat, how can you lead a revolution?

"This performance review is not about politics," said President Clinton. This is a pipe dream, a dangerous myth that all the public sector needs is a better theory of management. Public management is embedded in politics, and politics permeates public management. Even the National Performance Review itself was steeped in politics. According to David Osborne, the chief author of the NPR report, the task force had suggested eliminating the helium reserve and a number of other programs. "But each time it sent a list of program and subsidy eliminations over to [White House advisor] George Stephanopoulos and his team, the list came back in tatters. Too radical. Too dangerous. Too offensive to Congressman So-and-So," admitted Osborne.[25]

"The crucial steps in overhauling government involve political choices, not questions of managerial efficiency," writes economist Robert Samuelson.[26] If the Surgeon General efficiently discourages smoking while the Department of Agriculture efficiently subsidizes tobacco growers, that is not efficiency.[27] Bob Stone, the affable director of the National Performance Review whose heroic efforts to improve Defense Department operations have been detailed in *Reinventing Government* and *In Search of Excellence*, calls our criticisms "half legitimate." Admits Stone, "Sure, there are all kinds of things the government is doing that it shouldn't be doing. I think it's stupid, for example, for the federal government to make payments to rich farmers to grow crops we don't need."[28]

We appreciate and admire the efforts of Stone and the NPR staff to make the federal government operate better. But by ignoring the first principle of what the federal government should do in the first place, the NPR became at best a marginally useful exercise in improving bureaucracy.

It took the vote of November 1994 to finally get the federal reinvention effort to focus on the core problem of the federal government: its size. Round two of the NPR, announced within a month of the Republican landslide, will look at what the federal government should get out of; privatization, program elimination, and devolution to states will be key components. "Why the sudden shift?" we asked the federal reinventers. "The election changed everything," said one NPR staffer. "What seemed bold before, now looks rather timid in light of both the message the American people sent and what the Republicans in Congress are proposing."[29]

Core Within a Core

A 1994 study by the National Education Commission on Time and Learning found that just 41 percent of the public school day is spent on academic subjects. The report found that "the traditional school day must now fit in a whole set of requirements for what has been called the 'new work of the schools'— education about personal safety, consumer affairs, AIDS, conservation and energy, family life and driver's training."[30]

Government schools are asked to address more and more of society's ills, but are neglecting the basics. In the meantime,

4,500.—

Am. Gen. 350.—
House (2) 1900.—

Gas * 250.—
Elect.* 250.—> pay soon
H2O * 250.—
Cable 93.—
phone * 250.—
car (2) 500.—

LCCC 600.—

*

} pay
10/31/04

100.— Am. Gen
130.— Larmet
122.— gas
380.— ODCS
_____
732.00
100. car ins.
_____
832.00

} 10/14/04

car
ins. 100. pd. — 10/15

Rauser 209.— (my pay) — 10/23/04?

Alro Steel

Akron, OH	(330) 929-4660
Alpena, MI	(989) 354-4188
Battle Creek, MI	(269) 968-0234
Cadillac, MI	(231) 775-9336
Dayton, OH	(937) 253-6121
Detroit, MI	(313) 366-8000
Flint, MI	(810) 695-7300
Ft. Wayne, IN	(260) 432-3524
Grand Rapids, MI	(616) 452-5111
Grayling, MI	(989) 348-3350
Indianapolis, IN	(317) 781-3800
Jackson, MI	(517) 787-5500
Lansing, MI	(517) 371-9600
Louisville, KY	(502) 635-7481
Muncie, IN	(765) 282-5335
Niles, MI	(269) 687-4000

Alro Specialty Metals

Buffalo, NY	(716) 877-6242
Charlotte, NC	(704) 529-6880
Chicago, IL	(708) 343-4343
Detroit, MI	(313) 892-1212
Milwaukee, WI	(262) 781-5615
Pittsburgh, PA	(412) 279-1660
Redford, MI	(313) 534-1300
St. Louis, MO	(314) 726-3080
Toledo, OH	(419) 666-4899
Tulsa, OK	(918) 227-1456

Alro Metals Service Ctr.

Boca Raton, FL	(561) 997-6766
Orlando, FL	(407) 678-2576
Tampa, FL	(813) 661-1646

Alro Industrial Supply

Cadillac, MI	(231) 775-9336
Clearwater, FL	(727) 572-4344
Grand Rapids, MI	(616) 656-2800
Jackson, MI	(517) 787-5500
Kalamazoo, MI	(269) 343-9575

Alro Plastics

Grand Rapids, MI	(616) 656-2820
Jackson, MI	(517) 787-5500
Louisville, KY	(502) 968-9980

Alro Metals Plus

Clearwater, FL	(727) 572-4344
Jackson, MI	(517) 788-3190
Kalamazoo, MI	(269) 343-9575
Sarasota, FL	(941) 952-1918

Alro delivers...everyday

schools are doing an increasingly poor job of teaching children the three R's. Because of political pressure, the schools' core purpose is obscured by numerous distractions.

New Jersey's Education Commissioner Leo Klagholz says that much of New Jersey's highest-in-the-nation $9,429 per-pupil school costs are the result of mandates imposed on school districts from the state legislature and federal government. Klagholz says schools are directed to eliminate "all of the social problems that might inhibit a student's learning." He explains, "Last year, 600 bills were introduced requiring schools to do different things. Is it reasonable to expect any one institution to do so many complex things and do all of them well? I don't think so."[31]

Schools are not the only public institution that strays into peripheral activities. Why? Sometimes, concerned groups put political pressure on elected officials to address their pet issues. Sometimes public managers use their positions to pursue *their* pet issues. And sometimes a desire for media coverage prompts a foray into noncore activities. Whatever the cause, there are few mechanisms to keep public departments from expanding their activities beyond their central purpose.

Without question, police protection is a core function of government. Nonetheless, too many police officers spend too much time engaged in tasks that have little to do with keeping a community safe. Greenwich, Connecticut, for example, requires its police officers to act as crossing guards. In New York City, uniformed officers do everything from running public relations to budgeting to information services.

Sometimes public unions push for requirements that ensure additional work, often at overtime pay. In Boston, union rules dictate that a police officer must be on detail when an electrical or gas crew works on street repairs. (Thus the classic tableau of a cop peering into a hole at several less well-paid individuals hard at work. On a radio show, we once had a patrolman defend this practice because "a crime could occur." Maybe a crime is already occurring.)[32]

THE FALSE ALLURE OF ENTERPRISING GOVERNMENT

The hottest trend in public-sector management is the idea that every public official ought to be an entrepreneur. The term was coined by the French economist Jean Baptiste Say. "The entrepreneur," wrote Say, "shifts economic resources out of an area of lower and into an area of higher productivity and greater yield."[33]

Adhering to Say's definition of an entrepreneur, of course it makes sense for everyone, including public officials, to act as entrepreneurs. A public official could, for example, shift resources from an area of lower to higher productivity simply by discontinuing an activity that the government does not do as well as the private sector. Leaving money in the hands of taxpayers rather than spending it inefficiently on their behalf qualifies as "entrepreneurial government."

Unfortunately, that sense of the term has been largely overlooked. Instead, *entrepreneurial* government has often been used to mean *enterprising* government. Enterprising government generally involves a public investment in a noncore activity in hopes of greater future payoff. The confounding is understandable, since in common usage the word "entrepreneur" is associated with business people who invest in new and exciting ventures: Ted Turner and CNN, Bill Gates and Microsoft, and fashion mogul Liz Claiborne. These entrepreneurs are admired for their courage and praised for their vision.

Some public officials have enthusiastically embraced enterprising government but have forgotten one crucial element of private-sector entrepreneurship: risk. Private entrepreneurs risk their own funds, while enterprising public officials risk the taxpayers'. There's a big difference.

Commissioners in Josephine County, Oregon, illustrate the pitfalls of enterprising government. Their first enterprise was a

"Soup D Nuts" store, purchased for $270,000, that was sup-posed to make the county money. But the county spent more on rent payments than it took in.

County officials were undeterred by this initial failure. After thinking long and hard, the would-be entrepreneurs of Josephine County government came up with another enterpris-ing idea: the county would hold a rock concert. In October 1993, Josephine County sponsored a three-day rock 'n roll blowout called "Howling Through the Years." The rockfest featured recycled headliners of the 1960s such as Eric Burden (without the Animals) and Country Joe McDonald (without the Fish). They were joined by a number of local bands. Josephine County did not make a bundle on the concert. In fact, it didn't even break even. The county lost over $75,000 on the event, including $22,000 on an audit to figure out how it lost so much money.

The audit turned up several items of interest. First of all, the county hadn't printed up enough tickets to break even. In addi-tion, more food was consumed by people to whom the commis-sioners had given free meal tickets than by paying concert goers. It turns out that county officials were no better at promoting rock concerts than at running a restaurant. But more than just the money, Josephine County officials lost the trust of Josephine County taxpayers. Says county resident John Testler. "If the concert had been a big success (and the facts clearly show that no one expected it to be, i.e., only $29,000 worth of pre-printed tickets were printed up), that wouldn't change the fact that Josephine County government doesn't belong in the rock and roll business. If private investors, promoters, or whoever want to invest private money, that's fine, but the function of govern-ment is not to hold rock concerts, no matter how noble the cause. The concert was a series of bad decisions—the worst of which was made by the county commissioners when they approved the initial $8,000 of county funds."[34]

County residents were so upset over county officials' foray into enterprising government that they passed a series of initiatives requiring voter approval of all but the most routine government spending items. "The word around town was that the county was buying everything from Soups D Nuts to whatever with our taxpayers' money," says Testler. "We had to put a stop to it." The county government became so scared of further inciting the voters' wrath that in 1994 it actually held a special election to ask voter approval for spending $7,000 to replace broken office furniture.

There is nothing wrong with public officials trying new ideas, but there is a critical distinction between taking advantage of new opportunities in the pursuit of core activities on the one hand, and gambling with taxpayer's money on the other. This distinction is often lost. The authors of *Reinventing Government* point admiringly to California cities like Fairfield, which made money by taking part in developing a shopping mall, and Santa Clara, which bought an amusement park. They sympathetically quote an official arguing for the amusement park purchase who complains that "people are always willing to push on to government losers in this country. The winners are always to be preserved to the private sector."[35]

Many other governments have gotten the enterprising government fever. At the Redwoods National Park in Northern California, the government-owned Freshwater Lagoon campsite has caused a 30 percent drop in business at nearby private campgrounds.[36] Public libraries, whose only plausible claim to government funding is as an educational resource, now lend popular videotapes and compact discs in competition with the private sector.

VISALIA'S EXPERIMENT WITH
ENTERPRISING GOVERNMENT

Perhaps the most enterprising government of all has been Visalia, a city of a little over 75,000 in California's Central Valley where *Reinventing Government* co-author Ted Gaebler was city manager for much of the 1980s. Putting city money at risk in return for potential profits was a guiding vision for City Hall both under Gaebler and his successor, Don Duckworth. The city went so far as to purchase a minor league baseball team. Almost no activity seemed beyond the imagination of Visalia's profit-minded city officials. Gaebler once even tried to convince the city council to get into the business of selling fire insurance. "It makes no sense anymore to distinguish between public and private sectors," proclaims Gaebler. "That old axiom, 'The best government is that which governs least,' is nonsensical now."[37]

The citizens of Visalia don't seem to agree with Gaebler anymore. Today, entrepreneurial government, particularly of the enterprising variety, is a bad word in town. In its zeal to turn a profit, the city of Visalia went into the hotel business. Visalia taxpayers now own a Radisson Hotel, the tallest building in town, having shelled out $24 million (in actual spending or debt) on a hotel appraised at $10 million.[38]

The Radisson debacle shows the danger of mixing investment with politics. Originally, the city was to invest $4 million—the cost of the land—towards the cost of building the hotel. From there things snowballed. The developer convinced the city to lend him $3 million and guarantee future loan payments. Despite the loan, the developer couldn't attract private investors.[39] Though private investors weren't willing to risk their own money, City Manager Duckworth was ready to risk taxpayers' money. He refused to throw in the towel. Duckworth paid a public relations firm out of city funds to boost the developer's image, whose image needed boosting because of a succession of previous lawsuits.[40] At several points the city could have cut its losses, but that would have been embarrassing politically. With losses mounting, in 1991 the city council bought the hotel.

Visalia voters pronounced final judgment on enterprising government. By 1994, Visalia had a new mayor, a new city manager, and a new city council, all of them promising a back-to-basics, limited government agenda. It is not likely Visalia will be risking taxpayer money on speculative real estate deals again anytime soon. "An entrepreneur is a person who risks his own money for gain," says Basil Perch, the city's mayor. "What I believe is that in government, we can't risk taxpayers' money, because it's not ours; that's not the function of government."[41]

The philosophy of enterprising government embraces a view of government without limits. If an enterprising government can sponsor a rock concert, run an amusement park, and build a hotel, what's to prevent it from making shoes or operating pizza parlors? Argues Indianapolis Mayor Stephen Goldsmith, "The problem with Osborne and Gaebler is that they believe government can be good in a whole range of things, when the truth is it can't. Government isn't set up that way. The private sector is better than the public sector in many ways in delivering goods. The public sector should only be involved when the private sector isn't working."[42]

Government officials need to pause before venturing into the for-profit world and recall that they are caretakers of government, not owners. They are risking OPM—Other People's Money. Private risk-taking causes people to do their homework before investing. Moreover, private risk-takers are under constant pressure to improve the efficiency of their ventures. Government lacks these important market disciplines. Government won't go out of business if a venture flops; it will just raise taxes. In addition, enterprising government also risks creating unfair competition with the private sector.[43]

The original concept of the entrepreneurial public manager—that is, one who shifts resources from areas of low to high value—is a commendable one. But enthusiasts of enterprising government should remember that a public manager can also be entrepreneurial by shifting activities from the public sector to the private.

A CHANGING VISION

Politicians often dance around their views on what government should and should not do. Being vague on this issue has been smart politics, because every existing program has its entrenched interest groups. In America today, however, a new breed of mayors and governors of both political parties is starting to talk about the limits of government.

Cleveland Mayor Michael White, a Democrat, is one of these new thinkers. Says White,

> *The city of Cleveland operates a convention center, two golf courses, and a host of other assets which would make a private-sector operator a profit—but we operate them at a loss. We are probably the only operator of parking lots in our area who doesn't know how to make a profit on parking. Is it the height of heresy to suggest that companies who run convention centers, manage jails, and manage parking lots can deliver our constituents a better service at a better price? If they can deliver a better service at a better price, then they deserve the opportunity.*[44]

New York City Mayor Rudolph Giuliani, a Republican, also knows that city government is overextended. During his campaign for mayor, he repeatedly pledged to focus on core activities such as reducing crime, building a healthy economic climate, and making city government more efficient. It's hard to focus, however, when you're ultimately responsible for everything from gambling payouts to radio programming to running a hotel. So Giuliani has decided to take the city out of some activities entirely.

City enterprises such as city-owned parking garages, gas stations, the city's radio license, and the city-owned United

Nations Plaza Hotel—the hotel alone is valued at between $55 million and $65 million—are all slated for sale. "I don't think having a bunch of city employees choosing hotel bathroom wallpaper patterns is the best use of their time," says Tom Hershfeld, who was in charge of the mayor's asset divestment program.[45] The Off-Track Betting Corporation and two waste-water treatment plants are also privatization candidates, as are some of the city's hospitals. "New York City shouldn't be in the business of running a hospital system," says New York City Deputy Mayor Peter Powers.[46]

New reform governors such as New Jersey's Christine Todd Whitman and New York's George Pataki contend that states should reduce their sizeable portfolios. "Getting government out of the way of the private sector is the goal," says Governor Whitman. "We're trying to get government to do only what it should do. I believe the public is truly ready to make some of these tradeoffs that they have been reluctant to make before."[47] Pointing to a shelf chock full of intimidating government reports, Peter McDonough, a New Jersey Treasury official, explains the new thinking: "Every one of those studies are management studies on 'How to Do Dumb Things Cheaper.' They never asked the fundamental question, 'Should we be doing this at all?' We're going about this differently. Sometimes we say yes, the state should provide the service . . . But there will be other cases where the state should not be in that business, period. If someone else wants to provide it, God bless them and let them do it."[48]

SHIFTING FROM PUBLIC TO PRIVATE

If a business decides to get out of a certain product line, it gets out. It is not an enjoyable process, but when a firm's management chooses to discontinue an activity, it gets discontinued. It doesn't work that way in government. Politics makes it extremely difficult for government to discontinue even the most extraneous activities.

Madsen Pirie, a prominent British economist who has advised over 36 governments on transferring functions from the public to the private sector, has identified 21 different techniques and political strategies that governments all over the world have used to "get out" of a particular activity (see Table). Most of these techniques fall under the general rubric of privatization. More specifically, Pirie's techniques are ways to transfer activities to the private sector and eliminate government support. An example would be British Steel, which was formerly government-owned but now operates as a private, for-profit enterprise.

Various privatization techniques have been used by governments worldwide—from Britain to Mexico to China—to unload themselves of activities best left to the private sector. In the decade between 1984 and 1994, $458 billion worth of state-owned enterprises have been sold or turned over to private owners—around $70 billion in 1994 alone.[50] Privatized industries include electrical power, telecommunications and water systems, sports stadiums, railways, ports, highways and bridges, zoos and museums, and airports. In an August 1993 editorial, *The Economist* called privatization a "a global economic revolution." No longer can nations afford to subsidize inefficient government monopolies and stay competitive with other nations. Even Libyan leader Muammar Gaddaffi has joined the movement, privatizing the country's camel industry. Transferring 6,000 government-owned camels to the private sector is expected to save millions of dollars per year in subsidy costs.[51]

Total privatization is a permanent cost-limitation measure. Unless a government budget is "zeroed-out," interest groups will apply intense pressures to restore appropriations each year thereafter. The Small Business Administration (SBA) of the federal government demonstrates the point. Serving a small, spe-

GETTING OUT TECHNIQUES AND STRATEGIES

1. Selling the whole by public share issue
2. Selling a proportion of the whole operation
3. Selling parts to private buyers
4. Selling to the work force or management
5. Giving to the work force
6. Contracting out the service to private business
7. Diluting the public sector
8. Buying out existing interest groups
9. Charging for the service
10. Setting up counter groups
11. Deregulation via voluntary associations
12. Encouraging alternative institutions
13. Making small-scale trials
14. Repealing public monopolies to let competition grow
15. Encouraging exit from state provision
16. Using vouchers
17. Admitting demand pressures
18. Curbing state powers
19. Applying closure procedures
20. Withdrawal from the activity
21. The right to private substitution

Source: Madsen Pirie, *Privatization, Privatization: Theory, Practice and Choice,* (Aldershot, England: Wildwood House Limited, 1988).

cial-interest constituency, it is a classic unnecessary federal program; according to the General Accounting Office, there is little or no evidence that the SBA has helped small business expansion since it was formed in 1954.[52] In 1980, the SBA was a $2 billion welfare program for business. During the Reagan presidency, budget-cutters fought hard to reduce the size of the SBA, eventually whittling it down to a "mere" $85 million in 1989. But the SBA fought back, rallying the troops and lobbying hard for restored funding. By the final year of the Bush administration, the agency's budget was back up to $975 million.[53]

In 1994, the SBA was being touted by the National Performance Review as a reinvention success story:

> *Fifteen years ago, when Mama Jo's and Zeno's Pizza in Witchita Falls, Texas, was getting started, it took the owners four weeks to work with a bank loan officer to fill out the forms for a Small Business Administration loan, gather all the documents, and wait for the government to respond. This year, when they wanted to expand, the whole process took only three days, start to finish.[54]*

Rather than being proud of this, the federal government should be embarrassed that it is taxing a single, working mother in Detroit to grant loans to a pizza parlor in Wichita Falls. Don't they have any banks in Wichita Falls? We shouldn't reinvent the Small Business Administration, we should take it behind the wood shed with an ax.

The United States Postal Service (USPS) represents a prime candidate for privatization: there is no reason the government needs to serve as the nation's letter carrier. Supposedly, self-funding, in the fiscal year ending September 1994 the USPS lost $914 million.[55] Competition would enhance efficiency, and privatization would eliminate the sometimes absurd politics of the post office. In 1994 Postmaster General Marvin Runyon came under fire when the USPS decided not to issue a POW/MIA stamp, and President Clinton became involved in a brouhaha over an Atomic Age stamp. Privatization would allow politicians to focus on more important matters.

Transforming state enterprises into private entities can turn dormant physical capital into financial capital, which can be used for pressing needs such as rebuilding infrastructure, paying off debt, or reducing taxes.[56] Governments also benefit financially by putting the asset on the tax rolls. A year after the state of Connecticut privatized its Off-Track Betting operation in 1993, it was netting more revenues (via a 3.5 percent tax on the company's gross revenues) than it would have been making as owner of the operation.[57]

The case for privatization has been bolstered by a substantial body of evidence, including a major 1992 World Bank study. "So, did divestiture make the world a better place, or not?" asks the eight-volume report. "Our case studies answer this with a resounding 'Yes'." The report, which looked at 12 privatizations in four countries, found that "in no case did divestiture make workers as a whole worse off."[58] From airlines in Malaysia to telephones in Chile, privatization of enterprise was found to be a win-win proposition.

America has thousands of government enterprises that are potential candidates for privatization. These range from infrastructure assets (such as Amtrak, electric utilities, bridges, and wastewater treatment plants) to cultural institutions (such as zoos and museums) to commercial enterprises (such as marinas and liquor operations). State and local governments own over $226 billion in infrastructure assets alone.[59]

Many government-supported activities can thrive without government involvement. On January 1, 1993, Norfolk, Virginia, turned its city-run botanical garden into a private non-profit operation. It received its first $1 million donation the same day. Zoos in Atlanta, Boston, and San Francisco have all successfully made the jump from government to the private sector. The San Francisco Zoo received $12 million in donations contingent on the zoo's going private, which it did in October 1993. People don't need government to sustain cultural institutions. The Dallas Arboretum, for example, has 600 steady volunteers. Lacking a public library, citizens in Sedona, Arizona, have run their own private library since 1958. "The magnitude of what we are doing without government funding is almost unbelievable," librarian Joan Duke told *Sedona Magazine.*[60]

One of the biggest political obstacles to privatization is public employees and their unions. But such transfers can be structured so as to consider the interests of public workers. Privatization practitioners have designed sophisticated strategies that reduce the potential negative impact on employees, and thus reduce opposition.[61] Under Margaret Thatcher, Britain's numerous privatizations often included incentives for public employees, such as discounted shares and outright giveaways to the work force. They also changed some of the rules governing union operation, requiring, for example, a direct secret-ballot polling of members on privatization actions. This helped give union members greater control over their own leadership and prevented union leaders from opposing changes that were in their members' interest but not their own. When Ohio privatized state-owned liquor stores in 1991, it offered employee buyouts and early retirement benefits to current workers in order to reduce their opposition.

CASE STUDY: PRIVATIZATION OF THE BRITISH AIRPORT AUTHORITY

In the United States, every major commercial airport is owned and managed by a government authority. What would happen if an airport were sold to a private operator?

The international experience shows the benefits of private ownership. Since 1987, the United Kingdom has sold 11 airports. Austria, Denmark, and several other countries have also privatized airports. The British government started the trend in 1987, when it sold, via public stock offering, the British Airport Authority, owner of three major London airports (Heathrow, Gatwick, and Stansted) and four Scottish airports for $2.5 billion.

Since going private, the British Airport Authority (BAA) has made numerous improvements in the airports. Annual capital investment doubled within the first three years. Output per employee has increased. New terminals have been opened and others expanded. By entering into a joint venture with British Rail, BAA is constructing a much-needed rail link to Heathrow that will slash the journey from downtown to Heathrow from one hour to 15 minutes.[62] BAA made all these improvements without raising landing fees or airport user fees (these fees are regulated by the government). In fact, from 1991 to 1994, charges to airlines actually declined 8 percent overall.

BAA has succeeded by, among other things, improving airport shopping. In most airports, you can expect to pay double or triple the normal price for food, drinks, and other concessions. Selection is limited. Airport layovers are universally dreaded because they generally mean sitting in a bar paying $5 a drink. Unlike the previous owner—the government—BAA sees its travelers as customers to be served.[63] Explains one BAA executive:

> We believe we can only sustain a growing and profitable revenue system by satisfying the wants and needs of our primary customers, the passenger. In the retail context this means recognizing that the passenger/terminal user is fundamentally the same as a shopper in a mall. They both respond to merchandising range, choice, branding, service, and value for money.[64]

BAA has transformed its London airports into combination shopping malls and business centers. Retail operations in terminals have nearly doubled since privatization and now generate nearly $500 million a year, generating more revenue than airport charges.

Airport customers can now shop to their heart's content at BAA airports. In one terminal at Gatwick, travelers can grab a snack at the Caviar House, rent a camcorder at Travelcam, and shop for ties at the Tie Rack. Sales average $25 per emplaning passenger at BAA airports, compared to a dollar or two in most U.S. airports.[65]

There has been considerable talk of privatizing airports in America. New York Mayor Rudolph Giuliani, Los Angeles Mayor Richard Riordan and Indianapolis Mayor Goldsmith have all proposed privatizing their airports, either through sale or lease. To date, however, no American airport has taken the privatization plunge.

If you've been through Pittsburgh's airport in the last few years, however, you might have noticed a big improvement. The large new terminal has over 100 restaurants and shops, including Waterman's (the British bookstore chain), a chiropractor, a banking services center, and a 1,000-square-foot Meditation Room, complete with soft music and images of clouds. So what happened? In 1992, the Allegheny County Airport Authority contracted with BAA to develop and manage all retail operations.

Pittsburgh's new terminal, managed by BAA, is America's only airport with a suburban-style shopping mall, dubbed the Air Mall. Like BAA's British airports, stores must sign a pledge promising to charge the same prices as they do outside the airport (coffee is 49 cents a cup).

"We monitor prices to insure compliance and we write it into the contract," says Michael Bell, who heads BAA's U.S. operations. "The old attitude is that you had to charge high prices because only a few of the people going through the airport stopped and lingered. But the reason they didn't linger is that they thought they were being ripped off."[66] Airport customers are not the only ones getting a good deal from BAA. The county gets a guaranteed minimum payment about equal to the amount it was earning from airport sales in its old facility. On top of that, the county shares in the mall's sale profits after BAA recovers its costs.

Some government airports are reasonably well run, others less so. But few can approach BAA's "world-class" orientation.

Government managers have little incentive to innovate, and with all their other tasks governments are unable to devote much attention to airport operations. Nobody has ever been elected by promising 49 cent coffee at the airport. BAA, on the other hand, only does airports. Chairman Sir John Egan has insisted BAA stick to its core business: being the world's most profitable and successful airport owner. In fact, before Sir John arrived in 1990, BAA had diversified its operations into hotels, property, and freight handling.[67] Sir John soon returned BAA to its core business: running airports.

PULLING THE PLUG ON UNNECESSARY GOVERNMENT PROGRAMS

The only time government ever kills programs is by refusing to feed them. This is policymaking by neglect. City officials need to go back to first cases, look at everything city hall does, and ask whether government has to do this at all.[68]

Ron Henry, *Former Executive Director,*
Pennsylvania Intergovernmental Cooperation Authority

THE STORY OF THE TEXAS CANCER COUNCIL

Pulling the plug on an existing government program can fail even with the most elaborate strategies and precautions. Texas State Comptroller John Sharp, a Democrat, is the mastermind behind the Texas Performance Review (TPR). Sharp's TPR takes a microscope to every nook and cranny of state government, looking for waste and duplication. Sharp's team inspires fear in other departments, which worry that they may be next on TPR's hit list. To prevent the Performance Review recommendations from being "cherry picked" by special interests, the reviews are conducted in James Bond fashion.

Sharp, a wily Texan with a gift for joke and storytelling, is no stranger to the workings of interest-group government. Knowing that leaks could kill a proposal before it is given a public hearing, he cloaks the audit process in a web of mystery to ensure that affected departments and interest groups do not find out about TPR recommendations before its reports come out. Even among his own staff, Sharp limits the portion of a report any one person can work on. Only four people—Sharp and his three top staffers—get to see the big picture.

But even the savvy Sharp got a lesson in political reality when he tried to shut down a tiny state agency called the Texas Cancer Council, which educates Texans about cancer risks and prevention. Sharp's CIA-type operation proved no match for the passionate defenders of the little council, which was duplicating work going on at the M.D. Anderson Cancer Center at the University of Texas. Texas Performance Review Director Allen Polleck tells the story:

We never thought it would cause a big headache. Texas already had the M.D. Anderson hospital, one of the biggest cancer research centers in the country. We felt the Texas Cancer Council was just duplicating Anderson's work, so we recommended it be eliminated. We even tweaked the recommendation so the director of the council would be transferred to M.D. Anderson.

Oh, man! People came out of the woodwork from all over to say that these people were performing duties and functions that were unique, that there would be this gaping hole in the education of citizens about cancer and in prevention, and all this kind of business . . . Once a government program gets up and running it's very difficult to eliminate it.[69]

When word got out that the Texas Cancer Council might come under the knife, interested parties swung into action. Legislators were called, favors exchanged, and strings pulled. In the end, Texas taxpayers were still footing the bill for an agency that benefits very few. As the Texas Cancer Council showed, organizations as well as organisms cling to life with formidable tenacity when their existence is threatened.

In the private sector, an individual owner or executive has the authority to close a failing unit, but closing the Texas Cancer Council would have been a public action. In a democracy, such a public choice demands political consensus. Obtaining the consensus to take tough but beneficial action can be almost impossible. Nobody in political life wants to be associated with closing anything, and for good reason. Those who are not directly affected are unlikely to know or care about your political courage, and those who are affected will never forget your role in closing a beloved institution.

Author Jonathon Rauch has a name for this phenomenon: demosclerosis. In his book of the same name, Rauch writes,

> *Demosclerosis, if it goes on unchecked, turns government into more and more of a rambling, ill-adapted shambles which often gets in the way but can't be gotten rid of . . . Liberals may not get new poverty programs that work, but conservatives also can't get rid of archaic banking regulations.*[70]

Rauch's book tells of dozens of failed attempts to eliminate obsolete government programs. This inability to reduce produces a ratcheting effect, creating a government that knows how to add but can't subtract. Contributing to this ratcheting effect is the view held by some that any program that produces *any* benefit is a good program—regardless of the cost. This view was expressed by Ted Gaebler, speaking critically of efforts to change the culture of government:

> *The first mistake was that elected officials decided we needed business acumen in government. . . . The [business experts] said we will need to identify our weak product lines and services, [and] stop producing those . . . We said, in government*

we exist to do good. Doing good is a moral absolute. As long as one person is benefitting, we keep those programs going.[71]

This is a dangerous sort of morality, for it sees only half the picture. Government can give only after it has taken. While the benefit of a public program is usually readily apparent, the costs are often hidden. Burdensome taxes prevent working families from being able to afford better education for their children, or braces for their children's teeth, or other desirables. A good provided by government is not obtained without cost. If we rob Peter to pay Paul, we shouldn't take credit for our impact on Paul without considering our impact on Peter.

CONGRESSMAN ARMEY'S BASE-CLOSING STRATEGY

One of the most successful recent examples of overcoming interest-group opposition to close obsolete government facilities was the federal base-closing effort fashioned by Representative Dick Armey of Texas, now the House Majority leader.

A military base is like any other government program: once established, it is difficult to close. Dozens of the military's 3,800 or so bases had been rendered obsolete by modern communications and transportation. Fort Monroe in Virginia, first garrisoned in 1823, still sports an eight-foot-deep moat to deter attacks.[72] Other bases occupy valuable real estate yet provide minimal military value. But no member of Congress wants to tell constituents that the local base is closing.

Many times before, senior members of Congress had tried and failed to enact legislation to close dozens of the obsolete bases. Armey was determined to succeed. "Too many members of Congress look at the defense bill the way Jimmy Dean looks at a hog: as a giant piece of pork to be carved up and sent to the folks back home," said Armey.[73] Armey knew that if members were allowed to vote on each individual base, none would ever be closed because legislators in the affected districts would horse-trade for votes. Armey hit upon the idea of establishing an independent, bipartisan commission that would suggest base closings without considering political pressures. Congress and the Defense Secretary would then have to pass or reject the entire package without changes.

Thanks to Congressman Armey's ingenuity and sheer will, the base-closing legislation passed (on the second try) and two rounds of base closings have now taken place, saving taxpayers the expense of maintaining nonessential facilities (Savings are expected to reach $4 billion a year once the bases are closed). Armey's base-closing strategy succeeded because it took the hard choices out of the hands of politicians. Senator Connie Mack (R-Florida) has called for the creation of an independent commission modeled on the base-closing commission to assemble a package of federal spending cuts which would be presented to Congress on an up-or-down vote—no amendments allowed.[74] The Democratic Leadership Council's think tank, the Progressive Policy Institute, wants to establish a similar commission to get rid of a couple hundred billion dollars worth of business and special-interest subsidies and tax breaks.

Nonetheless, Congress (like any legislature) is loathe to surrender its authority, and Armey himself—as determined a budget-cutter as there is in Congress—opposes applying the base-closure model to spending programs, believing that setting spending levels is a legislative branch function that should be voted on specifically by Congress, not by an outside commission or the executive branch.

Under the leadership of revolutionaries like Armey and Speaker Gingrich, in 1995 Congress was looking to eliminate scores of wasteful or unnecessary programs—possibly for good. The strategy? To "zero-out" entire line items. "They're going to hate you anyway," says Steve Bell, an advisor to Senate budget chairman Pete Domenici. "So why not cut it all so it doesn't grow back?"[75]

JOHN ENGLER'S BOLD USE OF THE EXECUTIVE ORDER

Michigan Governor John Engler's first year in office in 1991 marked the beginning of a new era in Michigan politics. After squeaking out a win (17,595 votes) over Democratic incumbent James Blanchard, Engler immediately started downsizing Michigan's bloated government. Within months of taking office, Governor Engler had cut back the Michigan Council for the Arts (savings: $11 million); closed down the Department of Licensing and Regulation (savings: $25 million); cut the budget for the Department of Commerce in half; eliminated four gubernatorial councils; and ended welfare for able-bodied adults (savings: $150 million).

Even with a Democrat-controlled house, Engler was able to achieve these politically volatile reforms through executive order. In Michigan, overturning an executive order requires a majority vote of *both* houses of the legislature. With Republicans controlling the Senate, all 13 orders signed by Engler in his first three-and-a-half months were sustained. "It's a remarkable tool for consolidating functions and eliminating superfluous commissions, of which Michigan has hundreds," said Bill Wittbeck, Engler's legal advisor.[76]

The governor's reductions at the Michigan Council for the Arts were immensely controversial. The media attacked Engler, a middle-class guy who grew up on a farm, as a philistine. The *Detroit News* called Engler an "arts ogre ... whose idea of high culture is a weekend with [his wife] at Boblo" (Boblo is a honky-tonk amusement park).[77] The Governor's gutsy termination of the General Relief program and closure of five underutilized state mental hospitals (one hospital housed six patients and had a staff of 120) were also widely decried. Still the Governor held firm. After the media storm blew over, voters liked the results, and in 1994 Engler cruised to reelection with 61 percent of the vote.

Several lessons emerge from Engler's success. First, downsizing requires bold, decisive action. The governor did not spend years studying whether the Department of Licensing and Regulation was truly providing value for the taxpayer. After 20 years in the state legislature, Engler knew very well that it wasn't. So he simply pulled the plug.

Secondly, unlike more timid politicians, Engler made the tough decisions knowing they would be unpopular in the near term, especially with the media. Engler did what he thought was right, hoping that Michigan's electorate would respect him for it. He gambled right. John Engler has demonstrated that downsizing can be good government *and* good politics. "I think there's a huge constituency out there for shrinking government," says Engler. "I think we've shown you can take risks beyond what was thought politically possible."[78]

PRIVATE-SECTOR RENEWAL

Whenever someone proposes discontinuing a service, it is often assumed the service will no longer be provided, period. Not so, says David Riemer, chief of staff to Milwaukee Mayor John Norquist, "The private sector, possibly now suppressed by the city, will usually spring to life to fill the gap."[79]

This happened in the Southern California city of Rancho Palos Verdes when a budget shortfall in 1993 prompted it to reconsider its priorities. Pressed for cash, Rancho Palos Verdes eliminated its recreation programs. Before getting out of the recreation business, the city surveyed the surrounding area and discovered that private for-profit and nonprofit organizations were already providing—at reasonable prices—most of the recreation services the city was running.[80] After hearing the city would be dropping the recreation programs, many of the class instructors came to the city and said, We will continue the programs if you will rent us your facilities. The end result: many of the city recreation classes are still being offered. The only difference is they are being run privately and without subsidy from the city. In fact, the city is now making a small net profit from the facility rental.

CONCLUSION

The most important public issue of all—the debate about what government should and should not do—has been avoided by all too many politicians and reformers. It is downright danger- ous to reinvent government while ignoring questions concern- ing the essential mission of government. The result can be a government furiously striving for useless efficiency.

Without a guiding philosophy of what government should do, and at what level, the natural tendency is for government to expand. Too many groups are ready to exercise political influ- ence to use the power of government to favor their cause. Overburdened by a smorgasbord of activity, governments at every level across America are in a state of crisis. There is no better time to rethink the purpose of government. The last time this nation engaged in such a debate, the decision was made to establish a government of limited powers. The evidence of his- tory has confirmed the wisdom of such an approach. A success- ful democracy requires a vigilant citizenry. It is time for a renewed public debate on the proper role of government in a free society.

CHAPTER 3

DEVOLVING POWER AND RESTORING COMMUNITY

Our problems go way beyond the reach of government. They are rooted in the loss of values and the disappearance of work and the breakdown of our families and our communities. We can't renew our country until we realize that governments don't raise children, parents do.

President Bill Clinton[1]

According to popular mythology, Democrats are progovernment, Republicans probusiness. These alternatives are less than totally satisfying. The government is institutional, bureaucratic, and predicated on the coercive power of the state. The free market is money-based, commercial, and predicated on the selfish interests of consumers and producers. Isn't there anything more to life?

Fortunately, there is. The false dichotomy of government and business ignores a crucial realm of human activity. This "third pillar" of society encompasses relationships that are voluntary but not for commercial gain, such as religions, charities, associations, and community groups. It includes friends, families, and kind strangers. Variously referred to as "mediating institutions," "civil society," or "community," by addressing human concerns that cannot be satisfied either by government or by economic exchange, this sphere enriches our lives not as consumers, but as human beings. This third pillar of society is vital to a healthy democracy, yet is often overlooked in examinations of public policy.

MARKETS, GOVERNMENT, AND BEYOND

Though a powerful mechanism for creating and distributing goods and services, the free market cannot satisfy every human need. You can buy a good car, but you can't buy a good friend. With enough money a person can buy sex, but money can't buy you love. Markets don't work that way. Even history's greatest champion of capitalism, Adam Smith, was under no illusion about what made markets work. "It is not from the benevolence of the butcher, the brewer, or the baker that we expect our dinner," wrote Smith, "but from their regard to their own interest." Free markets work so well precisely because they rely on the dependable spur of self-interest, rather than the more noble (but less dependable) motive of altruism.

It would be a poor society indeed, however, if every individual's every action were devoted solely to commercial gain. In the *Communist Manifesto*, Marx and Engels criticized "capitalist" society because it "left remaining no other nexus between man and man than naked self-interest, than callous 'cash payment.'" Marx and Engels were wrong about this, of course. There is much more to a free society than free markets. Given the liberty, individuals not only engage in commercial exchange, but also voluntarily give to others. In *Free to Choose*, Milton and Rose Friedman explode the myth of 19th-century America as a society of capitalist exploitation dominated by cruel "robber barons":

> *The charge of heartlessness . . . is belied by the flowering of charitable activity in the United States in the nineteenth century. Privately financed schools and colleges multiplied; foreign missionary activity exploded; nonprofit private hospitals, orphanages, and numerous other institutions sprang up like weeds. . . . Voluntary cooperation is no less effective in organizing charitable activity than in organizing production for profit.*[2]

The combination of free markets and robust, informal helping networks has long made America the greatest nation on earth in which to be poor, the destination of millions of poor immigrants from around the globe.

Unfortunately, private philanthropy and mutual aid couldn't eliminate all of America's social woes. As our nation became more affluent following World War II, anything less than perfection became intolerable to those who saw poverty and other social ills amidst plenty. Rather than seeking to improve society through private, voluntary efforts, a number of influential intellectuals and politicians decided that the way to deal with these imperfections was through government action.

In the 1960s, the Beach Boys had a hit song called "Wouldn't It Be Nice?" At about the same time, America adopted the Wouldn't It Be Nice? philosophy of government.

Wouldn't it be nice if government ended poverty? Wouldn't it be nice if government ended racism, tended the sick, and cared for the aged? Wouldn't it be nice if the government transformed urban ghettos into orderly housing projects? At the time, America's faith in government knew no bounds. Youthful, energetic President Kennedy epitomized a government ready to save the world through the Peace Corps. Wouldn't it be nice if government could do all these wonderful things? And why not? After all, Kennedy had brought the best and the brightest to government. They put a man on the moon. They could do anything.

But there is no "they." To paraphrase Pogo, "We have met the government, and they are us." The cynicism Americans now feel toward government is the crash and burn of the high hopes of the 1960s. We fooled ourselves into thinking that government experts would take care of problems for us. But the autopilot approach to democracy didn't work, as House Speaker Newt Gingrich reminds us:

The long experiment with professional politicians and professional government is over, and it failed. You cannot hire a teacher to teach your child, and then walk off and blame the teacher. You cannot hire a policeman to protect your neighborhood, and then walk off and blame the police . . . My challenge to the American people is real simple. You really want to dramatically reduce power in Washington? You have to be willing to accept more responsibility back home. You really want to reduce the bureaucracy of the welfare state? You have to accept greater responsibility back home.[3]

With government assuming many of the responsibilities previously left to individuals, families, and communities, America has deviated from its tradition of self-governance.

BIGGER GOVERNMENT, WEAKER COMMUNITIES

The New Deal marked the first major foray of the federal government into areas of charitable aid to individuals. The Great Society of the 1960s saw a major of expansion of these programs. Responding to nearly every societal imperfection, government established job training programs, arts programs, substance abuse programs, and daycare programs.

In 1930, government spending at all levels totaled about 12 percent of GNP; in 1990, total government spending stood at about 37 percent of GNP. Moreover, this boom in spending has mostly been in the area of welfare and transfer programs. In 1950, social welfare spending consumed about 12 percent of the federal budget; by 1992, such spending consumed roughly 40 percent of federal spending. (Over the same period, the share of the federal budget going to defense *declined* by over 30 percent.)[4]

The centralization of government power has been equally dramatic, distancing individuals and communities from the decisions that affect their lives. Public schools, for example, are more costly and more centrally controlled than ever before, a break from the traditional approach of local funding and local control.[5] Today, Congress sets national education goals and state committees—not teachers—choose textbooks. The result? Parents have less influence over what their children are taught, which helps explain why the number of children in home schooling has increased roughly twentyfold since 1980.

In 1930, the federal government spent less than 4 percent of GNP; by 1992, the federal government spent about 25 percent of GNP.[6] In effect, every American works one of every four days for the federal government.

While government spends more than ever, our nation is in the throes of a terrifying social decline. In 1993, former Secretary of Education William Bennett documented this decline in "The Index of Leading Cultural Indicators" (see box).

America's Cultural Decline[7]

Violent crime rate	1960:	16.1
(per 10,000)	1991:	75.8
Fraction of children on AFDC	1960:	3.5%
	1991:	12.9%
Births to unmarried women	1960:	5.3%
(as percentage of all births)	1990:	28.0%
Teen suicide rate	1960:	3.6
(per 100,000 15–24-year-olds)	1990:	11.9
Average SAT score	1960:	975
	1990:	900
Total social spending	1960:	6.7%
(as % of GNP)	1990:	14.4%

The intentions of those who expanded government and centralized aid programs may have been noble, but the unintended consequences have been catastrophic. The problem is not that the programs are too costly in dollars and cents. Instead, the costs are too high in terms of their effect on communities' ability to help themselves. Not only have people become less able to deal with their own problems, but able individuals have lost the habit of helping.

The civic institutions that strengthen community have deteriorated, collapsed, or retreated—especially among America's urban poor. The growth and centralization of government has contributed to this collapse, crowding out voluntary self-help efforts. Rather than enhancing community efforts, government has often displaced them. "The power to replace an institution like a family or a neighborhood is the power to destroy it," notes former HUD Secretary Jack Kemp.[8]

Like the free market, government has limitations as well. The failure of various communist countries showed what happens when government controls the economy. The problems America now faces show the problems that occur when government takes over those areas best left to families and communities. In his classic work, *Democracy in America*, Alexis de Tocqueville presaged the dangers of overdependence on the government: "The morals and intelligence of a democratic people would be in as much danger as its commerce and industry if ever a government wholly usurped the place of private associations."[9]

Democracy is more than just majority rule. American democracy was premised on the idea that each individual, absent compelling evidence to the contrary, is assumed to be the best judge of his or her interest.[10] In the past several decades, Americans have ceded a great deal of power to government in the name of compassionate paternalism. We've seen the results. It is time to return to the simple virtues of self-governance. Individuals need to be given the power and the responsibility to run their lives, their families, and their community institutions without the heavy hand of government. The term applied to such a power shift is "devolution."

DEVOLUTION: GIVING COMMUNITY INSTITUTIONS
THE ROOM TO GROW

Devolution means two things. First, it means decentralizing government, moving authority down to local levels of government and thus involving individuals more in their own governance (this aspect of devolution will be the focus of Chapter 11). Second, devolution means transferring responsibility from government to individuals, families, and voluntary associations. Each is appropriate in certain cases. Both are crucial as Americans struggle to regain control of their lives, and community builders try to revitalize America's now weakened local civic institutions, the traditional source of mutual assistance and support.

In 1994, Vice President Gore's National Performance Review reported that "the terrible truth is that most Americans don't trust government to do the right thing."[11] While certainly true, it is also true that government doesn't trust the American people to do the right thing. Parents aren't trusted to choose the best schools for their children. Washington doesn't trust local governments to police their communities. Government micromanages every aspect of our lives, from raising children to managing our businesses to planning for retirement.

Over time, government has taken more authority from families; states have taken power from cities and towns; and the federal government has assumed power from states. Reversing this trend won't occur without a struggle. Those who wield power are loathe to transfer authority downwards. Devolution is a revolutionary change. As Arizona Governor Fife Symington aptly notes, "The great divide in American politics today is between those who would relish power, and those who long to relinquish it."[12]

FIRST, DO NO HARM TO COMMUNITY

*The true greatness of any nation is not found in the appara-
tus of government or state power. It is found in the people
and all their spontaneous social, economic, and spiritual
associations—in their families, churches and synagogues,
fraternal and neighborhood organizations and all those
"mediating institutions" that are the real source of economic, social and cultural progress.*

New York Governor George Pataki[13]

What would happen if the government didn't have massive
programs to answer every societal problem? To answer this
question, we must first look to history.

For the first century and a half of America's existence, government didn't do much to help people; the federal government did virtually nothing. When problems arose, Americans
looked to themselves, their families, their churches, and their
neighbors to overcome them. (If government did provide aid, it
was usually at the most local level.)

Since the early days of the American republic, strong, active
voluntary associations of self-governing communities have been
the glue that holds American society together. Traveling
throughout America in the 1830s, Alexis de Tocqueville
described these self-reliant groups.[14] Tocqueville considered the
impulse to mutual aid as one of America's most salient features:

*The Americans make associations to give entertainments, to
found seminaries, to build inns, to construct churches, to diffuse books, to send missionaries to the antipodes; in this manner they found hospitals, prisons, and schools. . . . Wherever at
the head of some new undertaking you see the government in*

France, or a man of rank in England, in the United States you will be sure to find an association.[15]

The voluntary institutions of Tocqueville's America flourished in an environment of limited government. There is every reason to believe they would do so again today. Amitai Etzioni, author of *The Spirit of Community*, tells of his experience as a White House senior advisor during the Mariel exodus of 1980, which saw 125,266 Cuban refugees arrive in Florida. At the time, Etzioni argued that existing charities could deal with their resettlement, but he was overruled. Instead, a federal bureaucracy took over. Writing in *National Review*, Etzioni describes what happened next:

> *The U.S. Resettlement Agency, with [Victor] Palmieri at the helm, took on the mission. Congress appropriated additional funds and authorized additional bureaucrats. Palmieri hired people, drafted plans, prepared guidelines, contacted federal agencies, and so on. . . . By the time he got to Miami, most of the 125,000 Cubans had disappeared.*[16]

Before the bureaucracy arrived, the problem had largely solved itself. Where had the refugees disappeared to? "Most of them were taken care of by their own," writes Etzioni, helped by "family members already settled in the United States, friends, Catholic Charities, and Cuban-American associations. . . ."

While the informal resettlement process was not perfect, it did work remarkably well, especially for those refugees who were willing to work for their own betterment. Within nine months, all but 6,900 Cubans out of the original 125,000 were settled to the point that they stopped being public charges. This success rate is stunning when one considers that the refugees included an estimated 5,000 hard-core criminals or mental patients. Writes Etzioni, "To sustain such community endeavors, we need to prevent government from pre-empting communities. The more the government takes over providing services, the flabbier and more anemic communities become."[17]

The weaker communities become, of course, the greater the apparent need for government assistance. This brings us to the Iron Law of Community Destruction: a supply of government aid creates its own demand. Alexis de Tocqueville anticipated this vicious cycle nearly 150 years earlier: "The more government takes the place of associations, the more will individuals lose the idea of forming associations and need the government to come to their help. This is a vicious cycle of cause and effect."[18]

In the past, voluntary community groups arose out of necessity; economic survival demanded cooperation and mutual assistance. For example, barns could not be raised without a cooperative effort; therefore, neighbors held barn raisings. The great paradox of government aid is that by relieving hardship it weakens self-reliance. Recipients of aid come to believe that they are incapable of bettering their condition. Psychologists call this phenomenon "learned helplessness."

The recent government approach of airlifting in resources to distressed communities encourages dependency and weakens what's left of existing self-help mechanisms. "The evidence is overwhelming in developing societies that if outside plans and resources dominate and overwhelm local initiatives and associations, massive social and economic disasters result," says Northwestern University professor John McKnight.[19]

In effect, government aid can destroy a village in an effort to save it. In Steinbeck's *Of Mice and Men*, the dimwitted but powerful Lenny consistently crushes the life out of his beloved mice; similarly, the "helping hand" of government has clumsily crushed the fragile spirit of community. Ineffective government programs tend to crowd out effective private ones.[20]

Our Lady of Victory's homeless shelter in Brooklyn was a casualty of such government aid. For 13 years, Our Lady of Victory had operated a shelter for homeless men, many of them alcoholics. Our Lady of Victory not only provided shelter, it had helped 1,400 men put their lives back together. "There was no order in their lives," Monsignor Nugent told the *New York Times.* "We had to show them how to put that order and discipline back." Soon after the city opened two shelters within walking distance, the church shelter didn't have enough demand and closed its doors.[21]

Why did so many homeless men choose the city shelter over Our Lady of Victory? Because church counselors demanded that those seeking aid change their behavior. Guests at Our Lady of Victory had to avoid alcohol, receive counseling, and look for jobs. At the city shelter, clients didn't have to put up with such "hassles."

The story of Our Lady of Victory illustrates two important points. First, in a twist on Gresham's Law, bad charity often drives out good charity. Second, community-based programs are more likely to require effort on the part of recipients—to challenge people to reach their full potential.

If America's trend toward bigger government and weaker communities is to be reversed, government must begin doing less. This means returning to first principles. Tough questions must be asked about the whole panoply of well-meaning but self-defeating government programs established over the past 30 years:

- Is the program undermining community self-help efforts?
- Is the program providing indiscriminate material aid for a problem that is primarily behavioral in nature?
- Would the object of the program be better met by mediating institutions in the absence of a government program?
- Are there government-imposed barriers preventing or discouraging a community response?
- Are there ways to increase the supply of mediating institutions?

Many Americans have problems. But rather than top-down government solutions, the best policy for government is to foster an enabling environment in which individual, familial, and community solutions can flourish. Strong societies are built from the bottom up.

Community, Technology, and Modernism

Government policies are not the sole cause of the weakening of America's community institutions. Technology, affluence, and enhanced mobility have also played an important role.

Social bonds require nurturing. It takes time for people to develop caring networks, and today's highly mobile population works against the stable framework needed for community. In simpler times, many people would live their entire lives without traveling far from their village. Not so today.

"It is rare to the point of being bizarre to have the bulk of one's peers living in one neighborhood," writes Joel Garreau in *Edge City*.[22] Garreau notes that many people living in the suburban edge cities that have sprung up in recent years frequently complain of a lack of community. Like their shopping malls, some of these new communities are sterile, impersonal, and lacking in character. Mobile modern professionals often lack social fulfillment and complain of isolation.

Rather than neighbors and relatives, more people are cultivating relationships through their work. Companies are striving to provide their employees with social networks and meaningful labor. Information workers establish relationships by logging onto the Internet, where they experience "virtual community." These social networks are more transitory than in times past, and the bonds formed more tenuous. While liberating, affluence has also had the effect of weakening community cohesion.

Cities suffer built-in obstacles to strong neighborhoods: a large portion of transitory residents and renters. Cities are typically made up of small numbers of young, single professionals— yuppies—who enjoy the bustle of the city for a few years before heading off to the suburbs to raise a family. Joining them are the bulk of urban dwellers, the very poor—often minorities, the elderly, and newly arrived immigrants. Because many of these people are renters who move frequently, social affiliations are more difficult to preserve. The high incidence of broken families exacerbates the problem of social stability. Working class, homeowning families—an essential ingredient for strong neighborhoods—have overwhelmingly abandoned the city for the suburbs.

Changing social customs also work against community stability. Divorce, illegitimacy, and the increase in two-working-parent families have eroded the single most important community institution, the family. More than a quarter of all babies are born to single mothers, and over half of American children will spend at least a substantial part of their childhoods living apart from their fathers by the time they reach the age of eighteen.[23]

The forces of modernism unquestionably contribute to the unraveling of community bonds. There is nothing that public policy can or should do to reverse these trends—you can't keep the boys on the farm after they've seen the big city. But there is no reason for government to pursue policies that exacerbate the problems of establishing communal bonds.

WHY COMMUNITY HELP IS BETTER THAN GOVERNMENT AID

Not what we give, but what we share, For the gift without the giver is bare.

James Russell Lowell

Earlier we noted that the free market can't satisfy certain human needs; for example, you can't buy a friend. In addition, we saw that the profit motive is often held in scorn, especially when contrasted to the noble intentions of government programs. Noble intentions, however, are an overrated virtue.

Government programs may arise out of compassion, but they are administered by bureaucracies. Most government programs are ill-suited for providing for those human needs that deal with behavior and attitude, largely because government programs are constrained by the laws, rules, and regulations by which they are carried out. Only the third pillar of society, families, friends, associations, charities, and the like, can provide the sort of guidance, dedicated caring, and support that can effectively deal with people's nonmaterial needs. This third pillar combines noble intentions with the freedom to effectively achieve their objectives.

The "little platoons" of the third pillar work in myriad ways: coaching a Little League baseball team, teaching Sunday school, establishing neighborhood crime watches, or looking after a neighbor's child. The third pillar includes the nexus of human relationships that shape an individual's values, attitudes, and beliefs, providing an individual with a sense of purpose and belonging. Writes philanthropist Michael Joyce of the Bradley Foundation, "Our civil institutions give form and substance to the everyday qualities and values without which life itself would be impossible: honesty, perseverence, self-restraint, personal responsibility and service to others. These institutions act by rewarding us when these values appear, punishing when they do not, and by mercifully and willingly sustaining those who fall behind."[24]

It is in this last area—help for those in need—that the third pillar contributes something neither the market nor government can. Markets ill serve those without resources, while rule-based governmental efforts to provide aid typically establish destructive incentives by rewarding nonproductive behavior.

Private mediating institutions, in contrast, are often able to provide aid while simultaneously promoting independence rather than dependence. They help people to be functioning, productive members of society. Unlike the therapeutic philosophy often promoted by government social programs, many community groups emphasize individual responsibility and make demands on those they help. Unlike impersonal institutional assistance, community groups often dispense aid with love, judgment, and personal attention. Unlike government's tendency to rely on outside experts, community rebuilders are often "nonprofessionals"—parents, relatives, neighbors, recovering drug addicts—armed only with a commitment to provide aid and a personal familiarity with those they help. Unlike a rule-based system, these caregivers will do whatever they think is best for their charges—*including withholding aid*.

Not all community institutions exhibit such characteristics, but government programs almost never do.[25] The problem is systemic. Government is good at dispensing a check, meal, or lodging but is not good at exercising discretion. Government agencies are ill-suited to provide caring, nurturing assistance or to practice tough love, challenging people to improve themselves by conditioning aid on changes in behavior.

In most cases, the only requirement for receiving aid from government programs is that recipients remain in a dependent condition. Moreover, government programs treat all recipients alike, even those with very different needs. Rules that ensure equity prevent dispensers of government aid from making personal judgments about what might be best for those seeking help.

Consider how the government "helps" substance abusers. Through the Supplemental Security Income (SSI) and Social Security Disability Insurance (SSDI) programs, the federal government hands out about $1.4 billion a year to a quarter-million adults, most of whom are alcoholics or drug addicts. Not surprisingly, many addicts use this money to feed their habits. Numerous studies have shown that only about 1 percent ever recover or get jobs.[26] The majority get off the dole by dying or going to jail. "Hundreds of millions of scarce federal dollars are flowing directly to drug addicts, who are turning around and buying heroin, cocaine, and other illegal drugs on the street the very same day," says Senator William Cohen of Maine, who led a year-long investigation into the program."[27]

It doesn't take a Senate investigation to find the horror stories. We learned of one 21-year-old from an upper middle-class background, able-bodied, who was a heavy drinker and casual drug user. His own mother, who is quite well off, refused to support him because she felt he needed to pull himself together. Eventually, this young man applied for social security support because he had "anxiety." Initially turned down, ten months later his case was approved on appeal. As a result, he got a $7,000 lump-sum payment for the ten months between his initial application and the appeal. He now gets $700 a month to support his life-style of watching television, drinking, and sleeping. Neither taxpayers nor this pathetic young man are benefiting from this arrangement.[28]

Eloise Anderson, director of the California Department of Social Services, would like to end this sort of destructive charity. "I don't believe in giving a substance abuser a check for one minute, because most of them use it to support their habits."[29] Eligibility rules, however, require Anderson's department to mail out the checks against her better judgment. In fact, despite the destructive impact on recipients, the "dollars for drugs" program was expanded by the Social Security Administration; between 1989 and 1993, the SSI rolls skyrocketed 150 percent.

"I really believe that SSI stands for 'Some Sort of Insanity,' says Bob Cote, a recovering alcoholic who directs a Step 13 addiction recovery center in Denver. Cote, whose Step 13 houses over 100 homeless men, calls the SSI program "compassion without logic." His center conducts regular drug tests and requires residents to work at regaining control of their lives. "Make 'em work for their keep before you feed them," says Cote. "This something for nothing is a bunch of crap. Instead of coddling these guys, make 'em do what they're capable of."[30]

Pushing people to improve themselves is the stuff of real compassion. After all, life is nothing but a series of obstacles. When set upon by the slings and arrows of outrageous fortune that are the daily fare of human existence, people respond in one of two ways: they give up or they get tough. Either approach is habit-forming.

There is a natural inclination to help those in need. Sometimes, however, helping doesn't help.

The First Lutheran Church's soup kitchen in Sandpoint, Idaho, closed its doors in 1993 after only three years of operation. Why? Because volunteers decided their aid was doing more harm than good. Rather than helping people escape poverty, the soup kitchen was encouraging dependency. "We saw the same people coming year after year. They aren't learning anything and they aren't being helped by being given a free meal," says Brigitte Sanborn, the head of the soup kitchen committee. "I'd like to see where we can be of help in teaching them how to take care of themselves."[31]

Supporting dependence is anathema to those dedicated to rebuilding broken lives. "When charity creates a disincentive for an able-bodied person to work, it leads this person down the wrong path," declares Father Robert Sirico, president of the Acton Institute for the Study of Religion and Liberty. "It encourages indolence."[32] Dispensing money blindly can cause more harm than good. As the Bible puts it, "If you do good, know for whom you are doing it, and your kindness will have its effect."[33]

THE INADEQUACY OF PROVIDING MATERIAL AID FOR SPIRITUAL PROBLEMS

We just quoted the Bible. If we were a government agency, we could get in trouble for that. Government is prohibited from delving into issues of religious values, and this limits government's ability to deal with certain issues. In November 1993, Clinton told a black congregation in Memphis: "Unless we say some of this cannot be done by government, because we have to reach deep inside to the values, the spirit, the soul, and the truth of human nature, none of the other things we seek to do will ever take us to where we need to go." You can't address problems of attitude with material assistance.

Though some may find meaning outside a faith-based religion, many individuals find a sense of purpose through religion. Individuals such as Step 13's Bob Cote and self-help groups such as Alcoholics Anonymous seek to *transform* lives, and they do so by calling on a higher power than that which resides in Washington, D.C.

The growth of government has undermined religious institutions. "Black churches stopped doing their job because people oversold the role of government during the civil rights movement," says the Reverend Lee Earl, the pastor of Detroit's 12th Street Baptist Church.[34] According to Reverend Earl, once black officials were elected, parishioners came to expect the government to "do all those things for our people that the churches had done previously." With both anger and disappointment in his voice, Reverend Earl explains what happened: "We had been looking to the church, which provided leadership on the condition that you were a moral person. When government became the institution that you looked to, at best you looked to an amoral institution, at worst you looked to an immoral institution. With government, you don't have to live a moral life to get help. In fact, the more immoral you are the more help you can get."[35]

Reverend Lee Earl knows firsthand what a community can do for itself through its church. Earl became pastor of the predominantly black 12th Street Baptist Church on the northwest side of Detroit in 1981. "The Lord was calling me to do some work in low-income communities," says Earl.

When Earl arrived, 12th Street was a war zone. Police officers referred to the 12th Street neighborhood as "the Hole." An open-air drug market operated in front of the church. Prostitutes used the church parking lot to meet their customers, and there was a crack cocaine processing plant two doors down from the house of worship. "It's hard to talk about the hereafter when you are so overwhelmed by the here and now," says Reverend Earl.

On a shoestring, Earl formed a company called REACH, Inc.[36] One by one, REACH bought up the former crack houses and kicked the drug dealers out of the neighborhood. Whereas Jesus cleared the temple with a corded whip, Reverend Earl used cash. "I reasoned that the best way to close the dope house was to buy the dope house. If we own the house, we decide who lives in the house."

After buying a rundown crack house, volunteers would renovate the building. REACH would then sell or lease it to church members in need of housing. Many of these buyers were single, working mothers who were unable to obtain traditional mortgages. Reverend Earl nonetheless considered them a good risk. "The bank does not know my neighbor like I know my neighbor," says Earl. Under Reverend Earl's leadership at 12th Street Baptist Church, a community arose. The church offers child care, senior services, Bible studies, and other mutual aid services and activities to its members. Giving seemed to beget giving. A decade after REACH purchased its first crack house, it had bought and rehabilitated over 50 houses; neighborhood crime had dropped 37 percent.

But Reverend Earl offers a warning to those who would attempt to duplicate his success:

> *In the past thirteen years, I have learned a very difficult lesson, which is that addressing material poverty without addressing behavioral poverty and spiritual poverty is spitting in the wind. We have a poverty of spirit which leads to a poverty of behavior which leads to a physical, material poverty. You can fix all of the houses you want, but until you fix the hearts and the souls of people in them you are spitting in the wind, because those same people will cut your throat when you get done building that house for them.*[37]

It's easy to repair a house. All that is needed are hammer and nails, but for those problems rooted in the attitudes of the individual, government lacks the tools to make the needed repairs.

Whether explicitly religious or not, successful community-building organizations focus on *healing* those they help. This is why radical devolution is critical. Local efforts and private institutions of caring are what's needed to cure what ails many American communities. In Boston's depressed Roxbury neighborhood, YouthBuild Boston, a nonreligious organization, is engaged in a process of human reclamation that reaches deep into individuals' lives. On one level, YouthBuild takes crumbling properties owned by the Boston Redevelopment Authority and helps young men rebuild them. On a deeper level, YouthBuild takes young men with crumbling lives and rebuilds them from the inside out. YouthBuild teaches these young people a trade, the responsibility of hard work, and the pride of accomplishment. YouthBuild also teaches basic classroom academics such as reading and mathematics. Most important of all, however, YouthBuild teaches students a new outlook on life.

YouthBuild deals with men 18 to 24 years of age who are in deep despair. Often gang members and drug users, over half of YouthBuild's students have been in jail. When a new student enters the YouthBuild program, the very first thing he receives is two weeks of "mental toughness" training. This training is a form of intensive counseling that attempts to improve the new student's attitude toward life by purging his psyche of years of accumulated negativity. "We don't let the students into a classroom or onto a construction site until they complete mental toughness training," says Jackie Gelb, the program's director. "That means becoming mentally, spiritually, and emotionally ready to take on something that is challenging and disciplined."[38]

YouthBuild brings hope to the despairing. What makes it work? "It's like a family here. It's an environment of people that care about them," says Gelb. "Our counseling, mental toughness training, and leadership development—the core of what we do, really—is geared to develop the internal strength to help students go after what they want . . . We also demand a lot of the students. We tell students, 'You have to do it yourself.'"[39]

UNPROFESSIONAL BEHAVIOR

As of 1994, YouthBuild Boston received only a fraction of its operating costs through government. Each year, students are turned away for lack of funds. But YouthBuild's success has drawn the attention of the federal Department of Housing and Urban Development, which may funnel millions of dollars to fledgling YouthBuild programs across the country. It would be nice if YouthBuild's success could be replicated with just a supply of federal dollars, but success won't come so easily. The key to YouthBuild is an intangible sense of caring that cannot be purchased at any price. In the hands of federal experts, the YouthBuild program is likely to be replicated in form but not in substance. There are dozens of government-run education, training, and counseling programs that fail to produce Youth-Build's kind of results. *Newsweek* columnist Joe Klein offers an explanation:

> *Traditional social work has been elevated from a calling—that is, a quasi-religious, charitable activity—to a "profession" in the 20th century. The results have not been inspiring. Most members of the "helping professions" begin with the best intentions but ultimately drift into less strenuous realms. They tend to be bureaucratic processors, paper shufflers, 9-to-5ers.*[40]

Compassion and commitment are more important to success than money. "We've played out the outside strategies, developed by outsider elites. It didn't work," says Northwestern Professor John McKnight. "It's time to go back to what works. All community development of any consequence has always been based on local people and local assets—it's how every community in North America got started."[41]

It is remarkable how often successful rehabilitation programs are staffed by former substance abusers and other amateurs with a personal, maniacal desire to help others. Unlike government administrators, these community builders come from within the community, armed with common sense and commitment rather than academic training.

"Dealing with gangs is not a nine-to-five job. You really have to get into it," says Leon Watkins, who has worked with young gang members in South Central Los Angeles for over 20 years. "You can't slide in for a haphazard study . . . you have to put your time into it and you have to put yourself into it."[42]

Outside-expert solutions have not worked as well as the messy, quirky assistance of untrained but caring family members, neighbors, and friends.

AMATEUR PARENTS

The most essential social institution is the family. Families are the main conduit for transmitting values and preparing the next generation for responsible adulthood. As President Clinton put it, "Governments don't raise children. Parents do."

How true. Why then is the federal government's number one education goal that every child shall enter school ready to learn? Does the government intend to influence this by taking over the raising of children? (Some experts go further, urging the government to establish licensing requirements for potential parents.[43]) Unfortunately, the paternalistic state is increasingly encroaching on the realm of child rearing. According to *Business Week*:

Increasingly, early-childhood experts agree that children and their families need a host of services—education, health care, social support—if kids are to thrive and prosper . . . Some 30 states have major reforms under way to help young children and their families . . . At the same time, the federal Health and Human Services Department is encouraging Head Start to run full-day programs where needed. Separately, it is launching "Early Head Start," to serve families with kids under three . . .

*In 1993, [Hawaii] unveiled a vision for creating and financing
a state-wide system of early-childhood education and care, similar in scope to its system of universal health care.*[44]

This is Tocqueville's vicious cycle revisited. As governments
take over child-raising, family bonds weaken, increasing the
need for government aid. Such an approach makes virtually no
demands on the part of those receiving aid, treating them as
helpless children rather than responsible parents. Instead of
stepping in like a comic-book hero, government needs to
respect parents. Absent compelling evidence to the contrary,
parents should be assumed to be the best judges of their children's well-being. As mother Thelma Moton of Little Rock,
Arkansas, put it at a citizen forum, "Our children belong to us.
Uncle Sam is just that, an uncle . . . Uncle Sam is not to replace
me in my home and my husband as head of my home, and we
need to shout loudly as a group of people and tell Uncle Sam
where his place is, and then demand that Uncle Sam stay in his
place."[45]

Bureaucracies simply aren't very good at raising children.
Children need special attention. "I love my children, but it's a
real sacrifice to do it right," one parent told us. "You couldn't
pay me to do this for some stranger's kid."[46] Raising children
isn't easy, but anyone unprepared to raise children shouldn't
have them.[47]

Devolution means expecting individuals to take responsibility for their offspring. Instead of appealing to the government,
18 African-American fathers in Omaha, Nebraska, took matters into their own hands and formed MAD DADS (Men
Against Destruction—Defending Against Drugs and Social
Disorder). "This strong group of men paint over gang graffiti,
and challenge drug dealers and gang members to get out of the
area," says group member Eddie Stanton. "These loving
fathers also provide positive community activities for youth,
chaperone community events and provide street counseling
for those in need."[48] Over 800 fathers now belong to MAD

DADS in Omaha, and local chapters have been opened in eight other states.

SELF-GOVERNED COMMUNITIES

If anyone will restore civility to America's ravaged neighborhoods it will be the people who live in them.

Located in an upper-middle-class Indianapolis neighborhood, Holiday Park was a modern urban nightmare. Drug dealers and male prostitutes had set up permanent shop, and local residents were afraid to go anywhere near the park. After dark, not even the police felt safe in Holiday Park.

In 1990, a courageous group of neighbors finally said, "Enough." They banded together and asked Indianapolis for permission to take back their park. They proceeded to raise $300,000 in private donations for new equipment, a security guard, and better upkeep. The former drug-infested park is now safe enough for family picnics.

The story of Holiday Park must become the story of our future. For just as our communities have decayed one neighborhood at a time, rebuilding community institutions, if it is to occur at all, must proceed one neighborhood at a time as well. Personal involvement of local residents is essential to revitalization.[49]

It won't be easy. Mayor Goldsmith's attempts to replicate this experience in other Indianapolis communities have not been terribly successful.[50] In several cases, Goldsmith has tried to transfer responsibility for park maintenance to local residents. Unfortunately, Goldsmith found that many neighborhoods lacked the necessary community institutions to accomplish even this simple task. "Over time, governments have essentially taken the place of the private leadership of neighborhoods," says Mayor Goldsmith. According to the mayor, many communities had lost the capacity and will to solve their own problems.[51]

Like individuals, communities may need to be pushed toward excellence and self-reliance. Government must return to the community those functions that give it purpose. Ultimately, the strength of America's communities hinges on their having something important to do. Ordinary people are capable of extraordinary achievements if challenged to make meaningful contributions.

Delivering Public Services with Volunteers

No one knows for certain what percentage of work now performed by public employees could be handled by volunteers, but it could be a lot more than people might imagine.

"I don't think there has been a time in the history of this country that there weren't volunteers when you asked for volunteers," says San Diego Mayor Susan Golding. Unfortunately, nowadays many governments often limit or even prohibit the use of volunteers for many public services. In some cities, union contracts prohibit the city from using volunteers if public employees could do the same job. For example, the San Diego police department's extensive use of volunteers would be blocked by police union contracts in most cities.

Moreover, government lawyers often discourage the use of volunteers because of liability issues. Mayor Golding recounts what happened when the city was forced to look at closing numerous libraries during the early 1990s recession: "I was hearing from lots of San Diego citizens who said, 'Don't close the libraries. Don't cut the hours, I'm willing to volunteer.' The city attorneys told me they can't do it because they'd have to handle money, and because of the liability, and so on. There's always a reason they give you why we can't use volunteers. My attitude is that it's all nonsense!"[52]

Libraries are a good example. California's recession of the early 1990s forced the closure of dozens of local libraries. Palm Springs, despite its reputation as a playground for the very rich, didn't escape the hard times. In June 1992, the city closed the

Welwood Murray Memorial Library and removed every book from its shelves. A day later, the library started a new life as a private volunteer library, run by a newly incorporated nonprofit foundation.[53]

"They left us with nothing," says library trustee Jeanette Hardenburg, gesturing towards the library entrance now filled with glass cases of Indian jewelry and pottery. "And the building hadn't been properly maintained for years. Volunteers did everything you see here—refinished the ceiling, donated display cases."[54] Palm Springs' volunteer library now has more than double the number of books it had as a public library.

Perhaps you are thinking, Well, sure. There are a lot of book lovers out there, and library work isn't that difficult. Nobody would volunteer for the hard jobs. Think again, and try to imagine work more demanding and dangerous than putting out fires. Firefighters have to be a little bit crazy, for while most people are running out of burning buildings, firefighters are running *into* them. But there are obviously a lot of crazy Americans, for the *majority* of our nation's fire departments are manned by volunteers.

That's not a misprint. Over three-quarters of all the fire departments in America are staffed entirely by volunteers.[55] About 1.5 million Americans serve their communities as volunteer firefighters; they think it only natural that neighbors help each other out.[56] Their only pay is the gratitude of their communities, but there is often a waiting list. These groups not only put out flames, they ignite a spirit of community.

Perhaps you are thinking, Well, sure. Firefighting is tough work, but it's exciting. Nobody would volunteer for the *dull* jobs. Tell that to the citizens of San Juan Bautista, California. When city officials there ran up a $120,000 deficit on an $850,000 yearly budget, townspeople took matters into their own hands. First, they fired the entire city staff—six full-time and six part-time workers. Next, townspeople simply stepped in and volunteered to run virtually the entire government. (Sheriff services are rented from the county.) Not just the library and the fire department, but even the public works department was staffed by San Juan Bautista citizen volunteers.

THE TENANT MANAGEMENT MOVEMENT

Housing projects are synonymous with high crime, drug abuse, and domestic violence. Yet even within these forlorn dwellings the inhabitants have what it takes to create healthy community. Rather than accept their hellish conditions, some government-housing residents have decided to change them.

Empowered by the Housing and Community Development Act of 1987, residents at some of the worst housing projects in the nation have taken control of their environments. The movement, termed "tenant management," gives residents a chance to run, and eventually own, public housing projects.[57] The idea was pioneered in Great Britain, which under Margaret Thatcher sold 1.2 million public housing units to their tenants, increasing the fraction of British citizens owning their home from just about half to roughly two-thirds.

Having a sense of ownership matters. Cochran Gardens in St. Louis used to be known as a hellish den for narcotics dealers. Residents have made Cochran Gardens livable again, making it a model tenant management corporation.[58] Over 250 residents have been employed in the tenant management corporation's enterprises, which include janitorial services, a child care center, and a health clinic.

Tenant management also transformed the A. Harry Moore public housing development in Jersey City, New Jersey. Responsible for their own building maintenance, tenants improved it. Dissatisfied by inadequate police protection, the tenant corporation formed resident patrols to combat crime. The A. Harry Moore project has become a place where people can live decent lives. Vacancy rates, which hovered around 20 percent in the early 1970s, have dropped down to less than 2 percent. A. Harry Moore is a place residents care about. Delinquent rent payments are a third what they once were.[59]

An illuminating paradox emerges from these stories. The negative environment of public housing—the drugs, crime, etc.—is created by the people who live there. At the same time, people living in public housing must be the source of their revitalization. The challenge for those living within such communities is daunting, but we believe every community has what it takes to create positive change. Says Jersey City Mayor Bret Schundler, "What's plaguing life in our housing projects isn't material deprivation, but a lack of a sense of meaning. They don't have a sense of what they can actually become on their own."[60]

Tenant management gives individuals a stake in their own environment and creates habits of responsibility. It gives tenants both the power and the responsibility that will enable them to improve their situation.

When individuals and groups must provide for themselves they learn not only self-reliance but the importance of cooperative effort. In Sun City, Arizona, a private residential community association catering to senior citizens, the residents largely police themselves. Sun City's 183-member "police force" is an all-volunteer unit called Sun City Posse—and it has far more members than the local police could ever provide. "In the days of the Wild West, the sheriff would go into a bar and pick out four or five people and deputize them and go out and catch the bad guy," says Sun City Posse Commander Jack Goodrich. "Now bring it up to modern status, why, we are on a continuing posse status. They don't let us go when the job is done. We're a permanent crime-control posse."[61] The Sun City Posse offers security and a sense of community involvement. The psychological impact of involving people in providing services to their community has a positive ripple effect that cannot be discounted.

SUPPORTING NONPROFITS: A TRICKY BUSINESS

Since nonprofit community institutions are so important to community revitalization, it is tempting for government to funnel funds to these groups. But government has to be careful not to kill the goose that lays the golden egg.

The golden egg is the direct involvement of community volunteers. "You can't ignore the multiplier effect that volunteers have," says Massachusetts Governor William Weld. "Voluntarism is a tremendous untapped resource. There are battered women shelters where the volunteer-to-staff ratio is ten to one. People care about these things, and are willing to pitch in. Nonprofits can be of tremendous help to the community, as long as they're organized in a good way and don't get caught up in the government bureaucracy."[63]

That last part is tricky. It is very easy for government funding to entangle nonprofits in a bureaucratic web of rules and regulations. Government money and strings that come with it can alter the essential nature of these nonprofit groups. Some nonprofits are not motivated by charity, but by commercial interest. If governments are to assist charities, they must be sure to do so in ways that don't destroy their personal, compassionate orientation—and hence their special healing abilities.

The rise of government-funded nonprofit charity is a recent phenomenon. For most of America's history, nonprofits were privately funded. In some cases, local governments would provide a small subsidy to groups providing social services (federal aid was virtually nonexistent). Private charities preferred it that way. As Steven Rathgeb Smith and Michael Lipsky note in their book, *Nonprofits for Hire*:

> *It is instructive to note that the widely heralded settlement houses of the Progressive Era avoided public subsidies ... Dependence on private funds was consistent with the settle-*

*ment house philosophy that the community should take care
of its own citizens . . . Hostility toward government led Progressive Era reformers to campaign against public subsidies to
nonprofit organizations. By 1930, twenty-six states had constitutional limits on public funding of nonprofit agencies.*[64]

It is difficult to imagine many of today's nonprofit agencies
lobbying *against* government funding. But dependence on government funding is relatively new; the authors note that "even
in the mid-1960s nonprofit agencies were still overwhelmingly
reliant on private funds."[65] Then came a dramatic shift in the
relationship between governments and the nonprofit sector.
Governments began to use nonprofits to deliver the services of
the welfare state.

Catholic Charities U.S.A. received over $1.25 billion in gov-
ernment funds in 1993, 65 percent of its revenue.[66] The Child
Welfare League of America says that its members get 59 percent
of their revenue from the government.[67] The United Way of
America estimates that affiliate agencies treating substance
abuse received 62 percent of their funding from government,
and those working in mental health 64 percent.[68] Some nonprofits get 100 percent of their funding from government. Others
were established specifically to tap into a government funding
source. "The old concept of the charitable organization as local
do-gooder has been replaced by the nonprofit as government
vendor," write Robin Kamen and Steve Malanga, looking at
New York City's government-supported nonprofits.[69]

Just as continued dependence on public funding erodes the
spirit of individuals, government funding can fundamentally
alter the nature of nonprofit groups. Like his Progressive Era
forerunners, nonprofit executive Bertram M. Beck warns nonprofits against relying on government support: "Truly voluntary associations are desperately needed for the revitalization of
the democratic process, but they cannot be supported by governments since governmental funding immediately contami-
nates their nature and is self-defeating."[70]

In 1968, only 10 percent of Volunteers of America's (VOA) funds came from government. By 1994, 69 percent of VOA's $289 million budget was gleaned from government coffers. With the government money have come changes in the agency's operations. "Government aid is actually restrictive because the money can only be spent in one way and limits our activities," says Art Smith, VOA's director of communications. "It also impairs your ability to go out and raise funds. That's a real danger all nonprofits face—just sitting back and figuring the government will take care of you."[71] A private charity can be gradually transformed by the influx of government cash until it resembles a government bureaucracy.

"That scenario has probably been played out time and time again," says Charlie Baker, Governor Weld's Secretary of Health and Human Services. "Though the presence of government money doesn't necessarily guarantee that scenario, it certainly leads to that scenario in some cases."[72]

Massachusetts has contracted extensively with nonprofits for social services since the early 1980s. Private service agencies receiving state funds employed over 66,000 people in Massachusetts in 1991, far more than were actually employed in state human service agencies.[73] While admitting the risk, Baker contends that contracting with nonprofits can be a win-win scenario. "I would almost always rather have the state act as a purchaser than as a provider," says Baker.

The Massachusetts experience with using nonprofits to deliver social services is decidedly mixed. Some nonprofits, especially those with strong governing boards, haven't allowed government funding to diminish their charitable purpose. But many nonprofits become more interested in the funds they are provided than the aid they are providing. They are charities in name only. Stories abound of six-figure salaries for nonprofit contractors, and private human service providers in Massachusetts have become a well-organized and highly effective political lobby for higher taxes.

PAID VOLUNTEERS

Just as some nonprofits aren't really nonprofits, some volunteers aren't really volunteers, either. Take for example Ameri-Corps, Bill Clinton's $1.5 billion national service program that reimburses "volunteers" for taking federally approved community service jobs. Each AmeriCorps "volunteer" receives an annual stipend of between $7,945 and $15,890, plus $4,725 towards paying higher education debts—and don't forget the bureaucratic overhead costs, as the money for these "volunteers" is funneled through hundreds of nonprofit groups across the country.

President Clinton has defended AmeriCorps, claiming it's "changing the way government works because there's no bureaucracy at all."[74] One multisite AmeriCorps director, who agreed to an interview on condition of anonymity, heartily disagrees. "The federal role is stifling," this director told us. "We spend all our time completing paperwork and filling out reports."[75]

It's the little rules that drive you crazy. Initially, to receive an AmeriCorps grant every local group had to require each of its paid "volunteers" to obtain training in CPR, first aid, conflict resolution, and communications skills. "They made a big deal about it; we had to divert people from the program to get all the training," the AmeriCorps director told us. "After all this, two months ago they waived the requirement. That's how it's been."

Though she characterizes herself as a liberal Democrat, this AmeriCorps director's experience has prompted her to rethink the government's role in community programs. "I don't think the federal government should have their hands in local programs and grassroots efforts," she says. "It's not their expertise. Members of Congress sit behind their desks in D.C. all day. They don't visit the programs. It should be left to people who have the passion to do it—people who are in the communities." On a last reflective note, she lets it all out: "I've lost faith in the government. The AmeriCorps programs should be moved out to the private sector where taxpayers have a choice about what they want to fund."

Governments want to fund programs that can be boiler-plated and replicated, yet the most successful community programs are usually unique and quirky—they are tailor-made to meet the challenges of local circumstances, making use of local resources. Private nonprofits enjoy the advantage of being able to exercise discretion, deciding how and to whom they will dispense aid. Government has to follow the rules.

Governments wishing to provide social services face a difficult dilemma. On the one hand, they want to encourage private charities. On the other hand, they don't want to destroy the spirit of philanthropy that informs these groups. One solution, discussed in more detail in Chapter 8, is to allow Americans to take a charitable tax credit for donations given to community groups that are involved in fighting poverty. This would allow people to send some of their tax dollars to charities instead of the government.

Another option is to strictly cap the amount of public funding of a nonprofit at a certain fraction of total revenue, perhaps one-third. In that way, an organization would still depend on private contributors for the majority of its funds. Since its growth and future would depend on attracting private funds, such a nonprofit would be reluctant to behave in a way that leads potential donors to believe that it is anything other than a true charity. With a "one-third rule," the government might achieve its goal of encouraging private charity rather than replacing it.

ELIMINATING GOVERNMENT BARRIERS
TO COMMUNITY RENEWAL

In addition to crowding out community self-help efforts, government often impedes community renewal through misguided regulations. Velma Williamson and Theresa Taylor, for example, used to give free haircuts to destitute men at Duluth, Minnesota's, Union Gospel Mission. Used to, that is, until the State Board of Barber Examiners found out about it. Since Velma and Theresa don't have barber's licenses, the Board of Barber Examiners ordered them to stop or face 90 days in jail and a $700 fine.[76]

Occupational licensing regulations, high tax rates, and stringent building, fire, and zoning codes act as barriers to local entrepreneurship and home ownership for low-income residents. A HUD demonstration project found that excessive local government housing and zoning regulations can increase the costs of new homes by one-third.[77] This is destructive to communities because home ownership makes a difference in forging community. While renters often come and go with little attachment to the community, a homeowner tends to care not only about his or her house, but also about the local parks, schools, and neighborhood crime.[78]

Government regulations can also present daunting obstacles to community service delivery. Explains New Jersey Governor Christine Todd Whitman, "Government sometimes comes in with all the best intentions in the world just to make things safer but ends up making it impossible to deliver a service. We put so many restrictions on things such as home care for children or the elderly. We've put in so many requirements like fire escapes, back doors, the huge paperwork burden, and so on that we've eliminated many pretty safe environments. Many people just don't want to put up with the hassle."[79]

These restrictions end up decreasing the supply of informal solutions. Day care is a prime example. In many cities, day care is considered a small business—even if there are only a half-dozen or so children in the house—and therefore prohibited from operating in residential neighborhoods without a special waiver. Even after securing a zoning waiver, a day-care provider has to comply with innumerable fire, building, and safety codes—usually written with schools in mind—that can require thousands of dollars in renovations. For example, neighbor-hood day-care providers are supposed to install a fire escape if the second story is used. And along with the rules come inspectors and paperwork that discourage informal arrangements.

The consequences of these rules can be tragic. In 1988, Mother Teresa's Missionaries of Charity were ready to spend $500,000 to convert a burnt-out building in the South Bronx into a much-needed homeless shelter. In addition to a vow of poverty, however, the sisters also avoid the use of modern conveniences, so they were perplexed when the city told them to spend upwards of $100,000 on an elevator they would not use. After almost two years of bureaucratic wrangling, the sisters gave up. The sisters were used to overcoming poverty and despair, but they proved no match for New York City's building code.[80]

RENEWAL FROM WITHIN

Those who hope for a brighter future for America shouldn't look to the government for salvation. Nor will free markets alone cure what ails the people of our nation. America's future depends greatly on the vitality of the third pillar of society—the private, voluntary arrangements that create strong community.

The breakdown of the family—the main building block of strong communities—is symptomatic of a larger breakdown of society as a whole. There is a crisis in American society that goes beyond crime, drug abuse, and violence; there is a human disconnect at the individual, family, and neighborhood level. The dissolution of these basic social bonds robs civil society of its civility.

The good intentions of many government programs haven't been enough. Too often, government programs have caused more harm than good, especially for those they were intended to assist. If history is any guide, renewal from within is the strategy that has the best chance of working. Devolving power from the government back to individuals is an important first step. As we shall see in future chapters, devolution is a key principle underlying many of the radical reforms under way or being discussed in areas such as crime, welfare, and education.

"Americans, especially the poor, are sick and tired of being told they're incompetent to run their own affairs; that they're helpless victims of social forces beyond their control," says Michael Joyce of the Bradley Foundation. "People are ready to seize control over their lives once again and become contributing citizens."[81] Americans are a compassionate and resourceful people, and what we need are policies that bring out the best in people. Unlike the grandiose promises of large-scale government programs, we do not pretend that this approach to community regeneration will save neighborhoods overnight. Community renewal takes time. But we have greater trust in individuals working out their own problems than in the government doing it for them. The future depends on each and every one of us. As Mahatma Gandhi put it, "We must live the change we wish to see in the world."

CHAPTER 4

COMPETITION: THE KEY TO EFFICIENT GOVERNMENT

It is better for the public to procure at the common market whatever the market can supply; because there it is by competition kept up in its quality, and reduced to its minimum price.

Thomas Jefferson[1]

A MATTER OF SOCIAL JUSTICE

"Efficiency in government is a matter of social justice," declares Milwaukee Mayor John Norquist.[2] Social justice? What does efficiency in government have to do with social justice?

Everything. Social justice may be a murky concept, but it is crystal clear that government shouldn't squander the hard-earned wealth of its citizens. After all, each dollar spent by government is a dollar taken from a taxpayer. When the government sends tax money down the drain, going down the drain with it is the sweat and toil of a productive citizen.

"If government does not provide its customers with a dollar's worth of service for every dollar it takes in taxes, then it isn't helping them out—it's ripping them off," says Indianapolis Mayor Stephen Goldsmith.[3] Efficiency is not an end in itself, but a truly just government will strive to be as efficient as possible.

And as Mayor Norquist reminds us, efficiency in government isn't just about money and taxes, it's about people. "You

Alro delivers...everyday

Alro Steel
Akron, OH .... (330) 929-4660
Alpena, MI .... (989) 354-4188
Battle Creek, MI ...... (269) 968-0234
Cadillac, MI .... (231) 775-9336
Dayton, OH .... (937) 253-6121
Detroit, MI .... (313) 366-8000
Flint, MI .... (810) 695-7300
Ft. Wayne, IN .... (260) 432-3524
Grand Rapids, MI .... (616) 452-5111
Grayling, MI .... (989) 348-3350
Indianapolis, IN ...... (317) 781-3800
Jackson, MI .... (517) 787-5500
Lansing, MI .... (517) 371-9600
Louisville, KY .... (502) 635-7481
Muncie, IN .... (765) 282-5335
Niles, MI .... (269) 687-4000

Alro Specialty Metals
Buffalo, NY .... (716) 877-6242
Charlotte, NC .... (704) 529-6880
Chicago, IL .... (708) 343-4343
Detroit, MI .... (313) 892-1212
Milwaukee, WI .... (262) 781-5615
Pittsburgh, PA .... (412) 279-1660
Redford, MI .... (313) 534-1300
St. Louis, MO .... (314) 726-3080
Toledo, OH .... (419) 666-4899
Tulsa, OK .... (918) 227-1456

Alro Metals Service Ctr.
Boca Raton, FL .... (561) 997-6766
Orlando, FL .... (407) 678-2576
Tampa, FL .... (813) 661-1646

Alro Industrial Supply
Cadillac, MI .... (231) 775-9336
Clearwater, FL .... (727) 572-4344
Grand Rapids, MI .... (616) 656-2800
Jackson, MI .... (517) 787-5500
Kalamazoo, MI .... (269) 343-9575

Alro Plastics
Grand Rapids, MI .... (616) 656-2820
Jackson, MI .... (517) 787-5500
Louisville, KY .... (502) 968-9980

Alro Metals Plus
Clearwater, FL .... (727) 572-4344
Jackson, MI .... (517) 788-3190
Kalamazoo, MI .... (269) 343-9575
Sarasota, FL .... (941) 952-1918

alro.com

can actually end up screwing the poor with inefficiency. By having a government that focuses on feeding itself, feeding its own bureaucracy, you end up delivering rotten service to people who deserve better," says Norquist. "In some cases, people are struggling to get out of poverty, and with great expense we force them back down."[4]

When government takes on a task, whether it is paving a street, providing education, or caring for the insane, real people receive this service. If the government doesn't provide them with the best service possible with the resources available, that, too, is unjust. Too often, our government has served those within government and forgotten the people paying the bills.

THE WAY GOVERNMENT WORKS—AND DOESN'T WORK

Economists don't agree on much, but just about every economist agrees that monopolies don't function very efficiently. It doesn't matter whether it's a private or government monopoly, customers often get neglected. That's what made Lily Tomlin's "Laugh-In" character, the sadistic telephone operator Ernestine, so funny: "When can we expect the $23.67 you owe us? You don't understand. This is the Telephone Company. We are omnipotent!"

In a few cases, monopolies may be the best way to accomplish a needed task. As a general rule, however, monopolies should be avoided if at all possible. Fortunately, there are few monopolies in the private sector. Unfortunately, government monopolies are as plentiful as post offices.

Our government has a schizophrenic attitude towards monopolies. On the one hand, government aggressively roots out monopolies in the private sector.[5] At great cost, the government waged a 13-year antitrust battle against IBM, which held about 70 percent of the market in computer mainframes. By the time the suit was dropped in 1982 (with the government admitting the case was "without merit"), Big Blue's market share had dropped to 62 percent in a market of rapidly diminishing importance.[6] Today, competition from hundreds of personal computer "clones" makes life difficult for IBM while making life pleasant for consumers.

On the other hand, government is equally energetic in *protecting* government monopolies. It is illegal for anyone but the U.S. Postal Service to carry first-class mail. The Postal Service has successfully sued companies that have tried to compete. Incredibly, in December 1993, postal inspectors were auditing companies and fining them if they used Federal Express or another carrier "for non-urgent" mail. One company, Equifax, was fined $30,000 by the Postal Service, essentially for using the competition.[7]

When customers don't have any options they aren't treated like customers. Your local post office is only open 9AM to 5PM Monday to Friday with special stand-in-line hours on Saturday morning because they know you can't go anywhere else. It doesn't work that way in a competitive market. In order to stay in business, IBM has to make its customers happy every day. A customer-support hotline that operates from 9AM to 5PM Monday to Friday just won't cut it, which is why IBM offers 24-hour-a-day on-line assistance. IBM works hard so its customers don't become someone else's customers.[8]

The free enterprise system has always been the economic engine of America's historic prosperity. Competition spurs producers to develop innovative ways of delivering products and services. Sam Walton's Wal-Mart revolutionized retailing, but Wal-Mart didn't come into existence after a congressional hearing on the "Consumer Goods Crisis." Wal-Mart began when a brash kid from Arkansas thought he could do things better than Sears and J.C. Penney. There was no way of knowing beforehand whether he was right or crazy. It turned out he was right. Sam Walton did all right for himself, and he did all right by his customers, who enjoy quality goods at low prices.

Unlike public monopolies, private firms have powerful incentives to cut costs and satisfy demanding consumers. "Growth stems from trial and error, competition, and the survival of (and imitation of) the successful," says management guru Tom Peters.[9] Traditionally, government hasn't worked that way. When the government wanted to do something, it established a monopolistic operation—and that was that. The Post Office delivers mail. Forever. Whether performing well or poorly, monopolistic government activities are shielded from the hurly-burly of the marketplace.

The absence of competition has a devastating effect on efficiency. With some heroic exceptions, government has performed as one would expect a monopoly to perform: with little innovation, little regard for customer welfare, and escalating costs. Virtually everything government does has been done somewhere at some time by private firms in a competitive market, from job training to street lighting, from trash collecting to dog catching. Even police and fire services have been provided by private firms. We know the productive power of competitive markets. The challenge is to extend markets throughout government.

COMPETITION IN THE PUBLIC SECTOR: CHANGING THE GOVERNMENT LANDSCAPE

In Chapter 2 we explored the idea of total privatization, in which government leaves an activity entirely to the private sector. But for those functions that government does need to perform, there are a number of privatization techniques that inject competitive forces into government operations (see box). The most common practice is to contract with a private firm to perform a specific service, such as trash collection. This is called contracting out, outsourcing, or competitive bidding.[10] Governments can also embrace competition by allowing in-house government units to compete with the private sector. Another technique that brings market forces to government service delivery is to issue vouchers, as for education. The unifying theme of all these approaches is to replace a government monopoly with a competitive market.

Privatization Techniques

Service Shedding. A form of total privatization in which government stops providing a service entirely.

Contracting Out. The state contracts with a private organization, for-profit or nonprofit, to provide a service.

Public–Private Competition. Public in-house units compete against private firms to provide a public service.

Franchise. A private firm is given the exclusive right to provide a service within a certain geographical area for a limited time.

Vouchers. Government provides individuals with certificates redeemable for purchase of a good or service on the open market.

Subsidy. The producer of the service is subsidized by the government contributing financially or in-kind to a private organization to reduce the cost of private provision to consumers.

Internal Markets. Government departments are free to purchase services from either the private sector or internal support units.

Asset Sale or Lease. Government sells assets such as airports, gas utilities, or real estate to private firms, thus turning physical capital into financial capital.

Volunteers. Volunteers are used to provide all or part of a government service.

Self-Help. Community groups and neighborhood organizations take over a service or government asset such as a local park.

Private Infrastructure Development. The private sector builds, finances and/or operates infrastructure such as roads and airports, recovering costs through user charges.

Deregulation. Government regulations are eliminated to allow private providers to compete against a government provider; for example, allowing firms to compete with the U.S. Postal Service.

Governments typically save between 20 and 40 percent through competitive contracting.[11] It is growing more and more difficult to justify delivering services through public monopolies. After all, taxpayers don't spend 30 percent more than necessary to have their own lawn mowed. Why should their government?

Phoenix has been making competition between city units and private providers an important part of public works delivery since 1979. From then until 1993, total savings from competing trash collection totalled $21 million.[12] Los Angeles County estimates it saves over $50 million a year by contracting out.[13] The success of privatization is having a snowball effect; the more governments save through competition, the more officials are willing to give it a try. In a 1992 survey, over 90 percent of state agencies said they already used privatization as a management tool and most said that privatization will be an even more prominent tool in the near future.[14]

Competition isn't foolproof. Political pitfalls, corruption, poor communication, and other problems can occur. (See Appendices A and B for some suggestions on making competition a success.) But the track record of privatization has shown that it successfully boosts productivity like no other public-sector management tool.

COMPETITION CITY

In the past many politicians, especially urban Democrats, secured favor among public employees by protecting monopolistic public services. Lately, however, several big-city New Democrat mayors, such as Cleveland's Michael White and Philadelphia's Ed Rendell, have discovered that taxpayers are just as important a constituency as municipal employees. These leaders have made competition an integral part of their management approach. This takes political courage, since it alienates an historic source of Democratic support: municipal unions.

Promising that he will not back down from plans to privatize services no matter how strong the opposition, Mayor White says that someone needs to stand up for the taxpayers. "While we have 8,000 employees, there are 500,000 Clevelanders, and they pay for this," said the mayor. "I think that somebody, somewhere, ought to stand up for them, since they're paying the tab."[15] In early 1995, White pushed to bring competition to several city services, including road repair, golf course operations, and convention center management.

Mayor Rendell has opened up over over two dozen services to competition, saving about $34 million annually. Rendell says he's been surprised how easy—and popular—privatization has been.[16] Cost savings from putting services out to bid have averaged between 40 and 50 percent. Just as important, the possibility of privatization has had a ripple effect across city government: to stave off privatization, in-house units are finding ways to save 20 to 30 percent from their previous costs. "Savings that weren't possible before suddenly materialize once you put a service out to bid," says Linda Morrison, who headed up the city's competitive-contracting program for two years. "Competition brings unconscious managers to consciousness and makes recalcitrant workers cooperative."[17]

The shift between the old generation and new is best illustrated in Chicago, where Democratic Mayor Richard M. Daley now heads a city long synonymous with his father, Richard J. Daley. The elder Daley, known as "The Boss," was legendary for taking care of "his people," the city workers. It is said that he approved every hire made by the city and personally met each new employee, raising patronage to an art form. At election time, Daley enjoyed the loyalty of a virtual army of supporters.

Richard M. Daley has a management style more in keeping with the times. "City government has to be run like a business or it will go out of business," says Daley the younger. "The government that recognizes its limitations and establishes cost-saving partnerships with the private sector to overcome these limitations can successfully give people something real, concrete, tangible, and useful for their money."[18]

Since taking office in the spring of 1989, Daley has privatized over 40 services, including water customer billing; drug and alcohol treatment; sewer maintenance; and health care services at selected city clinics. Before Daley, the city used to tow away abandoned cars at considerable cost. Today, Chicago is paid $25 per car from private companies for the privilege. Just by privatizing its towing service, between 1989 and 1994 the city brought in over $6 million and improved the service.[19] "To survive," says Daley, "government managers must attack the systematic inertia of bureaucracies, in which employees are penalized for creativity and rewarded for the status quo."[20]

Mayor Daley treats municipal employees fairly, but he certainly doesn't tolerate inefficiency. After bureaucratic bungling by city engineers allowed a flood that caused hundreds of millions of dollars in damage, the frustrated mayor chewed out city administrators and threatened to privatize the whole department. (The late Richard J. Daley must be gazing down from the Big City Hall in the sky, shaking his head in wonder.) City employees aren't as comfortable as when The Boss was in City Hall, but Chicago's citizen taxpayers like the results.

Urban politics has long been dominated by the Democratic party, but the popular shift toward market approaches to government has helped elect a number of big-city Republican mayors. Rudolph Giuliani (New York City), Richard Vinroot (Charlotte), Steve Bartlett (Dallas), Bret Schundler (Jersey City), and Susan Golding (San Diego) all tout the benefits of privatization. "In the 21st century," says Bartlett, "City Hall will be more a catalyst for services. The number of public employees will be dramatically reduced and services provided much more on an outpartnering [privatized] basis."[21]

State-Level Competitive Government

Because of their size, state bureaucracies are often harder to transform than City Hall. Nonetheless, more and more states are embracing the idea of a government that steers rather than rows. Republican governors such as John Engler of Michigan and Christine Todd Whitman of New Jersey have made competition major themes of their administrations.

It is Massachusetts, however, that has established itself as the leading state in the competitive government movement. When he took office in January 1991, Governor William Weld inherited a state in dire fiscal condition. The state was facing an $850 million budget deficit, and Wall Street was about to downgrade state bonds to junk bond status. A Republican governor in an overwhelmingly Democratic state, Weld had vowed that he would not raise taxes. Instead, the Harvard-educated Weld would take the sort of frugal Yankee approach that would do his ancestors proud. (Governor Weld carries a beat-up briefcase that looks like it was handed down by his ancestors). To help him bail out the good ship Massachusetts, Weld brought on board a staff that shared his vision of a trim, competitive government.

In his first two years, Weld privatized everything from skating rinks to mental hospitals, from zoos to prison food service. According to Weld, "Entrepreneurial government is discovering what the private sector has known all along: When private vendors compete for the state's business, quality goes up and costs go down."[22]

It hasn't been easy. Powerful political forces have fought competition fang and claw. But the state's woeful condition and crisis atmosphere helped make change possible. Secretary of Transportation James Kerasiotes described the highway system he inherited as literally crumbling:

The lawns were being mowed once a year, instead of four to six times. The highways hadn't been swept in three years. Lit-

ter wasn't being picked up at all. There were bridges that were 20 years old that hadn't been washed, with the result being that they were in worse shape than 40-year-old bridges that had been properly maintained. We were using capital funds to mow the lawn, meaning we were using borrowed funds to cover operating expenses.[23]

A successful businessman, Kerasiotes challenged the status quo and tried to get long-time state employees to seek better ways of doing business. Initially, his efforts met with a wall of resistance. Says Kerasiotes, "I kept asking, 'Why can't we do this?' And I'd be told: 'We don't have the people, we don't have the money.' That was the constant refrain: 'Give me more money, give me more people, and I'll solve the problem.' Well, we didn't have any more money."

The lack of funds, and Kerasiotes's stubborn insistence on efficiency, forced change. The test case was highway maintenance in Essex County in northeastern Massachusetts, which was notorious for its inefficiency. There was one foreman for every two workers, and some foremen were making $40,000 to $50,000 a year just in overtime.[24] But it was "The Tale of the Very Dead Dog" that finally pushed Kerasiotes over the edge (see box).

Kerasiotes waxes passionate discussing highway maintenance. "Catch basins aren't sexy," he told us, stating the obvious. "But they're important." Supported by Governor Weld, Kerasiotes explored competitive contracting:

We were spending $5.5 million a year in Essex County on road maintenance. We developed a list of services that we needed to do that weren't being done, which we estimated at $2 million worth of service, and added it to everything we were doing. Then we put the whole thing out to bid. A private contractor came back with a bid of $3.6 million, meaning we'd pay $2 million less than we were paying and get $2 million more in services than we were getting. We issued the contract.

*After the first year, the contractor came in $700,000 less than
the bid price.*

The Tale of the Very Dead Dog: A True Story

Once upon a time there was a highway worker, let's call him Joe,
who worked in Essex County. Joe owned a stuffed dog, and
sometimes on his way home from work, he would toss his
stuffed dog out the window. Eventually the Highway Department would be notified about a "dead dog" on the highway,
and Joe would get a call. Grief-stricken, Joe would go out and
collect his beloved pet—and a contractually guaranteed four
hours of overtime. Sometimes, Joe would call a partner to help,
because, well, you know how heavy those stuffed dogs can be.
Not to mention the grief. And the overtime.

Kerasiotes took over the Transportation Department just
about the time Joe retired, but he had heard rumors of the overtime pup. He sent an aide to retrieve the infamous beast, which
the citizens of the Commonwealth had spent untold dollars
removing from the highways of Essex County. Finding a stuffed
dog in a shower stall, the aide was leaving the Essex building
with it when he was questioned by a highway worker.

"Where you going with that?" he was asked.

"Secretary Kerasiotes wanted Joe's dog," replied the aide.

"But that's not Joe's dog," he was informed. "That's
George's dog!"

According to Kerasiotes, the state employees union never
believed that Weld would actually privatize. "The political
infrastructure still didn't get it," says Kerasiotes. "They didn't
believe we'd pull the trigger."

In addition to Essex County, Massachusetts has brought
competition to seven other highway sectors. Convinced of the

governor's resolve by the experience in Essex County, the state unions made concessions in contract work rules and were awarded three of the seven sectors. "They've brought their productivity up and the costs down. They've really changed the way they operate," says Kerasiotes. Annual savings from competition in highway maintenance: $19 million.[25]

Unfortunately, it would be difficult for the Weld administration to generate such savings today. In December 1993, the state legislature passed a bill that makes it almost impossible for the governor to bring competition to state services. The bill, which requires legislative review of future privatizations, was backed by the state employee unions who, not surprisingly, would rather not compete if they didn't have to.

CASE STUDY: THE INDIANAPOLIS REVOLUTION

From the heartland of America come the most revolutionary changes in the field of public management. Mayor Stephen Goldsmith, a mild-mannered visionary, has made America's twelfth-largest city a working model of competitive, 21st-century government.

Goldsmith is not your typical big-city mayor. Whereas his predecessor loved to work the crowds and once dressed up in a leprechaun suit at a St. Patrick's Day parade, Goldsmith is not an enthusiastic baby-kisser. It is difficult to imagine him in a leprechaun suit, and his personality is more cerebral than charismatic. He's surely no political schmoozer; it took him six months into his first administration before he sat down with the two leaders of the city/county council, both of them fellow Republicans. Goldsmith was too busy revolutionizing Indianapolis.

Goldsmith is a serious policy intellectual. He teaches a graduate course on public policy at Indiana University one night a week (in his "spare time"). Unassuming and unfailingly polite, Goldsmith is an unlikely guru. Yet more than 100 other gov-

ernments—including several of the country's top mayors—
have made the pilgrimage to Indianapolis to learn from Goldsmith.

Underlying many of the mayor's ideas is his belief in the
power of competition to positively influence human and organizational behavior. "Only reforms that tap the competitive
power of the marketplace will make government more efficient," he says. When you ask the mayor to name the thinkers
he most admires, he says without hesitation, "Those who write
and think about the importance of markets." Among Goldsmith and his top staff, the term "government monopoly" is
subjected to the kind of scorn usually reserved for one's moth-
er-in-law.

Mayor Goldsmith has created what he calls a "marketplace
for municipal services." Since taking office in January 1992, he
has turned over 60 services from government monopolies into
services that compete in an open market (a process he sometimes refers to as "marketization.") Instead of asking whether a
particular service should be competitively contracted, it is
assumed that everything should be subject to competition
unless there's a good reason why it shouldn't be. There are no
sacred cows in Indianapolis; as one city official put it, "Sacred
cows make the best burgers."[26]

When Goldsmith first came into office, he was thoroughly
committed to privatization "at all costs." The mayor and the
public employee union seemed to be on a collision course.
Everyone readied for a bloody battle, but the conflict never
materialized. Why? Because Goldsmith switched the emphasis
from privatization to competition and gave the city crews a fair
shot at winning contracts. "I was increasingly impressed with
the inherent ability of our own employees to perform better
when the system allowed them to," Goldsmith told *Governing*
magazine. "I underestimated what they could do if we
unloaded the bureaucracy off the tops of their heads."[27]

Privatization should be a means to greater efficiency, not an
end in itself, reasoned the mayor. What mattered was not

whether a bid was won by a city unit or private firm but that there was vigorous competition for the chance to provide the service. "There is no great value in and of itself for privatization, as contrasted to the competitive process," said the mayor.[28] Competition is the mayor's "core strategy," and Goldsmith communicates this vision constantly to his staff. Everyone on the Indianapolis team knows what play Coach Goldsmith wants them to run.

"Stephen Goldsmith has the ability to articulate a vision in clearer terms than any other politician I have ever heard," says Charles "Skip" Stitt, who directs the city's competitiveness program. While many of his employees may disagree with his vision, no one has any doubt about what that vision is. "His philosophy is so consistent. I feel like I know how he will react to a situation, a proposal, as much as I know what my wife would say—maybe more," says Mitch Roob, the former director of the city's Department of Transportation.

To get his feet wet, the mayor started off with some smaller competition projects. Competition czar Skip Stitt says the best services to start with are the smaller "transparent" services; that is, those that do not directly affect the public. One of the first was window washing on city buildings. Previously, these windows were washed by city crews exactly three times a year—whether they were dirty or not. The service was totally focused on inputs. Now a private company washes the windows—not three times a year, but when the windows are dirty.

Microfilm operations were also moved into the marketplace. The private contractor cut the city's cost by 61 percent, saved $400,000 a year, and improved the quality of the microfilm documents. Goldsmith moved sewer bill collections to the local water utility, saving about $1.8 million a year and saving consumers a stamp—Indy residents now mail their sewer bill in with their water bill.

Competition does not always result in privatization. In 1993, the city saved $15 million—25 percent—by making trash collection competitive. Some districts were already being served by private firms, but in a noncompetitive environment. In the new round of bidding, city sanitation crews won back some contracts from private firms. To do so, city crews discovered they had to work seven hours a day instead of four and managed to double their productivity.

LIFE INSIDE A COMPETITIVE GOVERNMENT

So what is life like working inside a government where a dedication to market principles is carried down from the head honcho with almost religious fervor? How is it different from the typical government?

For one thing, performance is measured against the best in the private sector. "As I compare us to industry, Indianapolis is behind the leading-edge industries and in front of most government entities," says Stitt. Like many top staffers, Stitt comes from the private sector rather than the city bureaucracy, bringing with him a different perspective on the question of what is possible.

Mitch Roob, Goldsmith's former transportation director who is now in charge of the county's Health & Hospital Corporation, is another transplant from the private sector. Goldsmith lured the 30-something whiz kid away from a prestigious consulting firm. A Notre Dame business school graduate, Roob shares the mayor's zeal for applying successful business management practices to government. Elaborate, poster-sized graphs charting performance, costs, and productivity cover his office. He enthusiastically explains how the city is now using GE matrices, strategic planning, and customer satisfaction measurements.

Like most of Goldsmith's closest advisors, Roob firmly believes in the productive power of the free enterprise system. Under Roob's strong direction, the city's Transportation Department rose to the challenge of competition to fundamentally restructure its operations. Employees and managers were trained to look at costs and were introduced to a host of strategic tools common in the private sector, including performance measurement, customer surveys, and a sophisticated cost-accounting system that helped city crews more accurately determine their costs. The result is that the Transportation Department has held its own in the city's competitive hurly-burly, winning at least six contracts against private providers—including contracts for pothole repair.

A SIMPLE QUESTION

When Stephen Goldsmith became mayor, Indianapolis had a great credit rating and slick, four-color glossy financial reports rivaling those of Fortune 500 companies. But Goldsmith refused to be complacent. Instead, he asked a deceptively simple question: How much does it cost us to fill a pothole?

No one could tell him. City staffers knew everything about their budgets and almost nothing about their costs. The city kept no information on how much it cost to fill a pothole, clean a sewer, or mow an acre of grass. Without this information, it was impossible to know whether city services were being delivered efficiently. Goldsmith had no way to compare costs in the public sector with costs in the private sector.

As a first step to revolutionizing Indianapolis city governance, Goldsmith introduced "activity-based costing" to measure the total *costs* of performing a service, including equipment, material, labor, and overhead costs. With activity-based costing, "all sorts of wonderful things occur," rhapsodizes Goldsmith. "It is the door by which competition and privatization has been opened up." Activity-based costing was first instituted in the city's Transportation Department under Roob's direction. The first service to which the department applied activity-based costing was, of course, pothole filling.

Since the Mayor had decided to open the task to competition, the department had to submit a bid, and to submit a bid they had to know their costs. The line-level union workers knew that if they didn't come in with a low price, they would lose the business to a private contractor.

Forced to compete, city workers streamlined operations, dropping from eight workers on a crew to four, and going from two trucks to just one, but still their costs weren't competitive with private firms. Then one of those "wonderful things" happened. In reviewing their costs, city employees discovered that the overhead costs of indirect management were enormous. There were 92 truck drivers and 32 management supervisors. "We can't compete if you are going to attribute their salaries into our costs of doing business," the union told the mayor. The frontline union employees asked Goldsmith to unload them of the burden of the supervisors.

Goldsmith knew that they were right. The workers couldn't compete if they had to carry unproductive overhead. So, despite the fact that the managers were Republican patronage employees, Goldsmith laid off most of the supervisors. Goldsmith caught a lot of flack from the local Republican party, but he won the respect of the city workers, who were given a fair shot at competing.

The city unit won the contract. With the assistance of outside experts, they did intensive full-cost accounting on all the services they performed, from chuck-hole filling to crack sealing to line painting. Today, they can tell you exactly how much it costs to fill a pothole, seal a crack, or put up a street sign.

They have also gone through something called the GE Dot Matrix. In plain English, this means that city crews have evaluated their strengths and weaknesses compared to other competitors in the marketplace. In the private sector, this sort of benchmarking process is fairly common; it's unheard of in government. The city determined it was efficient at crack sealing but not as cost-effective at street resurfacing. City crews use this information when they compete on contracts. If a service is not one of their strengths, they won't bid on it. The road company operates much like independent business units in a private corporation.

Steve Fantauzzo, Indianapolis's local American Federation of State, County, and Municipal Employees (AFSCME) spokesman, says that all his union workers want is a level playing field in the competitiveness process, and even admits the in-house units really have a built-in advantage over the private sector; they pay less for fuel, have no capital start-up costs, and don't have to make a profit or pay taxes. All told, the in-house units start out with about 28 percent lower costs. "If we still can't compete, shame on us," says Fantauzzo.[29]

Just because the union has accepted competition doesn't mean it loves the idea. Fantauzzo has suggested that the Transportation Department's success in winning contracts means that continuing to bid out the services is not needed. "If you bid out ten times and the city crews win it ten times, maybe you're wasting everyone's time if you keep bidding it out," says Fantauzzo. But Roob doesn't buy this argument for a second. "You don't ever stop competing the work," he says. "The only way to measure yourself is in the marketplace every day."[30]

The marketplace is the *only* way to truly test your ability—not against other governments, not by undergoing a consulting study. Consider the story of Indianapolis's wastewater treatment plants. Though widely considered to be one of the best-run, most advanced wastewater systems in the country, Goldsmith thought it could do better. As he tells the story:

An accounting firm was hired and produced a study that said we were one of the most efficient plants in the country, and that we could save maybe five percent if we managed it better. I said thanks but no thanks, because what's relevant is what the marketplace will do with the management of our plants, not what a consulting company says we can do. So we bid it out, and four of the largest firms in the country bid on the job. The winner brought down our costs by 44 percent [about $11 *million a year]. Not five percent, but 44 percent, for one of the most efficient plants in the country. They have technologies we don't have, research we don't have, scale we don't have. It's not that our employees are bad, but our technology and research and scale are limited. The decision to compete created value in unexpected ways.*[31]

Though many of the city workers were offered positions with the winning firm, privatization of the wastewater plants did result in some layoffs (the city has provided these employees with retraining and outplacement services). While any layoffs are unfortunate, public officials must remember that their top priority is to serve the citizens of Indianapolis, not to be the employer of last resort. "My job is to create jobs," says Goldsmith, "and the private sector is a much more efficient way of doing it."[32] Echoes Mitch Roob, "If we hadn't privatized the wastewater plants, we would have been flushing over $11 million a year of taxpayer money down the White River."[33]

"The Mayor Has Rocked Our Boat."

Not all Indianapolis employees were tickled pink about Goldsmith's movement to the market—especially at first. "Abject fear" is how one city employee described his initial reaction to Goldsmith's competition and downsizing programs. "It's kind of scary because you never know what's going to happen next," said a city worker who paints traffic lines on roads.[34] In the public works department, about 20 engineers left the first year. "No good engineer wants to work for this city anymore," said former public works administrator Pete Chavol in December 1992.[35]

Part of the reason for the morale problem is simply that employees must work harder and smarter, and not all are used to that. A Parks Department employee admitted that "a lot of people coasted under Hudnut (the previous mayor). Now they have to work and many people feel miserable and threatened."[36] "There used to be joke in the city: What's white and sleeps twelve? A Transportation Department truck," says one department manager. "It wasn't far off the truth."[37] In the city sign shop, co-workers told a productive worker to slow down because he was making the rest of them look bad.

Passing "The Yellow Pages Test"

Nobody does everything well. That's why so many private companies contract, or outsource, tasks that are beyond their core competency.

Consider MCI. It actually manufactures very few products. Its research division surveys the market and finds the best products to connect to the MCI network. MCI locates companies that specialize in certain communication technologies, thus tapping the dispersed knowledge of thousands of different firms. This allows MCI to specialize in what it does best, which is network.[38]

Specialization is a key reason governments should explore privatization. Consider the different activities in which a city government engages, everything from writing traffic tickets to giving tennis lessons, from printing documents to paving streets. No organization could do so many tasks well.

There are plenty of private firms in the marketplace, on the other hand, that specialize in and are passionate about services/activities that are far from the core businesses of government but that government must nevertheless perform. These firms can bring economies of scale, experience in dozens of other jurisdictions, the latest technology, and management and customer service innovations to the table.

As Mayor Goldsmith points out, a mayor is not really qualified to run a print shop, manage a golf course, or direct a road crew. That's why every city function in Indianapolis has to pass "The Yellow Pages Test." If there are private firms out there providing a service, you have to ask why the city doesn't make use of their existing expertise.

An intense fear of change, especially the fear of losing one's job, also contributes to the morale problem. Fear of change is part of human nature and exists in any large organization, but such fear is particularly prevalent in public-sector jobs, which are often sought by those who favor stability.

Roob wanted to show us that not all employees have been demoralized. He took us out in the field to see one of the department's pride and joys: a city road crew that underbid private firms and won a contract. We're supposed to hear from them how empowered they feel and how competition has energized them. Instead, with the boss standing not more than five feet away, we're greeted with a torrent of complaints. They're "much more stressed," "always afraid of losing their jobs," and their "sense of security has disappeared." One crew member summed up the feelings of the group: "The mayor has rocked our boat."[39] The crack-sealing crew, for all their griping about increased stress and tougher conditions, told us their major complaint was that it takes them a week to get supplies. The delay "slows us down and decreases our productivity."

Of course, the private sector perpetually operates in an environment of risk, and most Americans work without absolute job security. Nevertheless, Goldsmith worries about the morale problem. "Without successful buy-in from the employees, we can't succeed," he said. To bring city workers into the fold, the mayor set up an array of programs, including once-a-month department brown-bag lunches with the mayor, so the employees could "get the vision," and an electronic mailbag system in which employees send him messages directly. "I have 4,000 new pen pals," says Goldsmith.

Some employees have indeed caught the entrepreneurial fever. In fact, the disgruntled road crew talked to us about taking their unit private. "I'm ready to do it right now," says David Walderop, the alternate crew leader, "There's money to be made out there and we all know it."[40]

Moreover, after nearly four years of working in a competitive program, most employees were adjusted and no longer afraid. "When we first came in and started shaking things up, many of the employees felt that whatever they did was doomed to failure," says Roob. "Now they have come around to realizing we were sincere about giving them a fair shot to win the contracts." Employees who are competitive and work hard don't have much to worry about in Goldsmith's Indianapolis Inc., but unproductive employees are nervous—and they should be.

INTERNAL MARKETS: LEARNING FROM THE BEST IN BUSINESS

Government employees have been very slow to recognize that government has customers. In the private sector, modern business thinking stresses that a customer is anyone it is your job to serve. If you are a secretary, your customer is your boss. If you write a newspaper column, your customers include your editor and the general newspaper-reading public. If you are a surgeon, your customer is the patient on the operating table. If you are a nurse, your customer is the surgeon to whom you hand the scalpel.

When your customers pay you money directly, it is easy to remember they deserve special treatment. But when your customers work for the same company, it is easy to forget they are your customers—and easy to treat them less well than they deserve.

A recent trend in the private sector is the creation of internal markets for support products and services. Under such a system, market forces are brought to bear within a company. Internal customers can reject the offerings of internal service providers if they don't like their quality or if they cost too much. For example, if the marketing department needs a new ad, instead of automatically using the company's art department it will also consider using an outside design firm. Both the design firm and the art department will submit a price, and the marketing department will take the best deal. The purpose: to stimulate innovation, efficiency, and entrepreneurship within the firm. Tom Peters explains how "one of the last of the centrally controlled economies is coming under the market's sway—not Cuba, but the centrally controlled, nonmarket arenas (e.g. components, services) that dominate the inside of the traditionally vertically integrated corporation."[41]

Prices play a critical role in a market economy by providing information and incentives. As Goldsmith learned with the potholes, managers can't make good decisions without cost data. In this respect, large private corporations suffer from many of the same symptoms as government bureaucracies. Says Massachusetts Institute of Technology's Jay Forrester, "They [both] have central planning, central ownership of capital, central allocation of resources, and lack internal competition."[42] The solution, for business or government, is to break up these internal monopolies.

Feeling its internal support services weren't up to world-class standards, Clark Equipment, a South Bend, Indiana, manufacturer of construction equipment, instituted internal markets in 1982. For the first time, internal support services would be subject to market pressures. The changeover was difficult. "Nobody wants to undergo the pain of real change," explained one Clark executive. "You only turn to the market when there's no way to avoid it." But Clark Equipment's gamble worked. To keep their internal customers, Clark's business units fundamentally restructured their operations: unnecessary positions were junked, outdated assets written off, quality controls established, and products redesigned.[43] Clark's revenues and profits skyrocketed between 1982 and 1990.

Milwaukee's ISIP Experiment

In the public sector, the city of Milwaukee has introduced internal markets into city services to push support service units to lower costs and improve quality. The city's Internal Service Improvement Project (ISIP) allows city departments to purchase six different internal services, with a total budget of over $43 million, from private firms instead of city departments if they can obtain a lower price and/or better quality.

Rather than setting rules and guidelines for improving the quality of their services, the ISIP program essentially says to city units, If you want to survive you must become competitive. Ann Spray Kinney, Milwaukee's director of administration, explains,

> *We went with competition—using a market approach in which internal service agencies would survive based on their ability to attract customers and break even. Funding was moved to the customers and the rules of the game were changed so that customers decided, based on cost, quality, and timeliness, which supplier to choose. We wanted to use market forces—forces we all manage effectively in our everyday lives—to improve systems in City Hall.*[44]

The program, launched in 1992, quickly produced results. In the first few months, private-sector bids were much lower in every case—averaging 44 percent less and enabling city departments to cut costs and obtain better-quality services. Losing some initial bids spurred the internal units to get smarter about how to deliver services. Change, long avoided, was now embraced. The building maintenance division, for instance, started conducting customer surveys and began to offer lower bids than private firms. With customers knowing they have a recourse if they're not satisfied, complaints about internal services, once numerous, almost disappeared. Customers now get what they want rather than what the supply department has in stock. "They don't have to buy a Buick if they want a Jeep," says Kinney.

EMPOWERING THE CONSUMER OF GOVERNMENT SERVICES

Government's ultimate set of customers are taxpayers. These customers are often more ill-served by government than its internal customers. The reason is the same: there are no customer feedback mechanisms. Americans can choose among scores of restaurants, laundry detergents, and breakfast cereals. But in the public sector, customers are usually offered the same one-size-fits-all generic product. Especially if you're poor, the public monopoly is often the only game in town. Few parents would enroll their children in inner-city schools if they had a better alternative.

Taxpayers accept this kind of shoddy service from government agencies because they are "free." Jersey City Mayor Bret Schundler's goal is to raise taxpayers' expectations so they demand the same quality from government that they get from the private sector. The only way to do this, he reasons, is to use competition and make use of vouchers. Says Schundler, "We need to have a system where accountability is natural. The people who are paying the bills need to actually have the power to fire the firm if they don't do a good job."[45]

Vouchers have the advantage of providing clients with greater freedom of choice, empowering them to make decisions for themselves. Vouchers also create incentives for producers to supply high-quality, low-cost services. Moreover, vouchers provide a good way of measuring service performance: if the customer doesn't like the service, he can go elsewhere. While most of the debate on vouchers has focused on education, other government services are candidates for vouchers, including care for the mentally ill, disabilities rehabilitation, and some programs for the elderly.

CONCLUSION

The debate is over; it is clear that competition works. What remains is the difficult task of introducing competition wherever possible into the operation of the public sector. Entrenched interests will generate powerful opposition to privatization.

Larger forces favor an increase in a competitive model of government. The marked increase in privatization in America's cities and states in the 1990s is part of a much larger global trend. Around the world, government monopolies are yielding to the productive power of competitive markets. "The world is marching forward and that world is lodged in a competitive environment," says Cleveland Mayor Michael White. "Government cannot remain as a monopoly which constantly borrows against our children's future, a monopoly that cannot create new ways to deliver a product."[46]

A technological revolution has prompted dramatic changes in the private sector. Government is behind the curve, but is beginning to catch up. Nearly every public official we spoke with said outsourcing would increase in the future. Change is never easy, but new habits will replace the old. As Governor Weld puts it, "Many in public service, reared in the conventions of regulation and direct service delivery, find the principles and practice of privatization foreign. With time and experience, privatization becomes second nature, embedded in organizational culture and standard operating procedure."[47]

CHAPTER 5

UNDERSTANDING GOVERNMENT SYSTEMS

You can only have less bureaucracy if you have less government.

Professor James Q. Wilson

San Diego Mayor Susan Golding told us of her experience working in San Diego County government in the early 1980s. "There was an employee who physically attacked someone, physically assaulted them. I think it was the second time. The supervisor told the employee he was fired . . . the civil service commission reinstated the employee because there was no written policy that said you couldn't assault someone."[1]

Seeing our disbelief, Golding continued. "This is a true story. There was absolutely nothing the elected officials or chief administrative officer of the county could do about it. Now, think about productivity and work efficiency and multiply this case to other ridiculous examples. There's no way to make the government operate efficiently under that kind of a system."

The key word is *system.* When we think of systems, we tend to think of neat and tidy arrangements designed to produce desired outcomes. Some systems operate like clockwork. Government does not. Government is closer to a mud-wrestling match than a precision time-keeping mechanism. That's OK; all human systems are to some extent messy. But we need to recognize our limitations. We cannot rationally engineer government according to our grand design, no more than we can rationally engineer a family, a company, or a society.

Susan Golding presides over a city best known for great weather and less than great sports teams. Among those who study such things, San Diego is also renowned for its frugal and well-run government. The nation's sixth most populous city, San Diego has relatively low taxes and a lean city staff, with just one city worker for every 38 residents—a ratio far less than in other cities of comparable size.[2] Nonetheless, one can sense Mayor Golding's anger and frustration when she speaks about red tape.

"The bureaucracy! How much money we spend on paperwork, on reviewing the regulations, on reviewing the reviewer who reviews the regulations. It's an enormous amount of money. I found out that there was one regulation for which the state was employing people who reviewed city people who were reviewing performance," says Golding, eyes flashing. "That's not what people pay taxes for. When I talk about this to the average citizen, they are outraged and they have every right to be."

Citizens are angry at the bureaucratic inefficiencies of government. Unfortunately, this anger is often ill-informed. Angry citizens are often angry at those who work in government. But people are generally not the problem; the problem is the system. As Golding points out, "Overall good management and good public policy are frequently thwarted."

OPTIMISTS, CYNICS, AND REALISTS

When it comes to thinking about government, the world divides into three groups: the Optimists, the Cynics, and the Realists.

The Optimists believe deeply in government. Optimists think that if we all work together we can make government just as efficient as the private sector. Optimists call government employees public servants. Optimists represent a small but influential minority and include leaders of the reinventing government movement and the architects of Al Gore's National Performance Review.

The Cynics hate government. Cynics believe almost everyone in government is either corrupt, stupid, or lazy—or maybe all three. Cynics call government employees bureaucrats, or worse. Cynics want to "throw the bums out." Cynics are a numerical majority; when Americans were asked if government always manages to mess things up, two-thirds answered Yes.[3] Many Cynics listen to talk radio.

The Realists see government as somewhere in between. Realists believe that government can be improved, but maintain that inherent constraints limit the efficiency of democratic government. Realists are relatively rare, and include among their ranks the authors of this book (where else would we put ourselves?), some academics, and a growing number of politicians and public officials.

The media tend to focus on the battle between the Optimists and the Cynics, in part because battles are entertaining. Unfortunately, both the cynical view and the optimistic view miss the big picture.

Cynics see only the bad. Cynics are angry about high taxes, intrusive regulations, and poor services—as they should be. But Cynics are looking for someone to blame. Cynics avoid the hard work of figuring out *why* government often performs poorly; if something doesn't work then it must be somebody's fault. They don't want to understand that bad systems can lead good people to bad outcomes.

Optimists see only the good. The unlimited confidence of the Optimists is epitomized by *Reinventing Government* authors Osborne and Gaebler. As their book's title indicates, they think government can almost always be engineered to produce far better results. Like many Optimists they feel that with some tinkering government can be our nation's savior:

Think of the problems facing American society today: drug use; crime; poverty; homelessness; illiteracy; toxic waste; the specter of global warming; the exploding cost of medical care. How will we solve these problems? Collectively. How do we act collectively? Through government.[5]

The Optimists' faith in government knows no bounds. Most dismiss even the possibility that individual and/or collective *voluntary* action could address these problems. Likewise, they are reluctant to admit the possibility that maybe there are some problems government simply cannot solve.

Realists have a more *realistic* view of things. While they celebrate the islands of public excellence, they also see the ocean of red tape that surrounds them. Realists believe that government employees are about as noble and knavish as most other folks. Realists care deeply about making government better but recognize the constraints on government efficiency.

We ran up against two inescapable truths during our investigation of public management systems across the country. First, many intelligent, hard-working professionals are striving to improve the way public agencies work. Second, the nature of government severely limits their efforts. Public innovators are constantly running into the brick wall of political reality. Can government operations be improved? Yes. Has anyone discovered an enduring cure for bureaucratic inefficiency? Not on your life.

James Q. Wilson, professor of management at UCLA, put it well in his book *Bureaucracy*:

> *Public management is not an arena in which to find Big Answers; it is a world of settled institutions designed to allow imperfect people to use flawed procedures to cope with insoluble problems. . . . The greatest mistake citizens can make when they complain of 'the bureaucracy' is to suppose that their frustrations arise simply out of management problems; they do not—they arise out of governance problems.*[6]

Our political *system* wreaks havoc with public management. As a rule, it is much more difficult for a public manager to run an efficient operation than his private-sector counter-part. This is an important reason why government should focus only on functions that can't be performed in the private sector.

We ought not look at government simply as a group of people trying to accomplish a task. We should recognize that they are working in a system, a regime of rules, of power relationships, of incentives, of legal obligations and restrictions. Every government action, from buying a textbook to firing an employee, is a matter of public concern.

The democratic process creates problems in personnel, procurement, goal-setting, performance measurement, and every other aspect of management. In his book describing management reforms of the 1980s in the United States, Great Britain, and Canada, Don Savoie notes that in each nation, almost every career official he consulted wanted to discuss the barriers to good management:

> *They stressed how the constantly changing political environ-ment plays havoc with virtually every long-term planning exercise they ever engage in; how goals in government agen-cies are often vague; how past experience tells them it is more important to follow prescribed rules than dart off in an unchartered direction, even though it may well hold consider-able promise; how there are always many "bosses" in govern-ment; and how those at the top of the hierarchy are constantly managing crisis situations. All of this suggests that govern-ment managers are in the business of "coping," not managing in a private sector sense.*[7]

Government is a coping institution, and making government work better is a constant uphill battle. There are ways to make that struggle more successful, and some of the changes taking place across America represent real improvement. But we real-ists offer no miracles.

THE PERILS OF PERSONNEL

William Stack is something of a legend. Between 1971 and 1991, the Hartford, Connecticut, firefighter was fired three times for being drunk. He used 433 sick days, was suspended for 414 days, and was AWOL on two occasions. Throughout, Stack used the mediation and arbitration process to keep his job. He was finally fired for good in 1993 when he showed up for work intoxicated yet again.[8]

Though Stack's story is an extreme case, public managers universally complain of the difficulty of dealing with nonproductive workers. Though most government employees are ready to do an honest day's work, the indolent few can really drag down overall productivity. Public personnel rules also make it difficult to adequately reward good workers and to shift people from job to job as circumstances change. Mayor Susan Golding feels the squeeze. "What the civil service system really does is remove flexibility, making it difficult to promote people on merit rather than seniority. It puts a whole strata of rules on top of a plethora of rules that already exist to protect public employees."

Golding has one last story of how the multitude of rules tangles up government. "When I was at the county, our civil service commission, which we appointed, sued us. We then had to hire the civil service commission an outside attorney (because of conflict of interests) to help them sue us," says the mayor, shaking her head at the memory. "We are going to continue to push for changes, but that's the kind of idiocy that goes on because voters aren't aware of it."

Golding recognizes that public workers deserve protection from political or capricious dismissal, but she points out that the pendulum has swung way too far. "There have been so many laws passed since the civil service system was established to protect employees, to establish grievance procedures, and to forbid patronage, in many respects the civil service system is no longer needed," says Golding. "We can't do certain things that could improve on effectiveness, both because of labor agreement requirements but also because of civil service." Public employees are protected by a dizzying combination of civil service laws, union contracts, and general employment protections.

In many cases, public managers don't even bother trying to fire incompetent workers—it's not worth the effort. Even in what should be open-and-shut cases it can take over a year of legal proceedings to get a pink slip delivered. More often, skilled managers shift deadwood into other departments. When several nonperformers accumulate in the same department, it's called a "turkey farm." In public schools, the practice of rotating poor teachers is known as "the dance of the lemons."

LEGACY OF THE PAST

Today's restrictive personnel rules are largely a legacy of a corrupt past, when election winners would routinely fire workers and replace them with party workers. Rules for hiring and firing arose in response to this spoils system. Patronage jobs were the currency of corrupt political machines.

George Washington Plunkitt was a leader of New York City's Tammany Hall around the turn of the century. Tammany was the center of New York's Democratic party machine politics at a time when politics meant patronage. As Plunkitt put it, "You can't keep an organization together without patronage. Men ain't in politics for nothin'. They want to get somethin' out of it."[9]

The essence of machine politics was simple: organize to win elections and divide the spoils of public jobs. Plunkitt always described his style of politics as "honest graft":

The city owns the docks, and look how beautiful Tammany manages them! I can't tell you how many places they provide for our workers. I know there is a lot of talk about dock graft, but that comes from the outs. When the Republicans had the docks under Low and Strong, you didn't hear them sayin' anything about graft, did you?[10]

The spoils politics of the Tammany Hall era, operating in almost every major American city at the time, made reform necessary. The reformers of the Progressive Era wanted to remove the patronage from public employment and replace it with an objective test to screen for qualified applicants. The civil service laws were intended to take discretion out of the hands of public officials and to protect public workers from capricious dismissal.

Civil service laws reduced the spoils system, but at a cost. The same rules that stop managers from making corrupt decisions also prevent them from using common sense. Plunkitt's unforgettable description of the civil service examination strikes a truth:

For instance, if a man wanted a job as a motorman on a surface car, it's ten to one that they would ask him: 'Who wrote the Latin grammar, and if so, when did he write it? How many years were you at college? Is there any part of the Greek language you don't know? State all that you don't know, and why you don't know it. Give a list of all the sciences with full particulars about each one and how it came to be discovered. Write out word for word the last ten decisions of the United States Supreme Court and show if they conflict with the last ten decisions of the police courts of New York City.' Before the would-be motorman left the civil service room, the chances are he would be a raving lunatic.[11]

Plunkitt had a point: performance on a written test bears little relation to performance on the job. No private company seeking a qualified worker would rely *entirely* upon a written examination. Human judgment is needed to assess the candidate's enthusiasm, cooperativeness, and other hard-to-measure characteristics. But under our rule-based system, Albert Einstein couldn't teach physics in a public school without first getting a teaching certificate. And almost no government in the country could hire Microsoft whiz kid Bill Gates (who lacks a college degree) to write a simple computer program.

Of course, just as Plunkitt and his ilk once opposed enacting such rules, there are those who oppose their abolition. Public employees and their unions fight to continue job protections and oppose merit pay. "Unions are not blameless," admits the president of the nation's largest public employee union. "And nobody wants to work next to someone who is not producing. But you have to understand, job security is our bottom line."[12]

THERE ARE NO PANACEAS, BUT IMPROVEMENT IS POSSIBLE

In early 1994, the federal Office of Personnel Management (OPM) staged a photo-op of OPM Director James B. King throwing personnel rules into a dumpster. King was tossing the *Federal Personnel Manual*, the 10,000 pages of rules that dictate federal hiring. Said King, "It is written in such gobbledygook that it takes a team of Washington's finest attorneys to understand what is required to hire, fire, classify and reward employees . . . and that's nonsense."[13]

There was only one problem. The old rules had been tossed, but there was nothing to replace them. What's more, whatever does replace them will likely be just as complicated. These rules came into existence for a reason. Democracy is messy, and our messy political system naturally creates messy, political personnel rules. Why? Because government personnel rules attempt to achieve contradictory objectives: managerial flexibility and discretion versus fair and objective treatment.

No one has solved this conundrum. A 1993 survey found that 33 states were undergoing or planning civil service reform, and seven states described their efforts as "wholesale reform."[14] Some have been going on for years, but no satisfactory system has yet emerged. In 1992, amid much fanfare, Florida's Democratic Governor Lawton Chiles announced that his state would be "sunsetting" its civil service laws. Florida has so far been unable to develop anything with which to replace them.

In the early 1990s, Massachusetts had similarly looked at enacting sweeping personnel reforms. "The politics of that reform became very difficult," says Joe Trainor, assistant secretary of human resources. "Veterans preferences, racial preferences, preference for children of slain or disabled police officers or firefighters—these aren't easy to alter."[15] In the end, the Weld administration was satisfied with marginal gains in flexibility.

Nothing can "fix" government personnel systems, but greater authority for public managers is clearly in order. In the give and take between managerial flexibility and fair treatment, "fair treatment" has gone too far in the direction of protecting employees. There are now many laws that protect all workers, private and public sector alike, from capricious firing, discrimination, and the like. The additional protection provided by the civil service is hardly necessary.

REDUCING JOB CLASSIFICATIONS

As with hiring and firing, public managers need more flexibility in assigning work and rewarding performance. The current system is hamstrung by archaic job classifications. Texas, for example, classifies 1,339 different state jobs. New Jersey has 6,400, each with a detailed description of its duties. Until recently, employees of Philadelphia's Department of Human Services declined to use computers because it wasn't in their job description. At the Philadelphia airport, it took three union employees to change a light bulb: a mechanic to take off the light cover, an electrician to change the bulb, and a janitor to sweep up the dust.[16]

Government job descriptions make for entertaining reading. Federal guidelines for an electronics engineer classify as GS-11 those who can "apply broad knowledge of engineering concepts and procedures." A GS-12 can "apply deep and diversified knowledge to atypical or highly difficult assignments." To qualify for GS-13, applicants must be "highly knowledgeable specialists in their subject-matter areas." Can you tell the difference?

Reengineering guru Mike Hammer hates tightly defined job descriptions because they stand in the way of productivity. "I don't want to have to write a job description for a position in order to get it by some government bureaucrat to make sure I am being fair in its application. I don't want to define what the job requires," says Hammer. "Who the hell knows what the job requires?"[17]

Most jobs require that workers do whatever needs doing, making efforts to classify at best silly and at worst counterproductive. Reducing these classifications and instead "broadbanding" employees into general employment categories would be a good first step. Broadbanding would increase management's ability to assign existing employees to new duties, something that is critical in light of fast-changing technologies.

This, too, is politically difficult to achieve. The only cases we have seen of public employees agreeing to eliminate old work rules are in the face of competition. Only the prospect of losing the work altogether prompts unions to junk the rules that limit their productivity.

PAYING FOR PERFORMANCE

Classifications treat unlike employees the same. If one GS-7 is hard-working, dedicated, and intelligent, while the GS-7 in the next cubicle is doing crossword puzzles all day, they are still both paid as GS-7s. Employee raises will not be determined by their supervisor, who sits down the hall; rather it will be voted on by the 535 members of Congress, who sit in Washington, D.C. The hard worker and the crossword puzzler will get the same raise.

The China Lake Experiment

Evidence indicates that allowing managers greater discretion over compensation improves staff quality. In the 1970s, the Navy gave managers at the China Lake research station significantly greater flexibility over personnel decisions. For once, the rules were done away with. In several key ways, the experiment was a success. Outstanding workers received faster raises, and top performers were less likely to leave. Managers improved the quality of the work force.

Though the program at China Lake proved successful, it has never been replicated. It might be good management, but it wasn't good politics. Shortly after the project released its findings, the Federal Managers Association polled 20,000 of its members and found that 70 percent *opposed* extending the merit pay principle of China Lake nationally.[18] In government, how well you do your job makes virtually no difference in how well you get paid. Job performance is largely irrelevant; what matters for compensation is how the job is classified.

"My salary is approximately $40,000 annually, and I am the most underworked and overpaid individual I know. I have nothing to do. I am a talented person with a professional license and an advanced degree. My talents are wasted."[19] That's the response of a Kentucky state employee to an employment survey. Kentucky officials noted that "many survey responses reported idle employees who drew a paycheck without giving their employer a full day's work."[20]

As we said earlier, most government employees want to do a good job. Many grow disheartened because getting things done in government becomes difficult when uncaring co-workers ride the system. Individuals who in a different environment would be highly productive begin to coast. "It's like trying to swim upstream when everyone else is doing the dead-man's float downstream," said one exasperated state employee.[21] Everyone has been frustrated dealing with the Post Office, the IRS, or the Department of Motor Vehicles. Imagine how frustrating it is to work *within* such rule-based organizations.

The superachievers, those individuals willing to work long hours and take big risks in hopes of achieving great success, are not adequately compensated by civil service. One highly productive public manager said of himself, "I'm a private-sector guy." He often felt frustrated by the slow pace in his department, and he knew he could earn more money in the private sector.

Paying for performance through performanced-based contracts might help. Sunnyvale, California, has been successful with a performance-based compensation system that links a portion of managers' salaries with their department's output. In 1994, the Minneapolis Public Schools hired a consulting firm known as the Public Strategies Group (PSG) as their new superintendent. Under the terms of the three-year contract, PSG is paid an annual base salary, but could earn as much as $244,000 more each year if it produces certain outcomes.[22]

Moving perhaps further than any other government towards a private-sector model of employee compensation is the government of New Zealand, which makes extensive use of performance-based contracts for public managers. The minister of each department, a political appointee, develops explicit "outcomes" for the department. The minister then contracts with a "chief executive" whose pay is linked to achieving the specified outcomes.

In developing the contract outcomes, the minister provides the vision for the department, but is not actively involved in managing. That role is left to the chief executive. This approach attempts to separate policy from administration, much like many American cities with an elected council and a "permanent" city manager. This separation of responsibility is supposed to eliminate political interference, although as the American experience shows, this separation is never complete. As Norm King, City Manager of Moreno Valley, California, explains, "The City Council fails to respect the difference between policy and administration. That includes council members who want to be involved in micromanagement, that includes council members who prefer special treatment for friends or relatives to merit-based treatment."[23]

Nonetheless, the New Zealand approach can help reduce political finagling. The chief executive is given high relative freedom as to how to manage. Moreover, because pay is linked to performance (bonuses can reach up to 20 percent of a chief executive's salary), the chief executive has a strong incentive to produce the prescribed outcomes. The chief executive has direct responsibility for personnel issues, and in some cases, chief executives have largely abandoned the New Zealand civil service system. Instead, they have used performance-based contracts with their workers.[24] With this freedom comes accountability. "The penalties chief executives face can ulti-mately include losing their jobs. This contrasts with the old position, aptly summed by the title of 'permanent head,'" note treasury officials Graham Scott and Peter Gorringes.[25] The New Zealand system is far from perfect, and political con-tention has been high. It is notable, however, as an effort to link pay with outcomes as it abandons the rule-based approach for one that focuses more on outcomes.

The New Zealand model will face political opposition in the United States. Moreover, just as hiring criteria cannot entirely be reduced to testable, measurable attributes, neither can job performance. Suppose you went and had your hair cut. You could tell if someone did a good job or not, right? But now try to write a contract that will allow you to *objectively* measure how good a haircut you got and reward this accordingly. Rather difficult, isn't it? This problem also bedevils government con-tract writers. Of course, some activities lend themselves more readily than others to objective measurement. It is relatively easy to measure how clean a street is or how much trash has been collected. It is much harder to objectively measure a teacher's performance. Acknowledging the difficulty in measurement, however, does not imply that every teacher should be paid the same, only that such judgments will be subjective. Subjective judgments by a party who holds a vested interest in the outcome is sometimes the best that can be achieved. It is how you choose someone to cut your hair.

Despite the challenges, linking pay to performance is desirable. It means, however, that people in similar positions will not be paid the same. This will inevitably lead to charges of unfair treatment. For those who wish to avoid the heat of making judgments, classifications systems act as a firewall, insulating them from having to make distinctions between employees. Deregulating public managers to use some discretion in personnel is essential to better government. We shouldn't ask these people to be managers if we don't trust them to exercise some common sense in staffing and managing their departments.

THE DIFFERENCE BETWEEN UNION INFLUENCE IN THE PUBLIC AND PRIVATE SECTORS

New York City public school custodians earn an average of $60,000 per year—more than the city's average teacher. Their union contract has in recent years included some truly astounding benefits. For example, the city used to cover five-twelfths of the cost of a new Jeep, Bronco, or other utility vehicle, which custodians would get to keep after five years. Moreover, rules rather than school principals determined what custodians would do. When a district superintendent wanted to hold a meeting in his office in P.S. 137 on the Lower East Side, he couldn't use his own key to open the school's door; he had to call a custodian, who charged the city $400 to open the building. When, after negotiation, the custodians' union agreed to paint 20 percent of the schools each year, it was sued by the painters' union. In a compromise, custodians were allowed to paint, but only up to eight feet above the floor.[26]

Just as government is not like a private-sector business, public employee unions are not like private-sector unions. For one thing, public-sector unions do not have to consider the effect of their wage demands on the competitiveness of their employer—government can always just raise taxes. In contrast, autoworkers at General Motors know that outrageous salaries will be reflected in higher car prices, which means less business for GM, which means union layoffs. The discipline of market competition is almost completely absent in public-sector unions.[27] "One of the most destructive things to happen to cities is the corruption of the collective bargaining process," says Chris Carmody, a senior advisor to Cleveland Mayor Michael White. "In the private sector, management and labor are on a level playing field because the work force has to deal with the financial realities of the company. This constraint isn't present in government. What's more, politicians don't have a strong incentive to hold on to management rights."[28]

The growth of government in the past 30 years has resulted in tremendous gains in public-sector unionism, even while private-sector unions have declined. In the 1950s, about one in three American workers belonged to a union; today, only one in ten American workers belongs to a union. In contrast, however, about 43 percent of the nation's roughly 20 million public-sector workers belong to a union, and that number is growing.[29] When President Kennedy signed Executive Order 10988 in 1961 allowing federal civil servants to bargain collectively, he fundamentally altered the political landscape of public employment.

It is not a criticism to note that unions tend to act in their own interest, or to note that their own interest is not identical to the general interest of citizens and taxpayers. Since they depend on the dues of government employees to sustain their organizations, public-sector unions have little desire to see government downsized. Unions don't like the idea of competition, either. "Why do unions raise the issue of 'We're against privatization'? Well, because it's a threat to our existence," says Larry Scanlon, executive director of the Civil Service Employee Association.[30]

As we saw in Indianapolis, unions can be instrumental in making government work better, but they are likely to do so only when it is in their own best interest. Bob Stone, director of the National Performance Review, notes one union's response to a federal reinvention initiative to eliminate job descriptions: "What the union told us was that the job description was the protection that workers had against arbitrary acts by management. [They] agreed that this is stupid, but told us, 'If you want to take away that protection, you have to give us something. You have to make us partners in the enterprise, partners in deciding what it is that people are told to do.' The unions said they will throw away the job description, but only if they are made partners in the process."[31]

The idea of labor–management partnerships sounds nice. Instead of an adversarial atmosphere, government reform will be a cooperative effort. The problem is that public managers and public unions have different goals. What is good for citizens and taxpayers is not necessarily good for public employees or public employee unions. And it is naive in the extreme to expect a union representative to act against the interests of his or her organization.

TWO PHILADELPHIA STORIES

David Cohen, chief of staff to Philadelphia Mayor Ed Rendell, tells a story of trying to develop a labor–management partnership in the city's procurement department: "In our procurement department, we were trying to do a Total Quality Management (TQM) project. We brought in an outside consultant to help us reengineer and restructure our work processes.

We began by talking to the workers, to find out what they thought their job was and to learn their ideas for doing things better. There was no contemplation of contracting out. We were just looking to improve our systems.

"What's the reaction of the unions? Number one, we get a letter telling us this is an unfair labor practice. They don't want us to talk to workers. They want us to go through the union. Just how is it that you can do TQM without talking to the workers? Number two, before the process continues they want a guarantee that no jobs will be lost, either by individuals or by the union. That is, they want an employment floor in the procurement department. We can do [a TQM project], but we have to keep the same number of workers making the same money, and we can't talk to the workers. Well, that's not TQM."[32]

As is often the case, public-sector attempts to emulate the best practices of the private sector are frustrated by constraints unique to government.

Contrast this with another Philadelphia story. Philadelphia's sludge-processing plant was performing poorly, so Mayor Rendell put it on the list to be considered for contracting. Faced with the prospect of losing their jobs, in about a month the plant's managers—working with the union—came up with changes that reduced the number of workers by 79 employees (from 214 to 135), and cut costs by one-third, saving $8 million dollars annually. Those who knew the processes best, the managers and workers, restructured the system to enhance its efficiency.

Would this quantum improvement have come about in the absence of competition from the private sector? "Absolutely not," says Mayor Rendell. "It hadn't happened before."[33]

Because the employees saw contracting out as a credible possibility, they knew that it was in their own best interest to change the way things were done, including eliminating unnecessary positions—something no union will do unless there is no other choice. The looming possibility of privatization changed the essential system dynamics. "This wouldn't have happened if we hadn't demonstrated a track record that when we put something on the list, we actually would contract it out," says Cohen.

Change won't come without some confrontation. It is more pleasant to think we can all hold hands and work together to improve government, but we have to be realistic and recognize the existence of competing interests. New Jersey's Governor Whitman thinks competition and privatization would benefit the citizens of her state. What do the unions think? "I really cannot envision how privatization can ever work to the advantage of the employee," says Bob Pursell, New Jersey area director of the Communications Workers of America. "It puts people in the position of having to compete for their own job . . ."[34] Those who put the interests of taxpayers first will never see eye to eye with those whose chief concern is the well-being of employees.

SYSTEMS DYNAMICS AND DYNAMIC SYSTEMS: THE END OF BUREAUCRACY?

The behavior of government employees is not a result of personal inclination, but of systemic forces. Government can't "act more like business" unless the fundamental underlying forces are duplicated.

What defines life in the world of business? Two things. First, companies must please their customers. Second, they must turn a profit (not every year, but on average). Companies structure their internal organizations to satisfy these requirements.

Early in this century, bureaucratic structures did the trick. Rigid hierarchical systems with clearly defined rules, tasks, and responsibilities were effective organizational structures. Top managers set rules, workers followed them. Much work was repetitive in nature, technology was changing slowly, and centralized decision-making made sense. Bureaucracy was appropriate for the times. Not so today. Now, companies must meet the twin demands of customer satisfaction and profitability in a rapidly changing world. The competition changes. Technology changes. Consumer tastes change. In a rapidly changing world, the disadvantages of bureaucracy outweigh the advantages.

That is why so many corporate bureaucracies have given way to self-managed work teams, and rigid hierarchies have given way to employee empowerment. External forces have driven these internal changes. The world has changed, and the structure of corporations has changed with it. Successful businesses today have adopted a variety of innovative organizational structures, including radical decentralization, empowered line workers, self-managed work teams, quality circles, semi-independent business units, Total Quality Management, extensive outsourcing, virtual corporations, radical "delayering" (getting rid of several layers of middle management), reengineered work processes, and the introduction of work cells or work clusters. There is nothing magical about any of these reforms. Each approach is appropriate under certain circumstances, but not others. Form follows function. Businesses don't adopt structures because they're trendy, but because they work. Government tackles many very different functions—from providing care for the insane to writing parking tickets to national defense. There is no across-the-board model to use. Hierarchy is not necessarily a bad thing in and of itself. Creative risk-taking by frontline workers on an aircraft carrier can be fatal.

Companies are not efficient because they use these approaches; they use these approaches because they need to be efficient. The macrolevel incentives of the market reward efficiency. The twin demands of customer satisfaction and profitability drive the engine of change. Companies have to do whatever it takes—or go out of business. This urgency drives change. This is why governments must subject themselves to competition, even if layoffs result.[35]

The changes in the private sector have not been painless. Radical restructuring has brought layoffs. Between 1986 and

1993, IBM reduced its work force by 117,000, or some 30 percent. Sears Roebuck (22 percent), GE (31 percent), and GM (14 percent) each shed over 100,000 employees during that period.[36] These layoffs were difficult but necessary for profitability and future growth. Meanwhile, the economy as a whole strengthened to the point that by the end of 1994, unemployment was at a four-year low.

Unfortunately, it is almost impossible to *significantly* boost productivity without work force reduction. Doing more with less means just what it says. Recall the examples from this and previous chapters of radical productivity improvements in the public sector: the Philadelphia sludge-treatment facility, or the Indianapolis road repair crew, or the money-counting room of the Massachusetts Transit Authority. These stories all shared two key elements. First, they took place in response to competition. Second, the productivity improvements meant that fewer workers were needed to do a given job.

In the first 21 months of his administration, Governor Weld cut the number of state employees under his control by almost 7,000, a 14 percent decrease. In four years, Governor Engler cut the state payroll by 8 percent. Governor Branstead of Iowa laid off 1,200 workers in order to balance his state's budget during the recession.

In both business and government the major source of excess employment is often found in middle management. When the city of Charlotte, North Carolina, merged its 24 departments into nine key businesses (organized around city hall's core activities), the city manager discovered at least one layer of management could be removed in each department with ease.[37]

Why? Because the traditional function of middle management was to pass down the rules from upper management to the work force. Middle management made sure the rules were followed, and in today's information environment that role is unnecessary—or worse. The endless layers of middle management and their rules can make it all but impossible for frontline people to do their jobs. "We call them the useless, helpless, hopeless low-level bureaucrats who do nothing all day but warm chairs, and who never touch a product or provide a service," says Ed Keller, executive director of AFSCME Council 13 in Harrisburg, Pennsylvania.[38]

In contrast, today's successful organizations tend to be structured according to what Tom Peters calls the "simultaneous loose-tight model." Upper management tightly defines a corporate vision but allows workers wide latitude in fulfilling that mission. In the private sector, the two main outcomes of this shift are leaner middle management and worker empowerment. Middle managers are becoming as rare as the dodo bird, while pump operators at Dow Chemical provide input on the hiring process.[39] In government, there are too many middle managers still acting as umpires, stifling the creativity of frontline workers. In Boston, a police officer often has to make split-second judgments about whether or not to use deadly force. But in order to get a car towed out of a crosswalk, she has to get approval from her sergeant. In myriad ways, rules tell public workers that they cannot be trusted.

It's time to follow the advice of one of America's more effective public leaders, General George C. Patton: "Never tell people *how* to do things. Tell them *what* to do and they will surprise you with their ingenuity.[40] Companies have adopted this practice because it makes them more efficient.

Governments can imitate the trappings of corporate structures, but they will be ineffectual without the underlying, fundamental sense of urgency that only competition brings. The public sector often borrows strategies from the private sector and reduces them to little more than buzzwords: TQM, reengineering, "seamless" government. These attempts remind us of a cartoon we saw shortly after the breakup of the Soviet Union. A group of communist officials are in a classroom learning about capitalism. These would-be entrepreneurs are all paired off shaking hands, earnestly telling each other, "Let's do lunch!"

That may be what capitalism looks like, but it's not what

capitalism is all about. Republicans as well as Democrats are frustrated by government inefficiency. As Newt Gingrich has put it, "We Republicans see the efficiency of Wal-Mart and UPS; and we want to change the government to be as courteous, efficient, speedy, and effective as those companies."[41] While this is an admirable goal, don't expect government to duplicate the excellence of business by imitating companies. It is competition, the fact that customers can go elsewhere, that makes companies customer-focused. We do not mean to suggest that all attempts at improvement are futile. But we need to be sober about how much things can improve in the absence of competitive incentives. It will require exceptional leadership to effect the difficult changes entailed in restructuring.

REFORMING PROCUREMENT

Back in the days of Tammany Hall, there were two ways corrupt politicians funneled funds to friends: job patronage and procurement patronage. To safeguard the public interest, reformers instituted rules and regulations. We have seen the problems of public personnel systems. Not surprisingly, the same sort of problems plague public procurement.

In the late 1860s, Boss William Marcy Tweed used his political influence to build a financial empire by influencing the awarding of public contracts in New York City. Boss Tweed formed a printing company, to which he funneled lucrative municipal contracts.[42] Progressive Era reformers sought to eliminate such corrupt practices by introducing rules. Rules bring their own cost, however, and we are still paying for the legacy of Boss Tweed.

"In the name of fighting corruption we have created a very overbureaucratized, overcontrolled, distrustful procurement system. We've gone way, way overboard." says Steven Kelman, administrator of the Office of Federal Procurement Policy. "All kinds of controls and auditing and paperwork are rooted in distrust, distrust of both government employees and companies the government does business with."[43]

A professor of public management at Harvard, Kelman is taking a sabbatical to practice what he teaches. "We shouldn't make the system function horribly in order to deal with corruption. We should deal with corruption directly by very strict criminal sanctions. We should put corrupt people in jail for a long time. But you don't want to make the system so inefficient on a daily basis that it make the lives of the 99.5 percent of honest people impossible. You don't fight corruption by creating an awful procurement system."

Government at all levels has awful procurement systems. When Kelman taught at Harvard, he used to have his students examine the government's 15-page specification used to purchase chocolate chip cookies. In theory, Kelman told his students, it would make a lot more sense to just buy cookies from a commercial catalog. "A few years ago, this was a utopian account of how government might actually work," says Kelman. As of January 1, 1995, some army bases began purchasing their food this way.

Such monumental stupidity has been standard operating procedure in government purchasing. For example, the federal government used to ignore past performance when awarding contracts. "Looking at past performance was never illegal, but it was always discouraged," explains Kelman. "The idea has been if you choose one supplier over another because they have performed well for you in the past, this somehow restricts competition. Rewarding somebody for having performed well in the past was thought anticompetitive. Now this is really contrary to all theory. Rewarding good performance is exactly how the free market works to promote individual welfare, so it is a very strange theory of competition." A strange theory indeed. In real life, anyone thinking of getting a haircut considers past performance in choosing between potential suppliers.

Kelman describes an essential difference between procurement in the public and private sectors: "The government's approach to competition is more of a paper-based system, as opposed to the more informal, performance-based competition common in the commercial world. Selection of a supplier is much more based on objective things such as price, as well as how the company fills out a piece of paper saying what they are going to do. This is in contrast to the commercial world, in which you are judged much more on past performance and how you've delivered."

This difference is not something that can be completely eradicated. In the private sector, most purchasing actions are not taken through formal, competitive processes at all. Most of the time, companies purchase things from suppliers they have dealt with in the past. A change in supplier will typically occur only when the buyer is displeased with price or performance. This makes perfect sense, because it is time-consuming and expensive to conduct searches for new suppliers. For example, most people get their hair cut at the same place time and again. It isn't worth it to conduct a broad market survey of price and performance if you are happy with what you are getting.

In the public sector, however, you are not spending your own money. Because you are using public funds, you have to be fair when awarding contracts. Because of the possibility of kickbacks or other favoritism, new firms need to be allowed to participate in the bidding process. This raises costs.

The other big cost factor in public-sector purchasing is political and legislative interference—most of it well intentioned. "Any purchase, even for a stapler, had to be from a small business," says Kelman. "In the government context, how a small business is defined is a term of art. You have to have a big book in front of you to determine if a company is indeed a small business."

To sell copying paper to the government, at least before 1994, you had to first certify that none of your employees had ever violated the Clean Air Act, the Clean Water Act, or had committed any defense-related felonies. There are "buy American" regulations, rules that encourage minority- or women-owned enterprises, regulations against buying from companies that use convict labor, and rules that give preference to suppliers that encourage a drug-free workplace. All of this raises costs. Though the federal government has been the worst example, governments at all levels have the same sort of rule-based, formalized purchasing systems.

Though largely unheralded, one of the most significant reforms to come out of the first year of the federal reinvention effort was in the area of purchasing reform. Legislation in 1994 removed a number of statutory rules and restrictions on purchases under $100,000, and radically deregulated purchases under $2,500. Electronic commerce, including the use of credit cards, will free up a number of these smaller purchases. Though transactions under $2,500 represent only 2 percent of all procurement spending, they make up 70 percent of all transactions. "The administrative costs of making these small purchases are out of all proportion to the cost of what we're buying," says Kelman. "What we're trying to do is change the way government buys things and make it more like the way a successful private-sector company buys things."

This is a wonderful goal, and the changes taking place in this area merit praise. We should not delude ourselves, however, that public procurement can ever be conducted in the efficient and informal manner of private-sector purchasing. Demands of democratic government preclude the sort of behind-closed-doors, peremptory decisions that work well when people are spending their own money.

CHANGING THE RISK REWARD RATIO

Mistakes are embarrassing. Public mistakes are even more embarrassing. As Frank Lloyd Wright once noted, doctors can bury their mistakes, but architects can only advise their clients to grow vines. In hockey, a goaltender's mistake causes a flashing red light to go on in front of thousands of fans. But no professional's mistakes are more public than those of a public official.

In state capitals, newspaper articles about the goings on in government are copied and distributed to public officials on a daily basis. No public manager wants to drink his morning coffee reading a headline describing his latest screwup in 12-point type.

"In the private sector, if you are going to have innovation and an A-1 team, you have to allow your people to fail," says Joe Adler, secretary of Maryland's Department of Personnel.[44] Innovations always come with an element of risk, notes Adler. In the private sector, risky ventures bring big payoffs. This isn't true in government, and the media spotlight on screwups makes public officials reluctant to make changes. "There is an inherent caution when you are dealing with public money, a much greater reluctance to experiment, because if you don't make it, it's your neck on the line. The best way for a public official not to get in the news is not to do anything new," says Adler.[45]

"I can count on one hand the number of articles about the successes of Milwaukee's government, and we've had a lot of successes," says Milwaukee's Director of Administration Ann Spray Kinney. "I'd need a large truck to load all the articles about the possible failures and abuses."[46]

The public-sector environment, where every mistake gets jumped on and excellence is ignored, discourages change. Rather than taking risks, public employees have strong incentives to engage in "CYA" activities. ("CYA," of course, stands for "cover your assets.") Explains Mayor Goldsmith, "The media is the key. As long as they focus on input failures not outcomes, it's difficult to change. My complaint is not that they emphasize failures, which they should. My complaint is that they emphasize failures of process and input, rather than outcome failures. We won't get any radical change until we convince the media and the public that the costs of not changing are greater than the costs of input failures."[47]

The reality: the media's focus on failure is unlikely to change. Newspapers, after all, are in the business of selling newspapers, and smooth-running government bureaucracies are not news. ("Hey, honey, look at this! The city's sludge-treatment facility is cutting costs through competitive contracting. Wow!") Good government makes boring reading. With the possible exception of political sex scandals, the best government stories involve waste, fraud, and abuse.

What we can work to change, however, is government's internal definition of a mistake. This means making a clear distinction between mistakes and corruption. Within government, embarrassing screwups need to be celebrated as a necessary component of change. If an official is trying to accomplish *a core function* in a new and better way, even if things don't work out, that official (or line worker or whoever) deserves praise for innovating. Note the emphasis on the innovation's being within a core function. Public employees should be encouraged to use creativity in carrying out their organization's function; they should not employ creativity in defining their organization's task. The Josephine County officials we met in Chapter 2 merited criticism not because their rock concert lost money, but because they shouldn't have been sponsoring a rock concert in the first place.

As part of the federal reinvention effort, a number of departments have issued "permission slips" to all their employees: "Is it right for my customers? Is it legal and ethical? Is it something I am willing to be accountable for? Is it consistent with my agency's mission? Am I using my time wisely? If so, don't ask permission, you already have it. JUST DO IT!"[48] This is a step in the right direction, for it focuses employees on results.

CAPTIVE CUSTOMERS, ROSY PROMISES, GRANDIOSE PERFORMANCE GOALS

In September 1993, President Clinton signed Executive Order 12862, which requires the federal government to "provide service to the public that matches or exceeds the best service available in the private sector." The Executive Order goes on to say that "the Federal Government must be customer-driven."

Optimists believe this will actually happen. Cynics laugh derisively. Realists hope for some minor improvements, but recognize that government will never achieve the customer focus of the private sector. The reason is simple: most government services are monopolies, and monopolies lack the sort of life-or-death urgency that informs a competitive market.

In addition, monopolies have a harder time judging their own performance. Because their customers are largely captive, they can't look at sales or market share. Second, government agencies have no measure of profitability. Thus, the key measures of corporate success—satisfied customers and profitability—are not available to public agencies.

The National Performance Review is attempting to artificially simulate the customer focus that occurs naturally in a market. To do this, it had every department set customer service goals. For instance, NASA commits to "meet[ing] all major milestones on schedule and cost, more than 95 percent of the time," and the Equal Employment Opportunity Commission says that "businesses can expect us to treat you with respect and dignity."[49] That's nice. But the National Performance Review doesn't ask the nit-picking little question, *What happens if they don't?* The answer is, *Nothing.*

Promises of performance are meaningless unless there are consequences for failure. The greatest protection a consumer has is the ability to take his or her business elsewhere. That sends a message directly to the producer's pocketbook.

When the U.S. Department of Agriculture inspects chickens, nothing happens if they call substandard birds Grade A. But if Frank Perdue sells inferior fowl, he'll lose his customers. More than a government stamp, Frank puts his own name on the chickens he sells. "If you're not completely satisfied, write me and I'll give you your money back," Mr. Perdue tells his customers. If you're not happy with a government-inspected chicken, Frank asks, "who do you write in Washington? What do they know about chickens?"[50]

The performance goals established by various government

agencies are equally impotent, for there are no negative consequences for failing to achieve them. For example, the 1994 Goals 2000 federal education act established national education goals for the year 2000. Goal number four states: "The nation's students will be first in the world in mathematics and science achievement." And if we aren't? Well, there will probably be a push for greater funding. Goals 2000 is a wish list and nothing more. Some of the goals enter the realm of the absurd, such as "All children will start school ready to learn" and "Every adult American will be literate."

In the early 1990s, many states started producing grandiose wish lists for future government performance. Led by the Oregon Benchmarks program, about a half-dozen states have joined the bandwagon. Though they borrow the hard-nosed language of business, promising a "focus on outputs, not inputs" and stressing "performance measurement," these programs are mostly all bark and no bite.

The Minnesota Milestones program, for example, lays out 79 milestones for the future. In 1990, 42 percent of Minnesota twelfth-graders used drugs or alcohol on a monthly basis. Minnesota's goal is to reduce this figure to 15 percent by the year 2020. Such noble nonsense! How much influence does the government of Minnesota have over teen drinking? What happens if the goal is not achieved? The report is silent. Other Minnesota Milestones include increasing the life expectancy of Minnesotans, reducing teen suicide, and increasing the diversity of Minnesota songbirds.[51]

CONCLUSION

"Our fundamental problem today is not too much government or too little government," write Osborne and Gaebler. "Our fundamental problem is that we have *the wrong kind of government*."[52] The right kind being the efficient, customer-oriented, Osborne and Gaebler style of government.

We disagree. The real problem is threefold. First, government is too big. Second, government is too centralized. Third, *government management is embedded in politics, and is therefore inherently limited in efficiency.* There are ways that government systems can be improved, but we should not expect government to be as efficient as the private sector. That's not realistic.

If you've ever owned a dog, you know there are certain things that you can change about your pet's behavior and certain things you can't. With a lot of effort, care, and attention (by which we mean a rolled-up newspaper), you can train your dog to sit, to roll over and play dead, and perhaps to fetch your slippers. You cannot, however, teach Fido to drive a car, prepare dinner, or discuss Proust over cocktails.[53]

Though it can be improved, democratic government has inherent limitations. Nothing can make every government activity a paragon of efficiency. There are systemic reasons that prevent it.

Public administration in a democracy is fundamentally different from managing a private corporation. In government, you are spending the public's money, and thus the public deserves a voice in how it is spent. Of course, different factions have used and will continue to use political influence to benefit themselves. Consider Los Angeles city government as described to us by Deputy Mayor Michael Keeley: "Think of city government as a big bus. The bus is divided into sections with different constituencies: labor, the city council, the mayor, interest groups, and contractors. Every seat is equipped with a brake, so lots of people can stop the bus at any time. The problem is that this makes the bus almost undriveable."[54]

Political wrangling works against the best efforts of those in government as they attempt to provide service as well as the market does. The limitations of government efficiency we have outlined in this chapter provide powerful reasons for government *to stick to its core tasks, and leave the rest to the market.*

We asked many public officials, "Do you think government

can be as efficient as private business?" Our favorite answer came from Norm King, city manager of Moreno Valley, California, who said, "No. And I wouldn't expect it to be. It shouldn't be. There's a lot of room for improvement, sure. But aside from [outcomes], government is a process. There is no way we should let go of some of the built-in barriers to efficiency. Part of the democratic process is that we take the time to hear a lot of voices, to allow participation in the decision-making process."[55]

We wouldn't change that for the world—that's democracy. We could purchase greater efficiency, but only at the price of democracy. Mussolini, after all, did make the trains run on time. But we would be exchanging our birthright of freedom for a mess of pottage.

CHAPTER 6

SETTING LIMITS

The Chinese symbol for crisis combines the symbols for 'danger' and 'opportunity.' It has been true forever that crisis and danger and fear produce an opportunity to make things different.[1]

David Cohen, chief of staff
to Philadelphia Mayor Edward Rendell

Michigan Governor John Engler offers the first law of government: "The more tax money that flows into government coffers, the more money government will spend."[2] New Jersey Governor Christine Todd Whitman states the corollary: "As soon as you start limiting revenues, government will do more with less."[3] Without a driving force for organizational change, change won't often occur. Improving government efficiency requires a driving force, and the most powerful change agent is a limit on revenue.

These observations are not intended to be mean-spirited or antigovernment. They are true of all human systems, as valid for individuals, families, and corporations as for government. Think about it. If your salary suddenly doubled tomorrow, wouldn't you manage to spend the extra money? And if your salary were cut in half, wouldn't you change the way you lived to stretch every penny? Government is no different. Far from crippling government, less money often makes it more efficient.

In business, competition provides the driving force for organizational change. Businesses that don't change go out of business. In government, citizens, taxpayers, and voters must supply the impetus to change. In the early 1990s, a quiet revolt built across America, culminating in the historic election of 1994. Angry citizens asserted their democratic authority to keep government in line. This citizen-generated discipline may be the best hope for improving government efficiency.

CRISIS IN PHILLY

After a decade of teetering on the edge of fiscal catastrophe, Philadelphia hit rock-bottom in 1991. Nineteen times in the previous ten years Philadelphia's City Council had responded to a budget shortfall by raising taxes. But this was an election year, and the voters were restless. Taxes were not an option.

The bond rating fell below junk. Pension and vendor payments were suspended. *City & State* magazine ranked Philadelphia's financial health fiftieth out of the 50 largest cities, calling it "the city that has set the standard for fiscal distress." Philadelphia faced the prospect of declaring bankruptcy.

Mayor Edward Rendell came into office in January 1992, when the city was staring at a $208 million budget shortfall, projected to rise to $1.4 billion in five years. Rendell inherited a fiscal disaster of a magnitude not seen in Philadelphia since the Great Depression. Once elected, Rendell moved quickly. He immediately dismissed any thought that Philadelphia could tax its way out of its problems. Then Rendell started to cut the *costs* of government. Rendell used the crisis to take on a host of sacred cows. He took an approach considered political suicide for an urban Democrat—he took on the city's police, fire, and municipal unions.

Rendell took his case to the people. He told citizens about Philadelphia city workers' compensation packages. In almost every case, city workers enjoyed better pay, holidays, and benefits than the private sector—not to mention the job security. Rendell annoyed the unions immensely. During contract renegotiations, he proposed changing work rules and scaling down compensation.[4] In response, the unions struck.

The walkout lasted just 16 hours. Why? Public workers had

zero public support. Rendell wrested $353 million in wage concessions from the unions over four years, including a two-year pay freeze, reductions in vacation days, and changes in work rules. "Everyone said what a mean and rotten guy I was during these negotiations," says the mayor. "But I said that I thought that our city work force could overcome the emotional stress of being away from their families at Flag Day."[5] Recounts the mayor, "[F]rom the day I took office, I never stopped communicating two facts: that we were out of money and that the benefit packages, when compared to what the average Philadelphian gets, were outrageous. This worked enormously well."[6]

Rendell's 81-percent popularity rating after the strike demonstrated that ultimately the "population of this city cares more about fiscal stability and sanity than they do about giving generous benefits to the municipal work force," said Rendell's Chief of Staff David Cohen. These changes—as well as the privatization and productivity improvements that have occurred under Rendell—probably wouldn't have been possible without the fiscal crisis. Says Cohen, "Realistically speaking, it's hard to imagine that we could have accomplished as much as we did without the fiscal crisis. The vested interests that exist make it very, very difficult to bring fundamental change in the absence of some kind of compelling reason to change."[7]

Former Philadelphia Deputy Mayor Joseph Torsella concurs: "We are lucky we had such a terrible fiscal crisis in Philadelphia. It was an opportunity for the city. By making people understand that change was absolutely necessary and could no longer be avoided, in the long run, the crisis will be one of the best things that happened to Philadelphia."[8]

THE JOY OF BEING BROKE

A popular phrase among government reformers is, "Doing more with less." That can happen only if you have less to start with. Faced with the difficult choice of changing the way things are done or raising taxes, politicians have historically found it easier to raise taxes. Changing the way things are done is very difficult in a public bureaucracy; but most elected officials and public managers told us that a voter environment hostile to tax increases was an environment more amenable to change. Time after time, fiscal crisis has played a pivotal role in improving government efficiency.

In 1990, William Weld of Massachusetts was thought crazy for promising not to raise taxes when the state was confronting an $850 million deficit. Pro-tax advocates predicted dire consequences for needed services unless taxes were raised. Despite the pressure, Weld refused to buckle.

Skeptics had said it was impossible, but in his first year Weld balanced the budget without raising taxes, and Massachusetts actually spent fewer dollars than it had the previous year. Moreover, the predicted calamities never materialized. Instead, long overdue changes finally began. Services were contracted out to the private sector, saving millions. The state payroll was trimmed by 7,000. Eligibility was tightened on general assistance for the able-bodied, and the state stopped providing fertility drugs to welfare mothers. Says Charlie Baker, Weld's Secretary of Health and Human Services:

> *The fiscal crisis was in some respects the best thing that ever happened to the Commonwealth. Many changes that occurred because of that crisis—on the program side, on the service side, on the staffing side—were long overdue reforms, but they could not be achieved in the political dynamic of the status quo. Without crisis, the sense of urgency that dominates life in the private sector just wasn't there ... In the environment of the fiscal crisis, reducing overhead, reducing staff, closing facilities, and radically changing programs was good policy and good politics. Without crisis, it is much harder to promote that sort of agenda.*[9]

What triggered the fiscal crisis in the first place? Well, the legislature had spent more money than it had taken in. But in

Massachusetts, a budget shortfall was an almost annual event, like the Red Sox folding late in the season. What *really* triggered the fiscal crisis was a citizen-led tax revolt, galvanized by Citizens for Limited Taxation (CLT). In the 1990 election, the most talked about issue in Massachusetts was not the governor's race, but a CLT ballot initiative to roll back taxes (which Weld supported). In the final months of the lame-duck governorship of Michael Dukakis, bumper stickers and radio talk shows constituted a sort of government in exile. The discontent was enormous. The tax initiative untimately lost at the polls, but it had a profound effect nonetheless. Even those who opposed the rollback measure didn't support *higher* taxes. Their slogan against the tax rollback initiative was the less-than-rousing, "It goes too far."

The budget shortfall, coupled with voter sentiment and Weld's "no new taxes" pledge, forced change. These changes helped to restore a healthy Massachusetts economy. Unfortunately, the prosperity Weld helped create has made additional change more difficult. Working with a Democratic legislature, Weld has seen the state budget grow significantly since his first year in office. Some of Weld's initiatives, such as privatization, have been brought to a standstill by legislation passed over his veto. And though the tax rate hasn't been raised, a strong economy has brought in more revenues to government—which they've managed to spend.

Former Virginia Governor L. Douglas Wilder was staring at a $1.4 billion deficit on the day he became governor in 1990. Like Weld, Wilder refused to raise taxes and was able to pare projected government spending by 5 percent. Said Wilder, "I think the shortfall in revenues presents me with an opportunity to streamline government more closely to what government has a responsibility to do, without as much resistance as I would face if there were more ample funds to go around. Having been involved in state government for 20 years, I knew there was fat."[10]

Similarly, a huge budget shortfall gave Michigan Governor

Engler the help he needed to abolish numerous obsolete, unneeded or nonessential programs; with limited funds, marginal programs have to go.

Reengineering License Processing in Wisconsin

For years, Wisconsin's Insurance Department had a routine for handling license applications. When a request came in to the Agent Licensing section, someone would retrieve the microfilm record, stick it into a microfilm reader, and verify that the request was coming from a registered agent.

Next, a request for the agent's record was written up and *walked* over to the central data processing unit. A few weeks later, a record of the license was *walked back* to the Agent Licensing section, which then mailed it to the agent. Total elapsed time: three to four weeks.

"We weren't keeping up," recalls Randy Blumer, a manager in the department and a master of understatement.[11] Four people were handling applications from 60,000 insurance agents using a work process designed by the Marx Brothers. Small wonder that by the early 1990s the department was collapsing beneath a steadily increasing backlog.

The department's first reaction was: We need more people. But requests for additional personnel were denied by the budget office, which was under orders from Governor Tommy Thompson to keep a tight lid on department budgets. "Finally, we realized we weren't going to get any more people," recalls Blumer. "We were forced to become more innovative."

In 1991, the department purchased a Wang computer and restructured the license process from top to bottom. Today, when an agent requests a printout, department personnel can immediately look up his record in the computer, enter in the needed information, and print out the record. Total elapsed time: five minutes.

Necessity is the mother of innovation. Nothing ever would have changed if the Insurance Department's request for additional personnel had been approved. The technology to update the system had been around for a decade, but it took a crisis *with no easy way out* to achieve change. Without a crisis, license requests would still be hand-carried across town, from agency to agency. Luckily for Wisconsin's insurance agents, the Wisconsin Insurance Department ran out of money and was "forced to become more innovative."

CHANGE: THE LAST RESORT

Most people hate change. Our language is full of aphorisms warning of the dangers of change, such as "Don't change horses in midstream" and "Look before you leap." Makers of everything from computers to breakfast cereals strive to capture young consumers because they know how reluctantly human beings alter established habits. People are especially wary of changes in their work environment.

This is certainly true in the corporate world. "With a few exceptions, almost every major corporate restructuring has been in response to a crisis. Change is driven by the bottom line," says Professor Steve Postrel of the UCLA Anderson Graduate School of Management.[12] William G. Ouchi, chief of staff to Los Angeles Mayor Richard Riordan and also a business professor at UCLA, concurs. Ouchi has been studying business organizations for over 25 years. According to Ouchi, American businesses enjoyed rising revenue in the 1960s and '70s, but lost some of their competitive edge. "When revenues are constantly increasing, several bad things occur: organizations get fat, dumb, and lazy," says Ouchi. "Departments don't have to learn the art of steering resources."[13] Companies don't often undertake fundamental change or lay off excess workers during boom times. Cutbacks occur only when the competition begins to eat away at a company's bottom line.

In the public sector, privatization, productivity increases, work force reductions, dramatic reengineering projects, and most other innovations typically occur in response to fiscal crisis. In the absence of a fiscal crisis, there are few incentives for government to take the difficult steps needed to pare operations and reduce costs. "It's sad but true," says one city manager. "If money is coming in, we're going to spend it." Governments, of course, don't go out of business. If governments run out of money, they can always raise taxes.

Stop Us Before We Spend Again

Government is not a self-limiting system. Left unchecked, government will grow. Elected officials are under continual pressure to *expand* government. Most interest groups and lobbyists push hard for more spending. Artists want more spending on art. Parents want more spending on schools. Scientists want more spending on science. Farmers want more spending on farm programs. And the Gray Panthers and the American Association of Retired Persons are ready to pounce on any politician dumb enough to even *mention* cuts in social security. ("Social security is the third rail of politics," said one Washington staffer. "You touch it, you die.") Much government activity today consists of shuffling money away from general taxpayers to a particular happy recipient.[14]

Special-interest lobbying is only part of the picture. Most spending programs are not directly linked to taxes, so every government program gives the illusion of providing something for nothing. Economists such as Milton Friedman have explained that there is no such thing as a free lunch, but try telling that to the recipient of a school lunch program. Economic reality is not political reality, and it is unrealistic to expect politicians to vote against literal and figurative free lunch programs.

In addition, public managers are constantly screaming for more support for their departments. The police chief lobbies for more money, the head librarian does likewise. Public managers even find ways to spend public funds to expand government. For example, in 1994, the New York City welfare department spent $400,000 on an advertising campaign to increase the number of people applying for food stamps.[15] In 1989, the University of Massachusetts at Amherst spent over $20,000 to bus students into Boston to protest against cuts to the state's higher education budget.[16]

When budget cuts are threatened, public managers often threaten to eliminate the most visible service the department provides. The media loves this technique, affectionately dubbed the Washington Monument Game after an especially creative threat by the Parks Department to close the Washington Monument. When the U.S. Customs Service was told to take a two-percent cut, it announced itself ready to eliminate drug inspections at airports. In local governments, police, fire, and schools are typically held hostage.

We asked UCLA social scientist James Q. Wilson what he thought American government would look like in the future. His answer was scary. "It's going to be bigger, more complicated, more burdensome, and more costly. *No matter what point in human history you ask that question, the answer is always the same. Government gets bigger.*"[17] "Government is like a gas," explained one public official. "It expands to fill its container." But what is the container? If government cannot restrain its own growth, who can prevent government from growing without bound? People like Douglas Bruce.

COLORADO'S AMENDMENT ONE:
ROCKY MOUNTAIN UPRISING

"The issue is, who should decide how much government we can afford?" says Colorado Springs businessman Douglas Bruce. "The people who earn the money or the politicians who want to spend it? The people should be able to vote on how much government we want to buy."[18]

Douglas Bruce is the force behind Colorado's Amendment One, a 1992 state referendum to limit the growth of Colorado state government. Amendment One caps spending growth at the rate of inflation plus population growth, and requires taxpayer approval of all bond issues and tax increases—at both the state and local levels. If tax revenues exceed the growth cap, surplus revenues are refunded unless taxpayers vote to allow their government to keep it. Before Colorado government may grow, it must ask citizens' permission.

Like many voters, Bruce was tired of what he saw as runaway government growth. In Colorado, state and local spending grew by 135 percent in the 1980s and taxes jumped by over 60 percent.[19] For years, Colorado's political leaders had their foot on the accelerator. Taxpayers wanted a brake.

Amendment One faced a furious assault from the state's most powerful political interests, including public employee unions, the public education lobby, bond traders, representatives of local government, the Denver Chamber of Commerce, and many of the state's elected leaders. Opponents claimed that if Amendment One passed, schools would close, prisoners would roam the streets, the economy would be wrecked, and government services discontinued. One particularly imaginative bond trader even suggested that the Pope might be assassinated when he came to Denver if Amendment One were adopted (due to a lack of police). One notable opponent of tax and spending limits described Bruce as a "terrorist" who would "lob a hand grenade into a schoolyard full of children" and described opposition to Amendment One as the moral equivalent of "fighting the Nazis at the Battle of the Bulge."[20] That opponent was Roy Romer, Colorado's governor. (The terrorist nickname has stuck, and Bruce's business cards now list his occupation as "Terrorist.")

Bruce was undeterred, however, and despite being outspent more than three to one, Amendment One was approved by 54 percent of the voters in 1992. Would Bruce do it again, knowing beforehand all the abuse he would take? "Hell, yes," says

Bruce. "There was nothing in it for me. I did it for the love of my country."[21]

Over two years after its passage, none of the dire consequences predicted has come true, but Amendment One has brought changes. For one thing, citizens must now take more responsibility for their government, in that no longer can they clamor for more services and then blame politicians when taxes are raised to meet these demands. Notes a report from the Colorado Municipal League:

The passage of Amendment One on November 3, 1992, marked a revolution for state and local operations in Colorado. Far more than merely requiring a vote on new taxes, this new constitutional provision challenges traditional assumptions and practices on a broad front, ranging from budgeting to elections to contracting and far beyond.[22]

"A lot of folks propose tax increases without looking at other ways of doing things," says Fort Collins City Councilman Jerry Horac. "Amendment One forces us to work closer with the citizens and forces government managers to make sure they're getting greater efficiencies and higher levels of service."[23] The city of Blackhawk, for example, contracted out for transit, janitorial, and a host of administrative services. Arvada contracted out street maintenance, construction, and custodial services. Rangely has reduced the number of seasonal and part-time employees.

Some feared that Amendment One would make it impossible to respond to emergencies or unanticipated fiscal needs. But the amendment allowed for overrides, and voters haven't been unreasonable in approving spending hikes. In 1993, 34 ballot questions sought revenue and/or spending authorization; all but three were approved. Also in 1993, 17 municipal measures seeking sales or user tax increases went before voters. Ten were approved.

Because they know they must go before voters, officials have a strong incentive to run a tight ship. A wasteful government is unlikely to win approval for a tax increase. "Officials recognize we're the boss and that they're never going to get a tax increase unless they treat us like customers," says Bruce.[24]

THE MODERN-DAY TAX REVOLT

The initiative and referendum process gives citizens a direct voice in trying to limit the growth of government. The first wave of the modern tax revolt was in the late 1970s and early '80s, which saw the passage of California's Proposition 13, Massachusetts' Proposition 2-1/2, and tax and spending limitations in roughly 20 other states. There has been some debate over the effectiveness of these measures in actually keeping the lid on government growth.[25] The most recent study on the subject, a 1994 report by the Cato Institute found a small but significant reduction in government growth in states with tax and spending limitations.[26]

In addition to Colorado's Amendment One, between 1992 and 1994 voters approved tax and spending limitations in Arizona, Connecticut, Nevada, Oklahoma, and Washington state. In the face of furious opposition, limitation measures were narrowly defeated in three other states.[27] In 1992, Arizona voters passed an amendment called "It's Time," which requires a two-thirds supermajority vote of the legislature for any new taxes. Before "It's Time" became law, the Arizona legislature had increased taxes eight times in nine years. "These days the legislators don't even bother to propose new taxes," says Sydney Hoff Hay, one of the principal sponsors of the initiative.[28] Instead, Arizona taxes are being racheted *downward*. "The little secret [of the supermajority requirement] is that my income tax cuts are pretty much irreversible," says Arizona Governor Fife Symington.[29]

The most recent wave of initiatives could have a much greater impact than their forerunners in the late '70s and early

'80s. Initiative writers have learned from previous mistakes. For instance, many initiatives of the early 1980s used formulas to limit spending, but left legislators in charge of administering the formula. Politicians are wonderfully creative at fiddling with such limits. Studies by University of Colorado economist Barry Poulson found that the first wave of spending limitations had an effect for only about four years. After that, politicians found ways of working around the restrictions. (California, for example, now issues *revenue* bonds for prison construction, as though prisoners paid rent. New York State recently sold itself Attica prison.)

Poulson is more optimistic about the lasting power of the latest round of limitations. "The new round of spending limitations are working differently. They're being drawn so tightly that it's difficult to get around them. Also I think the politicians are beginning to realize the old days are over and they're going to have to be accountable for what they spend."[30]

Several of the initiatives of the 1990s require direct voter approval for additional taxes, giving ultimate control to the taxpayers. (Colorado's Amendment One actually goes further, requiring the state to ask voters' permission to keep any additional revenues it happens to take in.) Some folks predict a future without tax increases in the states with new tax and spending limitations.[31] "Voters are taking the power to tax away from politicians," says David Keating, executive vice president of the National Taxpayers Union. "Once you have it in one state, I can't imagine the people ever giving it up."[32]

Grover Norquist, president of Americans for Tax Reform, is a hurricane of energy, advising grass-roots activists across the country on tax limitation strategies. He believes that nearly every state with the initiative/referendum process will eventually adopt tax and spending limitations similar to Colorado's Amendment One. "Putting the power to raise taxes into the hands of people is as big a revolution as term limits," says Norquist.[33] Norquist also thinks these tax limitation measures will draw in businesses like a magnet. "Watch what happens," says Norquist. "Everything will tilt west," as business and taxpayers flow to those states with the initiative process.

LIMITING GOVERNMENT INTAKE DURING BOOMS

Perhaps tax limits such as Amendment One and "It's Time" can achieve what has heretofore been impossible: limiting the growth of government during economic booms. Doing so would avoid the dreaded "boom-bust" cycle of government spending.

The boom-bust cycle arises from the natural ups and downs of the economy. During good economic times, money flows into government coffers. Elected officials spend this money, starting new programs, hiring more workers, etc. When an economic downturn hits, money coming into government slows down while obligations typically rise, since a down economy increases unemployment and places a greater demand on government resources. Since it is very difficult for government to shed programs in the short term, it responds to the budget gap in a number of ways, none of them particularly effective. Short-term, gap-closing strategies include borrowing, deferring maintenance on infrastructure, freezing travel budgets, etc.[34] The most common "solution" to the shortfall is, of course, the "prudent" recourse of higher taxes.

The boom-bust cycle creates a ratcheting effect, whereby government intermittently grows but virtually never shrinks. By putting government on a tighter leash, a tax cap forces government to keep trim even during good times, so that when the economy goes sour and tax revenues dry up, governments don't face the massive structural imbalances they otherwise would have.

In theory, "rainy day funds" are supposed to achieve a similar purpose. In reality, things don't work that way. "You can talk about rainy day funds all you want, but as soon as there is a cloud on the horizon, that money is gone," says Barbara Anderson of Citizens for Limited Taxation.[35]

IT'S ABOUT MUCH MORE THAN TAXES

Unquestionably, limiting tax revenue is the best way to limit the size of government. But grass-roots activists are using other tools as well.

One of these tools is term limits. Passed in 22 states since 1991, term limits seek to reestablish a government of the people rather than an elite ruling class. Advocates claim that by creating a legislature of nonprofessional politicians more broadly representative of the American public and by making legislators less beholden to special interests, term limits will act as a check on government growth.[36]

As government has grown, politicians have increasingly viewed government as a long-term career rather than a short-term civic duty. Rather than serving the public interest, the goal of many politicians is to get elected and stay elected. Money is so vital to successful campaigns that all but the very wealthy must seek the support of special-interest PAC money. Once in office, such officials often buy "incumbency insurance" at taxpayers' expense. Writes Marlo Lewis, Jr., executive director of the Washington, D.C.-based Competitive Enterprise Institute:

> *The principal cause of the unchecked growth of government in America is the closing of our political system—the transformation of Congress and many state legislatures into exclusive clubs with lifetime memberships. A political establishment is a de facto ruling class, and every ruling class naturally seeks to expand the scale and scope of its power. The Washington establishment, with its corrupting subsidies, debilitating taxes, and invasive regulations, perfectly illustrates the point.*[37]

Some opponents of term limits believe they will merely increase the power of lobbyists and legislative staffs. But if this is the case, then why do lobbyists and legislative staffers detest term limits?[38] Lobbyists spent almost $3 million in 1991 to defeat term limits because they feared losing the "investments" they had made in long-time legislators.[39] "Special interests would go broke trying to buy off Congress if terms were limited," write James Coyne and John Fund in *Cleaning House.*[40]

There is yet a third tactic for limiting and reducing government. A grass-roots property rights revolt has begun in the last few years. Property owners are demanding compensation for government regulations that significantly lower the value of their property. Consider the case of Louise and Frederick Williams of Little Compton, Rhode Island. They saw the value of their land plummet from $260,000 to just $30,000 after the government categorized it as a wetland. Not only were they required to tear down the new home they had started to build, but they had to follow a 13-point restoration plan dictated by regulators. "I've lost my faith and trust in government," says Ms. Williams.[41]

The Williamses are not alone. Across America, thousands of property owners have chafed under the rough hand of government regulators, and property owners are banding together and fighting back. Over 500 property rights groups now exist across the country.[42] Between 1992 and 1994, 12 states passed property rights legislation. In addition, the 1994 Republican Contract with America calls for compensation for so-called regulatory takings; if new federal rules reduce a property's value, the government will have to compensate the owners. (The "takings" clause of the Fifth Amendment asserts that no "private property be taken, without just compensation." The intention is to extend this principle to cases in which new regulations "take away" the value of the property.)

Antidevelopment groups don't like this idea. "Republicans want a balanced budget, and then they propose a new multibillion-dollar entitlement program for property owners," says

John Echeverria, counsel for the National Audobon Society. "How they reconcile the two I have no idea."[43] We find it disturbing that Mr. Echeverria thinks the right of an owner to his or her property constitutes an *entitlement program*. The property rights revolution seeks to restore government to its traditional role as defender, not destroyer, of property rights.[44] "This revolution demonstrates that property is a foundation of a free society, that the right to acquire, use, and find security in property are among our most precious civil rights," says Clint Bolick of the Institute for Justice.[45] In the early 1990s, the Supreme Court appeared inclined to agree with Bolick, and several important "takings" cases have been won by property owners.

The property rights revolt is about more than just "takings." It is about the limits of government interference in the lives of citizens. In 1994, Massachusetts voters passed a referendum outlawing rent control in the Bay State. Even in traditionally liberal Massachusetts, voters have rejected the idea that government officials can set rent levels better than the market can.

As these various citizen movements seek to limit government, their grass-roots activism has been enhanced by the use of technology; the phone and fax brigades of small groups have helped to coalesce those opposed to government expansion. Unlike many other interest groups, taxpayers mostly lack an existing organizing structure, such as unions, professional organizations, and corporations. Thanks to technology, think tanks have been able to supply these small groups with the intellectual ammunition needed to make their case. Talk radio and low-budget newsletters have given ordinary citizens increasingly powerful voices in their government.

THE SPECIAL CASE OF THE FEDERAL GOVERNMENT

At the state and local level two additional mechanisms act to constrain governmental growth: the line-item veto and the balanced budget requirement. By 1995, 43 states had given governors the power of line-item veto, while 48 states and most municipalities require a balanced budget. The bad news was until early 1995 the federal government lacked either restraint, and still lacks a balanced budget requirement.

The line-item veto allows a chief executive to veto specific budget items. In effect, the line-item veto can be used as a scalpel to carve fat from the budget. As a result, pork barrel politics, while it surely exists, is not as prevalent at the state level as at the federal level. The line-item veto works because chief executives—who represent the entire population of a state—are usually more willing to oppose special-interest pork than legislators currying favor with narrow constituencies. In a 1992 survey of 118 former and present governors, the Cato Institute found that 92 percent of governors described the line-item veto as a useful or very useful tool. "Legislators love to be loved, so they love to spend money," said Massachusetts Governor William Weld. "The line-item veto is essential to enable the executive to hold down spending." Former New York Governor, Democrat Hugh L. Carey, concurs, "It is an antidote to pork."[46]

Calvin Coolidge once described the pressure of special-interest politics. Remember that Coolidge was president before the invention of the lobbyist's tasseled loafer, at a time when federal government spending was only about 4 percent of GNP rather than today's 25 percent of GNP. Even then, however, Congress was a slave to special interests:

It is because in their hours of timidity the Congress becomes subservient to the importunities of organized minorities that the President comes more and more to stand as the champion of the rights of the whole country. Organizing such minorities has come to be a well-recognized industry at Washington. They are oftentimes led by persons of great ability, who display much skill in bringing their influences to bear on the Congress. They have ways of securing newspaper publicity, deluging Senators and Representatives with petitions and overwhelming

them with imprecations that are oftentimes decisive in secur-
ing the passage of bills. While much of this legislation is not
entirely bad, almost all of it is excessively expensive.[47]

Though Coolidge could (and did) veto bills, he lacked the
authority to veto specific line items within appropriations bills.
Thus, presidents are often confronted with the unpleasant
choice of either vetoing a basically sound law because it con-
tains chunks of pork, or swallowing the whole bill, pork and all.

This explains why funding for moving sidewalks in Altoona
is tucked away inside massive transportation bills. With a line-
item veto, the president could reach in and eliminate the funding for Altoona's $30 million moving sidewalk, or North
Dakota's Lawrence Welk Museum, or a study of bovine flatu-
lence. (These humorous examples are, unfortunately, not hypo-
thetical.)

TOMMY THOMPSON'S POWERFUL PENCIL

In his office, Wisconsin Governor Tommy Thompson displays
two symbols of his commitment to limiting government
growth. In the corner of his office stands a ten-foot-tall "Governor's veto pencil." On Thompson's desk rests a sign that
reads, "What part of NO don't you understand?" Perhaps no
governor has used the line-item veto more effectively in stop-
ping excessive spending. Says Thompson, "I probably have the
strongest veto power in the country and I have not been tepid
about using it. I have had over 1,500 vetoes, all of which have
been sustained. It really helps me keep the legislature in check.
It allows me to really control spending and accomplish the
things that are needed for economic growth."[48]

In addition to the line-item veto, the governor of Wisconsin
also has partial veto power, which allows him to remove letters
or digits in an appropriations request. By erasing a single digit,
Thompson once cut a $500,000 appropriation to $50,000. On
another occasion, the governor used his partial veto to turn a

revenue-neutral tax swap into a tax cut. All in all, Thompson's aggressive use of his partial veto has saved state taxpayers $600 million in new taxes that would have been required to fund programs he vetoed. "The partial veto is an important tool for keeping spending increases within prudent and affordable limits, keeping taxes at competitive levels, and keeping special interest, pork barrel items from becoming law," says Thompson.

Can the line-item veto slow federal spending? Time will tell. In 1995, for the first time in American history, the GOP-controlled Congress gave the president the power of the line-item veto. Both President Clinton and the Republicans in Congress were happy with the arrangement. So, we expect, will be the American people.

BALANCED BUDGET AMENDMENT

Most cities and states are required to balance their budget every year. While many governments spend more than they take in during a given year, they must address the imbalance at year end, either by raising taxes or cutting programs. Only the federal government has long abused a third option: borrowing.

Until the 1970s, the federal government's power to borrow was used sparingly, typically during war or severe economic depression. When our government ran up a war debt, it paid it back. In the 21 years following the War of 1812, the federal government ran a surplus in 18 of them, virtually eliminating the national debt. After the Civil War, the federal government put together a string of 28 consecutive surpluses.[49]

What made federal legislators so conscientious about repaying loans in the past? Nothing more or less than a sense of duty. Lawmakers knew it would be fiscally irresponsible and morally reprehensible to saddle future generations with unpaid debt. Thomas Jefferson feared that this sense of responsibility would not always be sufficient to restrain the federal government from abusing its power to borrow. In 1798, Jefferson wrote, "I wish it were possible to obtain a single amendment to our Constitution. . . . I mean an additional article, taking from the federal government the power of borrowing."[50]

After the 1974 Budget Act, all restraint broke down. Like a teenager with a credit card, federal lawmakers learned the trick of funding programs without paying taxes. For 20-odd years running, the federal government has spent more—a lot more—than it has taken in. The result? As of 1993, our $4.2 trillion (and rising) national debt means that every man, woman, and child in the United States owes about $16,800. Moreover, about one of every seven federal tax dollars goes for interest on the debt.

In Washington, everything seems like play money. In 1991, two appalling scandals illustrated the depths of fiscal irresponsibility to which Congress had sunk. In that year, it was revealed that 250 members of Congress owed more than $300,000 for meals and receptions held at the Capitol restaurant.[51] About the same time it was revealed that 355 members had bounced more than 8,000 checks at the House Bank.[52] After spending time in Congress, members no longer believe that bills ever come due.

At the founding of our nation, a Constitution of enumerated federal powers was carefully crafted to limit the scope of the federal government. As we shall see in Chapter 11, parts of the Constitution have come to be ignored. The bloated federal government is a prime example of what government becomes in the absence of limits.

The balanced budget amendment is yet another way to limit federal growth (nearly all states, again, already have one). The balanced budget amendment is a constitutional amendment that would require Congress to balance its books. Except in special situations (such as war), Congress would have to collect the taxes for its programs, putting an end to the practice of "spend now, tax later." This would be an important step in putting the genie back in the bottle.

"We need an extra tool to require us to make the tough decisions," says Texas Congressman Charles Stenholm, the sponsor of a balanced budget amendment.[53] What Stenholm is essentially saying amounts to a cry for help: stop us before we spend again.

In addition to the balanced budget amendment, another way to give people greater control of federal spending is a national referendum on any tax increase. A 1993 poll by the *Los Angeles Times* found that 72 percent of those surveyed favored a constitutional amendment to require any federal tax increase to be voted on in a national referendum. "I predict that at least one presidential contender—and maybe more—will make a call for voter approval of taxes at the national level as part of his 1996 campaign," says John Fund of the *Wall Street Journal*.[54] One way or another, a lid must be clamped on federal spending.

"DON'T BLAME ME, I VOTED AGAINST PORK"

In a democracy, elected officials are supposed to represent voters. Unfortunately, they have. The irresponsible behavior of congressional representatives in the past has often accurately reflected the irresponsible voting behavior of their constituents. When polled, voters complain about high taxes and the growth of government. But they haven't wanted their programs cut. The story is told of the veteran congressman explaining the secret of his political longevity: "I vote in favor of every new program and against every tax increase." Don't blame the jaded politician; he was just giving the people what they want.

"People say, 'Why is Congress so out of touch?' We're not. We are responding faithfully to the schizophrenic signals you're all sending us, which is 'Cut our taxes and increase our entitlements,'" says former Republican Congressman Fred Grandy.[55] In the past, voters have not had to confront the inconsistency of those preferences. During the Reagan era, voters were told that these contradictory goals could be achieved by eliminating waste, fraud, and abuse. The Clinton administration promised a reinvented government capable of "doing more with less." The painful truth is that the only way to significantly lower taxes without raising the deficit will require an end to certain programs that benefit certain groups. If you are serious about losing weight, you have to say goodbye to the bacon, the hamsteak, and the Jimmy Dean sausages.

Historically, voters haven't always liked to hear the painful truth. (This is why diet books have such titles as "The Amazing Eat-All-You-Want-Hot-Fudge-Sundae Diet.") This is changing. Voters have largely accepted that they have a choice to make. Forced to choose between lower taxes and fewer government programs, and higher taxes and more programs, they want the former. Polls support this assessment, but a more accurate indicator is the behavior of politicians. One of the strangest scenes of the crazy and historic 1994 election season was the sight of candidates *promising* their constituents that they *wouldn't* bring home the bacon.

In New Jersey, Democratic Congressman Herbert Klein and Republican challenger Bill Martini entered into a debate about who was most committed to *killing* a proposed federal flood tunnel project that promised to bring $1.4 billion in federal largesse to the district. "We need people in Congress who will say, 'This is wasteful spending in our own district, and I don't want it,'" said Mr. Martini.[56] Representative Klein, who only a year before had called the tunnel "the only realistic solution" to the region's potential flooding problems, suddenly became a born-again budget-cutter during the campaign and also vowed to terminate the project.

In Iowa, Republican incumbent Jim Lightfoot had to *defend* his role in bringing a $2.4 million federally funded parking garage to Burlington, Iowa.[57] In years past, a candidate would have been *bragging* about it. "People are simply fed up with this kind of misuse of federal dollars," said Elaine Baxter, Lightfoot's Democratic Challenger, who ran on an antipork platform. Baxter was right; voters are fed up with the high-pork diet, and the list of losers in 1994 confirms it; House

Speaker Tom Foley, Ways and Means Committee Chairman Dan Rostenkowski, Judiciary Committee Chairman Jack Brooks of Texas, and Senator Jim Sasser of Tennessee were all turned out by voters. "In most of the campaigns that were in trouble, the candidate who ran on a pork-style platform lost," said pollster Frank Luntz.[58]

Traditionally, it has been almost impossible for a challenger to unseat the Speaker of the House, in part because of the speaker's ability to bring home the goodies for his district. But in 1994, challenger George Nethercutt attacked incumbent Tom Foley on exactly that point. Nethercutt pointed out that as the federal bureaucracy took its cut, tax dollars decreased in value during their overnight stay in the capital. Voters decided to give Nethercutt an overnight stay in Washington and keep Foley—and their tax dollars—home.

It's easy to favor low taxes. Polls have found that 69 percent of voters think federal taxes are too high considering what they get from federal government.[59] Nothing new there; people have always thought taxes were too high. What's new is that people now appear willing to forgo programs in exchange for lower taxes. A 1993 poll by ABC News and the *Washington Post* found that two-thirds of voters favor smaller government *and* fewer services. That's encouraging because we won't get the first without the second. (Of course, most voters would prefer it if you cut *someone else's* program.)

Someone once opined that democracy was doomed once the people realized they could vote themselves money from the treasury. Americans clued in to this some time ago, and our political and social well-being suffered for it. Now, after a decades-long spending binge, voters are rediscovering that you don't get something for nothing.

We applaud the example set by the town officials of Wakefield and Peterborough, New Hampshire, who voted unanimously not to accept federal disaster relief money after a snowstorm in March 1993.[60] In an act of maturity and self-discipline, these defiant, self-reliant New Englanders told the federal government that a snowstorm in New Hampshire is *not* a disaster. New Hampshirites have been shoveling their own snow since before there was a federal government, and they could deal with a nor'easter without the help of Congress or the American taxpayer.

In a democracy, people ultimately get the government they deserve. If we are to improve government, it must be voters who lead us to a better, more disciplined government.

THE NEW JERSEY EXPERIENCE

In many ways, the recent history of New Jersey offers a microcosm of our national experience—and it may provide a guide for our future. Like many states, New Jersey built up its government during the boom 1980s. When the recession hit, taxes were raised, creating an antitax backlash. Finally, voters installed leaders dedicated to reducing taxes, who now must govern within tighter fiscal constraints. Whether New Jersey can successfully downsize and improve its government may presage the future of American government.

In the mid-1980s, during the administration of Republican Governor Tom Kean, the economy was booming—and so was state government. Ginny Holt, now a top treasury official for Governor Whitman, who worked under Governor Kean, recalls the culture of New Jersey government during the halcyon 1980s: "The culture was: scheme up whatever you want, spend money, have conferences, take your whole department on a retreat, think up whatever project you want—no matter how grand—and there will be funding for it. There was kind of an attitude of, It's not my money. Money materializes out of nowhere when you're in government."[61]

New Jersey's budget rose from $6.1 billion in 1982 to nearly $12 billion in 1989.[62] This growth brought new programs, more employees, and larger departments. Like a growing teenager, New Jersey government was always hungry. When the national recession hit in 1990, something had to give. It turned out to be taxpayers.

By 1990, New Jersey's governor was Democrat Jim Florio. In the time-honored political tradition, Florio declared during the gubernatorial campaign, "I see no reason to raise taxes in New Jersey." In the time-honored political tradition, the people believed him. After his election, Florio saw things differently and pushed through a $2.8 billion tax increase, and the rest is history.[63]

Florio's tax increase energized taxpayers. Within two months, a newly formed antitax group called Hands Across New Jersey had over 70,000 members and had gathered 800,000 signatures calling for repeal of the tax and the recall of Florio.[64] A Hands Across New Jersey rally in Trenton drew a ten-mile motorcade. Police were eventually forced to close off entry into the city.

Everywhere Florio went, he was badgered by angry taxpayers. At a women's club meeting in Cherry Hill, irate female voters heaved toilet rolls at him. In Camden, the hapless governor was booed off the school stage by fifth graders.

In 1991, two years into his four-year term, voters expressed their anger at Florio at the ballot box. Over half the Democratic incumbents statewide were sent packing, giving Republicans, previously the minority in the Senate and Assembly, a veto-proof two-thirds majority in both houses.

Barely escaping with his political life was Democrat Bill Bradley, New Jersey's popular senator and holder of a supposedly "safe seat." Bradley had nothing to do with the Florio tax increase, but for New Jersey voters it didn't matter. They were hopping mad at anything associated with Florio. Campaigning hard against the Florio tax increase, the relatively unknown president of the New Jersey Board of Public Utilities—a home-maker by profession—came within one percentage point of knocking Bradley out of the Senate. Bradley's spirited challenger was none other than Christine Todd Whitman.

Two years later in 1993, political neophyte Whitman chal-

lenged Florio for the governorship. The passage of time had
cooled voter anger. And the incumbent Florio had strong support from New Jersey's sizable public employee unions and
other beneficiaries of the growing state budget. Just weeks
before the election, trailing in the polls, Whitman unveiled her
plan to cut the state income tax by 30 percent over three years.
The tax-cut proposal probably saved her campaign. "She needed a clear tax-cutting strategy or she wouldn't have won," says
Joe Donaghue, statehouse reporter for Newark's *Star-Ledger.*[65]
Until she introduced her tax-cutting plan, no one knew for certain where Whitman stood. Once she declared herself, in no
uncertain terms, voters responded warmly. By declaring herself
for limited government, Whitman won over New Jersey voters.

Once in office, Whitman came out swinging. Within months,
Whitman eliminated all income taxes for those earning under
$7,500 (10 percent of the population) and *retroactively* cut tax-
es 5 percent across the board. "If President Clinton can reach
backward into time and raise your taxes retroactively, then
your governor and your legislature can cut them retroactively,"
Whitman told New Jersey taxpayers in her inaugural address.
By January 1995, the Governor had announced the final round
of the tax cuts—one year ahead of schedule.

"There is only one way to cut government spending, and
that is to cut the amount of tax dollars that we take out of your
pocket," Governor Whitman told New Jersey taxpayers in her
1994 budget address. "The more money you have to spend, the
more the economy will grow."[66]

Whitman's first budget came to $200 million less in real
spending than the previous year's. Putting together such an
austere budget was no easy task. "It's easier to build a consensus for taxes because every time we raise taxes in New Jersey,
we give someone a program," said one Whitman staffer. "Last
year's budget had no friends." It did, however, have many well-
organized enemies.

Chief among them were the state employee unions, led by
the 144,000 state teachers union and the 35,000 member Com-

munications Workers of America (CWA). The unions raised $10 million to defeat the tax cuts and brought 30,000 protestors to the steps of the capitol. During the budget negotiations, they lined both entrances of the capitol with protestors who heckled and cajoled lawmakers on the way to their chambers. But the opposition, while loud, well-organized, and fervent, failed to sway opinion. "It was somewhat surprising," says the *Star-Ledger's* Donaghue. "It was the largest union protest ever in New Jersey, but it had the impact of a pop-gun blast." Donaghue attributes this failure of the once-mighty state employee unions to a fundamental mood change in New Jersey. "You can't overestimate how strong the antitax sentiment has been here over the last several years," says Donaghue.[67]

Whitman concurs. "If you consider what has happened in this state since 1990, when Hands Across New Jersey came together, it's been a massive sea change. It's largely due to the fact that the people said, 'Enough,'" says Governor Whitman.[68]

New Jersey, Part II: Now Comes the Hard Part

It's easy to promise lower taxes and push through tax cuts in the midst of a tax revolt. Now comes the hard part: governing on a budget. Can New Jersey change the way the government operates? Will Whitman be able to withstand political pressures from interest groups? How will the bureaucracy respond?

By mid-1995, it was still too early to tell. It was clear, however, that Whitman and her top staffers believed that the fiscal constraints imposed by the tax cuts would lead to improvements, not just cuts. Whitman was looking for smaller, better government: "Part of the reason for the tax cut is it forces the discipline necessary to make government smaller . . . The brutal reality of life is that as soon as you start limiting revenues, government will do more with less. We'll have to make some of the tough priority decisions."[69]

"In a comfortable environment, there needs to be an external force to convince those inside and outside government to change the status quo," says William Waldman, the commissioner of New Jersey's Department of Human Resources. "I wish I could say otherwise, but I think fiscal discipline is a primary driver of change and innovation in government."[70]

The sense of urgency created by the tax cut allowed Waldman to undertake reforms long considered too controversial to tackle. Government-run day care centers were privatized and large state mental health facilities were being phased out and patients transferred to community-based care.

Every nook and cranny of New Jersey's government was under the microscope. "We're questioning every post in the system," says one corrections official. "We're saying to wardens that we're going to challenge everything they do now."[71]

"Among the most insidious [factors behind growth] is the bureaucracy's tendency to self-perpetuate, to become insulated and unresponsive, not out of malice or contempt, but simply as a function of time and growth," notes New Jersey Treasurer Bryan Clymer. The fiscal crunch has forced New Jersey to undergo a fundamental reassessment not only of *how* it operates, but of *what* it operates.

Soon after taking office, Whitman shut down the Department of Education and the Office of Public Advocate, neither of which produced much value for the taxpayer. Also slated for closure were seven of the state's 39 armories. "The Russians are not coming—except hopefully as tourists," jokes the governor. Targeted, too, is New Jersey's public television station. "Public television cannot be truly independent as long as it is funded by government dollars," says Whitman.

Despite the tax cuts, thanks to an unexpected uptick in revenues due to strong economic growth, a year after Whitman was sworn in, the pace of change in overhauling New Jersey government was sluggish. The state's education system was largely unchanged, major work force reductions hadn't been made, and competitive contracting wasn't a routine way of doing business. It just goes to show how challenging a task changing the modus operandi of government can be.

Nonetheless, Whitman's tax cut inspired the emulation of candidates for governor across the country in the 1994 elections (her 78-percent popularity ratings didn't hurt either). Republican gubernatorial candidates from New York State, Connecticut, Maryland, and South Carolina all pledged substantial tax cuts if elected. The American people liked the message; all but one were elected. The Northeast is now miraculously being referred to as the tax-cut corridor. These are crazy times.

CONCLUSION

Cars run on gas, governments run on cash. In the 1970s, OPEC's oil embargo squeezed America's supply of fuel, so we traded in our gas guzzlers and switched to smaller, more efficient cars. In the same way, when voters shut down the tax pump, politicians are forced to switch to a smaller, more efficient model of government.

The changes suggested in earlier chapters—focusing on core services, embracing competitive government, devolving authority—won't just happen. Government, like any organization, requires a compelling reason to change. Limited revenues don't guarantee government efficiency, but unlimited revenues do guarantee government inefficiency.

For reasons unknown, opposition to taxes has been associated with a negativity, a selfish, mean-spirited lack of compassion. But individuals such as Douglas Bruce, and organizations such as the National Taxpayers Union, Americans for Tax Reform, Massachusetts' Citizens for Limited Taxation, and Hands Across New Jersey play a critical role in the democratic process. In a democracy, voters and citizens ultimately must control their government or lose their birthright of liberty. Without limits, government growth will grow unchecked. With limits, government is pushed to improve. As Cleveland Mayor Michael White put it: "Why the change across the country? Have we mayors all of a sudden got intelligent? What is the force behind this revolution? . . . That pressure, that change, that force has been in the form of six words from the people who pay our salaries. "No, we won't pay it anymore! . . . There's nothing wrong with that. There's nothing un-American about that. In fact, there's something very right about it."[72]

II

APPLICATIONS

CHAPTER 7

SAFER NEIGHBORHOODS, BETTER COMMUNITIES

We must restore a balance between citizen and police responsibilities, [for] effective social control cannot possibly be achieved by hired hands alone.

Herman Goldstein
Policing a Free Society

It is said that for every complex problem there is a simple and elegant solution that is wrong. For crime, the simple answer is: we need more cops and we need more prisons. Though extremely popular with politicians right now, such an approach won't do much to improve public safety.[1]

That's because the best police force in the world cannot make safe a community in which people have no regard for the lives or property of others. The most important determinant of whether a neighborhood is safe or scary is the people who live there, not the number of armed guards around. Good citizens act responsibly and teach their children to do the same. Without question, swift and sure punishment of criminal activity is an important component of an effective crime policy. But the best crime prevention strategy is a child raised in a loving home who learns respect for others.[2] By the time a cop is putting on the handcuffs, the damage has been done. The best defense against crime is not a thin, blue line, but a community of individuals respectful of others.

There is a great deal that the government can and should do to improve public safety, but first it must recognize that it

185

needs help; individuals, families, communities, and the police must all play an active role in creating a safe, ordered environment. Without the support of the community, police work is dangerous, frustrating, and ineffective. Restoring public safety requires a renewed partnership between the police and the community. Police must reacquaint themselves with the people in the communities they serve. Communities, for their part, also have a major role to play in taking neighborhoods back from criminals. Citizens must recognize that the brunt of the job of policing a free society does not lie with the police force, but with communities and citizens themselves.

A PARALYZING FEAR

Americans live in fear. We live in the most criminally violent times in our nation's history. The level of street crime is between three and four times what it was in 1960, and the rate of violent crimes quadrupled between 1966 and 1990.[3] People no longer feel safe walking to the corner store or letting their kids bike to the local park. "I wouldn't go out at night unless my apartment caught on fire," says one New Yorker.

"The pervasive fear of crime is a threat to organized society—it makes citizens suspicious of one another, erodes the sense of community upon which a decent neighborhood life depends, and weakens the confidence of the people in their government," notes James Q. Wilson, one of America's preeminent experts on policing.[4] The fear of crime keeps people (especially the elderly) shut up in their homes, cuts off commercial activity, alienates individuals from each other, and surrenders the streets to the very kind of criminal and disorderly activity that fuels crime in the first place.[5] Crime harms not only the victim, but the quality of life for everyone.

Fear of crime destroys communities. Fearful people are less likely to help strangers, less likely to involve themselves in their neighborhood. At some point, the balance of power shifts such that, instead of criminals living in fear of being caught, law-abiding citizens live in fear of criminals. In healthy communities, individuals establish and enforce codes of conduct, both formal and informal. Litterers get a lecture. Speeders get yelled at. Unruly youths get a tongue lashing. But if individuals are afraid to maintain order, the community loses its lawful environment. "If people believe their communities are unsafe, perception usually becomes reality," explains Madison, Wisconsin, police captain Mike Masterson.[6]

Until neighborhoods are safe again, they will not thrive economically or socially. Waiting for the government to make it all better is a losing strategy. People have to become more involved in ensuring their own security.

COMMUNITY POLICING: LEARNING FROM AMERICA'S PAST

The more laws there are, the more criminals there will be.
Lao Tzu, 6th Century B.C.

From the time of America's founding, law enforcement has had a strong neighborhood foundation. In the early years of the republic, male citizens of large cities were required to stand night watch with no pay. Throughout most of America's history, in fact, citizens were expected to police their communities themselves—at least part-time—as they went about their daily lives. The job of police officers was to support the community in keeping the peace. Alexis de Toqueville was particularly impressed by this:

In America, the means available to the authorities for the discovery of crimes and arrest of criminals are few. . . . Nevertheless, I doubt whether in any other county crime so seldom escapes punishment . . . During my stay in the United States I have seen the inhabitants of a county where a serious crime had been committed spontaneously forming committees with the object of catching the criminal and handing him over to the courts. In Europe the criminal is a luckless man fighting to save his head from the authorities. In America he is an enemy of the human race and every human being is against him.[7]

Direct community involvement doesn't mean vigilantes stringing up violators. Explains noted urban anthropologist Jane Jacobs, "The first thing to understand is that the public space—the sidewalk and street peace—of cities is not kept primarily by the police, necessary as police are. It is kept by an intricate, almost unconscious, network of voluntary controls and standards among the people themselves, and enforced by the people themselves."[8]

Except in extremely limited geographic areas, it is not economically possible to put a cop on every corner. No police department is large enough—nor should it be—to serve as an occupying army. There is no way that New York City's 37,000 police officers can control the city's 7.5 million residents. The police are there to help. For much of America's history, this was understood.

In the 1960s, however, the public began to forget its role in controlling crime, and became increasingly dependent on the police. Police departments became more professionalized and shifted their primary mission from peacekeeping to crime fighting. Rather than regular beats, foot patrols, and informal pressure on the unruly, police forces increasingly used motorized patrols, radio dispatch, and rapid response as their main tools. In the terminology of television sitcoms, the "Andy of Mayberry" model was replaced by the "One-Adam-Twelve" approach.

Americans began to think of crime fighting as the job of police. The riots of the 1960s showed in violent detail how America's historic partnership between police and community had broken down. Police officers—often in squad cars or behind desks at headquarters—were spending more time with other officers than with citizens. The new policing methods had the effect of divorcing them from the community. The divorce was mutual: many communities stopped policing themselves.

This alienation left everyone worse off. Americans are more dissatisfied with their police departments than ever before, and the police are straining under the weight of massive problems they are powerless to handle alone.

THE MUTUAL OBLIGATIONS OF NEIGHBORHOOD POLICING

SAN DIEGO'S TRAILBLAZING EXAMPLE

At its heart, neighborhood policing recreates the partnership between the police and the community. In essence, the police tell the community, We will help you do *your* job. Variations on the idea are being introduced all over the country, from Jacksonville to Madison to Seattle.

In San Diego, a bold effort is under way to restore the historic balance to public safety. The change isn't easy, as San Diego attempts to involve citizens to an extent unheard of in big cities. One San Diego official told us a story: "I told a group of our officers that we were planning to have civilian volunteers take crime reports and collect evidence in cases of petty thefts. About three-quarters of them were nodding their heads, saying 'Yeah, that makes sense.' If I tried that in New York or Chicago, they'd laugh me out of the room."[9]

Like a successful marriage, community policing involves responsibilities and obligations from both parties. The community's end of the bargain can take many forms, such as setting up community watches, getting landlords to screen potential renters, cleaning up vacant lots, reporting suspicious behavior, and making sure teenagers aren't roaming the streets. If citizens don't take responsibility for keeping their own community safe, the police can do little to assist them.

At San Diego's Eastern Division police headquarters, a group gathers around a conference table to discuss better ways to patrol a certain neighborhood. But these blue-shirted peacekeepers aren't police officers. They are grey-haired volunteers of the Retired Senior Volunteer Patrol (RSVP), and they are symbolic of San Diego's department-wide commitment to neighborhood policing.

"The partnership between the community and our department really works," says Capt. Dan Berglund.[10] In addition to 272 sworn officers, Berglund's division uses 115 senior volunteers, 20 reserves, and 40 other resident volunteers. "Their influence in their own community has been extremely beneficial," says Berglund.

Embracing neighborhood policing means changing the operating philosophy of the department. Police attention shifts from a preoccupation with rapid response to helping the community solve public safety problems, with more officers out on regular beats. Neighborhood policing also entails much greater use of volunteers and asking people about their concerns. In the language of Tom Peters, neighborhood policing means "getting close to the customer."

San Diego uses volunteers in a wide range of nonconfrontational situations, such as towing cars, collecting evidence (including fingerprinting), and checking on the homes of vacationing neighbors. Rather than having a uniformed officer spend 45 minutes gathering a report on a petty theft, San Diego uses volunteers trained at the police academy to do it, freeing up officers to deal with problems that require their special skills. "So long as volunteers are given meaningful work, and welcomed as a partner in the process, I will have an unlimited number of people in any community in this city to do that," Berglund tells us. Several others echoed his sentiment.

Neighborhood policing means listening to what citizens

want from their police and adjusting resources accordingly. San Diego actually took a survey of residents, says Pat Drummy of San Diego's Crime Analysis unit: "We found out that the community doesn't really care about nude entertainment, topless entertainment, or peep shows. They don't care about gambling or a lot of the stuff we're spending a lot of time keeping a handle on. They are saying that as long as this stuff doesn't spill out into the street and affect their children, they don't really care what goes on in these places."[11] San Diego police are rearranging their enforcement priorities accordingly.

The culture within the SDPD is unusual in its openness to accepting change, citizen input, and the assistance of volunteers. And admittedly, San Diego is blessed with many retirees who can volunteer. Though the sixth largest city in America, San Diego has a police force with a small-town feel. In most big cities, the idea of volunteers doing police work would be opposed by powerful police unions. But rather than seeing community volunteers as a threat, San Diego welcomes them.

This culture took years to develop and is partly due to Police Chief Sanders' deep commitment to community policing.[12] San Diego is the first large city to adopt a *department-wide* community policing approach. Nearly all SDPD officers are part of a team assigned to a discrete geographical area, where they are charged with developing a close relationship with that community. "We are using persuasion rather than coercion to get people on board," says a former San Diego neighborhood policing coordinator.[13]

Part of police departments' traditional resistance to the idea of community policing has been the fear that cops will be asked to do social work rather than fight crime—or even that the department will get soft on crime. That idea was dispelled early on by two San Diego cops who had been trained in neighborhood problem solving. After getting to know the residents on their beat, they learned that one particular section of an apartment complex had been taken over by a gang. Being close to their "clients"—the law-abiding residents in the building—

they gained the evidence and information needed to get search warrants. When the bust went down, complete with SWAT teams and swarms of patrol cars, it put an end to the worry that neighborhood policing was soft on crime.

Three Strikes and You're Out

Everybody wants to be tough on crime. In the view of many, the courts have grown too lenient. The popular remedy is mandatory sentencing. During the early 1990s, "three strikes and you're out" legislation passed in Washington state, California, New Jersey, and several other states. After three convictions for felonies, a criminal goes behind bars for life.

These laws appeal to the citizenry's offended sense of justice. Many people believe, correctly, that serious repeat criminals are not paying their full debt to society. Unfortunately, these inflexible sentencing rules can unintentionally frustrate, rather than further, the cause of justice.

Locking up the bad guys is a good idea. Career criminals, who constitute about 6 percent of all criminals in the country, commit around 70 percent of all crimes.[14] A relatively small number of repeat offender criminals account for a disproportionate amount of the problems handled by the police.[15] Putting these hard-core criminals behind bars is essential to keeping the streets safe and may be a bargain to boot.[16] But while "three strikes and you're out" is aimed at the career violent offender, it often misses the mark. Judges end up condemning someone to life imprisonment for passing a bad check, or passing a joint.[17]

"Three strikes" is especially problematic in the area of drug laws, where increasingly harsh "mandatory minimum" laws define possession of even a small quantity of drugs as felonies. Instead of drug kingpins, these laws are usually enforced on 19-year-olds at Grateful Dead concerts. Several federal judges have resigned rather than levy the draconian punishment called for by the law. By 1993, 50 senior federal judges (including a number of conservative, Reagan-appointed judges) were refusing to hear drug cases.[18] In 1982, drug offenses constituted about 8 percent of people admitted to state prisons; by 1994 over 60 percent of all federal and 25 percent of all state prisoners were there on drug charges.[19] If present trends continue, by the year 2000 half of all U.S. prisoners will be drug offenders.[20]

Filling prisons to capacity with nonviolent offenders can result in violent offenders never being imprisoned in the first place or released early to make room for nonviolent offenders. Recognizing this, in 1995, George Pataki, New York's conservative Republican governor, pushed through changes to give judges the discretion to impose punishment other than prison—such as drug rehabilitation or community service—on some nonviolent drug offenders. Pataki said this reform does three things. "First it frees up the cell space for violent felons [between 3,000 and 4,000 prison beds a year]. Second, it will allow those inmates who otherwise would simply become hardened convicts to have the treatment and the support services, so hopefully they could be led back to productive lives. Then third, we believe it could lead to lower costs to the taxpayers."[21]

The cost of committing a serious crime has dropped greatly over the past 30 years—the punishment for violent criminals is now shockingly low. After accounting for the likelihood of apprehension and conviction, the expected length of actual incarceration is only about two years for a murder, six months for rape, seven days for a burglary, and two to three days per car theft.[22] All too often, it turns out that crime does pay.

If mandatory minimums don't work, what might? There are no easy answers. In Virginia, Governor George Allen, signed a "truth-in-sentencing" law in September 1994 that requires violent criminals to serve no less than 85 percent of their sentences. This might help.

A system of swift and sure punishment for criminals is important, but we shouldn't fool ourselves into thinking that the courts can make us safe, any more than the police can.

We will never really get a hold on crime in America until we move back to a society where kids in trouble can be turned around before they get into more trouble and are sent away to prisons to become hardened criminals. "The total impacts [of public policy on crime] are not going to be that great in a free society," says James Q. Wilson. "A free society depends on the conscience and reputations of individuals and the social norms of communities to maintain order. That is what has collapsed in America."[23]

To use an analogy from the manufacturing world, we can't afford to depend on an outside referee to detect and rework the defective products of our society; better to create a system that isn't producing so many defects in the first place. From this perspective, product quality is no longer the responsibility of just the inspectors in the quality department; rather, it's the concern of everyone. Families come first, police and courts follow.

With its emphasis on crime prevention, community policing can be a part of the total picture. "We currently see ourselves as feeding the criminal justice system," says St. Petersburg, Florida, Chief of Police Daryl Stephens. "What if we saw our primary responsibility as starving it?"[24]

For community policing to work, the neighborhoods have to be willing to help themselves. Explains San Diego police officer Jim Coleman, "The community has to recognize it has a responsibility for governing its own value standard. It is not the teacher's fault, it's not the police officer's fault, it's not the courts' fault. It comes back to the individuals and the value standards they're living in. People choose the way they want to live, and police can't remove that responsibility. The police can't come in and restore order if the community doesn't raise its own value standard."[25]

To be sure, in America's toughest communities, where neighborhood control has been overrun by gangs, drug dealers, and a general sense of lawlessness, community policing on the San Diego model may not be enough. Community policing works best in the communities still controlled by law-abiding residents, not criminals. In the bad neighborhoods where criminals now hold sway, more cops may be needed to help citizens regain control and convince those who obey the law—a majority in even the worst inner-city neighborhoods—to come out from behind their locked doors to augment the police presence. In the long run, community members themselves must take responsibility for making their neighborhoods unfriendly to criminals.

Houston's Zebra Squad

In one poor, predominantly Hispanic inner-city area of Houston, several hundred community members have taken the notion of a partnership with the police one step further: by volunteering as cops.[26] Precinct 6, with a population of 150,000 and the highest crime rate in the Houston area, has only 13 full-time deputies. To keep the peace, Precinct 6 Constable Victor Trevino must rely on his department's 200 volunteer deputies, each one with full police training, a state license, and the authority to carry weapons. Trevino's average volunteer cop works four nights a week after putting in an eight-hour shift at his or her regular job.

Trevino's volunteer cops have effectively doubled Precinct 6's police services in the community—and crime went *down* 10 percent in the precinct, over a period that saw the city's overall crime rate *increase* by about 20 percent.

Houston's volunteer cops have shown a knack for crime fighting. By closely examining past crime records, one of the units—nicknamed the Zebra Squad—discovered that parolees committed over 50 percent of Houston area crimes. By going out every night in search of parole violators, the Zebra Squad managed to pick up about 2,000 felons wanted for parole violations. Crime by parole violators in the precinct has dropped 50 percent.

Constable Trevino believes volunteer forces like Houston's can be replicated in police departments throughout the country. "I am convinced that these volunteers are out there in every community," declares Trevino. "The challenge is to find them, organize them, train them, and then get them to work. They won't disappoint you."[27]

STREET PATROLS

A key component of community policing is getting more cops back on the neighborhood beat. By making a small group of officers responsible for a small jurisdictional area, "beat integrity" can return as a practice not seen since the 1950s. Patrols can be conducted on foot, on bike, in a car, or some combination of these. Having officers on the streets gives ordinary citizens an easy, inviting opportunity to express their concerns, and it increases the connection between law-abiding citizens and the police.

This sense of connection is certainly evident with community policing officer Mike Elder, whose beat for two years has been a three-square-mile, lower-middle-class area on Indianapolis's South Side. Elder's beat includes numerous vacant lots, some boarded-up buildings, and two of the city's worst public housing projects. As in many cities, the urban sprawl of Indianapolis makes it impractical for Elder to patrol his entire beat on foot. However, he makes up for this by spending a good part of each day walking around the housing projects and the neighborhood parks, checking in with store owners, and maintaining open office hours at his field office in the Clearstream housing project.

Officer Elder is a reassuring presence to public housing residents tired of living in fear. Before Elder set up shop at Clearstream, "there would be gunfights in the project in the middle of the street in broad daylight," says one resident. Says another Clearstream resident, this one a single mother, "Before Mike came in, I wouldn't dare let my kids play outdoors because of the shootings and drug deals going down at all hours of the day and night. People living in projects want a normal life, too—and we're getting there."[28] Since Elder started his beat, crime has dropped in the Clearstream projects, with service calls to the police dropping from 1,500 in 1991 to 550 in 1993.

By becoming intensely aware of the community, community-based officers can stop crimes before they happen. The officer on the beat gets to hear the gossip, to learn about what's going on from casual, informal contact with people. Elder knows most of the residents at his two housing projects. He'll know within a day if any drug dealing is taking place or any strangers are hanging around causing trouble; he can count on a dozen or so residents in each project to keep him informed of impending trouble by calling him on his beeper. If the adults don't tell him of trouble, the kids will. On the day we spent some time with him, Elder was mobbed by little kids screaming "Hi, Mike" on his way to his office at Clearstream, where he handed out toy cars and coloring books.

Assigning an officer to a regular beat and emphasizing community problem solving can also go a long way in getting residents of troubled minority areas to look more favorably on the men and women in blue. Before Elder was assigned to their beat, residents of Clearstream didn't have a lot of trust in the police. Residents only saw cops when they were responding to incidents; and so they viewed them as outsiders. By establishing steady links with residents, Elder has built up a relationship of trust. "If we tried to take Elder out of that beat, the residents would be marching on City Hall within hours," jokes Michael Beaver, Indianapolis's Director of Public Safety.[29]

Elder clearly takes a strong personal stake in maintaining order and safety in his beat area. He winces when he sees a stripped, abandoned car in the parking lot of Clearstream. He has abandoned cars towed away as soon as he spots them. "I have a more personal stake in things now than when I was inside working a desk job," says Elder. "Some officers like doing community policing, love the challenge of trying to help turn around a community. Others prefer the nine to five job. They don't want the added responsibility."[30]

That is an understatement. Most cops *loathe* beat patrols. Many police officers—particularly those in middle management—would far prefer to stay safely behind their desks than foray out onto the streets. Hitting the pavement is seen as a demotion by veteran cops, many of whom have worked hard to get off the beat and win assignment to a specialty unit or a desk job.

Jersey City Mayor Bret Schundler learned just how intense the opposition to community policing can be. When Schundler was elected in 1992, there was not a single cop on foot patrol in Jersey City; Schundler wanted 300. The idea did not go over well with the force. "Comfortable jobs in all city departments were given as a reward for political service and loyalty," says Schundler. "The patronage system has made assignments to street patrol intolerable."[31]

The new mayor found himself battling with Jersey City's police union. When Schundler learned that two police officers spent their days delivering interoffice mail, he had them reassigned to street patrol. The police union filed a lawsuit to prevent the switch, citing a contract that states, "Police work cannot be diminished except through contract negotiation." Like most people, Schundler can't understand how having officers patrol the street *diminishes* police work. He is fighting the suit.[32]

Schundler cites union contracts—supported by state arbitration rules—as his biggest barrier to successful policing. "Our crime problem is not the result of our spending too little on policing, but rather of our getting too little policing for our money—and the root cause of this problem is nonlocal government interference in police department management," he says.[33] Schundler knows it won't be easy to change the police culture. "They'll fight me today but thank me later. When you put a cop back in one neighborhood he knows that he's not accountable to the whole world—just to that community's residents."[34]

COMBATING DISORDER

Many urban areas are marked by evidence of physical decay: boarded-up buildings, vacant lots strewn with litter, and graffiti-covered walls. This sense of community despair creates an aura of lawlessness that encourages criminal behavior.

In a 1982 *Atlantic Monthly* article titled "Broken Windows," James Q. Wilson and George Kelling argued that the disorder of a community, if left uncorrected, reduces residents' own efforts to maintain their homes and neighborhoods and control unruly behavior. Wrote Wilson and Kelling:

> *If a window in a building is broken and left unrepaired, all the rest of the windows will soon be broken ... One unrepaired window is a signal that no one cares, so breaking more windows costs nothing ... Untended property becomes fair game for people out for fun or plunder.*[35]

Once disorder goes unchecked, it produces a vicious cycle. First it kindles a fear of crime among residents, who respond to their fear by staying behind locked doors. Their sense of involvement in the neighborhood declines; people begin to ignore rowdy and threatening behavior in public places. People cease to exercise social regulation over the little things: litter on the street, strangers hanging around, or kids playing hookey. People stop caring. With fewer law-abiding eyes watching the streets, criminals move into the vacuum. The social order breaks down and serious crime increases.[36] "Stable neighborhoods can change in a few months to jungles," declare Wilson and Kelling.[37] Disorder also can have dire economic consequences on a neighborhood. Shoppers will shun an area they perceive as being "out of control." One study analyzing crime in 30 different areas found that the level of disorder of a neighborhood—more than such factors as income level, resident turnover, or racial makeup—was the best indicator of its lack of safety.[38]

For decades, most big-city police departments have devoted little effort to combating disorder. By allowing an accumulation of small infractions, this neglect creates an environment that generates big infractions.[39]

The community policing movement is beginning to change this. Community policing emphasizes giving neighborhoods a greater say in determining police priorities, a surefire way to bring issues of physical and social disorder to the top of the police agenda. An important part of a community patrol officer's job is enforcing a community's norms of tolerable behavior and order. Much of this involves taking actions that are informal and tailored to local circumstances. "You have to be given the latitude to enforce the laws in different ways in different communities," says Indianapolis's Elder.[40]

Although calls for order maintenance have historically been associated mostly with white middle- and upper-class neighborhoods, today some of the loudest voices are coming from poor minority communities. Says Ace Backus, a Milwaukee community organizer, "In the nice white communities don't be drunk on the street, don't be throwing down litter, the cops will stop you. In the middle of the black ghetto you can do that and the police will drive past. It's reverse discrimination."[41]

Beat officers can't impose their personal rules on a community, but they can help a community maintain its own standards.

New York City's Subway

For years, litter, graffiti, vagrants, and panhandlers had combined to make New York City's subway seem like an underground netherworld. The transit agency's first reaction to this problem was a standard public-sector response: to add more inputs. Additional police officers were assigned to patrol the transit system. The results were unimpressive, and riders were afraid.[42]

In the mid-1980s a new transit authority president, David Gunn, decided to wage a war on the graffiti that covered nearly every foot of every city subway car. Vast amounts of time and money had previously been invested in trying to reduce graffiti by increasing patrols and surveillance—all to no avail. Regardless of how many "taggers" were caught, there were always more. The courts, already overburdened, never gave the taggers more than a stern lecture.

A deeper analysis of the graffiti problem revealed taggers got a big thrill from viewing their markings on future trips. By denying taggers the satisfaction of beholding their "art," Gunn figured many taggers would simply stop vandalizing the cars. He made graffiti removal from subway cars a top priority.

One line at a time, each of the graffiti-covered cars was cleaned. Any car found at the end of the day to have graffiti on it was removed from service and cleaned again. The taggers had no chance to see their artwork again or to show it off to their friends. Gunn's strategy proved successful. On May 12, 1989, five years after launching the Clean Car Program, the last of the graffiti-covered cars was removed from service. The Big Apple's notorious subway cars had become among the cleanest in the world.[43]

But removing the graffiti had solved only part of the problem; New Yorkers still viewed the subway as dangerous place because of the threatening and disorderly people who always seemed to be hanging out there.

In 1990 William Bratton, now the city's Police Commissioner, was hired as the new Transit Police chief to turn the situation around. Bratton, known as "a cop's cop," decided to try an untraditional approach; rather than fighting a quixotic battle responding to symptoms, he would go to the root of the problems that made riding the subway such a frightful experience. "Disorder was out of control. The number of people loitering or sleeping in the system, garbage and human waste were all on the rise," says Bratton. "We understood early on that the problems of crime, disorder and fare evasion were deeply interrelated, and that therefore we would have to form a coherent strategy to deal with them."[44]

Bratton discovered that fare jumpers not only cost the transit system over $120 million a year in income, but also that they were responsible for much of the crime, graffiti, and unruly behavior in the subway. He organized plainclothes sweep teams of four to six officers to look for problems and catch fare evaders. Relates Bratton,

> [T]he sweeps produced some interesting results. One of every six fare-evaders we stopped either was carrying a weapon or was wanted for another crime on an outstanding warrant. That was an incredibly high statistic, and it made us realize that by fighting fare evasion we were also making an impact on crime.[45]

At the same time, Bratton set out to greatly reduce the threatening behavior of criminals, panhandlers, and homeless people who spent much of their days in the subways. Monthly ejections from the subway went from 2,000 to 16,000.[46] In two years under Bratton's leadership, felonies committed in subways fell 30 percent; arrest rates for serious crimes also declined because there was far less serious crime in the subways.

SOLVING PROBLEMS INSTEAD OF TREATING SYMPTOMS

Random patrol duty is little better than sleeping on duty.
Former San Diego Police Chief Bob Burgreen

Conventional policing is incident-driven: a citizen calls 911 to report a crime and then the police show up. Much of the time, all officers can do at this point is take a report. By reacting to crime rather than trying to prevent crime, police treat only the symptoms, not the root causes of problems. The key to improving New York's subway was the emphasis on proactive problem solving, an example of what policing experts refer to as "problem-oriented policing."[47]

In one large city, for example, a trucking company had 32 trailers burglarized in less than 18 months. A predictable routine developed: the owner would report the crime, the police would visit the yard, take a statement, and then wait for the next call from the owner. In desperation, the owner finally threatened to move his $13 million company out of the city unless something was done to stop the stream of break-ins.

This prompted the police department to abandon business as usual and figure out a solution to the problem. An outside consultant was brought in, and police soon determined that the root cause of the break-ins was the physical layout of the trucking yard, which made it an inviting target. The officers talked the owner into improving the lighting and raising the fence. Police then worked with other city agencies to erect a barricade between the truck yard and the adjacent vacant city property that was being used as an escape route. Problem solved.

As this example illustrates, problem-oriented policing is a proactive strategy. Rather than treating problems as a series of unrelated, separate incidents, beat cops are encouraged to work with the community on recurring neighborhood problems. The emphasis is on the end product of policing (low crime and high order) rather than the means (rapid response and arrests).

Some level of problem solving occurs in every police department, but it is typically done in a haphazard fashion. San Diego is alone in making problem solving a focal point of each police officer's daily duties. Because it depends on identifying recurring patterns of disruptive activity, problem-oriented policing depends on good information. San Diego's crime analysis unit has set up a sophisticated computer tracking system that officers can tap into to get information on 60 types of problems, previous attempts to solve specific problems, and recurrent problems in different geographical areas. While problem solving gives police officers some tools and the analytical framework for approaching community safety problems, community involvement is still a key component. "There are no long-term solutions to problems unless the community is involved," says Nancy McPherson, Seattle's problem-oriented policing coordinator.[48]

REGAINING CONTROL OF SPACE

As we have emphasized throughout this chapter, people tend to equate the frequency of crime in an area with how the external environment "looks" and "feels." Visible disorder sends warning signals to our brains of impending danger. Disorder is a sign that the social mechanisms of control that characterize healthy neighborhoods have broken down, which in turn encourages lawlessness. To build safer neighborhoods, individuals and communities must exercise control of the physical environment in which they live.

EMPOWERING LANDLORDS

Police officers appreciate the role that landlords can play in keeping a neighborhood strong and safe. Historically, landlords in low-income, working-class neighborhoods adhered to the neighborhood's set of norms and refused to rent to individuals who, in the landlord's judgment, would not be a positive force in the neighborhood.[49] This is because landlords, for economic reasons, desire essentially the same thing as neighbors do for social reasons: responsible and conscientious tenants who will respect the property of others.

In recent years, government regulations, civil rights laws, and court rulings have made it almost impossible for landlords to turn away dubious renters or to evict destructive tenants from their apartments. The unintended consequence? Many working-class neighborhoods have been ripped apart by rental units that become crack houses.

The story of the Bronx's Elzie Robinson illustrates the disdain some public officials and judges have for landlords.[50] In 1972, the 71-year-old Robinson purchased nine buildings in the West 144th Street block of the Bronx. When Robinson first discovered drug dealing was taking place in his properties in the early 1980s, he tried to evict the dealers. His reward? A city Legal Aid Society lawyer helped one of the evicted tenants sue Robinson in Housing Court, and he was ordered to return the apartment keys to the tenant. A few months later, after more eviction petitions, the Housing Court judge threw Robinson into jail for refusing to provide heat and hot water to the growing group of drug-dealing squatters holed up in his buildings.

After Robinson was released from jail, the drug dealers began setting fires to his buildings. The city's response? Robinson was cited for violating the Housing Code. Soon, the respectable residents of Robinson's buildings began fleeing the growing disorder, and those who stayed wouldn't pay their rent. Finally, in 1987, City Hall, which had jailed Robinson for trying to exert control over his property, confiscated his buildings. His retirement nest egg was gone. "They took away everything I had in the world," said Robinson, now living in New Jersey with a daughter who supports him.

Giving homeowners control of their property can help reduce crime. Almost by accident, the city of Milwaukee came up with a simple yet effective way for government to assist, instead of frustrate, landlords who want to maintain neighborhood norms. Marty Collins, a fifteen-year city employee, was looking for a way to improve the city's drug-addiction prevention program. Knowing that most drug dealing in Milwaukee occurred out of rental properties, Collins reasoned that the people who could really control the situation were the landlords.

Collins surveyed Milwaukee landlords and found that 70 percent of them reported having had destructive tenants at one time or another, yet virtually no landlords were using tenant screening techniques.[51] Why not? "For fear of getting their butts sued," says Collins.[52] Milwaukee's landlords were largely unaware that legal methods were available to enable them to discriminate against prospective tenants with destructive histories. By taking simple precautions, such as requiring favorable recommendations from previous owners, running a credit check, and visiting the current home of prospective renters, homeowners can eliminate the bad apples and help keep their neighborhoods safe.

Most landlords were also unaware of three Milwaukee companies that provide a list of all tenants who have been previously evicted from rental properties. Milwaukee now informs all landlords how to be more discriminating.[53]

While Milwaukee deserves credit for giving landlords the legal leverage they need to protect their property, the city sometimes goes too far in holding landlords responsible for the actions of their tenants. If police receive two complaints about drug dealing at a rented property, Milwaukee undercover police will attempt a buy. If successful, the city sends a notice to the landlord instructing him or her to take actions to stop the property from being used for drug dealing. If the problem persists, the city takes the landlord to court and can ask for the property to be forfeited.

In essence, Milwaukee is asking the landlords to control their tenants' behavior or risk losing their property. Empowering landlords by allowing them to choose to whom they will and will not rent is one thing. Asking them to be responsible for the actions of their renters is quite another. Those landowners who knowingly aid, abet, or profit from illegal behavior should be held accountable. It is wrong, however, to punish an innocent landlord for the actions of others. Providing landlords with the legal assistance to screen and evict disruptive tenants is a step in the right direction, but we shouldn't expected landlords to act as chaperones for their tenants.

This trend toward relying on landlords to discipline tenants is ironic, for in many cases the most irresponsible landlord of all is the government. Much of the worst crime in America takes place in or around government housing projects. When Reuben Greenberg became police chief of Charleston, South Carolina in 1982 he thought it ludicrous that government routinely rented units to the lowliest criminals of society. "No other landlord has to rent to child molesters, robbers, rapists, and arsonists. Why should people in public housing have to live with them?" asked Greenberg.[54]

Working with city housing authorities, Greenberg set out to make the city's public housing the last place criminals would dare set up shop. Prospective tenants were screened for criminal records. Tenants who engaged in illegal behavior were swiftly evicted. Through mostly common-sense measures that any sensible landlord would take, Charleston's public housing projects are now "the safest places to live in Charleston," says Police Department spokesman Charles Francis.[55]

Closing Off Streets

Americans like to control their space. With their long driveways, high walls, and security systems, wealthier neighborhoods have never been known for their accessibility to nonresidents. Wealthy city dwellers have "doormen" that provide security for their apartment buildings. Middle-class suburbs have their own ways of discouraging strangers, including myriad cul-de-sacs and white picket fences. Residential community associations (RCAs) have taken the concept of designing for safety one step further. The typical RCA has walls, gates, cul-de-sacs, security systems, and an endless series of speed bumps.

In contrast, poor urban neighborhoods are typically laid out in a grid format. "By allowing for lots of through traffic, grids compromise a neighborhood's integrity," says Judy Butler, the city of Houston's neighborhood coordinator.[56] The grid format, while pleasing to city traffic engineers, makes neighborhoods susceptible to drive-by shootings and random through traffic.

While some criticize the suburbs and RCAs for having a "fortress mentality," these communities provide residents with the security they desire by means of physical barriers that give people greater control over their living environment. These barriers not only keep strangers out, they also define the physical boundaries that define communities.

"Why not try to redesign the urban area to recapture the quality of life in the suburbs?" asks Oscar Newman, a city planner and architect.[57] Newman is the country's leading expert on and proponent of creating "defensible space" in urban neighborhoods by closing off streets. Street closures, Newman has found, give residents greater control of the security of their neighborhood. Closures also broadcast a distinct message to potential criminals: this community is profoundly serious about deterring crime and antisocial behavior.[58]

St. Louis has a long tradition of street closures. Beginning in the late 19th century, many streets in the wealthiest neighborhoods were deeded to residents instead of the city. Each of the streets was represented by an association that often also owned the sewers and water mains. At the time, St. Louis had shoddy public services, so the private streets were a way of attracting homebuyers by assuring them of reliable services such as water and street lighting.[59]

In the 1950s, St. Louis was in decline. Crime was rising, property values were falling, and much of the middle class was fleeing to the safer and cleaner suburbs. Left behind were poorer residents, less likely to be homeowners and more likely to be transient. To stop the flight of middle-class homeowners out of the city, the city began to revive its private street program. Neighborhoods of all income levels were allowed and encouraged to petition the city to convert their public streets to private ownership. Many middle-class neighborhoods took the city's offer: they formed homeowner associations, put up gates, and assumed the costs and responsibilities for maintaining the streets themselves.

Fed up with prostitutes hanging around their street corners and cars racing up and down neighborhood streets, in 1974 Waterman Place, a lower-middle-class, integrated neighborhood, petitioned the city to vest it with deeds for its streets. In exchange, the neighborhood agreed to assume responsibility for an array of public services, such as street lighting and maintenance, sewers, rubbish collection, and security beyond standard police protection. After the petition was granted, the neighborhood made its first investment: $40,000 for a gate. Within 12 months of the ownership change, property values had doubled in Waterman Place, going from $30,000 to $60,000 for a typical owner-occupied home.[60] More importantly, the neighborhood stabilized and the quality of life improved.

Since that time, over 1,000 St. Louis streets have been closed off and become privately owned. By making these neighborhoods more distinct, street closures have made it easier to identify intruders and keep out unwanted visitors. The result: lower crime rates and higher property values compared to adjacent neighborhoods. It also has made the neighborhoods more cohesive, as the neighborhood has become a safe place for children to play and a conduit for social activity. "With traffic flow limited to an occasional moving car, the street has become an extension of the front yards of the abutting houses: an area where children play and adults can meet and socialize," writes Oscar Newman.[61] Street closures can restore the balance between mobility for cars and liveability for residents.

Until recently, St. Louis was about the only city that made use of street closures in urban settings. But the increasing levels of crime, gang activity, and drive-by shootings throughout urban America are prompting other cities to experiment with street closures. Cities as diverse as Dallas, Chicago, Houston, Dayton, and Fort Lauderdale are aggressively closing off streets. Though St. Louis is unique in allowing a transfer of ownership to residents, these urban enclaves are proving an effective way for a community to regain control of its environment.

With drug trafficking and homicides spiraling out of control, Bridgeport, Connecticut, in 1993 closed off streets in the Lower East Side, one of the city's worst neighborhoods. The city brought in the state National Guard to lay 16-foot-long concrete barriers across more than two dozen intersections. A string of neighborhood loops was established, each containing fewer than 100 families. The idea was to cut down on through traffic and create some neighborhood cohesion.[62] "What people don't realize is that there is a level of openness you can achieve by closing off," says Zane Yost, who designed the project. "Successful cities are really made up of little villages."[63]

Case Study: Dayton

Dayton, Ohio, is home to one of the country's most ambitious street closure experiments. Like many aging urban communities, Five Oaks, an integrated, lower-middle-class neighborhood, found itself in decline. Homeowners were leaving, rental properties were poorly maintained, and drug dealers and prostitutes had set up shop. Racially integrated and located near the freeway, Five Oaks was an ideal location for crack houses. Experts were predicting that within two years much of the neighborhood would be a disaster area.

In 1992, desperate neighborhood leaders turned to street closure. Oscar Newman was called in by the city to assist. A year later, 34 streets and 26 alleys were closed off in Five Oaks. Neighborhood residents divided Five Oaks into ten mini-neighborhoods in order to enable law-abiding residents to attend to the problems in their immediate area.[64]

Only a year after the streets were closed, substantial improvement was visible in Five Oaks. Cut-through traffic, previously a big problem in the neighborhood, fell by two-thirds. Traffic accidents and speed levels also declined dramatically. After dropping in the previous two years, housing sales rebounded, going up 55 percent, while the average purchase price of a home increased 15 percent. Violent crime was cut in half; overall crime was down 26 percent. Most importantly, Five Oaks residents felt much safer and in control of their immediate surroundings. "I have four little kids," said one neighborhood homeowner. "My kids can now play out in the yard. It's been a blessing for my family."[65]

Like all efforts to take back neighborhoods, Five Oaks' street closure experiment wasn't easy. "Everyone had an agenda that was personal. It's not easy getting people to change," says Jo Anne Means, a 30-year resident of Five Oaks. "Their first reaction is, 'Just don't inconvenience me.'"[66] To be sure, it's not easy getting a car around Five Oaks anymore; for a visitor it's like being a mouse in a maze. But that's just the point. It has forced drug dealers and prostitutes to move their trade elsewhere.

Depending on where you're standing, gates can represent different things. To some residents of Five Oaks, the gates symbolized an effort to keep criminals and undesirables out of their neighborhood. But to others, especially some in the neighborhood's black community, the gates were perceived as an attempt to fence them in. Dealing with these and other concerns and giving ample community input into the closures was a difficult year-long process, but worth it, according to a Dayton city official involved in the street closures. "You need to get as much citizen input as you can get or it won't fly in the long run," she says.[67]

The street closures have begun to bring back a sense of community to Five Oaks. About one-third of residents report more involvement in community activities and associations as a result of the closures, and the number of people who say they know at least half their neighbors has increased by nearly 20 percent. A number of families have moved in from the suburbs and a landlord association was formed to fix up properties and the neighborhood park. Most residents now view the closures as a success. Some see it as a godsend. "Without the gates, my area would have been gone by now," says Jo Anne Means as she points to the house across the street, which used to be a crack house. "To stay, I would have had to barricade myself in my home."

For street closures to succeed, they can't be forced down the throats of residents; the neighborhoods must assume some degree of ownership—if not of the streets themselves, at least of the idea. When Chicago Mayor Richard M. Daley announced in early 1993 that "we're going to cul-de-sac the city—all the wards," his announcement was widely criticized by residents and political leaders in the city's poorer black neighborhoods who feared it would isolate them from rest of city, trapping them in gang-infested areas.

Rather than fight against residents, Daley chose to make the program voluntary. Neighborhoods that wanted to close off their streets had to go through a tough four-step approval process, including getting two-thirds of the registered voters on a block to sign a petition requesting the closure. The process also required a local hearing to debate the cul-de-sac.

Making the neighborhoods work a little toward a closure had unexpected positive results: they had to take an active role in planning, which helped ensure its success. "Officials ought not to give in too easily," says Roger O'Conner, executive director of the American Alliance for Rights and Responsibilities. "Make the people lobby hard. I think the process of demanding this change helps to build a sense of community."[68]

RECLAIMING PUBLIC PARKS

Another problem of "space" in many cities (and some suburbs too) is local parks. Instead of serving as a place for kids to play and families to picnic, many parks have become gathering places for gangs and drug dealers. Instead of serving as a common area that knits the community together, many neighborhood parks are tearing communities apart.

City officials refer to such parks as "orphan" parks because there is no real or perceived "ownership" of the park; no one takes care of it. City Hall cannot possibly provide the same level of attention as the people who use the park every day. Local involvement is needed to make small parks a positive force in the neighborhood; only neighborhood residents, the people who use the park, can provide this.

The inspiring story of San Antonio's Lee's Creek Park proves the point. "It's not every 41-year-old that can leave a legacy for his children," says San Antonian Bill Lucas as he looks over the plans for Lee's Creek Park, a project that engrossed him for over a year.[69] Lucas does not work for the city planning or recreation department—he is a sales manager for Bekins Moving Systems.

Ten years after it was donated by the Lee family to the city, the park—located in a declining area of the city with swelling gang problems—was still little more than a vacant lot. Then along came Bill Lucas and the local chapter of Optimist Club International, the 75-year-old "friends of youth" organization. In conjunction with around 35 neighborhood families, the Optimist Club transformed the weed-infested vacant lot into a thriving community park—with no taxpayer money. Creating Lee's Creek Park was a true volunteer effort. A bridge over the creek was a gift from an Optimist Club member in memory of his wife. A running track was donated by a construction company. The sweat to clear the lot and plant the trees was contributed by neighborhood residents and even some nonresidents, such as Mrs. Lee herself. "All we are doing is recreating in a small way neighborhood involvement like it was in the 1800s in America, when people used to pitch in and help build their neighbors' houses and barns," says Lucas.

When the park was finished it was turned back over to the city, which agreed to maintain it. Lucas is confident the park will not fall victim to "orphan park" syndrome. "Our idea is for the neighbors to create ownership opportunities for themselves," he said. To do so, ownership committees were created and vested with control of certain blocked-out sections of the park that they are responsible for beautifying and maintaining. The sense of ownership is critical. "If the park were given to us we wouldn't respect it," says Lucas. "We can see it in our own children. Make them earn it and they own it."

Turning over partial ownership or management of city parks to nonprofit groups and neighborhood associations is often the best way to ensure they remain a public asset. New York City's Neighborhood Open Space Coalition has assumed control from the city of hundreds of abandoned lots and parks in this way, turning many dangerous eyesores into gardens. Nearly one-fourth of the city's nearly 1,500 public parks are now cared for by community associations under the Operation Green Thumb program.[70]

Private groups usually have more success ensuring a park is in constant use, the key to keeping it safe. The nonprofit Central Park Conservancy has raised over $100 million for New York City's Central Park since its founding in 1980, taking over the care of trees, lawns, and plants and providing over half of the park's operating costs.[71] By 1989, 72 percent of Central Park users said the park felt safer after the conservancy got involved. Crime dropped 59 percent and robberies plummeted 73 percent. The drop in crime is attributed to the large increase in park activities put on by the conservancy. Good uses drove out a lot of the bad uses.[72]

OPERATING DOWNTOWN BUSINESS DISTRICTS LIKE SHOPPING MALLS

Big-city downtown shopping districts—long a popular destination for visitors—have become another casualty of Americans' growing fear of crime. In deciding between going into the city to shop or going to the suburban mall, the mall increasingly is winning. Convenience may be partly behind this, but a major reason is the perception that downtown business areas have serious crime problems.

This perception is misguided: studies demonstrate downtown areas to be relatively safe. But again, it is the perception that is important. The sense that these areas are plagued by crime, filth, and disorder has driven away customers, which in turn has caused businesses to leave city downtowns for the malls, mini-malls, and office centers of the nation's suburbs, exurbs, and edge cities.

In some downtown areas, however, people generally still feel safe. A friend told us a story about shopping in a not-so-good part of downtown Washington, D.C.—the murder capital of America. When he came out of the store it was late and he had to walk a couple blocks past darkened, closed stores. Almost no one was around. Yet he was not at all afraid. Why not? Because he was in a mall.

Why did he feel safe in a mall when he would have been petrified out on the streets? Because the businesses in the mall own the entire shopping area, and they make sure that it is clean and safe. Cities are discovering that there is much to gain from giving downtown business some control in managing business districts. Giving businesses the authority to manage certain tightly defined business districts gives them far greater control over what they will look like. Rather than just complaining to City Hall, businesses can obtain their own security, street cleaning, and sanitation services for the downtown area.

Termed Business Improvement Districts (BIDs), these areas are given the legal authority to levy a tax on businesses, in effect allowing private landlords to augment municipal services with everything from additional security to better trash collection to social services. Over 1,200 BIDs now exist in America—24 in New York City alone. BIDs may be the best hope for reclaiming downtown areas from the feeling of danger that has motivated shoppers, store owners, and companies to flee to the suburbs.

Manhattan's Grand Central Partnership, with a $5 million annual operating budget and a capital improvement budget of $20 million, covers 53 blocks in midtown Manhattan. Grand Central's executive director Daniel Biederman is one of the pioneers of the BID concept and a firm believer that a clean neighborhood is a happy neighborhood. "If you remove all the graffiti, make the storefronts much cleaner and more attractive, remove the peddlers, light the area better, and get the homeless off the streets into shelters, you can get the public to feel that the area is not so dangerous a place after all," says Biederman.[73]

Subscribing to the broken windows theory, Biederman is *obsessive* about maintaining physical order in the district. Graffiti is removed within 24 hours—always. Pointing to city-owned trash cans with exasperation he says, "I've told the city many times, 'If you are not going to maintain these, they can't stay, they're going away.' I'm not putting up with this crap."[74] Grand Central's 55 unarmed security officers and dozens of sanitation workers maintain order in this heavily trafficked downtown area, particularly near the train station. Like a conscientious neighbor, they will speak up when they see someone littering in the street or being a public nuisance.

The Grand Central Partnership has achieved impressive results. The sidewalks and train station are so clean (littering has been reduced by 90 percent) that we were hard-pressed to find even a gum wrapper. The presence of the security officers has eliminated much of the petty crime around Grand Central Terminal—street crime is down by over a third and serious crimes have been cut in half since Grand Central Partnership took control in 1988, and the panhandlers and homeless have been moved into the Partnership's privately financed homeless programs.[75]

Biederman displays the kind of ownership pride over the Grand Central area that would be all but impossible to duplicate by even the best of the new reform mayors. "I have a good eye and I believe in dotting the i's,'" says Biederman. "We treat everything like they would in a small town. Even in urban areas like New York City almost everyone wants basically the same thing: they want somewhere pleasant and attractive where they can feel safe."

Other cities are also enjoying success with BIDs. In the 1980s, crime was bad in downtown Philadelphia, but the litter was worse. One local scribe began writing a column under the pseudonym Marquis of Debris. Philadelphians would often joke about the windstorms of trash and litter that afflicted the downtown area, and the newspaper tumbleweeds that gave the streets a "rustic" feel. The city finally admitted it was losing the war on trash, and ceded all responsibility for cleaning the sidewalks to local property owners.

In 1991, Philadelphia's Center City District was born. Each night, the sidewalks are vacuumed, swept, steamed, and power cleaned. By day you can observe workers in neat, bright orange jackets picking up litter. Center City District also has 48 of its own community service officers patrolling the streets and notifying Philadelphia police of any problems. In Center City's first two years, crime was down 16 percent.

The concept behind both street closures and BIDs is simple: define an area of manageable size and give the locals more responsibility for its maintenance and security. This gives people the power to control their environment and the future of their neighborhood. Maintaining physical order discourages crime. And giving people a voice in what happens in their own neighborhood helps build cohesion and a sense of identity. It is hard to feel connected to a city of seven million people, but it is easy to identify with your neighbors.

Hundreds of thousands of neighborhoods around the country already hire their own security to augment police services. In fact, businesses, individuals, and communities now spend almost twice the amount on private security as is collected in taxes for public police departments.[76]

Hiring private security firms can often sharply reduce burglaries and greatly increase the neighborhood's sense of security. What makes private security firms so successful? "We have more time to stay in the neighborhoods because we don't have the accidents to respond to, court dates to meet, or all the reports to write that the police department has," says James Dunbar, who heads Northeast Security in Indiana. "When we're in the neighborhood we talk to people more."

THE FUTURE

What is the future of public safety in America? One possibility is that we will continue to ask police to attempt the impossible: to create safe communities without the communities' help. Under this scenario, there will be more cops, more prisons— and more crime.

The other possibility is more appealing. We can learn from America's most innovative public safety models—San Diego's problem-oriented, neighborhood policing; Houston's Precinct 6 volunteers; New York's subway disorder reduction; Dayton's Five Oaks street closures; and Manhattan's Grand Central Partnership—to develop a new vision of policing America's neighborhoods and downtowns in which police departments are closer to the communities they serve and citizens take a more active role in protecting their safety.

In this scenario, America could see a future with fewer police and greater security. We are fast approaching a crisis point as crime and fear of crime paralyze our nation. How we respond as individuals, family members, and neighbors will go a long way in determining what we become as a nation.

CHAPTER 8

BEYOND WELFARE

We are making rules under AFDC which are separate from the rules of normal society. . . . Many do-gooders, in think tanks and in governments, make these dual rules and then later find in dismay and surprise that they have a dysfunctional society.

Larry Townsend,
Riverside County welfare official[1]

All Americans are supposed to play under the same set of rules, the rules of the free enterprise system. It's never been a perfect system, but it made sense to most people that the harder you worked, the more you made.[2] In the past, there were no free rides. Families stayed together and helped each other through hard times. The system rewarded effort, diligence, and self-improvement. The harsh reality of the world meant responsibility came naturally—if you didn't take care of yourself, you were headed for trouble.

The ethos of the welfare state is different. Initially conceived with the best of intentions to assist those unable to fend for themselves, it has become a destructive, multigenerational lifestyle. Welfare burdens working Americans with higher taxes. More importantly, welfare harms those it is intended to benefit. By providing assistance to mothers who have children as long as they neither marry nor work, the system subsidizes and thereby encourages unproductive, irresponsible behavior.

The result is a subculture laden with social pathology: poor parenting, an inability to work, and self-destructive behavior.

These social pathologies, in turn, have contributed to marked increases in America's most troubling problems: crime, drug abuse, violence, and the breakdown of the family.

One of the most popular platforms of President Clinton's 1992 campaign was his pledge to "end welfare as we know it." After several decades of seeing their tax dollars contribute to the destruction of families and the work ethic, Americans have seen enough.

Few would disagree that radical changes are needed. Welfare reform is at the top of Congress's agenda, but the challenge is daunting. Welfare doesn't work, but what should replace it? How do you provide government assistance without creating dependence?

The short answer is, no one knows. We certainly don't. Congress doesn't either and, in an historic shift, it may be ready to admit it. The Republican majority in Congress appears inclined to abolish more than 100 federal social programs and replace them with grants to states—in essence, making welfare a state responsibility. After six decades of federal failure, this represents a dramatic step forward. Across America, governors, policy experts, and frontline experts are searching for the future of welfare. Moving beyond our current welfare mess requires moving welfare beyond the Beltway.

HURTING CHILDREN

Whenever it is proposed that the welfare system be radically overhauled, supporters of the status quo contend that reducing AFDC (Aid to Families with Dependent Children) will hurt children. The implication is that dismantling the current welfare system is cruel and heartless. While it makes for a good sound bite, we don't buy it.

It is children who suffer the most under welfare. Adults who do not take care of themselves do not take care of their children. People who do not take responsibility for their own lives are not ready for the responsibility of raising young lives. During 1994, Chicago was the scene of three terrifying modern tableaux, providing a glimpse of a grim future in which teenagers and young adults who cannot care for themselves have children.

The first horror came in January, when police raided a Chicago apartment looking for drugs. Instead, they found 19 children living in inhuman conditions. Fifteen of the children were seven years old or younger. In addition to finding rat droppings, rotting food, and cockroaches, police reported a child sharing a bone with a dog. The children's six mothers were found guilty of neglect or abuse. (On the night of the raid, one of the mothers was at the hospital giving birth to her seventh child, born addicted to cocaine. Less than six months later, she was in prison and pregnant with number eight.) According to various reports, the children were fathered by up to 16 different fathers. The adults in the apartment were collecting $65,952 in cash and food stamps annually. Rent was $380 per month.[3]

The story shocked newspaper readers but it didn't surprise child welfare officials. "We've got 19 kids every day," a Cook County official told *USA Today*. "They're just usually from four different apartments."[4]

The second Chicago horror story came in September, when 11-year-old Robert "Yummy" Sandifer opened fire on a crowd of children playing football, killing a 14-year-old girl. Yummy himself was soon killed, allegedly by fellow gang members aged 14 and 16. Yummy's short life was worse than anything in "A Clockwork Orange." Yummy's mother was the third of ten children from four fathers. Yummy's mother had the first of her own six children at age 15, dropping out of tenth grade to move into an apartment and go on welfare. Twenty-nine years old when Yummy died, she had been arrested 41 times. Yummy himself had 23 felonies and five misdemeanors to his credit. At the age of 11, Yummy was a miniature monster, a feral, asocial being.[5]

The third Chicago horror came a few months later, when a five-year-old was dropped from a fourteenth-story window of a public housing project for refusing to steal candy for his alleged killers, two brothers aged 10 and 11.[6] Sadly, these events are not simply anecdotal anomalies; between 1983 and 1992, the juvenile arrest rate for murder and nonnegligent manslaughter more than doubled.[7]

These tragedies were not caused by welfare; rather, they are the consequence of bad parenting. We must ask ourselves, however, why so many people incapable of caring for themselves are becoming parents, and dangerously irresponsible parents at that. Poverty alone cannot claim credit, nor can racism, for the events in Chicago would have been inconceivable during the poorest days of the Great Depression, a time of far greater material want and far greater racial discrimination. Part of the answer may come from a 20th-century president who had campaigned on a platform of federal austerity:

Continued dependence upon relief induces a spiritual and moral disintegration fundamentally destructive to the national fibre. To dole out relief in this way is to administer a narcotic, a subtle destroyer of the human spirit.

Ronald Reagan, perhaps? No, that was Franklin Roosevelt's State of the Union address of 1935. This speech has been called the "founding document" of the welfare state, as it ushered in Social Security pensions, unemployment compensation, and assistance to the aged and elderly. Ironically, however, the speech stressed Roosevelt's rejection of the sort of direct relief the federal government had been administering since 1933. In its place, Roosevelt was introducing the Works Progress Administration to provide employment for the able-bodied. There would be no more free handouts. Roosevelt aide Harry Hopkins testified against direct relief, describing with frightening clarity its impact:

[I]t is my conviction, and one of the strongest convictions I hold, that the Federal government should never return to a direct relief program. It is degrading to the individual; it destroys morale and self-respect; it results in no increase in wealth to the community; it tends to destroy the ability of the individual to perform useful work in the future and it tends to establish a permanent body of dependents.[8]

With prescient clarity, the architects of the federal welfare state described the dangers of the dole, *which they believed they had avoided.* After all, the Works Progress Administration was a jobs program. The only federal program to offer direct relief was a tiny program called Aid to Dependent Children (now AFDC), essentially intended for widows. It would provide aid to families in which the breadwinner was "dead, disabled, or absent." That single word—*absent*—created a welfare infrastructure unimaginable even to the most ardent advocates of New Deal social welfare.

At that time, no one expected that programs intended to provide for widows would burgeon into today's monstrosity. Today, nearly one in seven American children is in a family receiving AFDC.[9] Beginning as a federal charity program, welfare became a legal entitlement with the 1970 Supreme Court decision in *Kelly v. Goldberg*, which held that welfare benefits were "an entitlement protected by the due process clause" of the U.S. Constitution.[10] Welfare became a right.

While the intention to help those in need may have been noble, the result has been calamitous. Forget about the $3.5 trillion spent since 1965.[11] The real calamity is the impact of welfare on human lives, especially children. While America has always had poor people, within a generation or two a hardworking family could usually break into the middle class. But with three of every ten babies being born to unmarried women, many children never learn the importance of work, commitment, and responsibility. Many never see a father or mother going to work to support the family. Many never see adults making their own way in the world and never come to see self-reliance as a value. By contributing to the stunning rise in illegitimacy and the creation of a subculture that doesn't value work, welfare has transformed a shortage of cash into a "culture of poverty." Reversing these trends and producing better lives for children should be top priorities for future policy.

REDUCING ILLEGITIMACY

"Illegitimacy is the single most important social problem of our time—more important than crime, drugs, poverty, illiteracy, welfare or homelessness because it drives everything else," wrote Charles Murray in a 1993 article in *The Wall Street Journal*. Murray contends that welfare contributes to the popularity of dependent single parenthood and calls for the end of all welfare support.[12]

Murray points out that "throughout human history, a single woman with a small child has not been a viable economic unit . . . In large numbers they must destroy a community's capacity to sustain itself."[13] Study after study has demonstrated that poor children who begin with only one parent nearly always stay poor.[14] Moreover, young males growing up without fathers is a recipe for social chaos. Almost two-thirds of rapists, three-quarters of teenage murderers, and the same percentage of long-term prisoners are young men who grew up without fathers in the house.[15]

Murray believes that so long as welfare makes it possible to have a baby out of wedlock and to live without working, many young people will choose that option.[16] According to Murray, the best way to reverse the alarming growth in illegitimacy is to restore the natural hardships that having a child without a father has always entailed. In other words, removing welfare will deter single young women from bearing children they cannot support.

Something needs to change. By the early 1990s, America had the highest teen birth rate in the developed world, and two-thirds of America's teen mothers are unmarried.[17] Considering the emphasis that urban public schools have placed on sex education and contraceptive advice (some public schools offer more than advice, distributing condoms at no charge, and, in cities such as Baltimore, providing Norplant contraceptive implants), and considering that the means to prevent and terminate unwanted pregnancies are widely available, we must accept that most of these pregnancies are not accidental. Nor does poverty alone promote young pregnancies; the lowest birth rates of the century for 15- to 19- year olds was during the Great Depression.[18]

Why then are so many young, poor, single women choosing to become pregnant? A better question might be, Why not? The comment of 14-year-old Taisha Brown explains everything: "Why do I need to worry about a father? My mother raised me and my sister just fine without one."[19]

Packed into this short quote is a lifetime of miseducation. Taisha, like many of her peers, never had a traditional father, one who loves and provides for his family. She has no understanding of the economic reality of earning a living. Her worldview, shaped by the invisible hand of welfare, has taught her that fathers, after their initial contribution, are superfluous to raising a child. Other than in a biological sense, Taisha is utterly unprepared to be a parent. Just as Taisha's mother learned that checks came along with babies, so has Taisha. As 19th-century essayist Herbert Spencer noted, "The ultimate result of shielding people from their own folly is to fill the world with fools." Taisha is not stupid, but she is foolish. The false lessons of welfare have taught her to be foolish, and no one in her life has taught her otherwise. The Progressive Policy Institute, the think tank of the Democratic Leadership Council, is even more critical: "It is *wrong*—not simply foolish or impractical—for women and men to make babies they cannot support emotionally and financially."[20]

Observers concede that Murray's "cold-turkey" proposal to eliminate welfare has the advantage of changing the environment that has so grossly misinstructed Taisha; eliminating welfare restores the natural consequences of irresponsible behavior. Many welfare experts, however, believe Murray's solution to be too draconian. For children like Taisha, having been raised under one set of rules (albeit a poor one), an immediate changeover is seen as unfair. And what about the babies? A transitional solution may be needed to prepare for the harsh reality of life without welfare.[21]

Indeed, several states are experimenting with intermediate approaches to reducing illegitimacy. Wisconsin and Arizona will require girls under 18 to live with their parents as a condition of receiving welfare. Another idea is the family cap. Arkansas, Georgia, Indiana, and New Jersey have ended the practice of providing supplementary cash benefits for the additional children the mother bears while she is on welfare.

In 1993, New Jersey was the first state to put the family cap into practice. "Nobody else in American society gets a pay raise when they have another baby," says Wayne Bryant, the African-American Democratic legislator who pushed the cap through the New Jersey legislature. "Why should welfare recipients be any different?"[22] The first year under the new law saw over a 10 percent decline in births to unmarried women on AFDC.[23] "Illegitimacy is something over which the parents have complete control," says Bryant. "Once we get the incentives right, families will form and couples will stay together."[24]

Others argue that the lure of independence must be eliminated. "Why would we as a state give money to a pregnant 17-year-old to go into her own apartment?" asks Eloise Anderson, director of the California Department of Social Services. "That is child abuse sponsored by the state, on two levels. It's child abuse to the teenager, and it's child abuse to the baby."[25]

Social scientist James Q. Wilson agrees that sending out checks encourages irresponsible parenting. Wilson believes that the overarching goal of public policy should be the welfare of the children. To this end, Wilson advocates what he calls a second-generation strategy for reducing illegitimacy. In order to receive government assistance, argues Wilson, a mother should have to sacrifice her autonomy and enter into a group living arrangement. There she would be supervised in the raising of her child and restricted in her actions: no drinking, no drugs, no late-night partying. Instead, young mothers would be introduced to the dull reality of diapers and dishes. Says Wilson:

The goal of this policy is to protect the children . . . For many of these children the only thing that will work is if they are raised in radically different settings. This means they are either raised by somebody else or they are raised by their own mother, but in an environment in which the mother herself is taught how to be a mother and the child is given a decent environment . . .

There are a lot of fifteen- and sixteen-year-old girls who have children who would like to be decent mothers. Most of them can be decent mothers provided they're put in an environment where they're taught how to be decent mothers and protected from those influences outside that make it impossible to be decent mothers . . . The key to these group homes is that the mother is providing the care.[26]

The concept is far from ideal. In the ideal, parents—whether single or married, rich or poor, and including both mothers *and* fathers—would take responsibility for raising their own children with their own resources. Unfortunately, the ideal is not an option. In making behavioral demands on the recipients of aid, Wilson's plan has merit. And the controlled environment of Wilson's group shelters could be far preferable to what many welfare babies know today.

Critics have called the proposal paternalistic. Wilson agrees. "Paternalism? Yes, that is exactly what it is. What these children lack is paternalism," says Wilson. On first consideration, the compromise of the young mother's freedom appears to be a major drawback to Wilson's proposal. On deeper reflection, it seems to be its greatest strength. Wilson stresses that no one should be forced to enter these group homes. If a mother, with or without a father's help, can make it on her own she should always be free to do so. If, however, she needs the government to bail her out, she gives up some autonomy. It is better to play by the rules.

The only model of how the group home might work is demonstrated by private charities.

SHELTER FROM THE STORM

Located on Chicago's devastated South Side, the St. Martin de Porres shelter offers refuge to single women and their children. Dealing with individuals who often have long histories of substance abuse, the program boasts a 95 percent success rate. How do they do it? *Their way.*

"We like to operate the way we feel we should operate," says Sister Connie Driscoll. Though the top staff are Roman Catholic nuns, the St. Martin de Porres shelter is incorporated outside the Catholic Church. "We don't want to be beholden to anyone. We're not a United Way agency, either. It is much easier for us to operate without the restrictions of a major organization over us."[27]

The shelter does whatever is necessary to help a woman who comes to them put her life back together. This includes strict rules that are the essence of tough love. On the day we called, the shelter had conducted random drug testing at 6 A.M. If someone fails the test, she is kicked out. On this day, all 110 residents had passed. ("It happens sometimes," says Sister Connie.) While staying at the residence, women live dormitory-style. Those in the substance abuse program are allowed to leave only with a pass that lasts a maximum of three and a half hours. They have to state where they're going, what they'll be doing, and who they'll be seeing. They either come back clean or not at all. With a gravely voice and a patch over one eye, Sister Connie is not to be trifled with. "We don't allow any cursing here," she says.

In addition to the tough rules, the St. Martin de Porres shelter offers something else: love. "Sister Theresa Sullivan personally does every single admission, and she sets the tone right off the bat. There is a kind of a spiritual attitude here of family, unity, community. We don't force people to attend services. But people know who we are," says Sister Connie. "When someone here is talking about leaving and looks to be heading for a relapse, the whole group will surround that person with support, saying, 'Don't do it. Wait.' No one wants anyone here to fail. They get a lot of community support here. The message is 'We care, we're family.'"

Sister Connie has nothing but scorn for government programs that simply send out a check. "Poverty is not the real issue. A lack of responsibility is the issue," says Sister Connie. "The government should get out entirely. Do you want to know how stupid the government is? If you're on welfare you can get a monthly check of $260 a month plus food stamps. But, if they find out you're on drugs, then you can go into SSI (Supplemental Security Income), and instead of getting $260 a month you can get $536 a month to spend on drugs, because they consider that a disability. So now you can spend twice as much on drugs. That doesn't help the person at all."

Food stamps are often converted to money for drugs, as well. Sister Connie recently found over 100 stores willing to swap stamps for cash at half value. "I can't go over to 63rd Street without being hounded by someone offering to buy food stamps at half price."

The women who come to St. Martin de Porres need help more than they need money. One woman came to the shelter after being on drugs for seven years, feeding her addiction by selling her food stamps and doing some stealing. Her children had been taken away from her. She is now employed, has her children back, and does volunteer work for the shelter. Such a turnaround is a little miracle, one repeated at St. Martin de Porres all the time. Such turnarounds are rare indeed for those trapped in "the system."

"The 30-day treatment programs don't work. That's not even long enough to get the drugs out of their system. But the government won't fund the in-house treatments," says Sister Connie, adding that the shelter wouldn't take their money anyway. "Dealing with the government bureaucracy is like putting a gun to your head."

St. Martin de Porres treats people as individuals, not numbers in a system. "The key is understanding each client and what their needs are, and looking at each person as an individual, and not lumping them into a group. We treat everyone with the same level of compassion and caring in this house, but every person has different needs and different goals. We have to find out exactly what that person needs to get them on the road to self-esteem."

Tough love means demanding responsibility. "Cut off this easy money," says Sister Connie. "People need to be pushed to decide what they want to make of their lives."[28]

Could the government successfully operate group homes? "These group homes can only work if the rules are serious," says *City Journal* editor Myron Magnet, an early proponent of the idea. "I believe these communal hostels ought to be run by private organizations, including and especially religious ones."[29] But Magnet admits that giving private shelters government funds would create a tangle of problems. If the government contracted with a private provider, who would set the rules? Would government officials be disciplined enough to actually cut off those who broke the rules? Would religious shelters be allowed to retain their religious character? Would women be allowed to choose from among various shelters? "These are tough questions," says Magnet. "But I think it's worth trying. The current system is a nightmare."[30]

ENCOURAGING ADOPTION

State-run foster care is a nightmare as well. Thousands of children drift through "the system" for years even though qualified families wait to adopt them. The trauma of being "owned by the state," as one 14-year-old put it, has its consequences; about 14 percent of inmates in U.S. jails are former "system kids."[31] Unfortunately, increasing parental neglect is creating a boom in foster care. "The population of children in state-run substitute care is increasing 33 times faster than the U.S. child population in general," says Conna Craig, president of the Cambridge-based Institute for Children.[32] In 1986 there were 280,000 children in foster care; by 1992, there were 442,000.[33]

"There are families waiting to adopt children of every age, every ethnic background, and with every type of disability. Yet about 50,000 children free for adoption are languishing in state-run care. That's unconscionable," says Craig, a former foster child herself.[34] She calls these children "hostages of the state," adding that "states are loathe to let go of these children because they represent an income stream."

As a partial remedy, Craig would require states to notify private adoption agencies within 30 days of a child's being declared legally free for adoption. "This simple step would enable private, voluntary institutions to step in and place children in loving families," says Craig. "That's what these children need, not more bureaucracy." In addition, Craig would welcome an end to the practice of restricting adoptions by race. Currently, many welfare agencies are reluctant to place a child with parents of a different race, delaying the possibility of adoption for the roughly 40 percent of children in foster care who are minorities.

WHAT ABOUT THE FATHERS?

Senator Daniel Patrick Moynihan of New York and others have offered a different solution for the welfare conundrum: make the fathers pay.

The idea has immediate appeal. After all, it is only fair that fathers take responsibility for their offspring. Unfortunately, it is not something the government can achieve by decree. In fact, government's track record in collecting child support payments is abysmal. In 1993, a little less than $9 billion of all money owed was collected, leaving between $20 and $40 billion unpaid.[35] Paternity is established in only about one-third of all births to unmarried women.[36]

The state of Mississippi, for example, spent approximately $32 million to collect $51 million in child support in 1993, leaving $300 million outstanding.[37] Hiring private collection firms rather than government agencies (as has been tried in Georgia and Tennessee) may improve this record, but no one should expect miracles.[38] The barriers to simply establishing paternity, not to mention exacting payment from fathers—who may be substance abusers, transients, or in prison, are daunting for out-of-wedlock births.

Increasing paternal support is desirable, but there are limits to government's ability to enforce responsibility. On the other hand, if single motherhood once again becomes a hardship, teenage girls will have an incentive to demand more responsible behavior from those who wish to enjoy their affection. While this may sound unrealistic, such informal social customs have worked in the past; teenagers in the 1950s had just as many hormones but a lot fewer babies. Once the hardship of single parenthood returns, so will the custom of females selecting mates on the basis of dependability.

Government has a hard time imposing responsibility after the fact, so it is far better to raise individuals who accept responsibility in the first place. Families must teach young men and women what it means to be a responsible parent. Responsible parenting is, after all, more than a matter of just economics. As social scientist Glenn C. Loury puts it, "A man's spiritual commitments influence his understanding of his parental responsibilities. No economist has yet to devise an incentive scheme for eliciting parental involvement in a child's development as effective as the motivations of conscience derived from the parents' understanding that they are God's stewards in the lives of their children."[39]

Irresponsible parents tend to raise children who are more likely to be irresponsible parents. Trying to break the intergenerational cycle of bad parenting isn't easy, but that's exactly what Charles Ballard and his National Institute for Responsible Fatherhood and Family Development (NIRFFD) are trying to do. Ballard is a former drug addict who served time in a Georgia prison. While in prison, Mr. Ballard decided to make something of his life and left prison feeling a duty to help young people heading for a future behind bars. After attending college and receiving a master's degree in social work, in 1982 Ballard founded Teen Fathers (now NIRFFD).

Ballard and his staff take young fathers through an intensive personal program designed to build up their sense of worth and tap their latent feeling of responsibility and love for the child. "We run our approach through the minds of these young men," says Ballard. "What comes out is all the garbage."[40] The counselors, all of whom live in the community, do not tell the young men how to live their lives. Rather, they seek to get them to look within themselves for answers.

In the early days, Ballard and his small staff would search basketball courts and street corners to find fathers to counsel. Now, 80 percent of those in the program come to Ballard of their own volition, having heard about the program from friends. Thanks to Ballard's organization, in a little over ten years some 2,000 unwed males in Cleveland have signed the birth certificates of the babies they have conceived, and 97 percent of them now regularly pay child support. About 200 of these young men have gone on to marry the mother of their child.

"We are standing between mass anarchy and the home, the family, and the community," said Ballard. "The best job training program is to reinstill the love of a father for his child." Ballard knows that turning a life around entails making changes in the values and belief systems of individuals—no easy task.

For efforts like Ballard's to have any chance, the attitudes of young mothers on welfare—many of whom believe they can make it fine without the child's father—must also change. "These women say, I don't need you, I'm going to make it on my own," complains Stanley Akers, a 22-year-old who lives with the mother of his second child. "But they're not making it on their own—they've got welfare. If it weren't for welfare, they'd need us men."[41]

WORK NOT WELFARE

Without work, all life goes rotten.

Albert Camus

Charity that encourages dependence is destructive of human character. Throughout most of American history, poverty warriors exercised discretion when dispensing aid. "Those who gave aid without requiring even the smallest return were considered as much a threat to true compassion as those who turned their backs on the poor," writes Marvin Olasky in *The Tragedy of American Compassion*.[42] Charity usually entailed a reciprocal obligation on the part of those receiving aid. In Buffalo, for example, S. Humphrey Gurteen's Charity Organization Society had a woodpile next to its offices, and able-bodied men seeking shelter were required to chop wood; women were required to sew. The aim was to assist those down on their luck just long enough so they could get back on their feet again and become self-sufficient. The "work test" also helped separate the able-bodied into two groups: workers and shirkers. In his 1882 handbook for charities, Gurteen noted:

When the managers of a Boston charity attached thereto a wood-yard, and announced that relief would be given to no able-bodied man, unless willing to do a certain amount of work, the daily applicants fell off at once from 160 to 49. . . . The attempt to distinguish between worthy and unworthy cases is at times extremely difficult; however, let the "labor axiom" be the test, i.e., whether or not the applicant is willing to do as much work as his condition will allow.[43]

The philosophy of entitlement changed all that. Government aid rarely requires anything of those receiving aid, nor does it encourage personal involvement by those giving aid to the poor, as in the past. It is easier just to hand out a check or a meal. For two days, Olasky posed as a homeless man and visited shelters. His experience was informative. "I was given lots of food, lots of pills of various kinds, and lots of offers of clothing and shelter. I was never asked to do anything, not even remove my tray after eating."[44]

Work is important to human beings for more than just economic reasons. A healthy adult derives pride from being productive. Individuals who do no work often suffer from a poverty of attitude and exhibit self-destructive behavior, a phenomenon that can be observed among those born to great wealth as well as those born to welfare families. Far from being enviable, a life of perpetual idleness is a pitiable existence.

Mickey Kaus, author of *The End of Equality*, believes the absence of work is the major problem of America's underclass. "I think if you could change the non-working single-parent underclass into a working single-parent class—you would have gone a long way to solving the problem of the underclass," says Kaus.[45]

Kaus may or may not be correct. So far, however, government efforts to change welfare into workfare haven't worked very well; nor have job training and other programs.[46] Writes Kaus, "Welfare doesn't work. Work 'incentives' don't work. Training doesn't work. Work 'requirements' don't work. 'Work experience' doesn't work and even workfare doesn't quite work. Only work works."[47]

FROM WELFARE TO WORK: THE RIVERSIDE COUNTY MODEL

Washington, D.C., in its own tepid way, has tried. The Family Support Act of 1988 was supposed to transform welfare by requiring work. The bill's chief sponsor, Senator Daniel Patrick Moynihan (D-N.Y.), hailed the act as a watershed event in welfare reform: "For 50 years the welfare system has been a maintenance program. It has now become a jobs program," said Moynihan.[48] That was the theory, anyway.

The main feature of the bill was the Job Opportunities and Basic Skills (JOBS) Training Program. Despite the nifty acronym, the program generally hasn't delivered. A bureaucratic federal program, JOBS allowed states to require individuals to participate in job search programs and could, in some cases, require public service work for benefits. In truth, little has changed under JOBS; nationwide, less than 7 percent of all AFDC recipients participate in job search, job training, or community service work.[49]

One exception was the welfare-to-work program in Riverside County, California. Riverside's version of the JOBS program, called Greater Avenues for Independence (GAIN), has actually met with some moderate success—and a lot of media attention. In 1993, *USA Today* wrote of the "dramatic success" in Riverside County, "where earnings increased 53 percent and welfare costs dropped 17 percent."[50] The *Los Angeles Times* noted that Riverside's program was "expected to shape reform of the nation's welfare system."[51]

Unfortunately, the Riverside program may not be easily

replicated.[52] That's because much of the program's success can be attributed to the philosophy of Lawrence Townsend, Riverside County's director of social services.[53] Says Townsend:

We are making rules under AFDC which are separate from the rules of normal society. As a result, we have two different societies. It's crucial to not make welfare rules different from the real world ... We ought to be encouraging and rewarding good, responsible behavior. We should never give welfare without getting something back for society ... We must stop this nonsense ... If I refuse to go to work, I shouldn't get anything. If I didn't go to work every day for the county of Riverside, do you think they would continue to pay me? No, they would not. So, if we have someone receiving public benefits who doesn't want to go to work, why should they get anything?[54]

The attitude expressed by Townsend is rare among welfare officials, but it is growing more common. It is also the view of the man and woman in the street, who may not be social scientists but who nonetheless understand certain enduring truths about human nature. Townsend continues:

Mankind for years has known that work is crucial to the quality of life for a human being. I think we have had individuals go to Congress in the past decades with kindness in their hearts to help the poor. But they weren't knowledgeable of how to help without destroying the character of those in poverty ... The most damaging part I see is that when recipients are getting something for free and are sitting at home, they are not part of society. After a while, they are not appreciative of what society is doing for them and they become more demanding. Behavior becomes more aggressive. Their attitude about themselves and the attitudes of those around them go into a downward spiral.[55]

The exclusive focus in Riverside County is on getting people into a job, any job. From the moment clients walk in the door, they are informed that they will be expected to work. The official handbook reads, "The Riverside County GAIN Program philosophy is based on a belief in a basic work ethic. We strongly believe that work has value over and above the obvious one of income."[56]

This is a far cry from the entitlement philosophy that has long imbued public welfare. Even the word "entitlement" conveys the wrong message. In contrast, the Riverside County GAIN booklet quotes Robert Jones Burdette: "Don't believe the world owes you a living; the world owes you nothing—it was here first."

Despite all the media attention and the hard work of Riverside officials, GAIN's gains have been dramatic only when compared with other welfare-to-work programs; in absolute terms, the results have been fairly modest.[57] The Riverside County program must compete with the hard reality that most welfare recipients can get nearly as much money without the "hassle" of work.

Riverside welfare recipient Kim Hatfield poses the crucial question: "Why should I go out and look for work when I'm going to earn less—plus get no benefits—than I would get on welfare?"[58]

Good question, Kim. Welfare-to-work programs such as GAIN must deal with the fact that welfare looks attractive compared to work. The only way GAIN could nudge people into working was, in most cases, to continue paying some welfare and medical expenses, as well as child care. People in the Riverside GAIN program still receive an average of $8,429 from the state, as opposed to the $9,825 for non-GAIN welfare recipients.[59] In other words, *at its very best*, job-based welfare reform has achieved only moderate positive results in reducing state assistance. In addition, Riverside's GAIN program has moved only a small percentage of recipients totally off welfare.[60]

Much was made of the fact that the Riverside GAIN program was found to return $2.84 for every dollar spent. But Riverside is one of six countries in the California GAIN program. On the whole, the six counties average a return of only 76 cents on the dollar—not a tax-saving strategy, and evidence that Riverside's success is due more to Townsend's leadership and the "jobs first" approach.[61] Replicating even the limited successes of Riverside will be difficult. Sad but true are the words of White House domestic policy aide Bruce Reed: "Riverside is a good example of how to get the most out of the current system."[62]

While taking nothing away from the effort of Riverside officials, this is a damning indictment of the current system. The root problem is that given the benefit levels of welfare, it doesn't make economic sense for people to work. The "rules of the game" are crazy, as former Education Secretary Lamar Alexander found out on a cross-country fact-finding trip:

> *Everyone has a welfare story. In Cassville, Missouri, I visited with a couple, both of whom are in their 20's and work on a production line, making $7.79 and $8.89 an hour. They know exactly what the federal benefits are in the Cassville area. They wonder why—when all the companies in the area are hiring— some of their friends make more money not working than they do working.*[63]

To change this situation, the incentives of welfare need to change in one of two ways. Either welfare benefits need to be reduced so that work becomes more attractive, or welfare recipients who are physically able to work must be *required* to do so.

REQUIRING WORK

Massachusetts Governor William Weld wants to require able-bodied recipients to go to work, not after two years but in just 60 days. Says the governor, "Our plan in Massachusetts is to abolish the cash grant entirely; to say to everybody who's able-bodied, You're going to work within 60 days, and if you can't find a job, we will pay you the minimum wage cost for a community service job. That would completely explode welfare dependency as we know it."[64]

Will Weld's idea work? It's too early to say. The welfare reform bill didn't pass the Massachusetts legislature until February 1995.

Weld's proposal resembles a program developed by Dick Wedt, an Oregon businessman. Wedt came to the conclusion that what poor people really needed was the chance to learn job skills by working. His simple solution: convert welfare and unemployment benefits to wages for real work. In 1990, Wedt went over the heads of politicians and presented his idea to Oregon citizens in the form of a ballot initiative. Approved by 58 percent of Oregon voters, the Full Employment Program, now called JOBS Plus, essentially pools the money from AFDC, food stamps, and unemployment compensation, and pays people to work at minimum wage at a public- or private-sector job.[65] (Arizona and Mississippi have enacted nearly identical programs.) Other states examining variations of JOBS Plus are considering making participation mandatory.[66]

It is too early to assess the results of JOBS Plus. Though passed by voters in 1990, the program wasn't implemented until the fall of 1994. First, there was opposition from then-Governor Barbara Roberts, who declared the initiative "dead on arrival" when it reached her desk before relenting to citizen pressure two years later; then there was a year of waiting for waiver approval from the federal Health and Human Services bureaucracy; finally, there was a last-ditch effort by Congressman Neal Smith to kill the program.

Even though it survived the tortuous implementation process, there is no guarantee the program will be administered as envisioned by the drafters of the legislation. Warns Charles Murray:

The government will screw up a program that replaces welfare with jobs. The day after it goes into effect we will start to see the erosion of it. The erosion will consist of all the different ways in which exceptions will be created, and the business of showing up at the job site will become a scam because it's so tough to make government bureaucrats act like job supervisors. Over a period of years it will become a joke.[67]

Murray might be right, and we wouldn't recommend putting all the eggs in the workfare basket. But rather than rejecting efforts such as those in Oregon and Massachusetts out of hand, why not allow each state to follow whatever course it thinks best? The states are mature enough to handle the responsibility. Different states could try workfare, group homes, time limits, or the complete elimination of welfare. Waiting for Congress to divine the perfect solution is the only guaranteed losing strategy.

ENDING AFDC: TOMMY THOMPSON'S WISCONSIN EXPERIMENT

When you think radical, the last place you think of is Wisconsin. Yet to get a peek at welfare for the 21st century, we traveled deep into the nation's heartland to meet with Governor Tommy Thompson. A Republican, Thompson has moved further than anyone else in America to dismantle the failed welfare system.

On December 31, 1998, Wisconsin's Aid to Families with Dependent Children (AFDC), will be history. Its replacement? No one knows for sure exactly what it will look like, though some of the outlines have become apparent. In an effort to come to terms with welfare's twin problems of enabling illegitimacy and discouraging work, Wisconsin's program will combine strategies aimed at reducing illegitimacy and fostering responsibility with tough work requirements. A family cap will be put in place, benefits probably won't be paid to teens under 18, and group homes may also be employed. Those who still qualify under the new rules will have to go to work to receive benefits. Thompson foresees a program providing "a 'self-sufficiency' (rather than a 'welfare') system—one based on independence through work."[68]

Tommy Thompson's election as governor of Wisconsin in 1986 surprised nearly everyone in the state. A state representative from the little town of Elroy (pop. 1,500), Thompson's gubernatorial bid was written off by the Wisconsin media. Neither a smooth speaker nor especially telegenic—he went through many razors in the campaign battling his 5 o'clock shadow—Thompson was considered too small-town and parochial. Though not very eloquent, Thompson's common-sense message played well with Wisconsin's voters, and he pulled off a huge upset over incumbent Governor Tony Earl.

Thompson soon made reforming the welfare system his top priority. Says the governor, "The welfare system as it now exists is one of the root problems of the breakdown of the family which has caused the breakdown of community. Set up originally to be a temporary program, the only real radical change that has been made to it has been to make it permanent. A system that doesn't support the family, or encourage work and doesn't require personal responsibility, is bound to fail."[69]

His first welfare reform was called Learnfare. Introduced in 1987, Learnfare required teenagers on AFDC between 13 and 19 to attend school regularly and complete high school or the equivalent, or the AFDC benefits for their families would be reduced. Learnfare was opposed by everyone from the Milwaukee Roman Catholic archdiocese to the NAACP, who called the program too punitive. Impressive results, however, quieted the critics. In Learnfare's first year, 8 percent of eligible teens lost benefits each month because they failed to regularly attend school. By the end of 1993, 97 percent of Learnfare teens were complying with school attendance requirements.[70] "We talked to a gal named Sonja who said Learnfare pushed her to go back to school and graduate, and now she wants to go back to college," recalled Thompson. "Everybody around the table, you could just see the little tears welling up in their eyes. Me, too. So many on welfare just don't have the self-discipline."[71]

Thompson felt that Wisconsin's generous welfare programs were attracting those looking for a free ride. "Wisconsin was paying 40 percent more than what the same family would receive in Illinois," said Thompson. Taking office in 1986, Thompson reduced the level of AFDC payments by 6 percent, and then instituted a freeze. "It was sending a strong signal that we were not just going to keep throwing money at the problem." By 1994, his seventh year in office, real, inflation-adjusted benefit levels had dropped by about 30 percent. Along with them, the Wisconsin welfare rolls had dropped by 21 percent—about 20,000 cases.

"The reality is that the governor's constant hammering away at welfare reform resonated successfully across every Wisconsin country," says Gerald Whitburn, Wisconsin's director of Health and Human Services. "In a way, what we have done is regenerate the stigma. We've said it's not okay to be on welfare."[72]

WISCONSIN WORKS

Thompson's early welfare reforms, while groundbreaking at the time, are moderate compared to what he is now embarking on: blowing up the entire framework of welfare. The Welfare Department is being eliminated, its functions transferred to the Economic Development Department. The message is clear: when someone comes seeking assistance, he'd better be looking for a job, not welfare.

Thompson's two-county pilot project, "Work Not Welfare," kicked off in January 1995, the nation's first welfare reform requiring work and strictly limiting the length of time an individual can receive welfare benefits. After a two-year period, all AFDC cash benefits end. No exceptions.

Here's how Work Not Welfare works. All AFDC recipients must sign a contract pledging to work for benefits. Within a month, they have to begin work or at least training for work. After a year, recipients must either be working for a private firm (for pay) or in a public job (for benefits). By the end of the second year, cash benefits are cut off. Child care and health care continue for an additional year. "We are saying, 'We've been nice to you so far, we've encouraged you up to this point, now it's time for you to break the welfare habit and get on with your life by working,'" says Thompson. "'After you start working we'll continue to give food stamps and housing and transportation—for a while.'"

Since the program was formally announced in the summer of 1994 (and even before it was put into place) welfare caseloads dropped an impressive 17 percent in the two counties.[73] What happened? Just like S. Humphrey Gurteen's woodpile, the "work test" weeds out those looking for easy cash. "We created the expectation that there would be no more free lunch," says Mark Liedl, a senior advisor to the governor.[74]

One knotty question always comes up with regard to proposals to end welfare and replace it with work: what will be done about the people who don't have jobs after two years? Worried that there aren't enough private-sector jobs to go around for all current welfare recipients, many politicians and bureaucrats are looking for ways of inserting exceptions into the two-years-and-out approach, or they argue that government must create scores of jobs for those on welfare.

Thompson thinks this is a big mistake. "I think it's tantamount to setting yourself up to fail if you say that you're just going to set up government jobs in the end," says Thompson, who is convinced most welfare recipients will move into private-sector jobs. Some critics contend that many welfare recipients are simply incapable of holding a real job. Thompson advisor Liedl contends that critics of Wisconsin's program suffer from "inside the box" thinking. They base their conclusions on the likely behavior of welfare recipients *under the current welfare system*, a flawed assumption because the welfare system will be gone in Wisconsin. In other words, when it's sink or swim, a lot more people will turn out to be swimmers than we might imagine today. "What will happen when there is really no welfare as we know it?" asks Liedl. "We think people's behavior will change dramatically."

Still, the question lingers: what happens to those who, for one reason or another, still are not working after two years? What happens to the ones who still don't swim? Thompson takes off his glasses, wipes his forehead and looks at us wearily. "If all else fails they're still going to get food stamps, housing, transportation, and day care and so on and so forth. All they're not going to get is cash, but believe me there are jobs out there."

ENCOURAGING PRIVATE CHARITY

When government pulls back on aid, the private sector often steps in. In 1991, Governor John Engler of Michigan discontinued general assistance (GA) for childless able-bodied adults, saving the state $250 million in benefits. This move spawned dramatic protests, including a "Tent City" at a park near the capitol in Lansing. When the shouting was over and the deed was done, however, the dire predictions failed to come true; and the move proved overwhelmingly popular with the voting public (one poll showed 81 percent support).

When he announced the end of the GA program, Governor Engler called for churches, civic groups, charities, private businesses, and families to fill the gap left by the state: "Taxpayers had neither the obligation nor the limitless resources to subsidize perpetually single adults."[75]

Dozens of private programs have sprung up—and existing programs have been expanded—to meet the increased demand. For example, a group of volunteers from Harrison, Michigan, opened up the Hard Times Cafe, a privately-funded center that offers companionship and job counseling to former GA recipients. Faith, Inc., a locally-initiated program out of

Grand Rapids, was formed to help the homeless get jobs and get clean. The key to the group's success is developing important skills such as hard work, self-reliance, and responsibility. The best way to inculcate these skills is through work. "At Faith, we don't send them to 'assessment school' for six months to decide what career they would like," says a Faith volunteer. "We help them start work immediately. It's essential to enhancing their self-worth."[76]

Despite the protests and uproar it caused, Engler doesn't regret cutting off GA. "I think we did the right thing," he says, "and the evidence is quite compelling that we did."[77] In 1991, 82 percent of Michigan's GA recipients had never held a job. By April 1993, 34 percent of all terminated GA clients had been employed at some point during the year, at least part-time.[78] (The disabled continue to be served by other state programs.)

An interesting by-product of Engler's elimination of General Assistance was that the state contracted with the Salvation Army to lodge any former GA recipients in shelters. "Because of this partnership, no one in Michigan need spend the night without shelter," says Engler.[79]

Private organizations such as the Salvation Army have historically been important poverty fighters. In 1992, the Salvation Army raised $762 million in private donations, served 69 million free meals, and provided 9.5 million nights of shelter to those in need.[80] More importantly, the Salvation Army provides care, not just cash.

At the Salvation Army shelter in Bell, California, homeless guests receive a free bed and hot meal—but only if they clean up their act. The boarders—many of whom are drug and alcohol addicts—must be sober to gain admission. Sex, alcohol, and provocative clothing are strictly forbidden. "If you've been here 45 days, you're expected to be in school or working," says caseworker Patrick Mellon, a recovering crack addict himself. This "tough love" approach works. In 1993, 113 of the 165 boarders who enrolled in training landed jobs.[81]

Some boarders don't like the shelter's strict rules. "You can't have no fun here—no sex, no alcohol, nothing," says Steve Jensen, 45, who was down on his luck when he came to the shelter. "I don't obey rules. I've already crossed the bridge as to whether I'd kill somebody." Shrugging he adds, "Hey, I probably need a structured environment."[82]

Jensen and other boarders stay despite the "hassles" because they want to lead independent lives. They also appreciate the family-like atmosphere produced by the sense of mutual obligation the shelter engenders. "Everybody here is like a family," says Royal Williams, a 35-year-old cocaine addict. "People know that if they go to [many] of these other shelters, you might as well be on the streets. You can't help but love this place."[83]

America is a wealthy country and has long enjoyed a generous network of private charities and aid societies. Government assistance, on the other hand, has been expensive and ineffective. In 1992, total social welfare spending topped $300 billion, meaning that every poor person in the United States could have received a check for about $7,500, or $30,000 for a family of four.[84] Even that figure is highly misleading, however, since it is based on a census definition that categorizes as "poor" those who are far from destitute: nearly 40 percent of all "poor" households actually own their homes; 60 percent own a car; 91 percent own a color TV; and 60 percent have air conditioning.[85] Sadly, of course, much of the money going into government poverty programs never reaches the intended recipient—it is swallowed up by the bureaucracy.

Moreover, as we have seen, the government assistance that does reach recipients often has harmful consequences for those it is intended to help. Whereas the government typically sends a check, private nonprofits like the Salvation Army are able to dispense caring on an individual basis and cultivate human aspirations rather than crush them.

Since private charities like St. Martin de Porres and the Salvation Army are often more effective than government programs, it makes sense to shift tax money to private charitable donations. The idea of a charitable tax credit could help. Rather than shipping their money to Washington, taxpayers could direct up to $300 to local nonprofit groups that are dedicated to fighting poverty. In arguing for this idea, *Wall Street Journal* editorial writer John Fund posed the following question with respect to government-sponsored welfare: "If you had a financial windfall and wanted to help the poor, would you even think about giving time or a check to the government?" A charitable tax credit, which would join existing charitable deductions, would allow taxpayers to send some of their taxes to charities rather than to Uncle Sam.[86]

Though it comes with no guarantees, allowing individuals to select charities based on their effectiveness has enormous appeal. Money would tend to flow to charities perceived as effective. "Dollars would follow people, not a system," says Representative Rob Andrews, a New Jersey Democrat. Because the donations would come from individuals, they wouldn't encumber such organizations with any restrictions or regulations. A charitable tax credit could prompt a flourishing of private philanthropic activity.

According to Salvation Army captain Sherry McWhorter, "[T]he Salvation Army tries to help wherever we can to correct societal problems, and the helping process is often hindered by the government." In Seattle, the health department ordered that donated food be thrown away, backing off only when Salvation Army officials threatened to invite a television film crew.[87]

Instead of hindering relief efforts the government could help them through a charitable tax credit. Not only large organizations but small community groups, for whom $300 often makes a big difference, would benefit. It would move towards transforming our centralized, top-down antipoverty programs into a decentralized network of giving. Instead of sending tax dollars for poverty alleviation to Washington, D.C., individuals could send some of it around the corner.

There is another important benefit to allowing individuals to designate tax money according to their choice. Just as giving affects the recipient in more than strictly economic terms, it also affects the giver. It embitters taxpayers to have money taken from them to support anonymous bureaucratic programs that don't work. In contrast, being able to direct their tax dollars allows individuals to support programs they believe are making a positive contribution to society.

LET THE STATES DO IT

The complexity of the task of replacing welfare is daunting. Our nation has dug itself deep into a hole from which there will be no easy escape. We do not pretend to have the answer. But we are fairly certain of the wrong approach: attempting to "fix" the system from Washington.

Welfare reform dictated from Washington will exhibit one crippling systematic flaw: the one-size-fits-all uniformity that produces an inability to learn from mistakes or adjust to circumstances. We need to compare various alternatives. As Mickey Kaus has argued:

> *We don't really know, after all, how many welfare recipients are simply incapable of working. We don't know the extent to which cutting off unwed mothers will encourage marriage, and the extent to which it will simply produce homelessness. We don't know if humane orphanages or group homes for single mothers are possible. The answers won't come from the study of the mincing, incremental reforms that have been tried. They will come from letting some states try the Republicans' radical ideas and some states try Clinton's radical ideas.*[88]

Ideally, responsibility for both funding and administering welfare programs would devolve to the states. Most of the nation's governors would be willing to accept reduced financing "in order to gain more freedom and flexibility," says Michigan governor John Engler.[89] But given the realities of tax structures and politics, that may not happen. Can Washington send the money without the strings attached? It remains to be seen, but it may require more self-discipline than Congress will be able to muster.

Moving beyond welfare requires moving beyond the Beltway. A diversity of approaches would allow the best reforms to emerge and be copied by other states. Failing policies can more easily be rectified or abolished. As James Q. Wilson puts it, "Any given state government may do no better than Washington, but the great variety of the former will make up for the deadening uniformity of the latter."[90]

CHAPTER 9

ECONOMIC GROWTH
FROM THE BOTTOM UP

"Jobs, jobs, jobs,"

George Bush

To hear politicians talk, you might think that jump starting the economy is easy, if not somewhat magical. Politicians pop in some money, pull a lever on a slot machine, and jobs and prosperity come pouring out. Candidates talk about "growing the economy," while "creating jobs" is universally viewed as a top government priority.

Such talk badly miscasts the role of government in economic growth. Government's role is not to "create jobs," but to create a healthy economic environment. A job, after all, is an *exchange* between two parties: money for work. Government can't *create* such exchanges (except by offering money for work—more on this later). What government can do is create an environment favorable to such exchanges. This means low taxes, reasonable regulations, and a dependable legal system.

Most quick-fix job creation strategies do nothing for the overall economy. But like drinking beer in high school, almost every politician experiments with such strategies. The construction of fancy stadiums and convention centers, corporate assistance programs, job training programs, or loans for favored industries are all approved with a sense of eternal optimism. These job creation gimmicks come with neat metaphors such as "priming the pump" or "jump starting" the economy, and are embraced in the vain hope that government spending drives economic growth. These efforts distract from the real reforms needed to create an environment conducive to wealth creation.

Of all the misguided notions concerning the economy, however, perhaps most destructive is the idea that government spending creates jobs. Humorist Dave Barry pillories this frequent claim:

> *Of all the wonderful things government says, this is just about my favorite. As opposed to if you get to keep the money. Because what you'll do is go out and bury it in your yard, anything to prevent that money from creating jobs. They never stop saying it. They say it with a straight face . . . On the other hand, [they] never say that the money removed from the economy will kill some jobs.*[1]

In one paragraph Dave Barry demonstrates more sophisticated economic understanding than most elected officials and members of the media. Barry's key insight: every dollar government spends, it first must take. In most cases, an individual who spends a dollar creates as many jobs as the government that taxes and spends that dollar for her.[2] Government spending on balance does not create wealth, it merely shifts resources.

Governors, mayors, and other public leaders have an important role to play in economic development, but it is not the glamorous role to which so many aspire. Rather than attempting to create jobs through direct government spending, the best job creation strategy is to create an environment in which more money-for-work exchanges take place. That means building a business-friendly environment.

Government needs to set the rules for exchange, resolve disputes, levy taxes, and provide public goods (such as certain infrastructure). Government should fulfill these functions as efficiently as possible, but otherwise allow the market to guide the economy. Doing so will promote a healthy economy, which ensures revenue for needed government services, reduces the demand for public assistance, and provides the economic opportunity necessary to revitalize distressed neighborhoods.

Economic activity is a complex process, involving the interaction of millions of producers and consumers in a world of changing technologies and tastes. Economic growth is fueled by innovation—discovering more productive uses for scarce resources and more productive processes to produce the same goods.[3] The "fatal conceit" of government economic planners is their misplaced confidence in their ability to manage these resources better than the market can. Political tinkering with the economy creates unforseen consequences that usually cause more harm than good.[4]

Technology is making the economy more global, interdependent, and decentralized. Government can't keep up, and shouldn't bother trying. Says Silicon Valley venture capitalist Don Valentine, "To Washington I say, please don't help us. The world of technology is complex, fast-changing, and unstructured, and it thrives best when individuals are left alone to be different, creative, and disobedient."[5]

Nations, states, and cities that fail to provide an environment congenial to the creators of wealth will lose out to their more unrestrictive competitors. Capital, including human capital, is more mobile than ever before. Some governments have clued in to this. Others are just learning—the hard way.

LOW TAXES: Rx FOR ECONOMIC GROWTH

Just as people used to flee the horrors of statism . . . in the former Communist nations of Eastern Europe, so in a less dramatic but still significant manner people have fled the high tax areas of America. Over one thousand persons a day moved into the low tax states from 1980 to 1988, while, on balance, people were departing the high tax states.[6]

Ohio University economist Richard K. Vedder

Philadelphia had a system. Every year, the mayor and city council would spend more money than they had. To close the budget deficit, they would raise taxes. As far as government officials were concerned, this system worked fine. During the 1980s, Philadelphia raised taxes 19 times. By 1991, the city's tax burden on the average family was the highest of all East Coast cities and twice as high as the surrounding suburbs. Philadelphia businesses paid the highest business taxes of the 25 largest U.S. cities.[7]

The citizens of Philadelphia didn't think this was such a great system, and over time, Philly's spend and tax strategy proved counterproductive. Despite nearly two tax increases a year in the 1980s, Philadelphia's tax revenues, in terms of purchasing power, stopped growing. Why? With each tax increase, more and more taxpayers and businesses fled the city; 20 percent of the population left during the '70s and '80s. Those staying behind were largely the nonworking poor. A 1987 study by the Wharton School of Business estimated that Philadelphia lost up to 130,000 jobs because of the higher wage taxes compared with the suburbs.

Philadelphia had literally reached its fiscal limit on taxes. A 1992 study by the Federal Reserve Bank of Philadelphia found that any increase in the tax rate would eventually result in lower tax revenues due to the erosion of the tax base.[8] Wall Street balked at issuing city bonds.

When he became mayor in 1991, Edward Rendell stopped the downward spiral. Instead of raising taxes, Rendell cut spending. David Cohen, Rendell's chief of staff, explains why:

When you raise taxes, in the first year you might raise enough money to cover a budget shortfall. In the second year, people— or businesses—start leaving; they go someplace where there are lower taxes. In the third year that accelerates. Five years or seven years of increases, and your tax base has disappeared . . . It's not like we're rocket scientists or anything, but we think we're among the first big-city governments to understand that tax revenue is a product of tax rate times base. It's time for us to increase tax revenues by bringing base back, not by increasing rates.[9]

Fleeing the Big Apple

"The only permanent fixtures in New York City are Grand Central Terminal and the Empire State Building," said a spokesman for Philip Morris as it contemplated leaving the city.[10]

Firms have been fleeing New York City's high taxes and excessive regulation for years. Between 1969 and 1994, 102 of New York's Fortune 500 corporate headquarters have left the city, taking half a million jobs with them.[11] In the recession of the early 1990s, New York City accounted for about one in five of all jobs lost in the U.S.[12] The city's Office of the Comptroller estimates that each $100 million in new city taxes destroys nearly 11,400 private-sector jobs.[13]

New Yorkers pay the country's second highest sales taxes (8.25 percent), the highest capital gains taxes (36.4 percent), and the highest taxes on personal income (11.4 percent state and local combined). New Yorkers' property taxes are 94 percent higher than the average in other large American cities.[14] These taxes support an enormous municipal work force, with one city employee for every 18 residents.[15]

These numbers were not lost on Mayor Giuliani, who upon taking office was determined to take a bite out of the Big Apple's 28 different taxes. "We've seen we can build government jobs better than any place in America," says Mayor Giuliani, "but our growth cannot be just government employment. Our economy is finished if that is the case." Despite a staggering $2.5 billion deficit, Giuliani pushed through $783 million in tax cuts over four years.

Giuliani joins the growing list of mayors who know that government spending can destroy more jobs than it creates. Overtaxed, overregulated companies can always pack up and head out of town.

Stemming the outflow of jobs in most big cities requires more than just holding the line on taxes; to compete with the suburbs, tax rates must be cut. Mayor Rendell knows this. "To bring back the tax base, we have to reduce rates," says the mayor. "We have no choice."[16]

When it comes to taxes, people would rather flee than fight. According to Barbara Anderson, executive director of Massachusetts Citizens for Limited Taxation, many of her members packed up and moved out during the Dukakis years. "You have to understand, a lot of my people have left," said Anderson. "I get postcards from Florida."[17] These hard-working, home-owning citizens are driven away by high taxes. Businesses act likewise.

HIGH TAXES AND ECONOMIC GROWTH

Dozens of academic studies have confirmed what most people suspect: there is a strong correlation between tax rates and economic growth (research tends to show that the direction taxes are moving has a stronger impact on economic growth than absolute tax rates).[18] Variations in state tax levels have a major impact on the rate of economic growth in state economies.[19] This is true whether growth is measured by income, by jobs, by the movement of capital, or by population movement.

Taxes are a drag on wealth creation and economic growth in two ways. High government spending leaves less capital available for savings, investment, and consumer spending. And high marginal tax rates discourage work, since the harder you work the more government takes.[20]

There is overwhelming evidence of the inverse relationship between taxes and economic growth. In an analysis spanning 61 years, economist Richard Vedder found that states with high tax burdens failed to grow as much as those with low tax burdens.[21] This pattern held true into the 1990s as well. The top ten income-tax-increasing states lost close to 200,000 jobs from 1989 to 1993, while the ten top tax-cutting states gained nearly one million new jobs.[22] Income taxes are perhaps the most destructive sort of tax for economic growth.[23] Vedder believes it is more than a coincidence that the three fastest-growing states in the union since 1929 are Nevada, Alaska, and Florida—among the few states without an income tax.[24]

Economic Turnaround in the Heartland

In the early 1980s, a group of Wisconsin business leaders grew disgusted with the state's attitude toward industry. Calling themselves the Bow Wow Association, they began advertising in the *Wall Street Journal*, advising companies against relocating in Wisconsin. Tommy Thompson, a state legislator at the time, recalls the mood: "Wisconsin had such a bad reputation in the business community. We had signs at the border saying 'Don't go to Wisconsin because it's an anti-business state. When the last company leaves Wisconsin please turn out the lights.' The first thing we had to do was turn around that attitude."

After being elected governor, Thompson worked to make Wisconsin safe for business. He lowered the state's capital gains tax by 60 percent and cut other taxes. Thompson wasn't even above making cold calls to business CEOs to convince them that Wisconsin appreciated their presence. While most of America was losing jobs during the recession of the early 1990s, Wisconsin was gaining jobs, nearly 450,000 of them since Thompson took office in 1987.[26] Under Thompson, formerly anti-business Wisconsin developed one of the country's best entrepreneurial climates.

It has been demonstrated repeatedly that cutting income-tax rates can spur economic growth. When Pete du Pont was elected governor of Delaware in 1976, the state's income-tax rates were the country's highest, unemployment was at 13 percent, and large deficits were an annual event. "We had a nearly bankrupt state with huge problems," recounts du Pont.[25] Governor du Pont cut taxes five times (lowering rates by 60 percent) and pushed a constitutional amendment through the legislature requiring a supermajority vote to raise taxes. The effect was dramatic. Jobs rose by 20 percent, the welfare rolls fell 40 percent, unemployment was nearly cut in half, and—despite the cut in tax rate—tax revenues grew by more than 7 percent annually. The moral? "States can improve their lot if they bear in mind that high taxes and opportunity don't mix," says du Pont.

It is not simply a matter of competition between states. Even if every state had identical tax policies, the absolute level of taxation makes a big difference to the economy. In today's global economy, low taxes are an essential part of making American industry competitive internationally.

FAULTY STATE ECONOMIC POLICIES

Some governors (and mayors) see the economy as a zero-sum game in which the only way to bring more jobs to your state is to lure them away from other states. They try to land big companies by offering special packages of tax breaks, loans, taxpayer-backed industrial bonds, and a host of other benefits.

Kentucky was one of the first states in the 1980s to enact legislation providing business incentives, including tax incentives that reimbursed up to 100 percent of construction and start-up costs over a ten-year period. The governor of Kentucky at the time, Brereton C. Jones, bragged about the package in a national commercial on CNN: "Locate your manufacturing plant in Kentucky, and the state could reimburse your *entire* investment. Call me for more details about Kentucky. In Kentucky, we're serious about jobs."[27]

Nearly everyone plays the incentive game, for when an economy goes sour, there is strong pressure on elected officials to "do something," especially something that will garner media attention. This pressure is not often resisted and crosses party lines. In 1992, South Carolina Governor Carroll Campbell, a conservative Republican, won the bidding war for a new BMW plant by putting up $130 million in incentives and subsidies. In 1992, Minnesota coughed up $270 million in loans to Northwest Airlines just to keep the company from leaving the state.

One of the most exciting state bidding wars was the 1993 battle for a new Mercedes-Benz plant. Over 20 states bid for Mercedes' new $300 million manufacturing plant and its 1,500 new jobs. North Carolina looked to be the winner after Democratic Governor Jim Hunt cajoled his state legislature into offering to build a $35 million auto-manufacturing training facility—immediately dubbed "Mercedes University" by local wags.[28] But they were outdone by Alabama's political leadership, which, on behalf of taxpayers, coughed up tax breaks and other incentives valued at about $350 million (that's over $200,000 per job, if you're counting).[29]

To get Mercedes to sign on the dotted line, Alabama also agreed to purchase over 2,500 Mercedes vehicles for state use, to rename a segment of highway the "Mercedes-Benz Autobahn," and to exempt the company from paying state income taxes for 25 years. The state also agreed to pick up the salaries of a thousand or so Mercedes employees for the first year while they trained at a facility built by the state just for Mercedes.[30] If that's not enough, now perched atop the scoreboard of the University of Alabama's historic Legion Field is a giant $75,000 Mercedes-Benz hood ornament. The crimson tide you see pouring across the field isn't the football team, it's red ink from the state's budget.

Why would state officials go to such absurd lengths? Jobs, and the positive publicity that goes with them. When United Airlines put the location of its new maintenance hub on the auction block in the late 1980s, states salivated over the chance to land the 6,000 jobs promised by United. The "winner" of the battle was Indiana, which—with the city of Indianapolis— agreed to pony up $230 million in up-front cash to get United.

It was also arranged so that United would pay no state or local taxes of any kind—ever. Thrown in for good measure was a parcel of land to site the facility—free of charge, of course.[31]

Landing the big company can be a Pyrrhic victory. Indianapolis economist William Styring has studied these bidding wars and concluded that the costs usually outweigh the benefits. He illustrates his point using the United Airlines package, with 6,000 jobs and a $230 million price tag:

> *Let's divide by 1,000. Suppose you walk into the mayor's office and say, "Boy, have I got a deal for you. If you'll buy up some ground, lease it to me tax-and-rent-free, promise me no sales, income, or property taxes forever, and give me $230,000 cash up-front, I'll promise to (maybe) hire six people in ten years." Care to take a guess as to your mayor's reaction? (How about, "No I don't think so.")*[32]

There is no evidence that these one-shot deals have a general positive effect on a state's economic growth.[33] An econometric study by Margery Marzahn Ambrosius of Kansas State University tested the impact of eight common state economic development policies.[34] Her findings: "None . . . had a demonstrable effect on . . . the economic health of the state."[35]

CORPORATE WELFARE

Incentive packages amount to little more than corporate welfare. Moreover, they are an affront to the rule of law, the idea that everyone should be treated equally. Why should one company get special privileges at the expense of others? Small businesses are unlikely to receive the tax breaks and other goodies offered to lure big out-of-staters—in fact, they'll be footing the bill.

While many governors and mayors agree in principle that bidding wars are bad news, they feel they have no choice but to enter battle. What should we do, they ask, unilaterally disarm? Our answer? No, choose a better weapon.

States should improve their competitive appeal across-the-board to every kind of business—not just the favored few. During his 1994 campaign, Connecticut Governor John Rowland vowed to eschew bidding wars in favor of lower taxes. Says Rowland, "Rather than giving particular incentives and particular grants to particular companies, let's make it cheaper, less expensive for everyone to do business here in the state of Connecticut by cutting taxes, cutting spending, reforming the welfare system and changing the attitudes about how we deal with businesses, small and large."[36]

Competing on a company-by-company basis is not only unfair, it is ultimately destructive to a state's overall economic well-being. As the *Wall Street Journal* put it: "The hand-out game, whether it involved steel mills or high-tech R&D, stops when politicians fathom or are made to learn that it doesn't pay in most cases and it isn't their role in life to bestow these favors anyway. They ought to attend to competitiveness by maximizing the appeal of their jurisdiction to every kind of enterprise, not just those with a big snout."[37]

A low-tax, lightly regulated business climate has allowed South Dakota to attract hundreds of out-of-state businesses while spurring local business creation and expansion—without cutting special deals with certain firms. South Dakota has no corporate income tax, no personal income tax, no personal property tax, no business inventory tax, and its unemployment insurance rates are the lowest in the nation. "Our business climate provides incentives and advantages, not subsidies," said former Governor Walter D. Miller.[38]

South Dakota's pleasant business climate has helped it rank second in job growth since the 1991 recession.[39] South Dakota's low taxes and regulations have also attracted out-of-state businesses. Over 320 firms have relocated to Sioux Falls in recent years. Even Minnesota Technical Research, a high-tech manufacturing firm, fled its namesake state because of the tax burden. "You cannot sell a product for enough to pay those kind of taxes and have anything left for growth," says MTR president Jerry Luetzow. "You just pay your taxes."[40] Unfortunately for South Dakota governors, when businesses move in because of across-the-board low taxes, the governor doesn't get a photo-op. The economy booms just the same.

The South Dakota strategy makes sense.[41] The way to compete with other states is by offering across-the-board tax and regulation policies that encourage business growth and formation. "All that government should do," says Michigan Governor John Engler, is create "a competitive tax and regulatory climate [and stop] trying to pick the winners and losers in the marketplace."[42]

Enterprise Zones for Everybody

Here's the idea. If we give economically depressed areas special tax breaks and regulatory relief, business will boom and local residents will get jobs. Simple, right?

Not quite. Though we appreciate the sentiment behind enterprise zones, in their current form they are more a boondoggle than a boon.

There are two problems with enterprise zones. The first is political. By definition, enterprise zones provide special treatment to particular regions. Political shenanigans are likely to turn enterprise zones into political prizes for the well-connected. Every state and local politician salivated at the chance of landing federally funded enterprise zones. And just like bidding wars, enterprise zones amount to special treatment for the favored few at the general expense.

The second problem is more subtle. Enterprise zone legislation assumes that attracting companies to poor areas will provide jobs for local residents. But as *Reason* editor Virginia Postrel notes, "The problem of the inner cities is not a problem of place. It is a problem of people."[43] Since the early 1980s, 37 states have established some 3,000 enterprise zones.[44] The results have been inconclusive at best.[45]

Philip Kasinitz and Jan Rosenberg, who studied hiring practices in the impoverished Red Hook section of Brooklyn, have an explanation. They found the lack of social networks a far greater barrier to employment than proximity to employers: "The idea of enterprise zones reflects a basic misunderstanding of the relationship between living space and working space in dense cities like New York. We do not, after all, expect middle-class New Yorkers to work within walking distance of their homes; why should we expect the poor to do so?"[46]

Reducing taxes and regulation is a great idea, but enterprise zones as they have evolved probably aren't the best way to do it. We would prefer to see someone experiment with making an entire city an enterprise zone. On this matter we agree with San Diego Mayor Susan Golding, who says, "The jury is still out on enterprise zones, because as far as I'm concerned none has been radical enough. If you want a great enterprise zone, look at Hong Kong. That's an enterprise zone that's far more radical than what our federal government is willing to give. . . . Say you're an African American looking to start a laundromat. [The government] says you have to pay this tax and that fee, and get this permit and that inspection, and by the time you're through, there's no way you can even dream of doing that."[47]

THE FIELD OF DREAMS STRATEGY

Just as states sometimes engage in destructive forms of competition, so too do cities. (Take note—this is one of the few occasions when we actually criticize competition.) The healthy response to a flagging economy is not more government, but less.

Some deteriorating cities look for miracle cures. The favorite quick-fix elixir is to spend tax money on a new stadium, convention center, or downtown construction scheme. This is called the "field of dreams" strategy: if you build it, they will come. Of course, many times they don't, leaving taxpayers the proud owners of an enormous white elephant.

"Most mayors are comfortable building big buildings. It's a fun thing to do," jokes one deputy mayor.[48] Call it the Edifice Complex. If you were a politician, would you rather spend your time streamlining the business permitting process, or cutting the ribbon on a new convention center? Would you rather stay late in the office working on reducing land-use restrictions, or throw out the first ball at a brand new ballpark? Building big buildings *is* fun, especially if you use other people's money.

Over three-quarters of a billion dollars has been spent for sports facilities since the mid-1980s. The growth in municipal convention centers has been even greater. The number of cities owning convention centers just about tripled from 1977 to 1987—and shows little sign of slowing down (some 300 cities have now built municipal convention centers).

It's the municipal equivalent of the arms race.[49] Less than two years after San Diego completed its convention center, city officials were talking about expanding. Why? Because Anaheim had just expanded *its* convention center, thereby leapfrogging San Diego's to become the largest on the West Coast. When St. Louis launched a $360 million expansion of its convention center, in-state rival Kansas City suddenly decided its convention center needed a $130 million facelift.

The theory of convention center building is straightforward. "Multi-million dollar convention centers are built in the expectation that hoards of free-spending conventioneers will bolster local economies and revitalize downtowns," writes Lawrence Tabak in the *Atlantic Monthly*.[50] The reality of convention centers is also straightforward, though quite different from the theory. In most cases, hoards of free-spending conventioneers don't materialize, and most convention centers are big money losers. One survey of 25 government-run convention centers found yearly operating losses average 42 percent of revenue.[51]

Consider Los Angeles' $500 million dollar convention center. Completed in 1993, it is the largest public-works project in the city's history.[52] "It has enough glass to make a crystal replica of the Washington monument and enough steel to build a monorail from New York City to Philadelphia," writes Charles Mahtesian in *Governing* magazine.[53] Its magnificent lobbies feature maps of the world in terrazzo and Milky Way galaxies.

Nonetheless, conventioneers are staying away in hoards. According to one city official, L.A.'s half-billion-dollar monument was "the worst pre-booked convention center in history."[54] One reason is location, for the center was plopped down next to a freeway in smoggy, dull, hotel-poor, downtown Los Angeles. Now, people who live in L.A. don't go downtown unless they absolutely have to, so it's a bit unrealistic to expect conventioneers to travel across the country for the opportunity.

Pointing to the shiny convention center (built during the previous mayor's administration), Richard Riordan's Deputy Mayor Michael Keeley says, "Every time I drive by it I hear a giant sucking sound."[55] That's the sound of tax dollars going down the drain. Think about the magnitude of $500 million. If the city of Los Angeles had spent $6,000 *every day* since it was founded as a Mexican village in 1781, it wouldn't have spent $500 million dollars until after the year 2000.

THE ECONOMIC MULTIPLIER DECEPTION

Those who push for city spending on convention centers, stadiums, and cultural enhancements such as zoos and museums often cite economic benefits from these "investments." Spending advocates claim that the indirect spending generated at shops, hotels, and restaurants makes such investments worthwhile.

Central to this argument is the magical multiplier effect. By this thinking, one dollar spent by a tourist tipping a waitress adds to her income, which means she can buy an ice cream cone, which in turn means the ice cream vendor—well, you get the point. Economic analyses of such government "invest-ments" can show virtually any economic returns.

As an example, the tax-funded California Arts Commission hired KPMG Peat Marwick LLP to evaluate the impact of arts spending:

> *Nonprofit arts organizations receive $254 million in grants and donations. As a return on this investment, arts organiza-tions and audiences generate more than $2 billion of spending in California ... Seven arts festivals analyzed in this study generated an average of $11 in economic activity for each $1 of cost.*[56]

Wow! This sounds too good to be true. How does this work? Well, the study explains that it used "an economic 'multiplier,' showing how dollars spent in one segment of the economy grow as they flow into other segments."[57] (As Dave Barry might say, we are not making this up—they are.)

With the right assumptions, you can generate almost any result you want. For example, most economic impact studies of, say, sports stadiums count every dollar spent at the stadium as "new" money (that is, money that wouldn't have otherwise been spent in the local economy). Robert Baade, an economist at Lake Forest College, says this amounts to bad economics. "It's not usually new money," he says. "The money would have been spent elsewhere in the economy—at local movie theaters or some other form of entertainment."[58]

Most economic impact studies—whether looking at gov-ernment arts funding or convention centers—don't even attempt to measure opportunity costs (whether the same invested dollars spent elsewhere would have generated more wealth) or the loss to the economy due to higher taxes. "Con-trary to popular belief," says economist Edwin Mills, "gov-ernment subsidies to convention centers do not 'multiply' into unique economic benefits that cannot be achieved by the private sector."[59]

When professional baseball-craving St. Petersburg, Florida, boosters (both public officials and private investors) were trying to get the city to build a stadium, backers commissioned an economic impact study that claimed the stadium would add a whopping $750 million annually to the local economy. This was all the "evidence" city officials needed. They hiked taxes to pay for the $110 million, 43,000-seat stadium.[60] Four years later, the citizens of St. Pete are still waiting for their baseball team. The $750 million boost to the local economy sounds like a cruel joke as the city tries to recoup a fraction of its investment by holding motorcross racing, monster tractor pulls, and rock concerts at the stadium.

A number of economists who have taken the time to study the *actual, after-the-fact impact* of sports stadiums on economic growth found the effects to be negligible. In a study of 30 metropolitan areas that built stadiums, Robert Baade found only three that demonstrated any significant change in economic condition. In those three cities, *the change was negative.* "Looking at pure economic benefit and pure economic costs, stadiums are not worth the limited resources put into them," says Baade.[61] Pepperdine University economist Dean Baim, who did an econometric study of 14 stadiums, agrees: "From a financial standpoint, the net present value of stadiums is invariably negative."[62]

Just Say No

In some cities, taxpayers are starting to hold overambitious officials in check. Little Rock taxpayers, for example, rejected a convention center two times in three years.

Citizen action also helped keep Tampa officials in check. The saga started back in 1990, when the city built a convention center without regard to its capacity to attract convention center business. By 1994, the convention center was costing taxpayers $14 million a year. Optimistic Tampa officials proposed a solution: they wanted the city to build a 900-room, $137 million hotel—using taxpayer dollars—in order to make the city's convention center a more attractive destination for conventioneers.

Some Tampa citizens thought this would simply throw good money after bad. Harry E. Teasley, Jr., a former board member of the Tampa Chamber of Commerce, helped lead a fight against the new hotel, noting that "Tampa had asked numerous hotel operators to bid on building on the site. All backed off saying that it was not the time for them to gamble their money on a risky hotel venture."[63] Though private entrepreneurs thought the venture too risky (hotel occupancy rates in Tampa average just 70 percent), in mid-1994 it nonetheless still appeared as though Tampa's public officials were poised to gamble taxpayer money on the project.[64]

The hotel deal appeared certain to sail through the city council on the basis of an economic impact analysis commissioned by the city. However, Teasley was determined to fight what he perceived was a misuse of political power. "For those promoters and vested interests who are looking for a government handout, my response is that welfare is for the poor and needy, not for the rich and politically powerful," Teasley told the city council, blasting the well-heeled special interests pushing the hotel scheme. "It is shameless and unseemly."

To rally public opinion, Teasley bought a full-page ad in the *Tampa Tribune-Times*. The ad featured a giant $140 million check from city taxpayers made out to the Tampa Convention Hotel. The ad's headline read: "On Thursday, October 27, Tampa City Council may Write a Check for $140,000,000 Out Of *Your* Checking Account."

Thanks largely to Teasley's efforts and media scrutiny of the economic impact study, in October 1994 the hotel scheme was voted down four to three by the city council.

LET THE PRIVATE SECTOR GO IT ALONE

Economist Baade's studies show that though they do little for the local economy, public subsidies for stadiums do benefit some people. "The beneficiaries of the public subsidies are clearly the owners and players," says Baade. "The major effect of the subsidies is to enable the players and owners to command more money in terms of their incomes because they don't have to pay for their own economic infrastructure."[65] Does it make any sense to tax shoe salesmen and cab drivers to subsidize billionaire team owners and millionaire ball players? We don't think so.

A promising trend: if they can't find a generous host, many teams will build stadiums with their own money (though cities sometimes provide infrastructure and/or other amenities). Chicago's new $175 million United Center, which houses the Bulls and the Blackhawks, was privately financed by a partnership between team owners. (United Airlines also chipped in with a 20-year lease on the name and logo.)[66] The new Arlington Stadium in Texas was also mostly privately financed.[67] Similarly, the new Boston Garden, named the Shawmut Center, is to be privately built, with government paying only for some additional mass transit infrastructure. Philadelphia's $215 million CoreStates Center is receiving only $20 million from local taxpayers.[68]

Sports teams need cities, but cities don't need sports teams. The story of Miami's Robbie Stadium illustrates this point beautifully. For years, Dolphins owner Joe Robbie (now deceased) had tried to get the city to improve the dirty, aged Orange Bowl. But Miami voters three times rejected bids to improve the stadium. So Robbie decided to build his own stadium.

Robbie was able to borrow enough cash to build the magnificent $115 million, 75,000-seat Joe Robbie Stadium without one penny of taxpayer money. Only football fans are paying for the stadium. "This stadium is a monument to a free, competitive enterprise system and showed that anything the government can do, we can do better," said Robbie at the stadium's opening in 1987. "What I have done is caused the politicians to look toward the private sector."[69]

If there is a market demand, entrepreneurs will build the arenas they need to entertain crowds. It is the opposite of the field of dreams strategy: if the crowds will come, someone will build it. Sports are an entertainment industry, and if entrepreneurs believe they can attract enough fans to turn a profit, they will invest in the stadium, incurring all the risk and reward of that investment.

"Catch Basins Aren't Sexy, But They're Important"

In a previous chapter we quoted these words of wisdom from Massachusetts Transportation Secretary James Kerasiotes. Rather than blowing hundreds of millions of taxpayer dollars on incentive packages, sports stadiums, and convention centers, state and local governments should concentrate on basic infrastructure. Most surveys of business executives list infrastructure quality as a key factor in locating their business. "If you don't have good streets and good sewers, the chances of having an economically viable city are nil," says one city official.[70]

The Chicago flood of 1992 was the most visible example of an infrastructure crisis that has been building up in cities for decades. The signs of decay are everywhere: potholed streets, collapsing sewers, crumbling curbs, and precarious bridges. Why has this occurred? Politicians get credit for cutting ribbons on new projects, not for repairing existing infrastructure. The result: maintenance is deferred on basic infrastructure such as sewer systems in order to pay for fancy new sports stadiums.

While not as sexy as big new facilities, maintaining existing bridges, sidewalks, roads, curbs, and sewers is essential to extend their life and preserve the asset value of a city or state's investments.

THE HIGH COST OF GOVERNMENT REGULATIONS

The past 30 years have seen a terrifying explosion in government regulation. Regulation scares more companies than competition. In its 1994 survey of America's 500 fastest growing companies, *Inc.* magazine reported that "regulation was most often identified as the No. 1 enemy."[71]

Los Angeles in the early 1990s was losing companies to places like Phoenix and Las Vegas. To find out why, a local business group surveyed thousands of Los Angeles companies:

Many firms simply wrote in capital letters, 'GOVERNMENT HARASSMENT!' . . . In interviews, company executives were frequently so angry about their relations with the government that they would vent their frustration on the project staff for several minutes before apologizing and more calmly responding to questions.[72]

The rule explosion extends beyond business, however. Rules and lawsuits are a daily feature of American life. Newspapers won't accept advertisements for apartments that say "female preferred," because the government can charge the newspaper with discrimination.[73] People are afraid to tell a joke at the water cooler for fear of being charged with sexual harassment or creating a hostile environment for some protected group. Americans today must obey 30 times as many laws as their great-grandparents did at the turn of the century.[74]

We are not even safe in our own homes anymore. Humorist Dave Barry tells how he got a ticket for painting his living room:

It turned out you had to have a permit if a job cost more than $50. I don't know what you can possibly do for less than $50. . . . The painter spent a day getting a permit to do a job that took about half a day to actually do.

Then I wrote a column about that and discovered that there were people in Coral Gables who would wait until 2 o'clock in the morning to replace a sink because to do it during the daytime you'd see two trucks outside. . . . People are afraid their own government will catch them fixing their houses.[75]

Americans are disgusted with this state of affairs, as evidenced by the 1994 election returns. Across the nation, voters went against intrusive government. In Massachusetts, citizens voted to repeal rent control laws. According to his own pollster, President Clinton's health care reform was resented by voters as big government interference.[76] On a special post-election program on CNN, the loudest audience applause was accorded an Angry Voter who declared, "The real issue was too much government and too much government regulations." The day after the election, President Clinton said he got the message: "People want fundamental change in the role of government in their lives." Let's be more specific: people want less government intrusion in going about their simple daily business.

Simple daily business, thanks to government regulation, isn't so simple after all. Consider that American tradition, the sidewalk lemonade stand. A lot of eight-year-olds pay scant attention to some very important laws. For instance, to sell lemonade by the book in Boston, you'd need to get permission from five different government entities, to fork over $335 on the necessary licenses and permits, and to obtain $500,000 in liability insurance. If the lemonade is made in a residential kitchen, only immediate family members may assist in its preparation. And don't forget that according to 105 CMR 590.009, the Massachusetts Board of Health now has jurisdiction over the length of your fingernails.[77]

Here's how Alexis de Tocqueville described the effect of overzealous rule-making:

It covers the surface of society with a network of small complicated rules, minute and uniform, through which the most orig-

inal minds and the most energetic characters cannot pene-
trate.... The will of man is not shattered, but softened, bent,
and guided; men are seldom forced to act, but they are con-
stantly refrained from acting. Such a power does not destroy,
but it prevents existence; it does not tyrannize, but it compress-
es, enervates, extinguishes and stupefies the people . . . [78]

Sounds like Tocqueville tried to sell lemonade in Boston. Or maybe he foresaw the fate of 15-year-old Monique Landers. Monique was named one of five Outstanding High School Entrepreneurs by the National Foundation for Teaching Entrepreneurship. Monique was earning about $100 a month braiding hair for her friends. Unfortunately, the Kansas Cosmetology Board read about her award. They sent Monique a letter explaining that it was illegal for her to touch hair for profit without their permission. If she didn't stop, the letter warmly told her that she'd be subject to "a fine or imprisonment in the county jail or both."[79]

In addition to the annoyance, the economic cost of overregulation is astounding. Economist Thomas Hopkins estimates the costs of regulations to be at least $581 billion, or nearly $6,000 per household.[80]

Without question, there are certain areas in which government regulation is necessary. Laws dealing with air and water pollution, for example, are an important government function. But we are in the midst of a regulatory madness that threatens to implode our economy. Says New Jersey Governor Christine Todd Whitman, "Government is responsible for protecting the general public safety, but is not responsible for micromanaging business and micromanaging the way people live. Government should set a standard as to what is safe emissions from a smokestack and enforce those emission standards, but not tell companies how to achieve those standards. If companies can come up with a better way to reduce noxious emissions and keep themselves economically sound then they should be able to do that."[81]

Lawmakers continuously enact regulations that micromanage business. In California, a state board determines the minimum acceptable size for tangerines. In Los Angeles, restaurants cannot allow diners to smoke. In Cambridge, Massachusetts, restaurants must put condom dispensers in the bathroom.

Author and management guru Peter Drucker calls the steady growth in government regulation "that dangerous and insidious disease of developed countries."[82] The cost of government regulations, Drucker points out, is invisible—it never shows up in government budgets—but this doesn't mean regulations are "free." Regulation isn't free when a fish company employs five people to advise on how to comply with government labor laws, or when a state college has 12 administrators working to comply with government mandates, or when a businesswoman spends most of her day filling out government forms instead of running her business.

It is consumers who ultimately pay. Regulation costs account for one-third of the price of a single-engine aircraft and 95 percent of the price of vaccines for children.[83] "When I started this business 15 years ago, I spent 95 percent of my time out front with customers," says Michigan restaurateur David Gillie. "Now I spend 95 percent of my time in back doing paperwork."[84]

In addition to these direct economic costs, regulation imposes substantial "opportunity costs," meaning whatever else people can't do (or capital that isn't available to spend) because of the resources expended complying with regulations. Consider the EPA's hazardous waste disposal ban, which costs $4.2 billion for every premature death averted.[85] Used for other purposes, such as improved sanitation, food, or medical care, this $4.2 billion could probably save hundreds of lives. Economists Bill Laffer and Nancy Bord estimate that including the indirect costs of regulations doubles their total costs to the economy.[86]

Overregulation has been a bipartisan trend, with President Reagan the only president to actually reduce regulation. His successor, George Bush, presided over a boom in new rules, including the 1990 Clean Air Act, the Americans with Disabilities Act, and the 1990 Pollution Prevention Act. These new laws add hundreds of billions of dollars to the costs of doing business, reduce the competitiveness of U.S. businesses, and lower America's GNP.

REGULATING ENTERPRISE TO DEATH IN CALIFORNIA

Many factors contributed to California's deep recession of the early '90s, including defense cutbacks and a national recession. But California's tax-and-regulate lawmakers shot themselves in the foot by creating a regulatory climate that was, in the words of Governor Pete Wilson, a "job-killing machine."

"California's economic wounds are mostly self-inflicted," declared Peter Ueberroth, the appointed chairman of Governor Wilson's special Council on California Competitiveness. "California has created a nightmarish obstacle course for business, job, and revenue growth."[87] Nearly 90 percent of the hundreds of manufacturing facilities that fled California between 1987 and 1992 cited the state's poor business climate as a major reason for relocating.[88] California is learning a hard truth: no business, no jobs.

California's workers' compensation system is an entrepreneur's nightmare. Though system costs were among the highest in the nation, California ranked forty-fourth in benefits paid to injured workers.[89] Where did all the money go? Mostly into the wallets of the lawyers, doctors, and system middlemen.[90] Workers' comp fraud is widespread, as a "60 Minutes" segment documented in 1992. Unlike all but a handful of states, California law allows individuals to file claims for workers' comp benefits by claiming "stress" as a disabling injury.

In addition to greatly increasing direct business costs, workers' compensation laws have also made it difficult to fire anyone in California. Companies are generally required to inform workers that their performance is unsatisfactory prior to dismissal, in order to give the worker an opportunity to improve. But under California's workers' comp system, fear of being fired creates "job-related stress," which entitles you to collect on a disability claim—and it's illegal to fire anyone on disability! This is a classic Catch-22. Employers are placed in an impossible situation, and consumers and honest workers pay for fraudulent claims as unscrupulous workers, doctors, and lawyers ride the system for all it's worth. When the Good Companies, an L.A.-based furniture manufacturer, moved to Mexico in the early 1990s, 600 workers were laid off. When the layoffs were announced, a law firm parked vans at the plant's door and carted workers to the firm's office. All but 70 of the 600 workers filed workers' comp claims against the company.[91]

California's environmental protection secretary James Strock described the state's environmental review process as "convoluted, overly complex, and unnecessarily burdensome."[92] In Los Angeles County, businesses were required to obtain permits from up to 27 local agencies and as many as 32 state agencies.[93] Adding in various federal agencies brings the possible amount of total approvals needed to over 70 agencies. "It's like being in a communist country," said Los Angeles Mayor Riordan soon after taking office. The situation is grim. San Diego Mayor Susan Golding says that her city's 2,000 pages of zoning code means that, "if you want to do anything in this city, you not only have to ask the government, you probably need to hire someone."[94]

Golding is fighting to roll back the rules. Under her leadership, San Diego cut the time involved in permit processing by 50 percent, eliminated the business license tax for small businesses, and junked a host of burdensome land-use regulations. Every three months the city council holds a regulatory relief day.

At the state level, mild workers' compensation reform and some business tax reductions finally passed the legislature in 1993. But Golden State legislators still don't seem to get it. In 1994, California became the only state in the nation to pass a law making it illegal for companies to require female employees to wear skirts. Writes *Reason* editor Virginia Postrel:

> *When he signed the bill, Gov. Pete Wilson declared, "Women make important business decisions everyday. Indeed, working women should be able to make the simple choice of the professional business attire they wish to wear." Neither Wilson nor the bill's sponsors imagine a situation in which a woman might "make the important business decision" to require her employees to wear skirts. Nor did they question whether workplace attire is really any business of the state of California.*[95]

Little wonder why California businesses are heading for Arizona, Colorado, and Nevada.

PARING BACK GOVERNMENT REGULATIONS

Government officials need to radically rethink the regulation of trade. While some rules are necessary, in a free society the two parties involved in an exchange should be given wide latitude in setting the terms of trade. Many regulations are nothing more than unnecessary meddling by government. Think about renting an apartment in New York City. First, rules dictate how you can advertise the apartment (saying, for example, "close to synagogue" may be illegal). Rules dictate whom you can and cannot rent to, forcing religious owners to rent to unmarried couples living together. Finally, in many cases the city of New York will dictate how much rent you can charge. Greater even than the economic costs of such regulations is the price we pay in lost liberty.

In too many other cases, regulations act as barriers to entry, aiding established firms by excluding newcomers. Governments, with help from the courts, restrict entry into professions, trades, and industry. In other cases, labor rulings favor unionized workers over lower-priced competitors. Often, such regulations work against poor and minorities seeking to move up the economic ladder.

Lawmakers need to assess the costs of regulations. A step in the right direction is the GOP's Contract with America and its proposals for regulatory reform. Contract provisions would require, for example, a regulatory impact analysis of any new federal rule affecting over 100 people. Also proposed is a requirement that the federal government compensate property owners if any new regulation reduces the value of their land by over 10 percent. It's about time we started putting some constraints on the rule-making apparatus, to bring rationality and fairness back to regulatory decision-making.

Putting a Break on Bureaucratic Rule and Regulation Making

Much of the blame for the regulatory binges we have indulged in for the last 30 years lies squarely with lawmakers who often pass regulations to curry favor with special interests. They don't consider who shoulders the cost. But legislators haven't been the only culprits. Contributing greatly to the regulatory onslaught is a system that has given bureaucrats—lacking any voter accountability—virtual free rein over writing and administering rules and regulations.

As the job of making laws has grown more complex and the number of laws have multiplied, the job of writing and adopting rules and regulations has increasingly flowed from elected representatives to government regulators. Federal and state agencies are seldom required to provide proof that a need exists, nor demonstrate that they have explored alternatives, before writing a particular regulation.

In the early 1980s, Pennsylvania's General Assembly established the *Independent Regulatory Review Commission* (IRRC) to review rules and regulations coming out of state agencies.[96] In the first 12 years of the IRRC's existence, it has killed or modified over a thousand administrative rules and regulations.

Richard Sandusky, director of regulatory analysis for the commission, says about two-thirds of bad regulations result from overzealous administrators. "Our mission is not necessarily to stop agencies from promulgating regulations," says Sandusky, "but to ensure that the regulations comport with the legislative statutes and that they impose the minimum burden on the regulated public."[97]

When Pennsylvania's Department of Labor and Industry proposed a comprehensive overhaul of the state's prevailing wage rules in 1993, the IRRC stepped in. The original 1960 Prevailing Wage Act required the state to pay above-market (union) wages on public-works projects. The Labor and Industry Department wanted to expand the law to cover a host of other construction projects, including road construction through private housing developments. The IRRC weighed in by concluding that the new regulation "had the potential to wreak a widespread economic reversal" in Pennsylvania. In the end the proposal was killed.

High-Cost Labor Laws

The prevailing wage law and the attempt by Pennsylvania regulators to expand its scope are but two examples of government interference in the labor market.

By requiring above-market wages, prevailing wage laws benefit union members at the expense of the general public. These laws hurt business, especially in distressed neighborhoods in need of new construction. At a housing conference in October 1994, Federal Reserve Board Governor Lawrence Lindsey criticized the federal prevailing wage Davis-Bacon Act and other government regulations. "These restrictions impede inner city development in two ways: They drive up the cost of construction and they tend to deprive local residents of job opportunities," said Lindsey. "The Davis-Bacon requirement effectively wipes out much of the good . . . bankers do when [they] lend to such projects at concessionary rates."[98]

"Closed shop" rules, which require workers in union shops to pay union dues whether or not they desire union representation, also hurt business. Companies avoid states where unions' monopoly on labor (enforced by government) allows them to force on employers the kind of featherbedding and work rules that raise a firm's costs, decrease productivity, and lower competitiveness.

In the competition for jobs, the 21 "Right-to-Work" states have a big advantage. Allowing employees to work without joining the local union has proven to be a powerful draw for business. The Fantus Company, one of America's leading industrial relocation firms, found that half of all businesses exploring relocating *refused to even consider* moving to a state without a Right-to-Work law.[99] A survey by *Area Development* magazine had similar results: over 71 percent of respondents said Right-to-Work laws were important or very important considerations in their relocation decision. The states with right-to-work laws created 92 percent of the country's manufacturing jobs between 1975 and 1985—over ten times as many as were created in the other 30 states.[100]

In 1987, Idaho became America's twenty-first Right-to-Work state. The economy has boomed ever since, even during the national recession. By 1993, over 103,000 new jobs had been created.[101] Jim Hawkins, Idaho's Commerce Department director who had worked under a governor opposed to the Right-to-Work law, was forced to admit that "the economic gains probably would not have been possible without Right-to-Work."[102]

DEREGULATING BUSINESS INFRASTRUCTURE: ROUND TWO

Companies depend on transportation, communication, and power to conduct business. Deregulating this "business infrastructure" drives down costs and makes American business more competitive.

Under President Jimmy Carter, the government deregulated interstate air travel and trucking. The result was better service at lower costs, for both businesses and consumers. This deregulation boosted American productivity and helped keep America's job market competitive. Round two of deregulation is about to begin.

This time it is state public utility commissions that are pushing for deregulation. Since the breakup of AT&T, the telecommunications industry has become increasingly competitive. In September 1994, the New York State Public Service Commission announced it would accelerate competition in all of Nynex's monopoly businesses; in October 1994, MCI filed for permission to compete for local service in Illinois and four other states. Why are states deregulating? Competition. "The larger states that have to compete on a global basis for business are moving ahead quite expeditiously on opening their markets," says Royce J. Holland, president of MFS Communications.[103]

For the same reason, states are deregulating their energy markets. Leading the way will be (surprise!) California, which now has some of the country's highest energy costs. In 1994, the state's Public Utilities Commission proposed radically deregulating the state's electric power system. By 1996, California's largest power users will choose their electrical supplier among competing vendors; households will get to choose by 2002. "California is getting itself out from the regulatory mess it created," says Robert Michaels, professor of economics at the California State University at Fullerton.[104] Other states, including Michigan and Nevada, are expected to take similar steps.[105]

CASE STUDY: THE INDIANAPOLIS DEREGULATORY SWAT TEAM

Indianapolis has the country's most comprehensive government deregulation effort. That's because Mayor Stephen Goldsmith hates stupid regulations. "Bad local regulations hinder job creation, stifle healthy neighborhood development, and chill business expansion," says Goldsmith. "In nearly every survey of local businesses, regulation appears at the top of the list of barriers to growth."[106]

Early into his term, Goldsmith created the Regulatory Study Commission (RSC). The mayor charged this deregulatory SWAT team with systematically weeding out unnecessary regulations. Moreover, all proposed regulations must pass the RSC's cost-benefit analysis.

The RSC is charged with fighting bad regulations. RSC deregulators have found reams of outdated ordinances in the city's 2,700-page regulation book. Shuffleboard operators in Indianapolis were required to obtain special licenses, as were residents with milk cows in their backyards. These requirements are now gone. Much of the RSC's deregulation work has benefited low-income and minority entrepreneurs. In early 1995, the city eliminated all business license requirements for used-goods dealers, movie theaters, and hotels/motels, which are often minority-owned.

The RSC SWAT team has also slowed the growth of regulation. "The cost-benefit analyses have imposed a chilling effect on the promulgation of new regulations—this is probably as important as our more proactive work," says Tom Rose, who codirects the RSC. "Every time we kill a bad one, another seems to come out."[107] Savings to business and government is estimated to be anywhere from $20 million to $50 million.[108]

What do the regulators at the city's Department of Metropolitan Development think about the RSC? "They loathe us," says Rose. Mayor Goldsmith thinks the competition between the two agencies can be healthy. "It keeps them both on their toes," says the mayor.[109]

Taxi Driver

The RSC's greatest triumph was deregulating the Indianapolis taxicab industry. Virtually every city has laws that regulate every aspect of the taxi service, including the number of cabs allowed in the city and the price for fares. These laws benefit established taxicab owners by stifling competition.

Until recently, Indianapolis was no exception. The twelfth largest city in America, Indianapolis allowed only 392 taxi licenses. Cabs were forbidden to cruise the streets for customers; it was illegal to hail a cab in the city. Why? "The regulations were written by the dominant cab provider," says Rose. Yellow Cab had "captured" the regulatory process and was using it to its advantage.

Mayor Goldsmith once called a cab from his house for a ride to the airport. After three follow-up calls, the cab finally arrived 90 minutes later. One imagines Goldsmith at the airport telling his driver in a Schwarzenegger voice, "I'll be back."

Goldsmith's proposal to eliminate most government entry and price restrictions on taxicabs encountered significant opposition from Dick Hunt, the owner of Yellow Cab. Hunt just happened to be a big donor to the local Republican party, which may explain how he had captured the regulatory process in the first place. Hunt went ballistic at Goldsmith's deregulation proposal. "It's just a bunch of liberals that want to do it," he groused. "They always say, 'Why can't you hail a cab?' I say where? Nobody's on the streets. Nobody's going to come out of those holes in the ground."[110]

James Chapman disagrees. A slender, older African-American, Chapman has been driving a yellow cab for Hunt since 1968. After years of driving someone else's cab, Chapman wanted the right to drive his own. Says Chapman,

> *I have lived in Indianapolis all my life. I have driven a taxi in the city for the last 26 years and have given its citizens my best years of service. I am getting on in years and have never asked for much. So why can't I make a go of it? The worst thing that can happen is that I will fail. And really, all I am asking from the City-County Council is the right to succeed or fail based on me—my decisions, my service, my prices and my hard work.[111]*

> *The owners of the taxi monopoly are scared of people giving*

service. I'm going to help senior citizen ladies in and out of the grocery store, help 'em with their bags. I'm not worried about Dick Hunt and Yellow Cab. If I give service, those people will call me back.[112]

In May 1994, almost all taxicab regulations were eliminated in the city of Indianapolis. By a vote of 21 to 7, the city council approved the taxi deregulation ordinance. (Six of the seven nay votes came from Republicans.) As of January 1995, the number of taxi companies in the city had nearly doubled, from 28 to 52, and all of the new companies are minority, or women-owned.[113] Fares have dropped nearly 7 percent and waiting times have fallen dramatically.[114] Lastly, an industry that was legendary for its poor service and customer complaints has not had a single customer complaint registered with the city since the ordinance took effect.

If you have a driver's license, a $100,000 insurance policy, a mug shot, and a $102 license fee, you, too, can go into the cab business in Indianapolis. Or you can just hail James Chapman for a ride. He's left Yellow Cab, and he's now leasing a cab from one of Indy's new taxi companies.

CONCLUSION

In many cases, the role of government in fostering a healthy economy has been misunderstood. When it comes to the economy, government should neither steer nor row. Economic prosperity depends on governments creating tax, legal, and regulatory environments that allow the market to work.

The unseen is often more important than the seen. Instead of flashy public-works projects, city governments can quietly improve the economy by easing the permitting process. Instead of hoping for thousands of jobs by offering special breaks to lure companies, states can quietly foster prosperity by lowering taxes. Instead of make-work government jobs, government can improve the legal system. Instead of jobs training programs, government can foster entrepreneurship by eliminating the regulatory barriers that prevent new business from competing. Just as important as the economic benefits of such reforms are the liberating effects on the human spirit.

CHAPTER 10

A COMMUNITY OF LEARNING

Never allow your schooling to interfere with your educa-tion.

Mark Twain[1]

W hen Americans talk about fixing public education, they talk about fixing the public schools. This is a mistake. We need to separate the concept of public *education* from that of public *schools.* Conjoined by long habit of association, these are actually two very different concepts. They need to be uncoupled, for equating public education with government-run schools has unduly limited our thinking.

What makes public education public? This deceptively sim-ple question strikes at the heart of the purpose of public educa-tion. Is the purpose of public education to impose a uniform educational orthodoxy through government-run schools? Or is the purpose of public education to make sure that all children have access to the sort of education their families desire? If the latter, then public funds should be provided not to control schools, but to empower students and their families. Says Terry Moe, co-author of the landmark *Politics, Markets, and Ameri-ca's Schools*:

Our goal should be to provide kids with the best possible education.... If they happen to get it in the private sector, then those private schools are providing a public service. We need to expand our notion of what public education is, to think beyond the current public schools and include all types

*of schools that could be providing a quality education to all
our kids.*[2]

What matters is that children learn; public schools are a
means, not an end. Before looking at the means of providing
education, it makes sense to examine the end. What should
schools teach?

ONE SYSTEM, MANY VALUES

*It is best that we should not all think alike; it is difference of
opinion that makes horse-races.*

Mark Twain

Ask 27 parents what constitutes a good education and you will
get 27 different answers. While there will likely be some areas
of general agreement, Americans don't all think alike. Among
these 27 parents there might be conservatives and liberals,
homosexuals and homophobes, believers and atheists,
technophiles and poets, hunters and animal-rights activists.
This diversity of thought and action is one of our nation's greatest qualities. But if you take the children of these 27 parents
and put them in the same classroom, all hell breaks loose.

If all parents wanted the same thing for their children, a
politically controlled education system might work just fine.
But it simply isn't so. "We" control the schools but "we" don't
agree on what they ought to be teaching. In a public school
classroom, every issue—from what gets taught in history class
to what gets served in the lunchroom—becomes a matter of
contention.

If you thought the debate over teaching evolution was settled with the Scopes trial, think again. Despite Clarence Dar-
row's skillful arguments, some parents believe that God played
a role in the creation of the universe and want their children

taught likewise.[3] In 1993, the Vista school board in San Diego County, home to many devout Christians, passed a resolution promoting discussion of creationist explanations for human life. On the night of the telecast of the final episode of "Cheers," some 500 parents packed a meeting hall to wrangle over the issue. These parents held a passion-filled debate over how life began, what role God may have played in the process, and what to teach the children. No consensus was reached.

Consensus will never be reached because *there is no consensus*. The "culture wars" that plague government-run schools can never be resolved. Parents have fundamentally different views on sex education, multiculturalism, prayer, Afrocentrism, animal rights, environmentalism, gender roles, homosexuality, the origin of the species—the list is infinite.

With so much disagreement over what makes for a "good" education, who decides what gets taught?

LOCAL SCHOOLS, CENTRALIZED CONTROL

Centralization of decision making has been the most important educational trend of America's public schools, especially in the 20th century.

In colonial times and the early days of the republic, families played a central role in education. Well into the 1800s, America's "common schools" were mostly financed by parents' fees.[4] Into the mid-20th century, American parents were highly involved in the operation of public schools. Public schools were run as a local, almost intimate affair; as late as 1948, half of all public elementary schools were one-room schoolhouses.[5] Parents had a strong voice in how their children's school was run.

This is no longer true. Today, government schools are much more centrally controlled than ever before. The basic political unit of American education is the local school district. Between 1940 and 1970, the number of school districts dropped from 117,000 to 18,000; by 1990, that number was down to 15,000.[6]

Districts are larger, schools are larger, and parents are more often passive observers than active participants in the decision-making process.

School boards do offer parents a measure of influence, but only in limited quantities. First, school boards are severely constrained by rules and regulations. Second, winning a seat on a school board is far beyond the reach of most parents. Consider: there are some 640,000 students in the Los Angeles Unified School District. To win one of the seven seats on the school board requires a professional political campaign reaching millions of voters. A parent who runs will have to campaign against people such as Jeff Horton, who one year collected $55,000 in campaign contributions from the teachers union.[7] Most parents are thus squeezed out of the school governing process.

School districts have also become increasingly dependent on state and federal sources for their revenue. In 1920, 83 percent of public school funding came from local sources; in 1980, only 43 percent did.[8] The shift away from local funding has been accompanied by a decrease in local control.

The centralization trend reached its logical conclusion in 1994 with the adoption of Goals 2000, the federal government's objectives for America's public schools. Unbeknownst to most parents, the National Educational Goals Panel is deciding at the federal level what the neighborhood school should be teaching. How does something become a goal? "Fierce lobbying by art teachers and support from the National Endowment for the Arts and the Kennedy Center were responsible for adding arts to the national goals as the seventh core area," reports *State Legislatures* magazine.[9]

The National Educational Goals Panel clings tenaciously to the myth that all Americans share a common vision of what constitutes a good education. According to the panel, "standards must be developed through a consensus building process." The panel states that the standards it develops should "not address nonacademic areas such as student values, beliefs, attitudes and behavior."[10] Good grief. Of course education will shape the values, beliefs, attitudes, and behavior of pupils. Otherwise why bother? The question is not whether government schools will teach values, but whose values will get taught.

TEXTBOOK FOLLIES

If you are an eighth-grade math teacher in Houston, Texas, guess who decides what textbook you'll use in your class next year?

You, the teacher, won't get to decide. Your principal won't decide. The district superintendent won't decide. And the local school board won't decide. If you teach in Texas or 20 other states, textbook decisions will be made for you at the state level by central boards. (Local decision makers are usually allowed to select from a short list of "state-approved" textbooks.)

Full of good intentions, the Texas state constitution requires that the state Board of Education provide "free text books for the use of children attending the public free schools of this state . . ."[11]

The "free text books" of Texas are very costly. Because districts don't pay for their own books, textbook publishers eschew price competition, focusing instead on being a winner in the all-important state-level selection process. This textbook design process can take several years while committee members offer input to create a "dream text" with little consideration of cost. According to a spokesman for the Association of American Publishers, "A publisher will sometimes have to spend over $1 million before they sell a single copy of a new textbook," adding that "the more complex the regulations and the selection process, the higher the cost of doing business."[12] This higher cost is passed on to taxpayers.

The Texas State Auditor's Office estimates that providing incentives for individual districts to consider costs could save $10 million annually. District textbook administrators also exercise poor inventory control: an audit of 35 of the 1,050 school districts in Texas found that over $500,000 in "free" textbooks were missing.[13] As Thomas Paine noted, "What we obtain too cheap, we esteem too lightly."[14]

Centralized decision making also tends to lead to a uniformity of pedagogical approaches. This centralized decision-making process doesn't eliminate the "textbook wars" that rage over content. It does mean, however, that these battles are waged at the state level, out of the reach of most parents. Only well-organized political factions can influence what goes into the ninth-grade history texts that your child will read.

Though textbook spending makes up only a small fraction of overall school spending, it illustrates the costs of centralized control—both the monetary costs and the costs in terms of democracy, as parents are robbed of a voice in how their children are educated.

We need to allow families to pursue their own vision of educational excellence, free from the stifling constraints of centralized control. When parents with different goals are thrown together by force, bitter discord ensues. When people come together by choice to pursue a common purpose, they create a community.

A COMMUNITY OF LEARNING:
L.A.'S MARCUS GARVEY SCHOOL

We called the Marcus Garvey School and asked to speak with Dr. Anyim Palmer, the founder and principal of the school.

"Does he owe you any money?" we were asked.

"Uh, no," we replied.

"Then you got him," we were told. Not only is Anyim Palmer the driving force behind the Marcus Garvey School, he also answers the phones. This was our first clue that the Marcus Garvey School is not your typical school.

The brightly painted green and red building that houses the

Marcus Garvey School stands in stark contrast to its depressed surroundings in South Central Los Angeles, an oasis of pride amidst a desert of despair. Across the street from auto repair shops and abandoned lots, bright green letters proclaim the Marcus Garvey School the "acclaimed number one private school in the nation." Surveying the surroundings, we are skeptical.

We visit a classroom. Amidst a sea of waving hands Jamal is chosen to spell words such as "humidity" and "exhaust." We call out three-digit numbers for the children to add and subtract, which the students handle readily. Then Derek reads for us from his history book: "Chapter One: Africa, The Beginning of Civilization. Africa has a land area of 12 million square miles. Africa is the second largest continent. Africa is in the tropics . . ." He reads without an error. Then Brandon takes over the reading chores: "Africa is the birthplace of humanity. The first man was from Ethiopia." Flawless.

We are in a *kindergarten* class. In *November.* "If you come back in the spring they'd be miles ahead of this," says Dr. Palmer.

Taking a tour of the Marcus Garvey School redefines the limits of the possible. At the Marcus Garvey preschool, three-year-olds are taught to name all 50 states and recite the alphabet in both English and Swahili. By the second grade, the children are reading capably from a text used at Cal State Los Angeles. (Eight-year-old Amber correctly spells "deinstitution-alization," and knows what it means.) The fourth graders are solving algebra problems. Sixth graders begin calculus.

Virtually all of the students and teachers are African-American. About one-fourth of the 400 students come from families that receive public assistance. The Marcus Garvey School costs only about $3,600 a year and receives no public funds. How do they do it? *Their way.*

None of the teachers has teaching credentials. ("We make it a practice not to hire teachers who are quote 'certified'," says Palmer.) The school doesn't teach art, or music, or physical education. ("That's the way we want it," says Palmer.) The school focuses on African heritage and African-American heroes. ("That's how we motivate our students," says Palmer.) Naturally, the Marcus Garvey School chooses its own textbooks. ("We use whatever works," says Palmer.)

Some people might disagree with the Afrocentric approach of the Marcus Garvey School. Others might object to the rigid discipline. But parents love it—if they didn't, their children wouldn't be there. Many families make significant sacrifices to come up with the tuition. One parent puts in a 100-mile daily round-trip so his youngster can attend the Marcus Garvey School.

The Marcus Garvey School successfully teaches those who are generally written off as uneducable. It is not money, but pride and love that fuels the learning. Anyim Palmer's office is cramped, the furniture falling apart. Teachers at Marcus Garvey earn less than half the money of their public school counterparts. But Palmer and his staff are proud of what they've accomplished. The children all know "Brother Anyim" (as Palmer is called), and he knows them.

Anyim Palmer founded the Marcus Garvey School in 1975 after 16 years in public education. Palmer has nothing but scorn for what government-run schools do to the African-American community. "I don't see any way that the current educational system can be saved or changed to help our children," says Palmer.[15] We ask Dr. Palmer what he thinks of a system that would give parents a choice of where to send their children. He smiles. "The first day this community would be allowed choice, we'd have 10,000 students apply here," says Dr. Palmer. "Do you understand now why the public schools resist it?"[16]

PUBLIC SCHOOLS: FAILING OUR CHILDREN

The public school system is characterized by two important features. First, it is politically controlled. Second, it is a virtual monopoly. Like most politically controlled monopolies, government-run schools tend to produce low-quality, high-cost outputs.

The woeful academic performance of many public schools has been amply documented elsewhere, and defenders of the current system are being buried under a blizzard of bad news. In 1983, the report "A Nation at Risk" likened public education to a plot by a hostile foreign nation to destroy America. Since government schools were doing such a poor job, they were given more money, and inflation-adjusted per-pupil spending skyrocketed by more than one-third between 1983 and 1993.[17] But the bad news blizzard rages on.

In a 1992 study, one-third of all public school eighth graders failed to demonstrate a basic level of reading proficiency, contrasted to just 16 percent of parochial school eighth graders.[18] The U.S. Department of Education in 1993 reported that "about 47 percent of the U.S. adult population demonstrate low levels of literacy."[19] Even our best students lag behind those in other countries. Comparing U.S. high school seniors taking Advanced Placement courses, the U.S. Department of Education declared in 1993 that America's "top-performing students are undistinguished at best and poor at worst," scoring last out of 13 nations in biology and algebra, and next to last in geometry and calculus.[20]

WHAT'S NOT THE PROBLEM: MONEY

Early in 1994, readers of the *New York Times* were treated to two delightful front-page stories on education. One told how a school in New York City was teaching classes in a bathroom.[21] The other front-page story described how New York City spent $185,000 in an *unsuccessful* effort to fire a teacher who was in prison for dealing cocaine.[22] The kids in New York City were being taught in bathrooms not because of a lack of money, but because available funds were being flushed down a dysfunctional system.

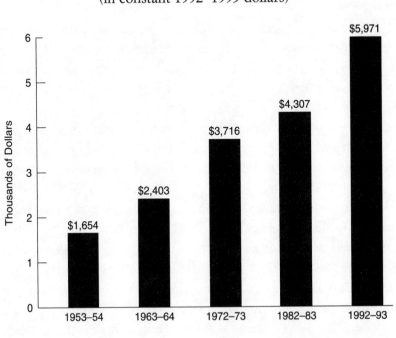

K–12 PUBLIC EDUCATION SPENDING PER PUPIL
(in constant 1992–1993 dollars)

Source: *Digest of Education Statistics*, 1993; U.S. Department of Education.

Despite a widely held perception to the contrary, public schools in America are better funded than at any time in history (see chart).[23] But if you pour water into a broken jar, you will never fill it, no matter how much water you pour in. Likewise, it doesn't matter how much money you pour into a dysfunctional school system.

In fact, many of the nation's worst schools have some of the highest per-pupil expenditures. In the 1990–91 school year, urban districts such as Boston, New York, and Pittsburgh all spent over $7,000 in current per-pupil expenditures (a figure that ignores capital costs).[24] Washington, D.C., ranks fifth in per-pupil spending yet ranks forty-ninth in SAT scores and fiftieth in graduation rates. In contrast, Utah spends less per pupil than any other state yet ranks fourth in SAT scores and fourteenth in graduation rates.[25] Money alone can't buy performance.

Kansas City is a case in point. A 1986 court order directed the district to remedy racial discrimination by spending more money—a lot more. Between 1986 and 1993, the program poured an extra $1.3 *billion* into a district of roughly 36,000 students. Kansas City's $32 million Central High School, for instance, now features a "computers unlimited" program with two computers for every three students, a $5 million swimming pool, a six-lane indoor track, a weight-training room, and fencing courses taught by the former head coach of the Soviet Olympic fencing team. Another school has a working farm area. The district even has a $900,000 annual budget to promote itself on local television.[26]

Though everything's up to date in Kansas City, the court-ordered spending spree has not translated into significant gains in either academic achievement or racial integration. The dropout rate hovers around 60 percent,[27] and even the school superintendent admits test scores at the middle and high school levels haven't shown "the progress that you would expect with the expenditures that have been made."[28]

Kansas City's lavish magnet schools do attract some white suburban students (the district sometimes pays the taxi fare), but minority enrollment is near its all-time high.[29] When the spending spree began in the mid-'80s, black enrollment was about 69 percent; ten years later, black enrollment was about 70 percent.[30]

The federal courts have exercised unprecedented control in providing Kansas City school officials with unlimited funding. In addition to the spending mandates, the court ordered the district to implement a full-day kindergarten and a summer school program, *doubled* local property taxes,[31] and, most remarkably, ordered a pay raise for every employee of the district, including janitors and cafeteria workers.[32] Observed

Supreme Court Justice Sandra Day O'Connor, "It seemed like it was just a convenient way for the school district and the labor union to get what they wanted without having to go through collective bargaining."[33]

The courts have also set up a classic set of perverse incentives for district officials. The district will continue to get extra money *unless* test scores improve.[34] Said Supreme Court Justice Anthony Kennedy, "I just don't see an end to this."[35]

NOT THE PROBLEM, PART II: PEOPLE

In the first place God made idiots. This was for practice. Then he made school boards.

Mark Twain[36]

When something isn't working, the first reaction is to find someone to blame. But what if people aren't the problem? After all, not many teachers head to their classroom each day looking to do a poor job. Nor do school administrators go to their offices thinking, "How can I mess things up today?"

The problem isn't people, it's the system. Whenever large numbers of people exhibit behavior that leads to undesirable outcomes, the problem is almost certainly systemic. School boards make idiotic decisions not because school board members are idiots, but because the process is flawed. Management expert Peter Senge describes it this way:

We must look beyond individual mistakes or bad luck to understand important problems. We must look beyond personalities and events. We must look into the underlying structures which shape individual actions and create the conditions where types of events become likely.[37]

In short, the system creates its own behavior.

The View from Beneath the Bureaucracy

Joann Wysocki is a first-grade teacher in the Los Angeles Unified School District (LAUSD). Since she began teaching in 1957, Ms. Wysocki has become an expert on bureaucracy.

Wysocki teaches from the bottom of an inverted pyramid. Above Wysocki is a principal, a district superintendent, a local school board, a state school board, the California Department of Education, and the U.S. Department of Education. Government-run schools mean bureaucratic schools. In the Los Angeles district where Wysocki teaches, over 1,800 employees earn over $70,000 a year. The district employs 16 central administrators who share the title of "temporary advisor," each of whom earns over $90,000 a year.[38] What does a first-grade teacher in the classroom think of all this expensive "assistance"?

"The district administration should be taken out and disposed of," says Ms. Wysocki. "The schools would do a lot better without them."[39] Wysocki sees administrators getting paid handsomely while her class goes without basic supplies such as paper and pencils, creating chaos in the classroom. Though the first grade ordered basic reading textbooks from the district in April, the books still hadn't arrived by October. Teachers were sharing or doing without. The way Wysocki tells it, she has an easier time dealing with the seven-year-olds in her class than with the district administration.

How about the federal Department of Education, we ask? Does it provide any assistance in your work?

"No, I don't think so," she replies. "And I don't think we get anything from the state, either. All they do is shove a lot of paper down on us." If Wysocki sounds bitter, it is because for 30-odd years she has fought against an organization that is supposed to help her. Her criticisms echo those heard again and again from public school teachers. Teachers wage a continuous battle against the bureaucracy. "You learn quickly how to nag and nag," says Wysocki, laughing. "I've become a good nagger. Really I'm a nice person. I was never like this when I started out."

When Wysocki talks about her students, her voice comes alive. But when she talks about the bureaucracy, her voice grows weary. The battles are so petty, so frustrating.

"There is a gate between our day-care center and the school, and it was locked. We asked the janitor to unlock it, and do you know what he said? He said, 'It isn't in my job description.'" She shakes her head and laughs. "I have to *negotiate* with my janitor to get him to clean the chalk tray once a week. They don't answer to the principals, either. My principal has fought quite a few battles with the janitors."

Wysocki claims that the views of classroom teachers are routinely ignored. Several years ago, California decided to go with the whole-language method of reading instruction rather than the traditional phonics. Like many educators, Wysocki dislikes the whole-language method, which she claims doesn't help her first graders learn to read. But because the textbook decision was made in Sacramento, Wysocki must make do with whole language. Teachers concerns were ignored by the central decision makers. "I think we've gone overboard by abandoning phonics. I think they made a mistake," says Wysocki.

A lot of students can suffer because of one bad decision. "The publishers are not dummies. They look at what the state says shall be the accepted way to teach, the accepted methods, the latest philosophy that's going to save us, and they cater their textbooks to it. They're just interested in selling textbooks," says Wysocki.

Wysocki claims she generally likes her work, but finds herself "tired" of fighting the system. "If we are supposed to be professionals, give us some credit," she pleads.

A NEW VISION OF PUBLIC EDUCATION

Good people, bad system. Unfortunately, it is much easier to understand individual failings than to fathom the complex interrelationships that cause large numbers of people, each individually striving to do a good job, to produce undesirable outcomes. Rather than affixing the blame, we should be fixing the system.

Research on effective schools has identified the characteristics associated with successful schools.[40] The Marcus Garvey School illustrates these key elements: a strong sense of mission; the freedom of the school's leaders to pursue that mission; a shared set of values; a high level of parental involvement; and a high level of cooperation among faculty and staff. In short, the Marcus Garvey School is a community of learning; it "feels" more like a family than a bureaucracy.

To be effective, schools need the freedom to be oddballs, to be special, to do things differently. An autonomous school can be as creative, as unique, and as energetic as its students. Those who lead such schools answer to parents first and foremost; they are not micromanaged from above.

Public schools are political institutions, so it makes sense to reflect back on the principles we outlined in earlier chapters for improving government operations: focusing on core functions, embracing competition, and devolving power to individuals and communities. The current public education system runs contrary to all these principles. Instead of focusing on core academic subjects, just 41 percent of the school day in the average public school is spent on academic subjects.[41] Instead of encouraging competition, public schools cling tenaciously to their monopoly status. Instead of devolving power down to parents, government-run schools centralize decision-making power.

In California, schools are governed by an education code that is 7,523 pages long and stands several feet high. This is absurd, but the education code is a symptom of the problem, not the cause. Bureaucracy is the natural consequence of political control. As author Terry Moe puts it:

The bureaucracy is there for powerful political reasons. Our political system naturally creates bureaucracy in response to the demands placed on politicians. It wouldn't matter if you cut the education code in half. Given the reality of politics, it would just grow back.

Eliminating bureaucracy is only half the problem. The other half is putting power in the hands of parents and letting them choose. I don't think you can have significant widespread improvement without choice.[42]

The problem is not the rules; the problem is the system that creates the rules. Mayor Bret Schundler of Jersey City agrees: "A reform is when you change *what* you are doing. A revolution is when you change *who* has the power to do things."[43] The revolution may be on the way.

Butting Heads with the Status Quo, Part I: Jersey City

Jersey City Mayor Bret Schundler wants to let parents choose where their children will go to school. "You can't ever effect a revolution if you leave power in the hands of politicians," says Schundler.[44]

Schundler is applying a full-court press on the New Jersey legislature for a citywide school choice program. It would be quite an accomplishment, but Schundler has already surprised a lot of folks. Schundler's election in November 1993 is one of the most remarkable events in modern big-city electoral history. Running in a highly Democratic, low-income city, Schundler ran on a platform of tax cuts, privatization, community policing, and, most importantly, school choice.

When I campaigned on a platform of school choice, it wasn't a sophisticated issue. . . . In one of our high schools, only 28 percent of the students can read and write. So I went to the housing project close to that school and said, "Listen, we're spending $9,200 per child. If I let you choose the school you

want for your child and I pay the bill, public or private, up to
$9,200, don't you think you would be able to get a great edu-
cation for your child?"[45]

Few big-city mayors push for such fundamental change, in
part because they fear political fallout from teachers' unions. In
contrast, the deeply religious Schundler has made a crusade
out of bringing school choice to Jersey City. The teachers
unions are not at all happy about Schundler's plans, but char-
acteristically the mayor—with the missionary's sense of eternal
optimism—seems not the least bit worried. "I'm not taking on
the unions," says Schundler. "I'm disregarding them."

In his inaugural address, Schundler laid it on the line:

> *The National Education Association is committed to fighting*
> *my proposal for a school voucher experiment in Jersey City. It*
> *is committed to fighting me, not because it fears that this small*
> *experiment with vouchers will fail. It is committed to fighting*
> *me because it fears this experiment will succeed. It fears that it*
> *will lose the near dictatorial control that its political power*
> *gives it over the current system, once schools become account-*
> *able to parents instead of being accountable to politicians.*[46]

Despite the support of Governor Whitman, Schundler's
campaign to give his constituents choice faces an uphill political battle against established interests. For choice to succeed,
Schundler says parents will have to fight to control their children's education. "Power is always taken, never given," says the
former sociology major.[47]

BUTTING HEADS WITH THE STATUS QUO, PART II: MILWAUKEE

Milwaukee Mayor John Norquist is frustrated with Milwaukee's public schools. He's ticked off because taxpayers, who
pay about $6,700 per student, aren't getting their money's

worth. Most of all, he's upset that kids in Milwaukee aren't getting a good education. In other words, Mayor Norquist is like a lot of parents.

"If parents had any control over where their dollars went to pay for education, they wouldn't buy this," says the mayor, referring to a 1994 reorganization plan by the State Department of Public Instruction (DPI). "They're just shuffling the deck chairs around on a sinking ship, and the DPI is a ship that oughta sink."[48]

John Norquist offers an alternative: school choice. Though school choice programs are common overseas, Milwaukee is one of the only places in the United States where parents of regular education students can use public funds to send their children to a private school.[49] The Milwaukee Parental Choice Program (MPCP) program was championed by Polly Williams, an African-American legislator. Williams, a Democrat and former welfare recipient, represents one of Milwaukee's poorest neighborhoods, and the program is limited to low-income families. As of the 1994–1995 school year, the MPCP enabled 830 children to attend 12 private schools at public expense.[50]

What do parents think of choice? They like it. According to an evaluation conducted at the University of Wisconsin: "[Parental] attitudes toward choice schools and the education of their children were much more positive than their evaluations of their prior public schools."[51]

Norquist wants to see the program expanded. He wants to allow religious schools, currently excluded, to participate in the program.[52] Norquist thinks that parents who want their children's education to include a moral or religious component should get it. "There are a lot greater threats to our children than religion," says Norquist.[53] When people argue that tougher standards can turn the schools around, Norquist scoffs. "The standard that's really missing in the system is parents, and what they think."

After years of battling the state's education establishment and legislators in his own party, Norquist may get his wish in

1995. The election of November 1994 gave Republicans control of both houses of Wisconsin's legislature. Assembly Republicans named Democrat Polly Williams chairman of the Assembly's Urban Education Committee in 1995 and they, along with Governor Thompson, are pushing to expand the Milwaukee Parental Choice Program. In January of 1995, Thompson included funding for choice at religious schools in his budget, meaning the issue will at least be debated.

THE DEMOGRAPHICS OF SCHOOL CHOICE

In the past, school choice has often been seen as a white, Republican issue. That's changing fast, in part because of the breakdown in education in poor inner-city areas, which disproportionately serve minorities.

The politically run public school system ill serves those on the political margins. Inner-city residents, often poor, often minority, attend the worst schools in the nation. In 1988, author Jonathan Kozol returned to teach in the inner city after a 20-year hiatus. In his book *Savage Inequalities*, Kozol writes of the "remarkable degree of racial segregation that persisted almost everywhere." Kozol continues:

> *I knew that segregation was still common in the public schools, but I did not know how much it had intensified. . . . Looking around some of these inner-city schools, where filth and disrepair were worse than anything I'd seen in 1964, I often wondered why we would agree to let our children go to school in places where no politician, school board president, or business CEO would dream of working.*[54]

Defenders of government-run schools describe the current system as a melting pot. *Reinventing Government* authors Osborne and Gaebler, for example, argue that public schools "bring children from all walks of life together."[55] Senator Barbara Boxer writes: "A great public school system is the heart of

America. It has always been the great equalizer—one way that each of us could get our opportunity to shine."[56]

The reality is starkly different. America's public schools have historically been separate and unequal, ill serving the marginal members of society. This continues today. University of Chicago sociologist James S. Coleman and his colleagues have found that "blacks and whites are substantially less segregated in the private sector than in the public sector."[57] Indeed, few aspects of American life are as segregated as our public schools. As Jonathan Kozol puts it, "Unless we have the wealth to pay for private education, we are compelled by law to go to public school—and to the public school in our district. Thus the state, by requiring attendance but refusing to require equity, effectively requires inequality."[58]

Not surprisingly, a 1992 survey in Los Angeles found the strongest support for school choice among poor and minority parents.[59] If you were trying to design a system that would rob the poor of hope, you couldn't do much better than the racially and economically segregated system we have today. Rather than a way out of the ghetto, public schools help trap the underclass in a cycle of poverty.

PRIVATE CHOICE PROGRAMS: LEADING BY EXAMPLE

Although almost every other democracy has some mechanism of state funding for private schools (even Poland and Russia now have school choice), the idea of letting parents choose their children's school scares Americans. Voters soundly rejected school choice referenda in three states in the 1990s.[60]

But school choice is being given some demonstration projects, thanks to the efforts of business philanthropists. In August 1991, Pat Rooney, the white-haired CEO of the Golden Rule Insurance Company in Indianapolis, took matters into his own hands. Wanting to help the disadvantaged children in Indianapolis and demonstrate the effectiveness of school choice, Rooney started the CHOICE Charitable Trust. Funded entirely by private donations, the program gives low-income parents half the tuition at the private school of their choice, up to a maximum of $800 per child per year.

The response has been overwhelming. Within three days of announcing the program, 621 families requested applications. By the 1993–1994 school year, over 1,000 low-income families were receiving scholarships. Moreover, philanthropists in Milwaukee, San Antonio, and nine other cities had started similar programs.

"This is the most significant gift we ever could have received in our lifetime," says Joy Smith, a mother of three who receives tuition assistance from Atlanta's Children Education Foundation (CEF) to send her children to a parochial school. "Your program is their lifeline."[61]

Even with help from CEF, Joy Smith and her family struggle to meet their share of the tuition payment. For the Smiths, having their children taught in a Catholic setting is important. In order to earn a tuition reduction, Joy works at the school as a teacher's aide, her oldest boy Billy works in the school cafeteria, and one Saturday a month the family cleans the parish church. Recently, the Smiths gave up health insurance. "My family thinks I'm crazy to be living this way, without medical insurance. They say we'd be so much better off financially if we put our children in public school. But this is our choice."[62]

A study of Milwaukee's two choice programs, the public MPCP and the private PAVE program, found that students performed better the longer they had been in private school.[63] The most important indication of success, however, is that parents are willing to make financial sacrifices to meet their share of tuition costs. One-quarter of the families in the Indianapolis CHOICE program earned less than $10,000 per year, and three-quarters earned less than $20,000.[64] As one parent put it, these private choice programs have "dispelled the myth that poor parents don't care about their children's education."[65]

That includes parents such as Maria and Antonio Chavez of San Antonio, who simply weren't satisfied with the public schools. "Vouchers were the only way out for us," says Maria. "If it hadn't been for the voucher, we'd have had to have taken them out and put them in the public schools."

Maria and Antonio struggle to earn their share of the tuition, but are willing to make the sacrifice so that their children might have a better life. "Take a look around and see where the better education is happening," says Antonio. "I didn't get a good enough education in the public school system for me to keep up with college. I got lost. I don't want that to happen to my kids."[66]

The more we give parents a chance and let them go shopping, the more options arise for those who otherwise are trapped in government-run schools. According to one study, the MPCP "has allowed several [private schools] to survive, several to expand, and contributed to the building of a new school which opened in 1993."[67]

Unfortunately, there simply isn't enough philanthropic money to give all families school choice. But imagine what could happen if some of the tax money currently being misspent in the public system were given to parents?

UNIONS AND COMPETITION

The biggest change needed to improve education is not choice, or charter schools, it's taking some of the autocratic power away from the teachers unions in our society. . . . I want to make clear this is not teacher bashing, because there are outstanding teachers who are being shackled and not given the opportunity to teach. They're being dictated to by mandates handed down by their union.

Wisconsin Governor Tommy Thompson[68]

Education unions are an enormous political force. The two largest, the National Education Association and the American Federation of Teachers, have a combined membership of roughly 2.9 million members, combined national budgets of over $230 million, and sent more than one of every ten delegates to the Democratic National Convention that nominated Bill Clinton.[69]

Teachers unions have used their considerable influence to oppose merit pay, the elimination of tenure, and school choice. Teachers unions focus on issues central to any labor union: wages, benefits, and job security.

In the early 1980s there were two American institutions that were performing quite poorly: the public schools and the automobile industry. Both are highly unionized. Today, the public schools are much the same. The American automobile industry, however, has transformed itself to better serve its customers. Why? Competition. Competition in the automobile market improved things not only for those consumers who bought foreign cars, but also for consumers of American cars.

Already, the threat of competition is fostering positive change in the way public unions behave. Consider the following excerpts from a newsletter put out by the Milwaukee Teachers' Education Association to its members:

> *If we don't take aggressive steps to support our membership in developing substantial school improvements now, the State Legislature will give . . . the privatization proponents everything they want. . . . If the MTEA does not become a catalyst for educational reform—for our own members and in the eyes of the community—we simply will not survive.*[70]

The threat of competition is prompting the teachers unions to be more flexible, and the children in Milwaukee's public schools will benefit. It is unrealistic, however, to expect unions to adopt this attitude without competition. As Mayor Schundler notes, "Powerful interest groups know a good thing when they have it."

FUTURE SCHOOL

Is choice a panacea? No. It's one of many things that you need to do. You also need to allow for and encourage charter schools, contracting out with the private sector, and to set up an opportunity to close down failing schools. Equally as important, you need to allow people to teach who are not certified by the Department of Education.

Wisconsin Governor Tommy Thompson[71]

No one knows exactly what public education would look like under a system of parental choice; markets are delightfully unpredictable. When computers were first developed at IBM, president T. J. Watson estimated the total worldwide market to be about five companies. With thousands of education entrepreneurs applying their ingenuity to the task, we believe the possibilities are limitless. We need to stop thinking that red brick buildings run by the government are the only places where children can learn.

We see hints of future possibilities in current reforms. For example, who will run schools in the future? In certain cases, private companies, colleges, and consulting firms are now managing public schools. The superintendent of the Minneapolis Public Schools is a consulting firm. In Baltimore, Hartford, and Dade County, Florida, public schools are also managed by a private company.

Charter school legislation, passed in 11 states by early 1995, offers possibilities as well. Rather than government officials, these schools are managed by parents, teacher groups, private companies, or nonprofits. In California, public charter schools use a network to link home-schooling families with teachers via computer. Interactive video instruction and computer-based curricula could revolutionize instruction through "distance learning."

In March 1994, Governor Weld announced that Massachusetts will allow 13 organizations to design and operate 15 charter schools, public schools that report directly to the state and
avoid much of the regulation that constrains other public
schools. "We have to break out of this attitude of telling parents 'You have to come to us'," says Weld.[72] These charter
schools will be competing with existing government-run
schools, attempting to attract students—and the funding that
goes with them.[73]

The Massachusetts charter school program shows the possibility of true educational diversity. Among the 14 schools
granted final charters for the 1995–1996 school year, several are
targeted for at-risk youth, including one granted to Youth-
Build, the program we described in Chapter 3; one is to be run
in conjunction with a museum and art officials; one embraces
the Reggio Emilia interdisciplinary, thematic approach to education; one doesn't start classes until noon; one will focus on
basic skills; one is open 210 days per year; one is structured for
homeless youth and wards of the state; and one will have
mixed-age grouping. None of these schools will have students
assigned to it—each will have to attract students.[74]

Giving parents more options would likely encourage more
schools to cater to the different needs of parents, especially
working parents. Already, a limited number of public schools
have been established at business work sites. Known as satellite
schools, such schools currently operate at an airport, a
Hewlett-Packard plant, a hospital, and a nuclear power plant.[75]

Other schools might be centered around the different needs
of students. The Honeywell School, a public–private partnership school in Minnesota, specializes in educating teenage
mothers in both academics and child care. Other schools might
cater to youthful offenders and other at-risk students. The Illi-
nois-based Ombudsman Educational Services, a private for-
profit company, contracts with public schools to educate at-risk
students in six states. Ombusdsman boasts an 85 percent reten-

tion rate and costs about half what public schools typically spend on these hard-to-educate youths.

Our nation's colleges offer an interesting model of educational diversity. There are liberal arts colleges and technical colleges, religious schools and secular schools. Similarly, we may see a greater variety of pedagogical approaches on the K–12 level, such as Waldorf or Montessori schools. Schools would be shaped by the desires of parents and teachers, who would work together with a shared vision. In the future, the occupation of "teacher" may look much different than it does now. Teachers are likely to have greater autonomy. We may come to think of teachers as skilled professionals, like lawyers or doctors, who offer their services to a variety of clients. We see the beginning of this transformation even today.

Elevating the Professional Status of Teachers

Every major company is going through restructuring and so is education. Either you're going to be a part of it, and make it happen, or you're going to be pulled along.
    Ellen Larkin Sternig, director of a Sylvan Learning Center[76]

Recall the frustration Los Angeles first-grade teacher Joann Wysocki experienced dealing with the public school bureaucracy. Wysocki loves to teach but loathes the politics and interference from central administrators. "If we are supposed to be professionals, give us some credit," she says.

A growing number of teachers around the country love to teach, but are frustrated by bureaucracy. Some of these teachers are setting up shop on their own in a movement known as private-practice teaching, providing educational services to public and private schools on a contract basis. These independent businesses range from Learning Styles, a one-employee

Massachusetts-based firm that provides special education teaching; to Berlitz Jr., a Berlitz International spinoff that supplies roughly 75 foreign-language teachers to public schools; to Sylvan Learning Systems, with 150 teachers who provide basic reading and math programs.

Private-practice teaching empowers teachers to make their own decisions. Private-practice teaching allows teachers dissatisfied with the public school approach to pursue their interests as independent professionals.

Teaching elementary school in the early 1980s, Robin Gross discovered she had a special aptitude and love for teaching science. For Gross, nothing was more rewarding than "seeing the utter delight of children mixing chemicals together and watching the colors change and learning chemical reactions," she says. "All I wanted to do was teach science."[77] But no public school would hire an elementary teacher to teach science full-time. So, in 1983, Gross started Science Encounters. "I decided to focus all my energy on teaching science and became a science specialist, which meant I had to go into practice for myself," Gross explains.

Now with a staff of 20 teachers, Science Encounters provides learning programs to schools in Maryland, Virginia, and Washington, D.C., thus enabling schools to offer specialized science classes without hiring a full-time teacher. Being the owner of a company has brought with it far more risk for Gross than she had in a traditional teaching role. "Every day is a risk. The greatest risk is having my name and reputation hanging out in the world every day. I am totally accountable. There's no place to hide."[78]

Risk is part of the price of freedom. For Gross, the challenge of being a professional is worth it: "I have tremendous freedom. I set my own schedule. I'm able to be home with my children when they're sick or bring them to the office. Even though things have been tough financially, certainly in the beginning, there's a lot to be said for having the flexibility I have. I'll never trade the benefit of having the freedom to run my life."

In addition to benefiting entrepreneurial-minded teachers, private-practice teaching also offers significant benefits for schools. By giving schools the opportunity to purchase the performance and output of a teacher professional at a given price, contracting for educational instruction enables them to increase accountability for *results*. It has also enabled schools to decrease costs, boost flexibility, and take advantage of specialized outside expertise.[79]

Superintendent Franklin Smith of Washington, D.C., has engaged Sylvan Learning Systems, another private-practice company, to help his *high school* students learn to read. Says Smith: "If Sylvan can come in and take those young people before they graduate and get them up to the sixth- or seventh-grade level, and we've had them for 10 or 11 years and all we do was get them to the third-grade level, I think it sends a very strong message to everyone in the system that says: we are not doing something right and we have got to change."[80]

Other Contracting Options for Public Schools

Habit is habit, and not to be flung out of the window by any man, but coaxed downstairs a step at a time.

Mark Twain

Some politicians are moving toward a competitive education market one step at a time. In 1992, Baltimore Mayor Kurt Schmoke prodded the city to sign a five-year contract with for-profit Education Alternatives to manage one middle and eight elementary schools. "We wanted to compare their approach with some of the other approaches that we have in our school system," says Schmoke.[81]

As a private company, Education Alternatives has the advantage of being able to act quickly. "We've freed them from the control of the central bureaucracy and given them more flexibility in their procurement procedures," says Mayor Schmoke. "They have introduced business principles to the school site."[82] Within Baltimore city schools, for example, any school purchase over $500 has to go before the Board of Estimates, a city agency, and schools wait about 40 days for a reply. With Education Alternatives, principals have the authority to go directly to vendors for purchases, and the turnaround time for approving large expenditures is usually 24 hours.

Contracting hasn't been an instant cure by any means, and early results on test scores have been mixed, in part because EAI has limited authority in choosing staff. "There is nothing magic about a private company if it's buried under rules and regulations," notes education expert Terry Moe, who nonetheless endorses the private management concept.[83] In the meantime, Schmoke, a Democrat, is paying a heavy political price for reaching outside the existing system for help. The trend continues, however. In the fall of 1994, Hartford, Connecticut, took the privatization plunge, signing a contract with Education Alternatives to manage the entire school system.

These contracting arrangements increase managerial flexibility in the area of physical plant, but Education Alternatives has no authority over staff. With personnel so critical to successful schools, this severely limits the ability of new managers to implement a coherent restructuring plan.

Recognizing this, Wilkinsburg, Pennsylvania, went a step further. Frustrated in reform by the school bureaucracy, the Wilkinsburg school board released a Request for Proposal to manage one of that town's four elementary schools that included a bold twist: new managers would be allowed to staff schools with new personnel if they so chose. Interest ran high, and Wilkinsburg received 16 proposals, ranging from a local nonprofit to Alternative Public Schools, a national for-profit firm. The reaction of the local teachers union followed a famil-

iar pattern: first there was denial, then anger, and finally acceptance. After months of fuming, the union eventually submitted
a joint management plan with the University of Pennsylvania.
In April 1995 the Wilkinsburg school board hired Alternative
Public Schools (which intends to bring on its own staff). Union
lawsuits are expected, and the battle of Wilkinsburg has important ramifications. "Wilkinsburg is one of the most important
cases in American education reform, because it gets at the issue
of who controls public education, the school board or labor,"
says John McLauglin, an education professor at St. Cloud State
University in Minnesota.[84]

Until the early 1990s, the kinds of reforms taking place within
public education were unheard of. School contracting, public
school choice, charter schools, and private-practice teaching are
all commendable efforts to bring market forces to the public
education system. These efforts should be applauded, but we
need to be sober about their potential impact. All these efforts
face strong political opposition, and all are limited in certain
critical respects. If competition among producers and choice for
consumers is the best way to supply education, why not go all
the way? Why not let parents choose any school they want?

SCHOOL CHOICE: FREEDOM OR CONTROL?

Time and again, we have seen how government funding has
led to government control, since he who pays the piper calls
the tune. Why wouldn't publicly funded vouchers used at private schools bring with them the kind of regulations that could
destroy their unique character? If students attending the Marcus Garvey School used tax money to attend, wouldn't government regulators attempt to control how the school is run?
"The law is very clear," writes David Frum in *Dead Right*.
"Take even a dime of federal money and all the federal civil
rights laws apply to every part of your school." Frum continues: "Voucher advocates intend to bring the virtues of the pri-

vate schools into the public sphere; there is a much more real risk that they will instead inflict all the vices of the public sphere upon the private."[85]

We share Frum's concern. Unlike Frum, however, we judge the risk worth running, partly because doing nothing carries risks of its own. While recognizing the risks, we believe that private schools could retain their independent character even in a voucher system—but it won't be easy. First, choice laws must contain legal language that erects a firewall against government intrusion. Second, parents will have to be vigilant in opposing government micromanagement of voucher-redeeming schools. There is reason to believe that such opposition will develop once parents develop a sense of ownership over their schools.

In France, tax money has long been used to support private schools, including private religious schools. In the early 1980s, France's Socialist President François Mitterand attempted to increase state control over the operation of these private schools. He thought he could impose uniform, secular standards on France's education system.

He underestimated parental outrage. The National Union of Parent Associations for Free Education had nearly a million members ready to man the barricades to maintain the independence of their cherished schools. In June 1984, over a million protesters jammed the streets of Paris to protect their schools. A month later, Socialist Minister of Education Alain Savary resigned and the plan to extend state control was abandoned. The ill feelings generated may well have contributed to the subsequent defeat of the Socialist government in 1986.[86]

In America, a burgeoning network of independent schools and home schoolers keeps vigilant watch over any attempts by the government to usurp control. In February 1994, Representative George Miller added an amendment to HR 6, the Elementary and Secondary Education Act. As written, the amendment could have been interpreted to require teacher certification even for private schools and home schoolers.

Texas Congressman Dick Armey informed the Home School Legal Defense Fund, and the alert went out. Within 48 hours, tens of thousands of home schoolers knew all about HR 6 and the threat it represented. The phone and fax brigades swung into action, deluging Congress. Capitol Hill switchboards were jammed. After receiving thousands of calls, the office of Congressman Miller stopped answering the phone. "You have shut down Capitol Hill," one staffer told a home-school lobbyist. "Nothing is getting done up here because everyone is answering calls from home schoolers." Another congressional staffer said, "Don't get me wrong, I believe in democracy, it's just that we have had about as much democracy as we can handle for one day." After ten days of being barraged by home schoolers, the amendment, which had been expected to pass, was defeated by a vote of 424 to 1. That one nay vote was cast by Congressman Miller.[87]

Though largely ignored by the popular press, the citizen response to HR 6 is legendary on Capitol Hill. An obscure amendment to a boring piece of legislation generated more calls than the controversy over gays in the military and the Clinton budget *combined*. When parents have a sense of ownership over their childrens' schools, they stand up for them.

THE FUTURE OF AMERICAN EDUCATION

The debates over educational reform will not go away. The current system, which views government-run schools as the only way to provide public education, will not fix itself. Without parental involvement, decentralization, and choice, we are doomed to fruitless efforts to accommodate fundamentally different visions of education. A centrally controlled, one-size-fits-all system cannot satisfy diversity.

Just as voters are striving to take back their government, parents are reclaiming control of their children's education. The failure of government-run schools has produced a boom in home schooling. As recently as 1978, children in home schooling numbered only around 10,000 to 15,000. As of 1994, conservative estimates put the number around 500,000.[88] Facing a failing public school system that they cannot control, many parents have opted out of the system. Rather than wringing our hands over this development, we should see it as a positive sign. Parents are ready to make significant sacrifices to ensure that their children receive the sort of education they envision. Lest there be any concern, children in home schools handily surpass their public school counterparts in academic achievement.[89] Uncertified but caring, parents generally do just fine.

It is disturbing to us that giving parents control over their children's education is considered an extreme idea. As President Clinton said, "Governments don't raise children, parents do." The government does not bring children into the world and is ill-equipped to guide them through it.

Behind most of the debate surrounding school reform is a dispute over power, and with whom it shall reside. But this is an issue that shouldn't be open to debate at all. We simply need to recognize the fundamental right of parents to determine how their children shall be raised and what they shall be taught. The most astounding feature of government-run schools is that parents tolerate other people deciding what their children will learn. People who would go bananas if the government told them what kind of car to drive meekly submit when they are told where their children will go to school and what they will learn.

After being locked in a bureaucratic stasis, education is ready for a revolution. Public education today is like a boiling pot with a lid clamped on it—and the political forces struggling to keep the lid on are losing their grip. Innovation will flourish once the political structures that keep public schools locked in the past finally lose out to the forces of the future.

CHAPTER 11

BEYOND THE BELTWAY

Tell us how much you're prepared to take back and we'll send it.

House Speaker Newt Gingrich[1]

THE DISTANT PAST

The political landscape of America was very different way back in 1994. The nation was at the dawn of a new political era—and nobody in Washington seemed to know it. Ignoring the obvious discontent of voters with Washington, the federal government continued with business as usual—drawing more and more power to itself.

President Clinton was elected after promising middle-class tax cuts and welfare reform. But the first two years of the Clinton Administration were marked by a series of federal takeovers: national service, national education goals, a federal crime bill, and the granddaddy of them all, the never-passed Health Security Act. If enacted, the Health Security Act would have been the greatest consolidation of federal power since the New Deal, putting an additional 14 percent of GNP under Washington's control.

There was a gap between White House rhetoric and reality. Al Gore's National Performance Review had proudly quoted Thomas Jefferson's maxim: "Were we directed from Washington when to reap and when to sow, we should soon want for bread." But when it came to policy, the Clinton Administration was pushing for greater federal control. As the National Perfor-

319

mance Review so eloquently quotes Ralph Waldo Emerson, "What you do thunders so loudly, I cannot hear what you say to the contrary."

While the National Performance Review described the federal government as a bureaucratic mess, the White House pushed for a gigantic new health care bureaucracy. With remarkable confidence, the White House claimed the federal government could guarantee high-quality, low-cost health care to every American. Even more remarkable than this outrageous claim was the response to this proposal. While various details of the plan were challenged, few people questioned whether the federal government had any business involving itself in the health care decisions of 250 million Americans. Virtually no one asked whether the Constitution gave the federal government the authority to assume control of health care. The thinking ran thus: Here was a problem. There was the federal government. Why shouldn't the two get together and work things out?

The same kind of thinking, or lack thereof, was applied to crime.[2] Crime was a problem, so why shouldn't Congress get involved? Why shouldn't car-jacking be a federal crime? Why shouldn't Washington pay to put cops on the streets of Bangor, Maine, and Walnut Creek, California? Similarly with education and community service. There seemed to be no limit to what the federal government might get into next.

After 60 years of growth, the federal government has become vast beyond comprehension, and it is growing larger (see charts). The growth of the federal government has come, as it must, at the expense of the private sphere. As of 1992, the 535 members of Congress (plus the president) were spending one quarter of America's GNP.[3]

Despite all the talk of change, not much was changing. Gore's National Performance Review was touted as a revolutionary reinvention of the federal government. But *by its own admission* the NPR did not question *what* the federal govern-

GROWTH IN GOVERNMENT SPENDING

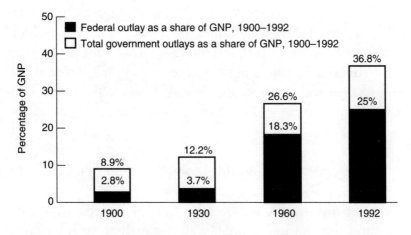

Source: The Institute for Policy Innovation, Lewisville, Texas, Policy Report No. 121, February, 1993.

REAL FEDERAL DEBT PER FAMILY OF FOUR, 1900–1992

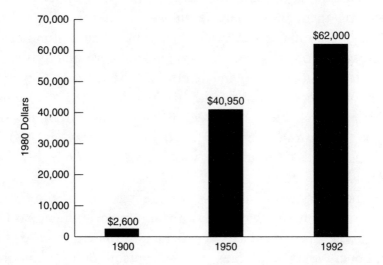

Source: The Institute for Policy Innovation, Lewisville, Texas, Policy Report No. 121, February, 1993.

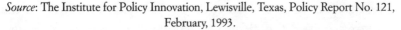

ment did; the NPR was a halfway measure, looking only at *how* the federal bureaucracy worked. And as Senator Phil Gramm of Texas notes, "When Washington takes 25 cents of each dollar earned by middle-class families, halfway measures won't save America or the American Dream." But organizations do not change without a strong driving force. What could impel the federal government to alter its course?

NOVEMBER 8, 1994: THE PEOPLE SPEAK

Ah yes, democracy! On November 8, 1994, Americans had their say, and they said, ENOUGH! "Well, we made history last night. Call it what you want: an earthquake, a tidal wave, a blowout. We got our butts kicked," said a despondent David Wilhelm, the chairman of the Democratic National Committee.[4] "Well, a lot has changed since yesterday," said President Clinton.[5]

The American people wanted less government, especially of the federal variety, and they saw Clinton and the Democrats offering them more. The result was an historic Republican landslide. A major national survey found that a stunning 73 percent of voters agreed that "the federal government is much too large and has too much power."[6] Republican Governor Pete Wilson of California said that Americans had "cast a massive, unmistakable vote to reclaim our country from an arrogant, out-of-touch, and dysfunctional Congress and federal government."[7] "I think they want a smaller government," said President Clinton.[8]

One clear trend emerges from polling data: as the federal government has grown, America's faith in government has fallen. Today, 59 percent say the federal government is more of an opponent than a partner in their pursuit of the American Dream.[9] Declared the Republican governors at their annual conference after the election: "The current, cresting feeling of frustration and futility among voters is not an inexplicable phenomenon. To the contrary, it is a direct and wholly predictable consequence of the shift of government power to institutions beyond the grasp of the people."[10]

That the overwhelming majority of Americans want a much smaller federal government is now virtually beyond dispute. Did Washington get the message? Maybe. At a press conference after the election, President Clinton said, "We propose to stop doing things that government doesn't do very well and that don't need to be done by government." So far, so good. But then the President continued, "What we really need is a new American government for this new American economy in the 21st century—one that is creative and flexible; that's a high-quality, low-cost producer of services that the American people need and that can best be provided at the national level."[11]

We're not sure what this means, but we are sure that the American public has no tolerance left for utopian one-size-fits-all fixes from Washington, of either the liberal or conservative variety. "The big risk is that we will seek to use the national government to achieve conservative prescriptions," says Congressmen Chris Cox, (R-Calif.), "rather than using our mandate to reduce the size and power of the federal government."[12]

Dictating a host of conservative national prescriptions to states, cities, and communities is not why the American people put the GOP in control of Congress. "We ought to show some humility," Lamar Alexander said after the 1994 election. "The biggest danger now for Republicans is that we'll substitute our own arrogant empire in Washington for theirs."[13]

CENTRALIZED POWER IN THE AGE OF DEVOLUTION

In the widening gyre . . . the center cannot hold.

W.B. Yeats[14]

The remedy for what ails the federal government is not another efficiency review. (Management improvements should be pursued, but don't expect miracles.) The fundamental problem with Washington is not *how* the government is run, but *what* it does.

Our swollen federal government is in large measure incompatible with the demands of a modern society. In today's Information Age, there is little rationale for the federal government to control as much as it does. Large, centralized bureaucracies—whether that be IBM headquarters, the Kremlin, or Washington, D.C.—aren't well suited to an age of rapid technological change. In business, companies are decentralizing, empowering workers, and establishing autonomous business units. (It's not just trendy, it's an economic necessity.) In politics, economic reality is relegating central planning to the dustbin of history.

Washington, D.C., is becoming increasingly irrelevant. Explain authors Alvin and Heidi Toffler:

> *It is not possible for a society to de-massify economic activity, communications and many other crucial processes without also, sooner or later, being compelled to decentralize government decision-making as well. There is no possibility of restoring sense, order, and management 'efficiency' to many governments without a substantial devolution of central power.*[15]

In today's rapidly changing world, the performance of the federal government looks worse and worse. There is a reason for this. As technology advances, decentralized decision making becomes more efficient in more and more cases. The problems of centralized decision making are inherent to *any* central authority, whether corporate or governmental, and are based on the relationship between knowledge, decision-making power, and technology.

As technology advances, productivity increasingly depends on knowledge. And, as communications technology advances, *general* knowledge—the kind that can be written down—becomes widely accessible. But *specific* knowledge—the kind that requires firsthand experience and that is difficult to communicate—is as difficult to obtain today as it has ever been. Other things being equal, *specific* knowledge—the kind that is dispersed throughout society—is growing in importance relative to *general* knowledge. Thus, as technology advances, it makes less and less sense to bottle up decision-making authority in a distant, centralized bureaucracy.[16] Dictating the "one best way" from Washington, whether in education, welfare, or crime fighting, makes less and less sense. In particular cases, there may be a compelling reason for maintaining centralized control, such as the need for a coordinated national defense. But as a general principle, for efficiency's sake we should be increasingly devolving power *away* from centralized bureaucracies.

More than simply efficiency is at stake, however. We need to return to our roots as a self-governing people. Democracy is not a spectator sport. In a healthy democracy, citizens are actively involved in their own governance—and not simply on election day. Americans need to reconnect with the political process. Numerous functions now handled (and mishandled) by the federal government should be transferred back to the states and, wherever possible, to communities and individuals. Radical devolution brings government closer to home.

Do political leaders in Washington understand the importance of devolution? Some do. Others cannot bear to accept it. Dispersing power has been proposed before, but Beltway politicians of both parties have proved themselves unwilling to relinquish control. While the economic forces favoring devolution are strong, the political obstacles are formidable. Even with a Republican Congress philosophically disposed to devolution, one should not count on a ruling body to voluntarily divest itself of power.

The revolution must come from the roots. A powerful movement whose aim is to seize power and authority back from the federal government has taken hold beyond the Beltway. Voters have been disgusted with Washington for some time, but now they are joined by governors and mayors who are in open rebellion as well. If Washington fails to voluntarily cede power, Americans may just *take* it back. Thankfully, in a democracy revolutionary change does not require violence, only concerted political action on the part of citizens.

THE REVOLT AGAINST WASHINGTON

When all government, domestic and foreign, in little as in great things, shall be drawn to Washington as the center of all power, it will render powerless the checks provided of one government on another, and will become as venal and oppressive as the government from which we separated.

Thomas Jefferson[17]

The legitimacy of the federal government is facing its most serious challenge since the Civil War. In some ways, the current challenge may be more severe. At least during the Civil War, *some* states took the side of the federal government. This time around, virtually every state is lined up in opposition to Washington, D.C.

From Pennsylvania to California, states are defying the federal government, ignoring federal requirements on everything from auto emissions inspection to voter registration rules. Six states have sued the federal government for failing to enforce immigration policy while requiring states to provide services to illegal aliens. Some counties are refusing to comply with the federal Brady Bill, which requires background checks on handgun purchases. Some 35 counties in five Western states have passed ordinances or other policies designed to strengthen local control of land claimed by the federal government; Nye County, Nevada, went so far as to literally *bulldoze* its way past the orders of federal officials.[18]

This open defiance of the federal government is reminiscent of the colonists' defiance of England's King George III over 200 years ago. In 1994, Governor Pete Wilson refused to implement the "motor voter" registration law because Congress passed down new rules but wouldn't pass down the money to pay for them. Says Wilson:

> *California is not a colony of the federal government. The [feds] should study their early American history and remember what happened to the last imperial government that handed down edicts and ignored the will of the people. If Washington continues to treat states like colonies, then it will seem like last week [the November 1994 elections] was just the tea party, and 1996 will be the real revolution.*[19]

Governors are tired of being treated as though they were midlevel administrators of the federal government. Wisconsin's Governor Tommy Thompson says he's tired of having to approach Washington "on bended knee, to kiss the ring, just to get a waiver in order to do something."[20]

Returning to the Constitution

The powers not delegated to the United States by the Constitution, nor prohibited by it to the States, are reserved to the States respectively, or to the people.

The Tenth Amendment

Every new president takes an oath, promising to "preserve, protect, and defend the Constitution of the United States." The Tenth Amendment is part of the Constitution, but it hasn't gotten the sort of protection it deserves. Maybe it's all those commas. Maybe it's the way the Tenth Amendment is tucked in there between the Ninth and Eleventh Amendments. Whatever the reason, the Tenth Amendment has been sorely neglected.

The Tenth Amendment affirms that the federal government is given authority to act only *through* the Constitution, and given only the specific, enumerated powers described *in* the Constitution. To know what those powers are you have to read the Constitution. We strongly urge you to take 15 minutes and actually read the Constitution of the United States, which is only about 12 pages long. You will see that it grants the federal government the authority to control a handful of tasks and prohibits it from doing anything except those tasks. In a nutshell, the Constitution grants the federal government the authority to wage war, conduct foreign policy, levy taxes, regulate commerce with foreign nations and between states, coin money, and, oddly enough, establish post offices and post roads. As James Madison put it, federal powers are "few and defined."[21]

When we mention this to people, we are often met with denial. "If what you say is true," we are challenged, "then most of what the federal government does is unconstitutional. That's absurd!"

Absurd it may be, but it certainly is true. Most federal activities dealing with domestic issues such as education, poverty relief, cultivation of the arts and sciences, business loans, and so on, are unconstitutional.[22] "[I]f judges started seriously striking down federal programs and statutes [that were] outside the founding fathers' intention, they would cause chaos," says Robert Bork, a former federal judge and Supreme Court nominee. "They would destroy about three-quarters of the statutes and all sorts of agencies."[23] Of course, many distinguished jurists disagree with a "strict interpretation" of the constitution. The interstate commerce clause especially has been interpreted in a manner that radically expands the realm of federal authority. In fact, since the New Deal a majority of Supreme Court justices have abandoned the view that the Constitution sets strict limits on the federal government. We are not claiming that these justices don't have a right to their opinion; we simply believe that they are wrong. Again, rather than take our word on this we urge you to take dramatic action and *read the Constitution*.

We need to return to our roots. For much of our history, adherence to the Constitution limited the growth of the federal government. Congress has always been prone to submitting to popular sentiment, but it is only recently that the courts have failed in their role as guardians of the Constitution.[24] Presidents, too, in former times honored their oath to defend the Constitution, which meant vetoing legislation that exceeded the federal government's constitutional authority.

In 1854, after years of lobbying by social reformer Dorothea Dix, Congress passed the so-called Dix bill, which called for federal funds to be earmarked for the care of the indigent insane. Now, there are few who would argue against government care for the indigent insane. But what level of government ought to be responsible? The Constitution provides clear guidance: it should not be the federal government.

When the Dix bill hit the desk of President Franklin Pierce, he expressed "deep sympathies" for "the humane purposes to be accomplished by the bill." Then he vetoed it, saying, "I cannot find any authority in the Constitution for making the Federal Government the great almoner of public charity throughout the United States. To do so would, in my judgment, be contrary to the letter and spirit of the Constitution and subversive of the whole theory upon which the Union of these States is founded."[25]

Though few modern justices would agree, we believe Pierce was correct. The Constitution precludes federal charity efforts, meaning that the vast federal welfare bureaucracy, and much else the federal government does, is unconstitutional.

We do not claim that the Constitution as written 200 years ago is a perfect document. We are obviously pleased that the United States has ceased to tolerate slavery, and has extended the protections of individual rights granted in the Bill of Rights to state residents through the Fourteenth Amendment.[26] Moreover, there are issues unforeseen by the founders, such as air pollution, which merit federal involvement. We do claim, however, that a constitution is of no value if no one defends it. The way to alter the Constitution is by amendment, not by stealth.

Today, Congress, the president, and the courts largely fail

to respect constitutional limits, leaving America with a central government that defines its own powers. This is dangerous, and our current constitutional crisis is an open invitation to democratic despotism. Many South American nations have constitutions that read much like ours, yet have governments that routinely trample individual rights. In the past 60 years, a gradual but dramatic shift has left nothing off limits to the federal government. The federal government has assumed unlimited power, and "We the people" have allowed it.

THE TENTH AMENDMENT REVOLT

Until now. Today, state after state is challenging the federal government's authority, and much of that challenge is centered on the long forgotten Tenth Amendment. People are discovering that much federal activity lacks constitutional authority. Even the Supreme Court, which for decades has ignored pleas to impose constitutional limits on federal power, may be ready to dust off its copy of the Constitution and support states in reasserting their legal prerogatives.

One modern-day Patrick Henry is Arizona Governor Fife Symington. Declaring that the federal government "is like this monarchy of old—King George III," Symington has set up a $1 million fund, the Constitutional Defense Council, for the purpose of challenging the federal government on the basis of the Tenth Amendment.[27] The governor's leadership in the fight against overreaching federal power prompted one writer to suggest that "Phoenix is to this movement [federalism] what Boston was to the American rebellion of eleven score years ago."[28]

Governor Pete Wilson has already filed a lawsuit against the federal government. The suit argues that "Defendant United States of America is a sovereign constitutional government of those limited enumerated powers specified in, and restrained by, the Constitution" and that the motor voter law "impinges on the state's sovereign right . . . in violation of the Tenth Amendment to the United States Constitution."[29]

Radical stuff, this. But it will be awfully difficult to dispute. A reading of the Constitution and history confirm California's claim: Defendant United States of America has no right, no authority, to involve itself in areas other than those authorized by the Constitution. As noted by Wilson's suit, states are *themselves* sovereign entities. Earlier in our history, this was understood. Until the Civil War, the United States took a plural verb, as in "The United States are located in the Western Hemisphere." Since the Civil War, states have increasingly come to be viewed as local offices of the federal government. But, as Virginia Governor George Allen points out, "The Tenth Amendment was not repealed at Appomattox."[30]

California's lawsuit is just the tip of the iceberg in the Tenth Amendment revolt. Colorado's legislature has passed a Tenth Amendment resolution commanding the federal government to "cease and desist, effective immediately, mandates that are beyond the scope of the constitutionally delegated powers." Similar resolutions have been passed in ten other states. Much federal activity by law ought to be the domain of the states. But don't take our word for it; listen to James Madison, the man who crafted the Constitution:[31]

> *The powers reserved to the several states will extend to all the objects which, in the ordinary course of affairs, concern the lives, liberties, and properties of the people, and the internal order, improvement, and the prosperity of the state.*[32]

In other words, states are supposed to govern on most issues. Consider, for instance, a law prohibiting anyone from carrying a gun near a schoolyard. Now, some people may think this a good law, others might think it a bad law. One thing is certain, however: according to the Constitution, it *cannot* be a federal law.

That didn't stop Congress from enacting the Gun Free School Zones Act in 1990. When this law was challenged, federal lawyers claimed that Congress's constitutional power *to regulate interstate commerce* granted them authority to outlaw firearms near schools. Using reasoning that only a lawyer could love, the feds claimed that the "adverse impact on interstate commerce" caused by the "decline in the quality of education" gave them the authority to ban guns near schools.[33]

This tortured reasoning caught the attention of Supreme Court Justice David H. Souter. "Presumably there is nothing left if Congress can do this, no recognizable limit," said Souter. The federal attorney replied that the legislation should be upheld as long as it had a "rational basis." To this Justice Souter replied, "If that's the test, it's all over. Benjamin Franklin said it's wonderful to be a rational animal because there's a reason for everything."[34] In 1995, in a 5–4 decision, the Supreme Court struckdown the 1990 law on the basis that it was unconstitutional.

A major focus of the Tenth Amendment revolt is unfunded federal mandates. An unfunded mandate is an ugly name for an ugly federal trick. Essentially, the federal government enacts laws that require states, cities, and counties to do something—and they don't send any money along to pay for it. Washington's arrogance in unleashing a flood of such mandates has angered not only the 50 state governors, but thousands of state and local officials who are ready to descend on our nation's capital carrying torches and pitchforks like the angry villagers in a Frankenstein movie.

UNFUNDED MANDATES

The revolution that gave birth to our country was fought over the principle of "no taxation without representation." Two centuries later, the federal government has figured out a much more clever way to impose a tax on cities than old King George III ever did. The method is to impose unfunded mandates and regulations. I call that "spending without representation."

Gregory S. Lashutka, Mayor of Columbus, Ohio[35]

Mayor Lashutka is mad. Members of Congress are passing laws that his constituents have to pay for. Congress gets the credit, Lashutka gets the bill.

It is a big bill. In 1991, Columbus, Ohio, figured out what it cost to comply with 22 different federal and state mandates. The costs of compliance were estimated at $850 per household per year.[36]

For example, the Environmental Protection Agency requires Columbus (and every other city in America) to test drinking water for dibromochloropropane. Now, dibromochloropropane is a pesticide that has been banned since 1977. Not only that, it was used mostly on pineapple crops. (The last time we checked, pineapples were not a major crop in Ohio.) Because the federal government issues a one-size-fits-all ruling, something that might make sense in Hawaii is imposed on the people of Columbus, Ohio.[37] Moreover, when city water bills rise, will anybody in Columbus blame the federal government? Not likely. They'll blame Mayor Lashutka. But when their representative in Congress sends them a little mailer explaining that he voted against higher taxes *and* supported the Clean Water Act, people will feel all warm and fuzzy inside. "An unfunded mandate is like having Uncle Sam take us out to dinner, order our food, and then hand the check to us," says Columbus Mayor Lashutka.[38]

Of course, most mayors and governors like the idea of being taken out to dinner, as long as the federal government is picking up the tab. Though they complain mostly about the *unfunded* nature of the mandates, as we will explain later, we have just as big a problem with the mandates themselves. Local officials like Mayor Lashutka need to begin declining the feds' dinner invitation.[39]

Everybody has a mandate horror story, and our favorite comes from Anchorage, Alaska. The EPA sets standards for cleaning wastewater before discharge, but Anchorage had a problem: because of snow runoff, its water was too clean to clean. In order to meet the EPA's demands, Anchorage officials asked local fish processing companies to dump fish guts into the water so the city could clean it up. This defies reason, but it's much easier to defy reason than to defy the EPA.[40] (Those of you thinking that this "creates jobs" should go back and reread Chapter 9.)

Unfunded mandates are booming. Prior to 1988 there were only about 40 major unfunded federal mandates on state and local governments, and some of these at least came with some money. Three years later, the number of mandates had tripled and the money to implement them had largely dried up. These mandates make the federal government look great while breaking the bank of state and local governments and the private sector.

As often happens when someone else is paying, there is no discipline on spending. Declares Tracy Mehan, a member of Governor John Engler's cabinet,

> There seems to be no priority or hierarchy among the various and sundry mandates emanating from the Congress, the courts, and the federal regulatory agencies. All risks are equal. Resources are deemed to be infinite, no need to choose, prioritized, or sequence programs. Washington takes a lesson from Nike: "Just do it." Just do the Americans with Disabilities Act. Just do Medicaid. Just do clean air, clean water, safe drinking water, leaking underground storage tanks, solid and hazardous waste control.[41]

The costs of unfunded mandates are staggering: about $150 billion a year for the private sector (environmental mandates alone) and $75 billion a year for states. "The federal Congress and courts now effectively tell us how to spend 35 percent of our total budget and over 80 percent of our new general revenues," said former Missouri Governor (now U.S. Senator) John Ashcroft in his 1991 State of the State address.

Ten unfunded mandates are estimated to cost cities about $13 billion a year.[42] For healthy cities such as Indianapolis, the mandates are "vacuuming up all the efficiency savings generated," says Mayor Goldsmith. For struggling cities, these mandates can be devastating.

In 1995, Congress made unfunded mandates a top agenda item on its reform program. That's wonderful. We are concerned, however, that much of the revolutionary opposition among state and local officials is centered around the "unfunded" nature of these mandates.[43] We are just as concerned about the mandate as the funding.

WASHINGTON KNOWS BEST

Mandates exemplify the "Washington knows best" thinking that dominates inside the Beltway. The federal government behaves as if cities and states were irresponsible children, and that left to their own devices they'd never behave responsibly. This paternalism irks many state and local politicians. "I'm not going to run for office saying that I'm going to pollute the city," says San Diego Mayor Susan Golding.[44] Ben Nelson, the Democratic Governor of Nebraska, says that federal mandates are based on "an assumption [by Congress] that states won't take care of these things, but [Congress] can take care of it."[45] Echoes Ohio Governor George Voinovich, "There's a tendency for people in Washington to think we don't care about clean air, we don't care about the environment in our community. We care as much as Congress does."[46]

State and local officials are grownups, and just as capable and intelligent as federal bureaucrats or congressional staffers. Moreover, there is an advantage to having 50 states. If the government of one state does grow inimical to the interests of residents, residents can always relocate. While difficult, this is not impossible. Recall Barbara Anderson of Massachusetts Citizens for Limited Taxation saying that many of her members had moved to Florida to escape high taxes. It is much harder to escape the federal government.

The problem with federal mandates goes well beyond the fact that they are unfunded; at root they represent abuses of federal power. Relates former Tennessee Governor Lamar Alexander,

> *Now we have a Senator from California, I understand, wanting to pass a federal law about what the weapons policy ought to be in all of America's 15,000 school districts! Well, why don't we go ahead and pass a law about what time school ought to start and who ought to empty the wastebasket and how to discipline a child who is disrespectful to a teacher. I mean do we not need parents or teachers or principals or school boards or governors or legislators anymore?*[47]

The battle is about much more than simply money. Funded mandates are still mandates, and contrary to the spirit of America's federal system of government.[48] "We are not focused merely on unfunded mandates, because we're not looking for more money from the federal government," says Brenda Burns, Arizona's House Majority Leader. "We're looking for a stricter interpretation of the Constitution and what it allows the federal government to do."[49] This is a battle worth fighting for, and one increasingly being joined by America's beyond-the-Beltway revolutionaries.

MODERN-DAY FEDERALIST REVOLUTIONARIES

Virginia Governor George Allen is among the most vocal of the federalist firebrands. "I am not willing to let the 'Federales' up in Washington run our lives when it is not what the people of

Virginia want," says Allen. Governor Allen spent much of his first year in office defending his state's independence, fighting against Washington on issues such as car emissions, access to state parks, and discipline in public schools.[50]

As is often the case, the federal government threatens to withhold funds from those who don't stay in line. Allen vows to forgo the federal dollars if that's what is required to maintain independence. "You can't just be following around the dollar bill like some goat in heat," says Allen.[51]

Seeking to reverse Washington's power grab, Allen has created a special advisory committee on federalism. In announcing the committee, he issued an "Executive Order on Self-Determination and Federalism":

Two centuries ago, the challenge to the liberties of Virginians came from an arrogant, overbearing monarchy across the sea. Today, that challenge comes all too often from our own federal government—a government that has defied, and that now ignores, virtually every constitutional limit fashioned by the framers to confine its reach and thus to guard the freedoms of the people . . .[52]

In Arizona, Governor Symington has locked horns with a federal judge over the issue of prison conditions. The judge has overturned a number of gubernatorial executive orders with regard to the prison system.[53] When we last spoke to him in December 1994, Symington seemed almost eager for a showdown:

If we decide to take them on then they'll have to take me on, not one of my political appointees. It shows you how far gone some of these federal judges and courts are in terms of their understanding of the limits of their power. The fact is, there are no limits to their power, and that's why we're in such trouble today. Jefferson and Madison would be groaning in their grave if they heard about a judge who was telling a state how to run its prison system.[54]

The lengthy and convoluted waiver process Washington forces states to go through for welfare reform was also trying the governor's patience. Arizona's welfare reform package, passed by the state legislature in April 1994, was languishing in the federal Department of Health and Human Service's (HHS) bureaucracy ten months later—and federal bureaucrats were telling Symington it would take another six to nine months to get the waiver. The governor was leaning towards implementing the plan without Washington's approval. "Maybe they should have to sue *me* for a change," he told us.

LAND WARS

The sense of outrage among mainstream Americans right now should not be underestimated. It is the stuff of which uprisings are made.

Former Tennessee Governor Lamar Alexander[55]

The federal government owns about 4 percent of the land in the Northeast, Midwest, and South. In the West, the federal government owns a bit more. On average, the states of Montana, Idaho, Wyoming, Colorado, New Mexico, Arizona, Utah, Nevada, Washington, Oregon, California, Alaska, and Hawaii are more than 50 percent owned by the federal government.[56]

This annoys the heck out of people in the West. Federal ownership means that this land can neither be taxed by state governments nor efficiently managed, thus limiting the economic potential and population base of some Western states. Federal lands are notoriously poorly managed, with special interests enjoying special logging, grazing, and mining privileges.[57]

In the Sagebrush Rebellion of the 1970s, westerners called for the federal government to turn over public lands to the states. Today's rebellion is even stronger, as grass-roots groups such as People for the New West! (which has over 30,000 members) and local politicians are fighting to wrest control of land from Washington.

In 1993, Nye County, Nevada, officials declared all federal lands to be under their jurisdiction.[58] Other western counties have followed suit. In Catron County, New Mexico, "the Forest Service has been run off at gunpoint," says a local environmentalist.[59] "If we didn't have the plan [for the county to take over federal land], there would have been bloodshed," says a local rancher. "Things have gotten to that point." The U.S. Department of Interior's Bureau of Land Management, the U.S. Forest Service, and the FBI have talked about the use of criminal lawsuits and prosecutions to curb the western land revolt, with the Nevada protest receiving "top priority" by the Department of Justice.[60]

Arizona's Fife Symington wants all federal land returned to the states:

> *The very situation which created the rebellion against King George III, we have in Arizona today. The federal government owns about 70 percent of our land. This dominant presence in our state is the very thing the founding fathers tried to prevent from happening. The federal government originally wasn't even allowed to own land except for the Post Office and military forts. Well, 70 percent of our land means that the federal government has a hell of a fort in Arizona.*[61]

Alaska Governor Walter Hickel—who believe it or not was elected in 1990 as the candidate of a political party advocating *secession*—filed a $29 billion lawsuit accusing the United States of locking up 100 million acres of Alaska's land in violation of the compact by which it became a state.[62] "There is no need for a U.S. Forest Service or a Bureau of Land Management," former Alaska Senate Majority Leader Robin Taylor wrote in a letter to Newt Gingrich. "The states can decide how to manage their land just as each of the first 28 states have made those decisions since they were admitted to the Union. Empowerment is a hollow phrase to those of us who have been forced to watch passively as the federal government mismanaged the land upon which we live."

CONFERENCE OF THE STATES

There was a feeling of revolution in the air at Colonial Williamsburg, the site of the Republican Governors' Conference, and it wasn't just because of the actors in revolutionary costume. Meeting in the aftermath of the November 1994 election, the governors in attendance were expressing revolutionary sentiment towards an overreaching federal government.

Newt Gingrich described it as "the meeting that crystallized the process of getting power out of Washington ... reversing the centralization which began in 1932." The governors called for a bipartisan gathering called the Conference of the States, now planned for fall 1996.[63]

The governors plan to submit a States' Petition at the Conference of the States.[64] The States' Petition will then head home to the 50 states, and, pending approval, will be presented to Congress. The states—acting together—will petition their government for a redress of grievances.[65] "We have to be willing to deal with the issue right up front and in a competitive, confrontational way," says Governor Mike Leavitt of Utah, who is heading up the effort. "We must be treated as equal partners as opposed to a master-servant relationship."

Some state leaders are looking to amend the constitution to ensure states greater autonomy.[66] Invoking images of Madison and Jefferson, Governor Symington argues that states must resort to such radical measures:

> If we are ever to truly straighten out the system, the states will have to band together to put Washington "back in the box." That's what the Conference of the States is really all about. We will come up with language to strengthen the

Tenth Amendment, and propose some constitutional amend-
ments that go right to the heart of the problem. We need to
restore a balance.[67]

If this doesn't force fundamental change, Symington is willing to support a constitutional convention. Keenly aware of the
risks such a convention would entail—many worry that a "runaway" convention could do permanent harm to the Constitution—the governor says it's a risk we might have to take. "The
issue is so important that if Congress is unwilling to act after
the states have expressed their needs and desires then let's go
have a constitutional convention, because if we don't we're
going to wreck this country anyway," Symington says. "We
can't let our great republic slip away from us through the further erosion of the federalist system."[68]

MAKING RADICAL DEVOLUTION A REALITY

In 1992, a highly respected economist wrote, "The federal government should eliminate most of its programs in education,
housing, highways, social services, economic development, and
job training."[69]

These radical sentiments come from Alice Rivlin, then a
Brookings Institution scholar and currently President Clinton's
director of the Office of Management and Budget. Writing as
an independent scholar, Rivlin called for a massive, radical
devolution of federal programs to states.

Devolution is not a partisan issue. It is a recognition that
centralized control and centralized decision making carries
unacceptably high costs, both in terms of efficiency and democratic accountability. It is not a question of Democratic dictates
from Washington versus Republican dictates. Following the
election of 1994, Republican governors seem ready to oppose
federal usurpation even when orchestrated by their fellow party members. "My priority is for Texans to be running Texas,"

says Texas Governor George Bush, Jr. "We're pretty good at what we do in Texas, and we like to be left alone by the federal government as much as possible."[70] It's time to end the unequal partnership and the whole idea of one-size-fits-all national prescriptions. The American people have said it's time to move power *and responsibility* out of Washington—for good.

Devolution would restore clearer lines of responsibility between state and federal tasks. By bringing government closer to home, citizens could once again understand what each level of government does and hold the appropriate officials accountable at election time. Radical devolution will make much of what goes on inside the Beltway redundant or unnecessary. "You have to get rid of a lot of those vested interests in Washington," says Mayor Goldsmith. "There are tens of thousands of people there whose only job in life is to control what I do."[71]

The Department of Education, for example, spends about $15 billion a year on 150 different elementary and secondary programs. Since the department was created in 1979, Washington has become fond of imposing top-down solutions on local schools. Ohio Governor George Voinovich says his state's school superintendents spend nearly half their time filling out federal forms to get money that makes up only 5 to 6 percent of their school budgets.

Recall Joann Wysocki, the first-grade teacher from the Los Angeles Unified School District whom you met in the last chapter. Ms. Wysocki told us that the federal government was providing money for school days lost due to the 1994 earthquake. The rules required a special form, so every teacher had to copy *by hand* the attendance register. Photocopies were not acceptable. That's the rule. Wysocki doesn't like to jump through hoops for money from Washington. "That 'federal money' is our money to begin with, on the local level," she says. "Please don't insult anyone's intelligence saying anything else. The money comes back to us with strings attached. Why should the money go in the first place? Let it stay!"

Former Education Secretary William J. Bennett concurs:

"We really do not need a Department of Education. We were educating our kids better before we had a Department of Education. Why do we have to pass the dollars from the states and locales to Washington and back out again?"[72]

Sending housing, welfare, and social service programs to the states, as Rivlin proposes, would mean that HHS and the Department of Housing and Urban Development (HUD) can also be dramatically downsized or eliminated. Even Housing Secretary Henry Cisneros has admitted that much of what HUD does is expendable. "Many aspects of this department are simply indefensible," said Cisneros. "Change is necessary."[73]

Privatizing some federal lands and turning over the rest to the states would unburden the Department of Interior.[74] Some of the most successful models of ecologically sustainable resource development have taken place in wilderness areas owned by locally based conservation groups. The nonprofit Hawk Mountain Sanctuary Association in eastern Pennsylvania, for example, fosters the conservation of birds of prey, while Sea Lion Caves, a for-profit company, protects the Steller sea lions of coastal Oregon. Allowing state control might encourage partnerships with these kinds of private environmental groups, and is likely to improve on the federal government's mostly dismal record in managing grazing, mining, and timber lands.

As for the Environmental Protection Agency (EPA), state environmental agencies are better positioned to know the problems of their states. "We don't need an EPA in Washington, D.C.," says Governor Symington. "We have a Department of Environmental Quality in Arizona that is better at dealing with environmental problems in our state. You don't need an EPA in Washington with a command-and-control structure dictating environmental policies to the states."[75] Though we believe the EPA's powers should be greatly curtailed, we're not as radical as Governor Symington in this regard. There are certain cross-border pollution issues that may require some form of federal involvement.

No More Federal Santa Claus

We will get out of the mandate business, but we will also get out of the money business.

Senator Bob Packwood (R-Ore.)[76]

For radical devolution to become a reality will require a fundamental change in mind-set not only in Washington, but also among state and local politicians. Since the beginning of the Great Society, state and local officials have come to see the federal government as a kind of Santa Claus, doling out money for all sorts of programs. Many mayors and governors became professional beggars at the Capitol's steps. Programs that would never be funded with local tax dollars become "vital" so long as they are paid for with "federal" dollars. Historically, state and local officials have wanted the money without the mandates. Explains Utah Governor Mike Leavitt,

States have traded their fundamental responsibility to govern in return for something that the feds seemed to have an endless supply of—money. Over and over again we've traded both our autonomy and independence as well as our constitutional responsibility. It's the Biblical story of selling one's birthright for a mess of pottage.[77]

Even more than states, big cities turned to Washington for help. Today, most cities are addicted to federal funds. Upon election, one of the first orders of business for both Mayor Giuliani of New York and Mayor Riordan of Los Angeles was a pilgrimage to Washington looking for a handout.

In the aftermath of the Rodney King riots, thousands of demonstrators marched down Constitution Avenue in Washington, D.C., in a "Save Our Cities, Save Our Children" march. Dozens of mayors, including Boston's Ray Flynn, New York's David Dinkins, and Baltimore's Kurt Schmoke led the marchers. What did these people want? Money from Washington, $35 billion to be exact. How did they plan to get it? By accentuating the negative. Homeless people were bussed in (at taxpayer expense) from distant cities to make the point.[78] Said former New York City Mayor David Dinkins, "We will continue to cry until Washington responds."[79]

Not all mayors thought that crying to Washington was the right approach. In an article titled, "Why This Mayor Isn't Marching," Lawrence J. Kelly, the Democratic mayor of Daytona Beach, Florida, wrote that he had "many reasons to oppose this effort, No. 1 being cost to taxpayers." Kelly continued, "[Mayors and cities] should face up to the fact that the checks we received from the federal government in the '60s and '70s were made out in red ink. . . . It's time for us to say: 'What can we do for ourselves?' rather than 'What can the federal government do for us?'"[80]

Local politicians fear the loss of federal funds, but where do they imagine this money comes from in the first place? France, perhaps? Jersey City Mayor Bret Schundler, one of the few big-city mayors to oppose the crime bill, did so because he recognized that all "federal money" comes from people living in one of the 50 states to begin with. Says Schundler:

> *Clinton wants to shift the burden of policing to the federal government and increase taxes. After he takes his big cut, he'll give us a portion of the money back for local policing. What a bonehead idea. The solution is not to shift taxes and make us pay more. The solution is reducing the cost of local policing.*[81]

Washington doesn't add any value to the tax dollars it receives and then sends back down to cities and states; in fact, the federal bureaucracy subtracts value as it takes its cut before sending money back to local governments.

Less federal money flowing out of Washington should mean less money flowing into Washington from the residents of cities and states. Keeping the money closer to home will also mean more flexibility, control, and accountability. "We understand this is going to mean less dollars from Washington," says New Jersey Governor Christine Todd Whitman, "but if you relieve us of some of the most onerous mandates, we will live with that."[82] State and local officials need to stop judging the worth of joint federal/state programs merely in terms of whether they are funded by "federal dollars." "We as Governors need to begin to ask a new question about programs," says Utah Governor Mike Leavitt. "Instead of asking is this a funded program, we should ask, should there be a federal role?"[83]

LOCAL MONEY FOR LOCAL PROGRAMS

A popular halfway solution for the welfare mess is to give states the responsibility for running the programs, and for Washington to send out the funding in "block grants." There are two problems with this. First, it maintains the subordinate position of the states. Despite claims to the contrary, the federal funds will bring with them rules, forms, and bureaucratic procedures. Second, it will induce states to structure their welfare programs so as to maximize their welfare reimbursements.

Consider what New Hampshire did with Medicaid reimbursement. Using a loophole in federal law, New Hampshire managed to generate an additional $366.6 million in federal funds in 1992 and 1993. Only about $44 million of that went to hospitals, while $322.6 million went to cover a state budget deficit. "It was a scam, no question about it," said one state legislator who helped devise the scheme. "We're funding our state judicial system, our highway program, and everything else out of a Medicaid loophole, which is being funded out of the [federal] deficit."[84]

The loophole wasn't an accident. New Hampshire's powerful Republican Senator Warren Rudman inserted provisions in a key Medicaid bill during the final hours of 1991 to make sure New Hampshire got its federal goodies. "My attitude was that if that's the way the game is played, we'll play it too," said Rud-man, defending his role.[85]

If cities and states paid their own way, there would be less of such chicanery. The funding and delivery of a service or program should be the responsibility of the lowest level of government possible. Getting to that point is likely to require a major restructuring of the tax system, including a substantial cut in federal taxes.[86]

In the transportation arena, for example, the federal government could get out of highway and airport funding by forgoing the gasoline tax and letting states raise construction money themselves—whether through a state gasoline tax, by raising landing fees or highway tolls, or by securing private debt. This approach would allow states to avoid a host of federal mandates—including the 55-mile-per-hour speed limit, the Davis Bacon Act, and the minimum drinking age—that accompany acceptance of federal highway funds.

The purpose of radical devolution is not to transform unneeded federal programs into unneeded state programs. Much of what the federal government does in the areas of housing, education, social services, transportation, labor training, and economic development shouldn't be done by government at all. "Rereading the Tenth Amendment might remind Congress that not every problem has a government solution," declares Goldsmith. "Any attempt to push authority out of Washington that . . . replaces federal bureaucracies with state bureaucracies isn't worth doing."[87]

In many areas the ultimate goal of policy must be to transfer as much power, authority, and responsibility as possible from government to individuals and local communities.[88] Once citizens see the true cost of local programs now being financed from Washington, they may not think they're worth the tax dollars spent on them.

Consider, for example, the uproar that ensued in Manhattan Beach, California, (where one of us lives) after the city council voted to spend money expanding a parking garage that residents felt would benefit only merchants. A front-page story in *The Beach Reporter* noted that "three dozen residents . . . bombarded the Manhattan Beach City Council on Tuesday . . ."[89] Another story noted:

> [M]*any residents complained that they were continually having to come down to City Hall to protect their interests. District 4 Councilmember Bob Pinzler told the residents that they should continue voicing their opinions and concerns. "You have to keep coming down here to protect your interests," Pinzler said, "because the special interest groups are here all the time."*[90]

This is democracy at its local, messy best, with vigilant residents watching over elected officials spending their tax dollars. Chances are no one in Manhattan Beach even knew that the federal government spent $2.5 million of tax money to build a parking garage in Burlington, Iowa. That little item didn't make the front page of *The Beach Reporter*, and no Manhattan Beach residents drove the 3,000-odd miles to Washington, D.C., to testify before a congressional committee. At the federal level, organized interests have an enormous advantage. Former Education Secretary William Bennett estimates that 285 education lobbying groups have offices within walking distance of the Department of Education headquarters. The average Manhattan Beach parent doesn't have a prayer.

The parking garage story illustrates the phenomenon known as "bill averaging." Imagine going out to dinner by yourself. When ordering, you'll closely watch the cost of each menu selection because you'll be paying the entire bill. Even if you were going out to dinner with one or two friends, you still wouldn't spend outrageously because you'd still be footing a good portion of the bill.

Now imagine that you are going out to dinner with 75 strangers, and that the bill is to be divided evenly. If you are like most people, you are going to order liberally, enjoy an extra drink, maybe even dessert and coffee. And why not? Your order will only affect your bill a minuscule amount; besides, you can bet that everyone else will be ordering big. The only way to get your "fair share" is to order lobster and Lowenbrau.

The federal government is like going to dinner with 250 million strangers. Rather than everyone paying his own way, a complex tangle of cross-subsidies obscures everyone's actual bill.

It's time to ask for separate checks. The good folks of Burlington, Iowa, got a new parking garage because Uncle Sam took about one penny from every Manhattan Beach resident—and every other American.[91] Because local taxpayers don't feel the bite, local officials love to spend "federal dollars." Would Altoonans have approved Altoona, Pennsylvania's, multimillion dollar moving sidewalk if Altoonan taxes were going to pay for it? Unlikely. But since the folks in Burlington, Iowa, and Manhattan Beach, California, are footing the bill, the Altoonans are happy to be carried along.

CONCLUSION

It should be clear that our goal is not just a change in government but a much broader transformation of our democratic life—a renewal of our public spirit.

New York Governor George Pataki[92]

The goal of the revolution sweeping American politics today isn't merely to improve America's government, but to improve American society. The same is true of this book. The revolutionary changes we describe have as their goal the renewal of our nation. While we focus on changes in public policy, we recognize the importance of individuals and voluntary associations in addressing the problems that afflict our country. We seek a smaller, better government as a means to a better society.

Like all upheavals, the current revolution ultimately depends on changes in the attitudes of individual Americans, not simply a change in who holds the reigns of power. Consider the comments of John Adams, writing of the American Revolution that created our nation:

> *The Revolution was affected before the war commenced. The Revolution was in the minds and hearts of the people. . . . This radical change in the principles, opinions, sentiments, and affections of the people, was the real American Revolution.*

Is the current political climate truly revolutionary? Yes. The political changes highlighted in this book, taken together with the revolt at the ballot box of November 1994, describe a sea change in the sentiment of the American people.

The last time such a dramatic change occurred was during the New Deal. In the throes of the Great Depression, Americans embraced a vision that called for a far more expansive role for government. Thirty years later, the Great Society extended the New Deal philosophy into many other areas of American life. Since then, American government has tended to operate under the theory that more government was the answer— regardless of the question. That approach has proven an abject failure, and many of today's problems are the result of yesterday's "solutions."

As during the Great Depression, Americans once again face a national crisis. But today Americans seek a much different path to renewal. The overarching aim of the current bottom-up revolution is to reduce, rather than expand, the size and scope of government.

Revolutionary times present danger as well as opportunity. Angry citizens are providing the driving force for dramatic change, but will that anger lead to *constructive* change? There are those who would use the current crisis to impose their values on others, to undermine our national commitment to liberty and equality of opportunity. Sadly, the tragic Oklahoma City bombing showed what can happen when ill-informed anger gives way to irrational hatred. In a democracy, revolutionary change does not require violence. But will voters embrace a vision of new and better governance, or will they lurch after a demagogue who taps into their anger without tapping into their minds?

Revolutions arise because conditions are bad, but not all revolutions lead to something better. For example, popular discontent sparked both the American and the French revolutions. The American colonists, however, knew not only what they were revolting *against*—British tyranny—but also what they were fighting *for*—liberty. The Declaration of Independence doesn't just present the colony's grievances against the king; more importantly, it describes the principles that would guide the new nation's government. America's founders had a realistic model for a process to achieve their vision. While not perfect, the system of limited government outlined in the Declaration helped establish one of the most prosperous and just societies in the annals of human history.[93]

The French people also knew what they were revolting against—royal tyranny. They even had a vision of something better, albeit the somewhat vague "liberty, equality, fraternity." But instead of a vision of limited government, the French believed that the "general will" of the people would express itself, though no one ever explained precisely *how* this would happen.[94] Unfulfilled expectations led to disappointment. Rather than visionary leaders such as Madison and Jefferson, the French turned to demagogues such as Robespierre. The anger that fueled the revolt was never given rational guidance. Rather than democracy, France deteriorated into a violent mobocracy. What began with high hopes turned into a "Reign of Terror," and finally degraded into the despotism of Napoleon.

Successful revolutions require not only a desire for change, but a practical blueprint of how to achieve a better society. It is not enough to be in favor of safe streets, good schools, and a strong economy. Just like our nation's original revolutionaries, we need to think long and hard about the political structures that can best achieve these goals.

This book has been an effort not only to describe today's revolution, but to ground it in firm principles. We have tried to ask the right questions. What is the proper role of government in a free society? What should government do, and at what level? What can government do and what can't it do to promote economic growth, reduce crime, and improve education? What is the appropriate role of the third pillar of society, the private, voluntary institutions that so enrich our culture? Rather than arguing from theory, we have attempted to relate concrete examples from across America of how limited government can succeed where big government fails.

"The American War is over; but this is far from being the case with the American Revolution. On the contrary, nothing but the first act of the great drama is now closed," wrote patriot Benjamin Rush many years ago. This is true today as well. America continues to be a work in progress, engaged in an ongoing struggle to determine if a nation conceived in liberty and dedicated to equality can long endure.

If America is to endure as a great nation, radical change is necessary. The word "radical," however, doesn't simply mean extreme. Like the word "radish," radical comes from the Latin word for "root." Today's revolution is truly radical because it addresses the root principles that govern our nation; its force comes from the grass-roots sentiments of the American people. After years of growth and centralization, for the first time in memory, Americans are demanding less from their government, not more. They want a government that is smaller, better, and closer to home. In the end, the American people themselves will determine if such a revolutionary quest can succeed.

APPENDIX A

SUCCESSFUL COMPETITIVE
CONTRACTING TECHNIQUES

When public officials decide to purchase a service, they still have two important tasks. First, they need to make sure they ask for what they want. Then they have to make sure they get what they asked for.

This isn't as easy as it may sound. When contracting fails, it is almost always because government has failed at one of these two critical tasks. Some contracting failures are inevitable, but as governments focus more and more on becoming smart shoppers, contracting problems can be kept to a minimal level.

Contract administration and monitoring requires a new set of skills for purchasing professionals within government. Governments in the future will be contracting extensively for services, and they need to develop more sophisticated systems to monitor and measure the performance of contractors.

Rather than inputs, the focus will be on results and customer satisfaction. Government today is very poor at monitoring performance, whether of outside contractors or in-house units. One city official told us of trying to get his managers to contract for grass mowing at public parks: "I had someone in the meeting stand up and say, 'My gosh, how are you going to track whether these contractors are mowing right?' I said, 'How are you doing it today?' I got a blank stare with no answer."

As governments strive to satisfy consumer demands, stepped-up monitoring systems are essential. The use of specific performance measures help to define exactly what the government wants. For instance, in the case of grass cutting, one city initially was contracting to have its grass cut every six weeks. But seasonal weather variations make such a criterion meaningless, and checking up on contractors is tedious—you have to track them down to make sure they're really mowing when they claim they are. Then the city grew more sophisticated. After all, the city didn't really want its grass cut every six weeks—it wanted the grass to be short. Now it contracts with a company to keep the grass less than eight inches high. Monitoring is easier, too. At random times, you just send someone out with a ruler.

Undoubtedly, some services lend themselves to performance measures more easily than others. Grass cutting and trash collection are relatively straightforward. But how do you assess the quality of a contractor's mental health care? Well, we might respond, how do you assess it today when it is provided by a public department? Embracing competition requires that government tackle these sorts of tricky issues, defining its goals and focusing on outcomes rather than inputs.

Another option is to steal ideas from the private sector, which has long experience developing the skills to monitor sophisticated contracting arrangements. Nike, for instance, doesn't even make its flagship product, Air Jordans. It outsources 100 percent of its athletic footwear manufacturing to production partners abroad. To ensure top quality, Nike puts its own people in each factory to monitor the contractor's performance. These Nike "expatriates" become permanent personnel in each factory producing Nike footwear, usually staying for several years. Successful outsourcers such as Nike have close personal contact with their contractors at the floor level and clear mutual understanding of needs and expectations at the top management level.

In addition to monitoring, governments can arrange contracts such that quality is ensured by market incentives. For instance, rather than contract with a private provider to deliver services to the mentally retarded, you can provide families with a voucher. In this way, the most important player in the process—the customer—monitors the quality of service and has options if he is dissatisfied.

Following is a checklist for successful contracting.

CHECKLIST FOR COMPETITIVE CONTRACTING

(The assistance of Linda Morrison, former director of competitive contracting for the city of Philadelphia and former advisor to the State of New Jersey, in preparing this checklist is gratefully acknowledged.)

1. *Identify the customer.* Focus on the individual, not a group. If the service is filling potholes, the customer is not the Highway Department, but the individual driver on that road. If the service is litter removal in a park, the customer is not the Department of Environmental Protection, but the individual citizen who uses the park. If the service is adoption placement, the customer is not the Department of Human Services, but the child who needs a good permanent home.

2. *Define the service in terms of outcomes, not process.* Keeping the customer in mind, briefly define the service in simple terms. Ignore inputs, such as the procedures, processes, equipment, or labor currently used in providing the service. Instead, focus on the objectives. Why is taxpayer money being used? This step will assist in preparation of the Request for Proposals (RFP).

3. *Consider how to measure the service.* To ensure that you get what you're paying for, consider how you will measure the product or service delivery; it may be an acre of grass mowed, a clean office building, or on-time delivery of mail. It helps to think in terms of how private businesses charge for the service on the open market.

4. *Establish quantifiable and measurable performance standards, if possible.* Try to define the performance standard using the desired end result in objective, measurable terms. This will not always be possible, but both the contractor and the government contract monitor will be more comfortable and confident if what is required is explicit. Remember, focus on outcomes, not process.

5. *Calculate the total costs.* This means determining the full in-house costs, including overhead, and the total contractor costs, including monitoring costs. Make sure you are comparing "apples to apples," and estimate costs for similar quality levels. And you can use these costs as a reference point for streamlining your in-house operation if you decide not to contract out.

6. *Plan to monitor the contract.* The most common failure in contracting is failure to adequately monitor contracts. Don't skimp on making sure you get what you pay for; monitoring plans should be quantifiable and specific. Include reporting requirements, regular meetings with minutes, complaint procedures, and access to contractor's records (if necessary). In rare situations, it may make sense to hire a separate private company to monitor the contractor.

NEVER renew a contract unless you have clear information that the service was performed well under the last contract. Don't assume this is the case without supporting evidence.

7. *Price smart.* Price isn't everything, but it is important, and there are a variety of ways to structure compensation. Guaranteed maximum prices for a defined end result are best if possible. Avoid "cost-plus" contracts. If possible, try to price based on the units of outcome. If applicable, use incentive pricing so the contractor can be rewarded for exceptionally good performance.

8. *Subject the service to regular competition.* Consider carefully before you award a sole-source contract. Very few services are so special that only one company can provide them. Even if you believe that one company is superior to the rest, subjecting the service to competition will make that company sharpens its pencils and gives you a better deal. Don't define the desired end result or scope of work so narrowly that only one contractor qualifies.

You can't have competition unless you have competitors. Don't just advertise in the back of one newspaper. Check the

Yellow Pages, industry groups, trade associations, mailing lists, and trade magazines. Contact other cities that buy this kind of service. It is important to call for the name and address of the particular individual in the private company who should receive the RFP, as opposed to mailing RFP's to "Dear IBM."

9. *Check qualifications and references.* One way is through a two-step process whereby contractors are first prequalified to submit proposals. Alternatively, ask contractors to include qualifications and references with their proposal. Customer references are most important (for similar-type work), but ask about credit, financial and supplier references, resumes of key personnel, and legal problems. However, don't insist on unnecessary qualifications or requirements that won't guarantee you a better end result. Doing this will merely serve to limit competition.

10. *Solicit feedback, suggestions, and comments throughout the process.* Consider sending out a draft RFP/bid to contractors for comment first. They are in the business full-time, and you want to take advantage of their expertise. Companies are not the enemy—they are potential future partners. Contractors are often reluctant to give unsolicited feedback. Therefore, you must actively solicit this information. Of course, keep your ears open for self-serving suggestions and don't talk exclusively with one contractor or become best friends with any one of them. Buy your own lunch.

11. *Use intelligent evaluation criteria.* Establish these evaluation criteria before proposals are in. This will keep your thinking organized and objective, and keep the process honest. Give sufficient weight to the thoroughness and responsiveness of the contractor's plan, references, and qualifications—don't just award to the lowest price.

12. *Be ready to accept tradeoffs.* When evaluating the impact of contract terms, do a cost/benefit analysis. Making something risk free can be very costly. (Remember that lawyers are only advisors in a business deal.)

13. *Give contractors enough time.* An unrealistic time frame can cost the government both in terms of dollars and uninterested contractors (reduced competition).

14. *Size the contract appropriately.* Make it large enough to capture economies of scale, but not so large that you eliminate a lot of smaller companies that could do the job. Don't automatically assume that a big contract performed by a big company is always the best way to go. Why eliminate competition unnecessarily?

15. *Set appropriate conditions for the contract.* If a service requires a large capital investment, a longer-term arrangement will be needed to allow contractors to amortize costs. Similarly, a performance bond can help ensure that a vital service is performed, but it can deter smaller contractors. The bond amount should not be excessive, because that will only serve to reduce competition. References and qualifications are a much better indicator of contract performance than performance bonds. Bonuses and penalties are appropriate in some contracts because they are a way to get the contractor's attention without having to take the drastic step of dismissal.

(For more information on competitive contracting in government and a list of How-to guides, contact the Renson Foundation, 3415 S. Sepulveda Blvd., Suite 400, Los Angeles, CA 90034, (310)391-2245.)

MAKING PRIVATIZATION A REALITY

Not every attempt to make government competitive succeeds. In fact, many fail. As we have examined scores of programs across the country at every level of government, we have discovered some surefire ways to stymie privatization and competition.

FAILING STRATEGY #1

Pick a Pilot Project

Avoiding failure is not the same as achieving success. To avoid failure, assign a committee to study whether competition in a particular service is a good idea. But to succeed with competitive government, make a firm commitment to acting on the principles of competitive government.

Remember that a wide array of forces don't want to see competitive government become reality. If you announce that you are going to study one particular service, the opponents of change will focus all available firepower on delaying, distracting, and derailing the effort. Many a privatization attempt has been killed when opponents of change have ganged up on the one unlucky manager who happened to have the only privatization proposal in town.

It does make sense to begin with low-profile projects, but don't think that you can slowly ease into competition. It's a lot like diving into a pool; unless you go all out, it is easy to belly flop. Caution, timidity, and hesitancy have no place in diving. But as in learning how to dive, it makes sense to start out from the low board before trying any high dives.

FAILING STRATEGY #2

Let's Study It to Death

Also known as "death by committee." This process gives the illusion of progress, then degenerates into an exercise in generating paper.

In the summer of 1992, Michigan created a commission to study privatization opportunities. By the winter of 1993, the state had introduced a process called PERM, by which every function in every department would be reviewed, and a recommendation made to privatize, eliminate, retain, or modify. For over two years, this ambitious effort chugged along with little real impact. The real progress that has occurred in Michigan has been the result of strong-willed individual administrators who have pushed for it.

FAILING STRATEGY #3

Hire Change Agents Who Are Afraid of Change

There is nothing harder than changing the way things are, and it requires a special person to make change a reality. According to management expert Peter Drucker, meaningful accomplishments are often the product of "a monomaniac with a mission."

There are so many barriers to change that only individuals with an evangelical commitment to competition will succeed. Without such a person, the weight of organizational inertia will gently suffocate any program: murder by bureaucratic asphyxiation. Linda Morrison, the former director of Philadelphia's competition program, is just such a zealot. Morrison has a single-minded commitment to competition. Behind almost every successful example of positive change you will find someone who won't take no for an answer.

FAILING STRATEGY #4

Ignore Your Public Employees

Public employees deserve to be treated with respect. It should be assumed that public workers are capable and willing to do a good job. In many cases, the best suggestions for how to improve a function will often come from frontline workers.

When considering a competition program, public employees should be kept informed about what will be occurring; after all, changes in the government work environment directly affect their livelihood. Public employees should be involved in the process early, they should be allowed to air grievances, and reasonable accommodation should be made to minimize any negative impact that competition may have on their situation.

Without the cooperation of both line employees and public managers, a competitive government can be almost impossible to achieve.

FAILING STRATEGY #5

Wait for Managers and Public Employees to Embrace Competition

Public workers are human beings. They are, in general, no more or less greedy, corrupt, noble, and generous than business people, college professors, or politicians. Self-interest is a strong human motivator, and almost anyone would prefer the guarantee of stable employment to the daily pressure of competition. Waiting for public employees to embrace the idea of competition is a losing strategy. Al Gore's National Performance Review boasted that it took its ideas from within government. In early 1995, project leader David Osborne admitted that a key shortcoming of the NPR was its dependence on insiders who were not committed to dramatic change.

Unless convinced that change is inevitable, public employees and their unions will enthusiastically fight any deviation from the status quo from sunup to sundown. If they come to believe that they will be fairly treated but that competition will be the way things are going to be, they will begin to work to make the process work. Why? Because it will be in their best interest to do so.

FAILING STRATEGY #6

Fail to Find Out Your Costs

In so many cases, governments have no idea how much they spend to provide a service. Without knowledge of costs, it is impossible to know if you are being efficient. Furthermore, since not even government has infinite resources, budget decisions are a matter of tradeoffs. These tradeoffs can't be made unless you know how much things cost.

Activity-based costing (ABC), which captures the "fully loaded" costs—direct, indirect, and overhead—of delivering a product or service, brings to light costs that previously were hidden, allowing managers to determine where they need to get costs down. Consider one city where there were 13 city crews sealing cracks in the roads. "If it's costing your crew a lot more to patch a crack than the other crews, you're out there and exposed. You're going to hustle to get your costs down," explains a department manager.

NOTES

Chapter 1: A New Era of Revolutionary Change

1. Richard L. Berke, "Anger and Cynicism Well Up in Voters as Hope Gives Way," *New York Times*, Oct. 10, 1994, p. A14.

2. Douglas Jehl, "One Hand Tied, Clinton Offers the Other," *New York Times*, Nov. 10, 1994, p. B4; for a transcription of news conference, see "Clinton: Voters Are Demanding That Parties Work Together" in the same section of the same issue.

3. John H. Fund, "The Revolution of 1994," *Wall Street Journal*, Oct. 19, 1994, p. A14.

4. Stephen Moore, "Read Our Lips: The Tax Revolt Lives," *Reason*, June 1992, p. 41.

5. Ibid.

6. Florio had stated, "I see no reason to raise taxes at this time." Several months later, after the election, the time seemed right.

7. Oct. 16, 1994. Joe McCarthy would probably suspect a massive conspiracy. Attendance at the same Georgetown cocktail party is the more likely explanation for the coincidence.

8. Ronald K. Snell, "Oh What a Relief It Is," *State Legislatures*, National Conference of State Legislatures, October 1993, p. 12.

9. Ron Suskind, "Michigan's School Aid Crisis Offers Crash Course in Convergence of Tax and Education Revolts," *Wall Street Journal*, Nov. 30, 1993, p. A16.

10. See for example, survey by CBS News/New York Times, January 12–14, 1993, and "The People, the Press and Politics: The New Political Landscape," Times Mirror Center for the People and the Press, Washington, DC, Sept. 21, 1994.

11. Sheri Erlewine, "What Californians Know About Their City Government," *Western City*, September 1993, p. 16.

12. George E. Pataki, Inaugural Address, Albany, N.Y., Jan. 1, 1995.

13. William D. Eggers, "Competitive Instinct," *Reason*, August/Sept. 1993, p. 22.

14. Ibid.

15. Stephen Goldsmith, interview with the authors, March 1993.

16. John Norquist, interview with the authors, March 1993.

17. John Norquist, interview with the authors, Jan. 1995.

18. William D. Eggers, "City Lights," *Policy Review*, Summer 1993, p. 70.

19. John Norquist, interview with the authors, March 1993.

20. "The Charlie Sykes Show," interview with John Norquist, radio station WTMJ, Milwaukee, Wisc., Jan. 12, 1995.

21. Thomas D. Hopkins, "The Cost of Regulation: Filling the Gaps" (Washington, D.C.: Regulatory Information Service Center, August 1992).

22. William J. Bennett, *The Index of Leading Cultural Indicators*, Vol. 1 (Washington DC: Empower America, The Heritage Foundation, and The Free Congress Foundation, March 1993).

23. George Melloan, "Why America Tops Europe on Job Creation," *Wall Street Journal*, Dec. 13, 1993, p. A15.

Chapter 2: Focussing on Core Functions

1. See Anne E. Kaplan, "Off-Track Betting in New York City," in *Privatization for New York: A Report of the New York Senate Advisory Commission on Privatization*, ed. E.S. Savas (New York, Jan. 1992).

2. In 1992, approximately 80 out of OTB's 90 branches were in the red, if you exclude the 5 percent surcharge (read, "tax") put on winning bets that is also collected by the city.

3. John Tierney, "For New York City's OTB, A Sure Bet Ends Up a Loser," *New York Times*, Oct. 23, 1994, p. 1.

4. Richard Schwartz, interview with the authors, August 1994.

5. Kaplan, "Off-Track Betting in New York City."

6. Tierney, "For New York City's OTB, A Sure Bet Ends Up a Loser," p. 1.

7. U.S. Dept. of Commerce, Bureau of the Census, *City Employment: 1992* (July 1994), Table 5.

8. Ibid. Incredible but true. New York City employs 52,393 workers in its hospitals (full-time equivalents). This is more than the total number of all city workers in Boston (20,768), San Diego (10,351), Seattle (10,168), and Cleveland (8,451) combined.

9. Carolyn Lochhead, "Fun and Games at the Consumer Affairs Department," *City Journal*, Summer 1992 (New York: Manhattan Institute), p. 63. A dozen undercover agents were used in a citywide sting operation.

10. Bruce Bender and Amy Klein, "Ten Ways to Trim the Budget," *City Journal*, Summer 1993 (New York: Manhattan Institute), p. 45.

11. Julia Vitullo-Martin, "The Livable City," *City Journal*, Autumn 1993 (New York: Manhattan Institute), p. 27.

12. "Radio Free Patronage," editorial, *New York Times*, Feb. 23, 1994.

13. "Don't Sell Out WNYC," editorial, *New York Times*, Feb. 28, 1994.

14. Harvey Robins, interview with the authors, August 1994.

15. John Franc, interview with the authors, April 1994.

16. Robert H. Waterman, Jr., *What America Does Right*, (New York: W.W. Norton, 1994), p. 182.

17. Adam Smith, *An Inquiry Into the Nature and Causes of the Wealth of Nations* (Oxford: Oxford University Press, 1979), pp. 26–27.

18. Anonymous interview with the authors, Jan. 1994.

19. Al Gore, "Report of the National Performance Review" (Sept. 7, 1993), pp. ii, 2.

20. Ibid., p. 93.

21. Billy J. Moore, interview with the authors, December 1993. Moore is chief of planning and analysis at the Federal Helium Reserve. The more you learn about the helium reserve, the crazier it sounds. The program was started in 1925 as a reserve for Army dirigibles. The major expansion came in 1960, at a time when there was no market for helium and no private suppliers. Since helium is a natural by-product of natural gas production, the gas producers convinced the government that it would require helium for the space program, and between 1961 and 1973, the government purchased over 30 billion cubic feet of helium.

Not surprisingly, it turned out that government estimates of future needs were wildly optimistic. Eventually, however, private demand for helium grew and private producers began selling helium on the open market—demand, rather than Congress, created a needed supply. At this point, you might expect the government to sell its reserves and cut its losses, right? Wrong. Someone (helium producers, maybe?) convinced Congress to set the price of federal helium above market rates. As of 1993, the federal government supplied only 10 percent of the helium used in the country, and charged about 12 percent more than private industry. Only federal agencies purchase from the helium reserve, and only because they are required by law to do so.

It gets worse. Because the reserve borrowed money for its purchasing binge between 1960 and 1973 (expecting to recoup the debt when the helium was sold, of course), the Bureau of Mines had racked up an accumulated $1.3 billion in debt by 1994.

22. James Risen, "Seemingly Wasteful Programs Not Easy to Cut," *Los Angeles Times*, August 8, 1993 p. A8. Kamarck contends that discontinuing the program would "instantly reduce the value of those assets held by the government." Given that the helium is already sitting there, and that sales income more than covers costs, Kamarck argues that the economics get "complicated."

23. Gore, "Report of the National Performance Review," p. 144.

24. Ibid.

25. David Osborne, "Can This President Be Saved?" *Washington Post Magazine*, Jan. 8, 1995, p. 15.

26. Robert J. Samuelson, "Government at Its Worst," *Washington Post*, Sept. 1, 1993, p. A23.

27. William D. Eggers and John O'Leary, "REGO No Go," *Reason*, April 1994, p. 53.

28. Bob Stone, interview with the authors, Nov. 1994.

29. Conversation with National Performance Review team member, Jan. 1995.

30. Catherine S. Manegold, "41% of School Day Is Spent on Academic Subjects, Study Says," *New York Times*, May 5, 1994, p. A13.

31. Celeste E. Smith, "Voucher System Likely Only for Failing Districts," *Asbury Park Press*, Sept. 2, 1994.

32. Recognizing that assuming too many tasks and missions has stretched their resources too thin, some police departments are shedding noncore activities. The Milwaukee police department, for example, decided that unlocking car doors for people who locked their keys inside was not part of its mission and wasted valuable police time. Now people who call the police for such assistance are given the phone number of a local locksmith.

In San Diego, the police department is training volunteers (mostly senior citizens) to take reports of nonviolent crimes such as burglaries, and most of the employees at police headquarters are civilians dressed in San Diego-casual.

33. David Osborne and Ted Gaebler, *Reinventing Government*, (Reading, Mass.: Addison-Wesley, 1992), p. xix.

34. John Testler, interview with the authors, August 1994.

35. Osborne and Gaebler, *Reinventing Government*, p. 216.

36. Marcia Berss, "Government Inc.," *Forbes*, August 1, 1994, p. 66.

37. Ibid.

38. Ibid.

39. Rob Gurwitt, "Entrepreneurial Government: The Morning After," *Governing*, May 1994, pp. 34–40.

40. According to *Governing* magazine, Duckworth also authorized an under-the-table payment to the developer out of taxpayer funds.

41. Gurwitt, "Entrepreneurial Government," p. 37.

42. Stephen Goldsmith, interview with the authors, June 1994.

43. Government units don't pay taxes or insurance premiums, they get subsidized postage, and they are often not required to comply with regulations placed on private firms (in fact, government officials can write the regulations in such a way that private firms cannot effectively compete with government ventures).

44. Michael White, speech at the Reason Foundation's "No More Business as Usual" conference, Chicago, May 9, 1994.

45. Ted Hershfeld, interview with the authors, July 1994.

46. Peter Powers, interview with the authors, August 1994.

47. Christine Todd Whitman, interview with the authors, August 1994.

48. Peter McDonough, interview with the authors, August 1994.

49. Madsen Pirie, speech to the National Citizens' Coalition, Halifax, Nova Scotia, Can., June 1992.

50. John O'Leary, ed., *Privatization 1995*, Reason Foundation, 1995.

51. John O'Leary, ed., *Privatization 1994*, Reason Foundation, 1994, p. 2.

52. Cited in Scott A. Hodge, "The National Performance Review: Falling Short of Real Government Reform," Heritage Foundation Backgrounder No. 962, Oct. 7, 1993, p. 9. For the GAO's data, see U.S. General Accounting Office, *Housing Issues* (GAO/OCG-93-22TR), Transition Series (Dec. 1992), p. 20.

53. David Frum, *Dead Right*, (New York: Basic Books, 1994), p. 45.

54. Bill Clinton and Al Gore, "Putting Customers First: Standards for Serving the American People," Report of the National Performance Review (Sept. 1994), p. 19.

55. David E. Sanger, "Clinton Proposal Gives New Life to Privatization," *San Francisco Chronicle*, Dec. 27, 1994, p. A3.

56. We do not pretend that asset sales are simple or easy to accomplish. In many cases, substantial federal, state, and/or local restrictions on sales of public assets must be overcome. This, in conjunction with the financial complexity of most sales, is a major reason why asset sales have to date been relatively rare. The international experience, however, suggests that such barriers can be overcome if there exists sufficient political will on the part of elected leaders.

57. George Wandrak, deputy executive director of the Connecticut Division of Special Revenues, speech at the Yankee Institute, (Hartford, Conn., Sept. 1994).

58. John O'Leary, "World Bank Study Shows Privatization of Enterprise Has Positive Economic Impact," *Privatization Watch*, Sept. 1992, p. 1. For the World Bank study, see Ahmed Galal et al., "The Welfare Consequences of Selling Public Enterprises," World Bank, July 1992.

59. Robert Poole, et al., "Mining the Government Balance Sheet: What Cities and States Have to Sell," Reason Foundation Policy Study No. 139, August 1992.

60. O'Leary, *Privatization 1994*, pp. 14–15.

61. John O'Leary and William D. Eggers, "Privatization and Public Employees: Guidelines for Fair Treatment," Reason Foundation How-To Guide No. 9, Sept. 1993.

62. Robert W. Poole, Jr. "Airport Privatization: What the Record Shows," Reason Foundation Policy Study No. 124, August 1990, pp. 10–12.

63. Pleasing the airport customer has become the overriding concern of BAA. The company surveys over 120,000 customers each year on everything from airport security to the quality of caviar at the airport shops. (Heathrow Airport is now Europe's largest seller of caviar.) Future customer-driven projects include full-blown shopping centers at all BAA airports and an aviation-theme visitors center at Gatwick that will have advanced flight and air traffic control simulators and an audio-visual history of flight.

64. Clive Lowe, speech to the National Council for Public-Private Partnerships, Washington, D.C., June 13, 1994.

65. Travelers don't have to pay double or triple price at BAA's airports. Retail chains must guarantee that everything sold at a BAA store will be priced at or below its price in other U.K. stores.

66. "Affordable Airport Shops?" Editorial, *New York Times* Nov. 8, 1992.

67. Ibid.

68. Ron Henry, interview with the authors, June 1993.

69. Allen Polleck, interview with the authors, Nov. 1993.

70. Jonathan Rauch, *Demosclerosis* (New York: Times Books, 1994), p. 232.

71. Ted Gaebler, "Managing for Results," University of Texas Conferences Proceedings, Austin, Texas, March 1994, p. 12.

72. Randy Fitzgerald, "This Congressman Beat the System," *Reader's Digest*, April 1989.

73. Ibid.

74. Stuart Butler and Scott Hodge, "The Politics of Cutting Spending," *F.Y.I.*, The Heritage Foundation, Oct. 13, 1994, p. 4.

75. Quoted in Paul A. Gigot, "Maybe They'll Even Succeed," *Wall Street Journal*, Jan. 6, 1995, p. A10.

76. Greg Kaza, "Lansing with Wolves," *Policy Review*, Summer 1991, p. 76.

77. Ibid.

78. Paul A. Gigot, "Michigan GOP Isn't Your Father's Oldsmobile," *Wall Street Journal*, Oct. 14, 1994.

79. David Riemer, interview with the authors, April 1993.

80. William D. Eggers, "Rancho Palos Verdes Commercializes Recreation Services," *Privatization Watch*, Reason Foundation, Sept. 1993, p. 5.

Chapter 3: Devolving Power and Restoring Community

1. State of the Union Address, Jan. 25, 1994.

2. Milton and Rose Friedman, *Free to Choose* (New York: Harcourt Brace Jovanovich, 1970), p. 37.

3. Newt Gingrich, speech before the Washington Research Group Symposium, Washington, D.C., Nov. 8, 1994.

4. Stephen Moore, "Government: America's #1 Growth Industry," The Institute for Policy Innovation, Feb. 1993. Social welfare spending as described here includes all forms of cash and noncash public assistance, health care, social security, veterans benefits, and assorted other transfer payment programs. Between 1950 and 1990, the share of the federal budget spent on defense dropped from 32 percent to 22 percent.

5. A similar scenario has been played out in law enforcement. The modern approach to fighting crime has been more police, more prisons, more cops, more squad cars, and less interaction with the community. With the bulk of their time spent speeding from one 911 call to another, police have become disconnected from the communities they serve. And many communities, for their part, have abdicated their responsibility to police themselves. Criminal behavior, after all, is often the reflection of poor upbringing, which is beyond the reach of government.

6. Moore, "Government."

7. William J. Bennett, *The Index of Leading Cultural Indicators*, (Empower America, The Heritage Foundation, and the Free Congress Foundation, March 1993).

8. Jack Kemp, "The Politics of the Impossible," The Heritage Lectures, The Heritage Foundation, Washington DC No. 511, Nov. 15, 1994.

9. Alexis de Tocqueville, *Democracy in America* (New York: Anchor Press, 1969), p. 515.

10. Robert Dahl calls this "the presumption of personal autonomy." See Robert A. Dahl, *Democracy and its Critics* (New Haven, Conn.: Yale University Press, 1989), p. 100.

11. Bill Clinton and Al Gore, "Putting Customers First: Standards for Serving the American People," Report of the National Performance Review (Sept. 1994), p. 5.

12. Fife Symington, Inaugural Speech, Jan. 6, 1995.

13. George E. Pataki, Inaugural Address, Albany, N.Y., Jan. 1, 1995.

14. The Europe of Tocqueville's time, with its centralized state power and established state churches, lacked a wide array of community institutions. In contrast, Tocqueville found in America a system of decentralized government and diffuse power. Most decisions affecting the daily lives of Americans were made at the township level (the government closest to the people), which operated in many ways like a voluntary association. Furthermore, within each municipality, power was also dispersed among many citizens. The typical American shared in the management of the township, thereby creating a sense of municipal spirit. Wrote Tocqueville, "When the public governs, all men feel the value of public goodwill and all try to win it by gaining the esteem and affection of those among whom they live."

For Tocqueville, strong citizen participation in local government and the diversity and strength of America's nongovernmental, nonprofit institutions—particularly its churches—represented a principal source of stability and vitality in American democracy. Left to their own devices, Americans joined together to help one another.

15. Tocqueville, *Democracy in America*, p. 198.

16. Amitai Etzioni, "Settling for Less," *National Review*, Dec. 19, 1994, p. 46.

17. Ibid.

18. Tocqueville, *Democracy in America*, p. 515.

19. John L. McKnight, interview with the authors, Oct. 1994.

20. Richard C. Cornuelle, *Reclaiming the American Dream* (New Brunswick, N.J.: Transaction Publishers, 1993), p. 198.

21. Esther Iverem, "A Church in Brooklyn Closes Its Men's Shelter," *New York Times*, April 18, 1987, p. 23.

22. Joel Garreau, *Edge City: Life On The New Frontier* (New York: Anchor Books, 1988), p. 279.

23. Daniel Blankenhorn, *Fatherless America: Confronting Our Most Urgent Social Problem* (New York: Basic Books, 1995), p. 1.

24. Michael Joyce, "Citizenship in the 21st Century," in *Building a Community of Citizens: Civil Society in the 21st Century*, ed. Don E. Eberly (Lanham, Md.: University Press, 1994), p. 5.

25. It is important to distinguish between private, voluntary charities and nonprofits that exist to provide government services. Receiving most of their funding from the state, many nonprofits have become virtual arms of government. It is not surprising that they display many of the same characteristics; treating people as clients or consumers of social services rather than as potentially self-governing individuals. Restoring the private nature of these nonprofits should be a goal of those concerned with revitalizing civic institutions.

26. Michael Rust, "Social Security Scam: Uncle Sam as Enabler," *Insight*, April 11, 1994, p. 7.

27. Ibid.

28. Anonymous interview with the authors, Jan. 1995.

29. Eloise Anderson, interview with the authors, Dec. 1994.

30. Rust, "Social Security Scam," p. 9.

31. James L. Payne, "The Promise of Community: Local Voluntary Organizations as Problem Solvers," Philanthropy Roundtable, 1994, p. 23.

32. Robert Sirico, "Samaritan's Dilemma," *Forbes*, April 25, 1994, p. 106.

33. Sirach, chapter 12, verse 1.

34. Lee Earl, interview with the authors, May 1994.

35. Ibid.

36. Robert L. Woodson, Jr., and Collette Caprara, "Self Help Initiatives on the Rise," *Agenda: The Alternative Magazine of Critical Issues*, Vol. 2, No. 1 (1992), National Center for Neighborhood Enterprise, pp. 5–6.

37. Ibid.

38. Jackie Gelb, interview with the authors, June 1994.

39. Like many successful programs, YouthBuild has tough rules that must be followed; drug use or unexplained absences quickly lead to dismissal. "We have had people who have been shot call us from the hospital. We had one guy with bullets in his stomach and his lungs call us, begging us not to give away his place in Youth-Build," says Gelb.

40. Joe Klein, "Shepherds of the Inner City," *Newsweek*, April 18, 1994, p. 28.

41. John McKnight, interview with the authors, Oct. 1994.

42. Leon Watkins, "Awakening Their Dreams," *Agenda: The Alternative Magazine of Critical Issues*, Vol. 3, No. 1 (1993), National Center for Neighborhood Enterprise, p. 27.

43. Since 1994, at least two books have called for parental licensing, including Jack Westman, *Licensing Parents: Can We Prevent Child Abuse and Neglect?* and David Lykken, *The American Crime Factory: How it Works and How to Slow it Down.*

44. Michele Galen, "Kids Need a Safety Net, Too," *Business Week*, Oct. 17, 1994, p. 232.

45. National Policy Forum, *Listening to America*, (Washington, D.C.: National Policy Forum, 1994), p. 13.

46. Anonymous interview with the authors, July 1994.

47. This is not to say that it is always wrong for parents to purchase child-rearing services for their children. But there is a big difference between privately purchased day care—paid for with private funds and selected by the parents—and expecting the government to provide quality, affordable day care as a matter of right.

48. Quoted in Blankenhorn, *Fatherless America*, p. 228.

49. Jersey City Mayor Bret Schundler has made citizen and neighborhood involvement in public service delivery a cornerstone of his approach to governing. To encourage neighborhoods to become more involved in protecting their own communities, he has set up 133 community-based police districts, where foot patrol officers are directly accountable to neighborhood committees. Police on night patrol talk daily to a designated neighborhood resident, who informs them about any problems. Schundler also advocates parental choice in education to give parents greater say in their children's education (see Chapter 10).

Dayton, Ohio, also has extensive citizen participation in local governance. Since the early 1970s, when Dayton established a system of neighborhood councils called "priority boards," neighborhoods have been integrally involved in governing the city. Run by elected citizen-members, the priority boards play a role in shaping most of the important (and many less important) decisions facing the city.

By reporting on trash collection complaints, making sure alleys are cleaned up and parks maintained, the boards help monitor the city's performance in delivering basic services, acting, in effect, as a halfway stop between the individual citizen and City Hall. Whereas City Hall often seems distant and removed, the neighborhood council is right there.

City dwellers universally complain about the difficulties of navigating the government bureaucracy when they have problems with service delivery. To address this problem, Indianapolis, Pasadena, Portland, and Houston each has designated a top city official as its "neighborhoods czar" to help citizens cut through the red tape. Some governments attempt to elicit community input by setting up mobile town halls, doing customer service surveys, and creating a complaint office. While these efforts are admirable, it is preferable to devolve control as much as possible so that accountability occurs naturally.

50. See William D. Eggers, "Competitive Instinct," *Reason*, August/Sept. 1993, p. 26.

51. Stephen Goldsmith, interview with the authors, June 1994.

52. Susan Golding, interview with the authors, July 1994.

53. Elizabeth Larson, "Library Renewals," *Reason*, March 1994, p. 37.

54. Ibid.

55. John R. Guardiano, David Haarmeyer, and Robert W. Poole, Jr., "Fire Protection Privatization: A Cost-Effective Approach to Public Safety," Reason Foundation Policy Study No. 152, Jan. 1993, p. 14. Since all-volunteer departments tend to exist in rural regions, about one in four Americans is served by an all-volunteer fire department.

56. Database of the National Volunteer Fire Council, Alexandria, Virginia.

57. The bureaucracy doesn't always want to relinquish control. In 1994, public housing residents in San Antonio filed a lawsuit; aided by the nonprofit Institute for Justice, residents are fighting for the chance to do for themselves what government officials have been doing for them.

58. Isabel Wickerson, "From Squalor to Showcase: How a Group of Tenants Won Out," *New York Times*, June 11, 1988.

59. David Caprara and Bill Alexander, *Empowering Residents of Public Housing: A Resource Guide for Resident Management* (Washington D.C.: National Center for Neighborhood Enterprise, 1989), p. 21.

60. Bret Schundler, remarks at the Reason Foundation's "No More Business as Usual" conference, Chicago, May 10, 1994.

61. Garreau, *Edge City*, p. 184.

62. Robert Nisbet, *The Quest for Community: A Study in the Ethics of Order & Freedom* (San Francisco: ICS Press, 1990), p. xxix.

63. William Weld, interview with the authors, June 1994.

64. Steven Rathgeb Smith and Michael Lipsky, *Nonprofits for Hire* (Cambridge, Mass.: Harvard University Press, 1993), p. 50.

65. Ibid., pp. 53–54.

66. This amounts to $1.2 billion out of its $1.9 billion budget. See William Tucker, "Sweet Charity," *The American Spectator*, Feb. 1995, p. 38.

67. Smith and Lipsky, *Nonprofits for Hire*, p. 4.

68. Ibid., p. 8.

69. Robin Kamen and Steve Malanga, "Nonprofits: NY's new Tammany Hall," *Crain's New York Business*, Oct. 31, 1994, p. 49.

70. Ibid., p. 57.

71. Tucker,"Sweet Charity," p. 39.

72. Charlie Baker, interview with the authors, April 1994.

73. Smith and Lipsky, *Nonprofits for Hire*, p. 6.

74. President Clinton, remarks to press, Denver, January 15, 1995.

75. Director of a multisite National Americorps program, anonymous interview with the authors, February 1995.

76. Charles Oliver, "Brickbats," *Reason*, December 1994, p. 13.

77. U.S. Dept. of Housing and Urban Development, "Housing Cost Reduction Demonstration" (HUD-606-H), Dec. 1980, p. 5.

78. As a way of allowing more first-time buyers to purchase homes, some cities have relaxed or modified housing and zoning regulations. A number of Long Island communities have altered their zoning codes and created special districts where houses originally built as single-family homes can be changed to include a so-called "granny flat" rental unit. The rental income and tax advantages from the granny flat allow many first-time buyers to purchase homes when they couldn't otherwise do so. To remedy the decline of affordable housing for low-income people, San Diego in the mid-1980s revised its building codes to allow private developers to construct buildings consisting mostly of 100-square-foot units with no kitchens. Called SROs, these units cost 50 percent less than a conventional studio apartment. See Howard Husock, "Humble Homes," *Reason*, April 1993, pp. 30–31, and Howard Husock, remarks to the Urban Development Institute, Toronto, Ont., Can., June 2, 1994.

79. Christine Todd Whitman, interview with the authors, August 1994.

80. Philip K. Howard, "The Death of Common Sense," *U.S. News & World Report*, Jan. 30, 1995, p. 57.

81. Michael Joyce, interview with the authors, Nov. 1994.

Chapter 4: Competition: The Key to Efficient Government

1. Thomas Jefferson quoted in Commonwealth of Massachusetts, Dept. of Administration and Finance, "Privatization in Massachusetts: Getting Results," Nov. 1993, p. 43.

2. John Norquist, speech at the Reason Foundation's "No More Business as Usual" conference, Chicago, May 9, 1994.

3. Stephen Goldsmith, interview with the authors, March 1993.

4. Norquist, speech at the Reason Foundation.

5. The government is somewhat inconsistent in its application of antitrust law; it often protects private-sector public utility monopolies.

6. "Why Big Business Is No Longer a Crime," *Financial News*, Jan. 11, 1982, p. 12.

7. John O'Leary, "How to Improve the Post Office," *Journal of Commerce*, June 23, 1994, p. 8A.

8. Tom Peters, *Liberation Management: Necessary Disorganization for the Nanosecond Nineties* (New York: Knopf, 1992), p. 507.

9. Ibid., p. 502.

10. There are about 20 different types of privatization techniques. Contracting out a service to the private sector is typically thought of as one of these types. Selling an asset to the private sector would be a "purer" form of privatization.

11. See, for example, John Hilke, "Cost Savings from Privatization: A Compilation of Findings," Reason Foundation How-To Guide No. 6, March 1993.

12. Ron Jensen, interview with Reason Foundation researcher Courtney Timberlake, March 1994.

13. William D. Eggers, "Rightsizing Government," Reason Foundation How-to-Guide No. 11, Jan. 1994, p. 1.

14. Apogee Research, Inc., Bethesda, MD. Survey sponsored by the National Association of Comptrollers, 1992.

15. Michael White, speech at the Reason Foundation's "No More Business as Usual conference," Chicago, May 9, 1994.

16. Edward Rendell, interview with the authors, Nov. 1994.

17. Linda Morrison, interview with the authors, Nov. 1994.

18. Richard M. Daley, speech at the Reason Foundation's "No More Business as Usual" conference, Chicago, May 9, 1994.

19. Richard M. Daley, "Chicago City Government: Smaller in Size, But Greater in Performance," *Business Forum*, Winter/Spring 1994, p. 9.

20. Daley, speech at the Reason Foundation.

21. Stephen Bartlett, interview with the authors, Nov. 1993.

22. Bill Weld and Paul Celluci, Preface, Commonwealth of Massachusetts, Dept. of Administration and Finance, "Privatization in Massachusetts: Getting Results," Nov. 1993.

23. James Kerasiotes, interview with the authors, June 1994.

24. James J. Kerasiotes, "Mass Privatization," *Infrastructure Finance*, Feb./March 1994, p. 55.

25. Commonwealth of Massachusetts, "Privatization in Massachusetts." Another Massachusetts example of cost savings from competition was in the money-counting operation of the subway system. After the state received bids from Wells Fargo and Brinks, employees came forward with suggestions to streamline. The number of workers dropped from 71 to 59, and annual costs went down from $4.5 million to $3.5 million a year. The job stayed in house. "If we didn't have the ability to competitively contract that situation, we would have had business as usual," says Kerasiotes.

26. Skip Stitt, interview with the authors, May 1994.

27. Rob Gurwitt, "Indianapolis and the Republican Future," *Governing*, Feb. 1994, p. 26.

28. William D. Eggers, "Competitive Instinct," *Reason*, August/Sept. 1993, p. 23.

29. John O'Leary and William D. Eggers, "Privatization for Public Employees: Guidelines for Fair Treatment," Reason Foundation How-To Guide No. 9, Sept. 1993.

30. Mitchell Roob, interview with the authors, June 1994.

31. Stephen Goldsmith, speech at the Reason Foundation's "No More Business as Usual" conference, Chicago, May 10, 1994.

32. Ibid.

33. Mitchell Roob, interview with the authors, June 1994.

34. Interview with the authors, June 1994.

35. Eggers, "Competitive Instinct," p. 25.

36. Ibid.

37. Comment of city sign shop employee, interview with the authors, June 1994.

38. See Peters, *Liberation Management*, Chapter 9.

39. Crack-sealing crew, interview with the authors, April 1993.

40. David Walderop, interview with the authors, March 1993.

41. Peters, *Liberation Management*, p. 337.

42. Michael Rothschild, "Coming Soon: Internal Markets," *Forbes ASAP*, June 7, 1993, p. 19.

43. Ibid., p. 20.

44. Anne Spray Kinney, "Using Competition to Improve Services in Milwaukee City Government," presentation to Public Policy Forum Trustees, Milwaukee, Wis., April 21, 1994.

45. Bret Schundler, interview with the authors, Dec. 1993.

46. White, speech at the Reason Foundation.

47. William Weld and Paul Celluci, Preface, "Privatization in Massachusetts: Getting Results."

Chapter 5: Understanding Government Systems

1. Susan Golding, interview with authors, July 1994. All the remarks of the mayor in this chapter are from this interview.

2. U.S. Dept. of Commerce, "City Employment: 1992," July 1994.

3. Al Gore, "Report of the National Performance Review" (Sept. 7, 1993), p. 1.

5. David Osborne and Ted Gaebler, *Reinventing Government* (Reading, Mass.: Addison-Wesley, 1992), p. xviii.

6. James Q. Wilson, *Bureaucracy* (New York: Basic Books, 1989), pp. 375–376.

7. Donald J. Savoie, *Thatcher, Reagan, Mulroney: In Search of a New Bureaucracy* (Pittsburgh: University of Pittsburgh Press, 1994), p. 29.

8. Jonathan Walters, "The Fine Art of Firing the Incompetent," *Governing*, June 1994, p. 34.

9. William L. Riordan, *Plunkitt of Tammany Hall* (Mattituck, N.Y.: Amereon House, 1905), p. 11.

10. Ibid.

11. Ibid., p. 55.

12. American Federation of State, County, and Municipal Employees president Gerald McEntee, in Walters, "The Fine Art of Firing the Incompetent."

13. Stephen Barr, "Washington Turns Over 10,000 New Leaves," *Washington Post*, May 9, 1994, p. A1.

14. National Association of State Personnel Executives, "Civil Service Reform Survey Results," Jan. 20, 1993.

15. Joe Trainor, assistant secretary of human resources, interview with the authors, Dec. 1994.

16. William D. Eggers, "City Lights," *Policy Review*, Summer 1993, p. 68.

17. Rich Carlgaard, "Interview with Mike Hammer," *Forbes ASAP*, Sept. 13, 1993, p. 71.

18. Wilson, *Bureaucracy*, p. 56.

19. "Wake Up Call for Kentucky," First Report of the Governor's Commission on Quality and Efficiency, 1993, p. 22.

20. Ibid., p. 22.

21. State employee, conversation with the authors, 1994.

22. Janet R. Beales, "Performance-Based Education," *Privatization Watch*, Reason Foundation, July 1994, p. 1.

23. Norm King, interview with the authors, Oct. 1994. Mr. King noted that he was not speaking of Moreno Valley, explaining that such political interference is widespread.

24. Frank P. Sherwood, "Comprehensive Government Reform in New Zealand," *The Public Manager*, Spring 1992, pp. 20–24.

25. Graham Mather, "Making Good Government Seem Easy: Lessons from New Zealand's Economic and Policy Reforms" (London: European Policy Forum, Oct. 1993), p. 16.

26. Peter Hellman, "How To Cut the Budget," *New York*, Jan. 21, 1991, p. 29. If you think it would be difficult to run a school efficiently under these conditions, you are right. Though the New York City janitors' situation is an extreme case, along with civil service rules, unions and collective bargaining agreements tie up public managers in a maze of rules. Union contracts can be several hundred pages in length.

27. In the private sector, unions have an incentive to fight for high wages and benefits, but they also have an incentive to eliminate work rules that diminish the company's productivity. In the monopolistic public sector, productivity is really not an issue. The private United Parcel Service union knows it is in its own best interest to keep UPS competitive. Unions at the United States Postal Service, in contrast, know that no matter how unproductive the Postal Service is, it will still carry every piece of first- and third-class mail in the country. It's the law.

28. Chris Carmody, interview with the authors, Sept. 1994.

29. John O'Leary and William D. Eggers, "Privatization and Public Employees: Guidelines for Fair Treatment," Reason Foundation How-To Guide No. 9, Sept. 1993, p. 25.

30. Larry Scanton, panel remarks, National Council of Public Private Partnerships Conference, June 1994.

31. Bob Stone, interview with the authors, Nov. 1994.

32. David Cohen, interview with the authors, Nov. 1994.

33. Edward Rendell, interview with the authors, Nov. 1994.

34. Ron Marsico, "State Unions Worry as Whitman Spreads Her Message on Privatization," Newark *Star-Ledger*, Oct. 2, 1994.

35. What distinguishes business from government? Government cannot go out of business. Only by duplicating that urgency through competition is widespread, *systematic* improvement possible.

36. "Jobs and Productivity," *Forbes*, April 25, 1994, p. 243.

37. Wendell White, interview with the authors, July 26, 1993.

38. Jonathan Walters, "The Downsizing Myth," *Governing*, May 1993, p. 35.

39. Ken Bryan, Dow Chemical, interview with the authors, Sept. 1994.

40. George S. Patton, *War As I Knew It*, from *John Bartlett's Familiar Quotations*, 14th ed., ed. Emily Beck (Boston: Little, Brown, 1968), p. 987b.

41. David Frum, *Dead Right* (New York: Basic Books, 1994), p. 95.

42. Eric Foner and John A. Garraty, eds., *The Reader's Companion to American History* (Boston: Houghton Mifflin, 1991), p. 1091.

43. Steven Kelman, interview with the authors, Sept. 1994. All subsequent remarks by Kelman are from this interview.

44. Joe Adler, interview with the authors, Sept. 1994.

45. Ibid.

46. Ann Spray Kinney, interview with the authors, Sept. 1994.

47. Stephen Goldsmith, interview with the authors, June 1994.

48. Donald F. Kettl, "Reinventing Government?" Brookings Institution, August 19, 1994, p. 10.

49. Bill Clinton and Al Gore, "Putting Customers First: Standards for Serving the American People," Report of the National Performance Review (Sept. 1994), pp. 88–90.

50. Television commercials provided by R. C. Auletta and Company, 1994. Frank Perdue also notes, "The government has more to worry about than just the quality of your chicken. Fortunately for you, I don't."

51. "Minnesota Milestones: A Report Card for the Future," by Minnesota Planning, Governor's Minnesota Milestones Advisory Committee, Dec. 1992.

52. Osborne and Gaebler, *Reinventing Government*, p. 23.

53. Putting a dog, no matter how well-trained, behind the wheel of a car is not a good idea.

54. Michael Keeley, interview with the authors, Oct. 1994.

55. King, interview with the authors.

Chapter 6: Setting Limits

1. David Cohen, interview with the authors, November 1994.

2. William D. Eggers and John O'Leary, "Tight-fisted governors take over spendthrift states," *Kansas City Star*, Dec. 4, 1994, p. K1.

3. Christine Todd Whitman, interview with the authors, August 1994.

4. Edward Rendell, interview with the authors, Nov. 1994.

5. Edward G. Rendell, "America's Cities: Can We Save Them?" *City Journal*, Manhattan Institute, Winter 1994, p. 28.

6. Ibid., p. 27.

7. Cohen, interview with the authors.

8. Joseph Torsella, interview with the authors, June 1993.

9. Charlie Baker, interview with the authors, April 1994.

10. "Low-Tax Liberal," *Policy Review*, Winter 1991, p. 28.

11. Randy Blumer, interview with the authors, Feb. 1994.

12. Steve Postrel, interview with the authors, Sept. 1994.

13. William Ouchi, interview with the authors, March 1994.

14. Economists call this the phenomenon of diffuse costs and concentrated benefits. The phenomenon describes legislation that benefits a small group greatly at the small expense of a much larger group. The uneven impact of the legislation produces incentives that encourage politicians to pass special-interest laws. For example, dairy price supports greatly benefit a small number of dairy farmers, while the cost to each of America's millions of milk drinkers may be only a few cents a gallon.

There is a strong incentive for dairy farmers to organize and lobby for these laws, while it's not worth it for milk drinkers to oppose them. It is often too much to ask of politicians to refuse the temptation of these special interests.

15. "Soundings," *City Journal*, Manhattan Institute Autumn 1994, p. 6.

16. University of Massachusetts Foundation officials, interview with the authors, 1989. The University of Massachusetts Foundation, Inc., a quasi-public nonprofit agency that accepts donations on behalf of the university, was authorized by Joseph Duffy, then president of the University of Massachusetts at Amherst, to rent busses for the student protest.

17. James Q. Wilson, interview with the authors, Sept. 1994.

18. Douglas Bruce, interview with the authors, Nov. 1994.

19. *Nuveen Research Report*, "Colorado's Amendment One: Update," March 1994.

20. Stephen Moore and Dean Stansel, "The Great Tax Revolt of 1994," *Reason*, Oct. 1994, p. 20.

21. Bruce, interview with the authors, Nov. 1994.

22. Colorado Municipal League, "Amendment One: A Municipal Guide to the Taxpayers' Bill of Rights," August 1993, p. 1.

23. Jerry Horac, interview with the authors, Sept. 1994.

24. Daniel T. Griswold, "Colorado Offers Hope to Tax Cutters," *Wall Street Journal*, Oct. 20, 1994.

25. In a study of tax expenditure limitation measures, Dale Bails concluded that states' TELs "resulted in virtually no success in limiting growth in their budgets." See Dale Bails, "The Effectiveness of Tax-Expenditure Limitations: A Reevaluation," *American Journal of Economics and Sociology*, Vol. 49, No. 2 (April 1990), p. 223.

Also see James Cox and David Lowery, "The Impact of the Tax Revolt Era: State Fiscal Caps," *Social Science Quarterly*, vol. 71, no. 3 (Sept. 1990), p. 507. In a study of three TEL states, Cox and Lowery concluded that "by and large, the behavior of the cap states has been similar to that of noncap states."

26. Dean Stansel, "Taming Leviathan: Are Tax and Spending Limits the Answer?" Cato Institute Policy Analysis No. 213 (July 25, 1994). The study found that the growth rate of per capita state and local spending in TEL states fell from 0.1 percent below the U.S. average to 4.4 percent below it in 1991. With regard to taxes, the change was more dramatic. Real per capita taxes expanded by nearly 12 percent in the five years before the enactment of limits in the TEL states, but fell by 2.8 percent over the five years after enactment. The result was on average a state tax burden per family of four that was $650 lower than it would have been without the limits. Missouri's 1980 amendment that limited tax increases to a percentage of the state's personal income has saved taxpayers more than $1 billion and increased their personal income an average of 1.75 percent.

27. Missouri, Montana, and Oregon.

28. Stephen Moore and Dean Stansel, "The Great Tax Revolt of 1994," p. 22.

29. Ibid.

30. William Tucker, "Tax Rebels Battle State Spending Through the Ballot," *Insight*, August 8, 1994, pp. 9–10.

31. Grover Norquist, interview with the authors, Dec. 1993.

32. Kenneth Silber, "Voters Take Control of Taxes, *Insight*, Jan. 3, 1994, pp. 7–8.

33. Norquist, interview with the authors.

34. This is what occurred during the boom 1980s. Between 1980 and the early 1990s, Arizona's budget more than tripled, Connecticut's expenditures quadrupled, and Florida's budget went from $7 billion in 1980 to $30 billion. "In the 1980s, tax dollars rolled into state treasuries in wheelbarrows, and were quickly spent," says former Connecticut Governor Lowell Weicker.

When the economy soured in the late 1980s and early 1990s, states were in a real fix: they had no way to pay for all the new programs created in the 1980s. What did they do? Some—like Massachusetts (under Governor Weld) and Michigan (under Governor Engler)—chopped state budgets down to size. Most, however, raised taxes, finding that less unpleasant than trying to cut out a recent program that had built up a constituency.

35. Barbara Anderson, interview with the authors, April 1994.

36. See, for example, James K. Coyne and John H. Fund, *Cleaning House: America's Campaign for Term Limits* (Washington, D.C.: Regnery Gateway Publishers, 1992). Also see Stephen Moore and Aaron Steelman, "An Antidote to Federal Red Ink: Term Limits," Cato Institute Briefing Paper No. 21. By examining the voting behavior of relatively newer members of Congress against those of more veteran members, the study suggests that term limits would "tilt budget policy outcomes in the direction of increased fiscal restraint."

37. Marlo Lewis, Jr., "Limit Terms to Limit Government," *UpDate*, Competitive Enterprise Institute, July 1994, p. 2.

38. A survey of legislative staffers by the Sindlinger Organization found that over 70 percent of them opposed term limits. Why? A higher turnover of committee chairman would ensure a higher turnover of staff, because most new chairmen would be likely to bring on their own teams. It is senior legislators who are most dependent on staffers. Freshmen are more likely to come in with a "let's slay the beast" attitude.

39. Payne and Fund, *Cleaning House*, p. 127.

40. Ibid.

41. Christopher Georges, "Wider Property-Owner Compensation May Prove a Costly Clause in the 'Contract with America'," *Wall Street Journal*, Dec. 30, 1994, p. A10.

42. Carolyn Pesce, "Private Property vs. Public Rights," *USA Today*, Feb. 6, 1995, p. A3.

43. Georges, "Wider Property-Owner Compensation May Prove a Costly Clause."

44. Some confusion arises from the term "property rights," which are often erroneously contrasted with "human rights." Property rights refer to the right of a human to own property. A tin whistle is made of tin, but a fog horn is not made of fog; similarly, human rights are rights held by people, but property rights are not rights held by property.

45. Clint Bolick, "Property Rights Are Moving to Fore of Legal Reform," *Locke Letter*, John Locke Foundation, Nov. 1994, p. 1.

46. Stephen Moore, "How Governors Think Congress Should Reform the Budget: Results of a Survey of U.S. Governors and Former Governors," Cato Institute Policy Analysis No. 186, (Dec. 1992), p. 10.

47. Calvin Coolidge, "The Autobiography of Calvin Coolidge," (New York: Cosmopolitan Book Corp., 1929).

48. Tommy Thompson, interview with the authors, Feb. 1994.

49. Alvin Rabushka, "A Compelling Case for a Constitutional Amendment to Balance the Budget and Limit Taxes," Taxpayers' Foundation, May 1982.

50. Rabushka, "A Compelling Case for a Constitutional Amendment," p. 2.

51. Angelia Herrin, "Deadbeats Owe House Restaurant," *Chicago Tribune*, Oct. 3, 1991, p. 3.

52. Kenneth J. Cooper and Walter Pincus, "Disclosure Urged in Overdraft Case; House Probers Fault 24 Lawmakers," *Washington Post*, March 6, 1992, p. A1. Members were not charged for the overdrafts, nor were they charged interest on the money.

53. Charles Stenholm, speech at the National Taxpayers' Union Annual Conference, Nov. 18, 1994.

54. John Fund, "The Revolution of 1994," *Wall Street Journal*, Oct. 19, 1994, p. A14.

55. "Blame the Voters First," editorial, *Wall Street Journal*, Oct. 19, 1994, p. A14.

56. Christopher Georges, "Playing to Growing Antigovernment Sentiment, Many Candidates Criticize Pork-Barrel Projects," *Wall Street Journal*, Oct. 28, 1994.

57. Ibid.

58. John Merline, "Debunking the Spending Myth," *Investor's Business Daily*, Dec. 2, 1994, p. 1.

59. *Business Week*/Harris Poll, Nov. 1993

60. Review and Outlook, "Living Free," *Wall Street Journal*, April 7, 1993, p. A14.

61. Ginny Holt, interview with the authors, August 1994.

62. State of New Jersey, Office of the Treasurer.

63. At the time, the largest state tax increase in the history of the nation.

64. Stephen Moore, "Read Our Lips: The Tax Revolt Lives," *Reason*, June 1992, p. 43.

65. Joe Donaghue, interview with the authors, August 1994.

66. Governor Whitman, Budget Address, Trenton, N.J., March 15, 1994, p. 3.

67. Donaghue, interview with the authors.

68. Whitman, interview with the authors.

69. Ibid.

70. William Waldman, interview with the authors, August 1994.

71. Steve Sassala, deputy director of corrections, interview with the authors, August 1994.

72. Mayor Michael White, speech at Reason Foundation "No More Business as Usual" Conference, May 9, 1994.

Chapter 7: Safer Neighborhoods, Better Communities

1. According to social scientist James Q. Wilson: "The sheer number of police on the streets of a city probably has only a weak, if any, relationship with the crime rate; what police do is more important than how many there are, at least above some minimal level." Moreover, according to Wilson: "very large increases in the prison population can produce only modest reductions in crime rates." For example, between 1980 and 1990 the state prison population more than doubled, yet the victimization rate for robbery dropped by only 23 percent. See: James Q. Wilson and Joan Petersilia eds., *Crime*, (San Francisco: ICS Press, 1995), chapter 21.

2. Summarizing the findings of the professional literature on juvenile delinquency, Kevin Wright, professor of criminal justice at the State University of New York at Binghamton writes: "Research confirms that children raised in supportive, affectionate, and accepting homes are less likely to become deviant. Children rejected by par-

ents are among the most likely to become delinquent." See: Kevin N. Wright and Kerne E. Wright, "Family Life and Delinquency and Crime: A Policymaker's Guide to the Literature," prepared under the interagency agreement between the Office of Juvenile Justice and Delinquency Prevention and the Bureau of Justice Assistance of the U.S. Department of Justice, 1992.

3. Though overall crime rates have not increased appreciably in the past 20 years, violent crimes are up somewhat and juvenile crimes are up a good deal. See, for instance, James Q. Wilson, "What To Do About Crime," *Commentary*, Sept. 1994.

4. Police Foundation, "Reducing Fear of Crime in Houston and Newark: A Summary Report," Feb. 1986.

5. Ibid., p. v.

6. Mike Masterson, interview with the authors, May 1994.

7. Alexis de Tocqueville, *Democracy in America*, ed. J.P. Mayer, trans. George Lawrence (Garden City, N.Y.: Doubleday, 1969), p. 96.

8. Jane Jacobs, *The Death and Life of Great American Cities* (New York: Vintage Books, 1961), p. 41.

9. Dan Berglund, interview with the authors, July 1994.

10. Ibid.

11. Pat Drummy, interview with the authors, July 1994.

12. In the 1970s, San Diego's initial efforts at introducing neighborhood-oriented policing met with limited success. Restricted to a few specialized units, the idea won some converts but left the overall department unchanged. Like most new ideas, even good ones, it was greeted with hostility. It was an idea ahead of its time.

In the late 1980s, community policing was reintroduced and this time it took hold. Like other cities that have pioneered the concept—such as Edmonton, Alberta, and Madison, Wisconsin—community policing in San Diego was at first limited to a few neighborhoods. As in other cities, this limitation created a deep gulf and some friction between regular patrol officers and the neighborhood policing officers. Partly in response to this, San Diego became the first large city to execute a department-wide culture shift to community policing, in a reform termed "team policing."

13. Nancy McPherson, interview with the authors, July 13, 1994.

14. For juveniles, 6 percent of all boys will commit half or more of all serious crime generated by boys of that age.

15. Herman Goldstein, *Problem-Oriented Policing* (New York: McGraw-Hill, 1990), p. 104.

16. See David P. Cavanaugh and Mark A.R. Kleiman, "A Cost Benefit Analysis of Prison Cell Construction and Alternative Sanctions," prepared for the U.S. Dept. of Justice, May 1990. The study suggested the financial benefits of incarcerating a single inmate to be between $172,000 and $2,364,000.

17. Also, even among the violent, three strikes is an insufficient test to determine careerism. Many multiple violent offenders are only violent in their youth. The peak ages of criminality are between sixteen and eighteen, while the average age of prisoners is ten years older.

18. Chris Carmody, "Revolt to Sentencing is Gaining Momentum," *National Law Journal*, May 17, 1993, p. 10.

19. James Q. Wilson, "What To Do About Crime," *Commentary*, Sept. 1994, p. 31. Also see Allen Beck et al., *Survey of State Prison Inmates 1991* (NCJ-136949) (Washington, D.C.: U.S. Dept. of Justice, March 1993), p. 11.

20. Stephanie Mencimer, "Righting Sentences," *Washington Monthly*, April 1993, p. 27.

21. Quoted in Ian Fisher, "Pataki is Pressing to Ease Drug Sentences in Some Drug Laws," *New York Times*, Jan. 30, 1995, p. B4.

22. Ernest van Den Haag, "How to Cut Crime," *National Review*, May 30, 1994, p. 30. Part of the problem is that criminals serve only a small fraction of their nominal sentences.

23. James Q. Wilson, interview with the authors, Sept. 1994.

24. Daryl Stephens, interview with the authors, June 1994.

25. James Coleman, interview with the authors, August 1994.

26. Victor Trevino, "Zebra Territory: The Courage of Houston Volunteer Cops," *Policy Review*, No. 68, pp. 21–26.

27. Ibid.

28. Bettie Cadou, "Innovator in the Heartland," *City Journal*, Manhattan Institute, Spring 1994, p. 58.

29. Michael Beaver, interview with the authors, June 1994.

30. Mike Elder, interview with the authors, June 1994.

31. Bret Schundler, "On the Waterfront: Police Unions are Arresting the War on Crime," *Policy Review*, No. 69, Summer 1994, pp. 40–43.

32. Ibid.

33. Ibid.

34. Bret Schundler, interview with the authors, Dec. 1993.

35. James Q. Wilson and George L. Kelling, "Broken Windows," *The Atlantic Monthly*, March 1982, p. 31.

36. Wesley G. Skogan, *Disorder and Decline: Crime and the Spiral of Decay in American Neighborhoods* (New York: Free Press, 1990), p. 10.

37. Wilson and Kelling, "Broken Windows."

38. See Skogan, *Disorder and Decline*, pp. 65–84.

39. Police resources and internal recognition have been almost exclusively focused on murder, robbery, rape, assault, and the other serious crimes. Although no system can ignore violent crime, this approach sometimes treats symptoms rather than the cause.

40. Elder, interview with the authors.

41. Ronald Brownstein, "Taming the Mean Streets," *Los Angeles Times*, May 4, 1994, p. A21.

42. The aura of disorder led passengers to believe that crime was extremely high on the subway. About 97 percent of passengers said they took some kind of defensive action when riding the subway, according to surveys conducted by George Kelling in the 1980s. Less than 10 percent believed that the subway was safe after 8:00 P.M.; while 62 percent said that fear of crime keeps them from riding the subway at night. All in all, it was estimated by respondents that around 25 percent of all the city's serious crime occurs on the subways.

These perceptions were completely off base. In reality, the subway system was a relatively safe place: only 3 percent of New York City's recorded felonies occurred there. What accounted for the profound safety fears regarding the subway? High levels of disorder. Subway riders were "constantly exposed to disorder and left with the impression that no one is in charge. Broken turnstiles, litter, graffiti, the homeless, and panhandlers threaten riders and lead New Yorkers to believe that serious crime is more frequent," according to Kelling. This fear also contributed to that head-down, eyes-averted posture that is the hallmark of subway riders. Fear distances individuals from one another in a deeply disturbing fashion. See George Kelling, "Measuring What Matters: A New Way of Thinking About Crime and Public Order," *City Journal*, Manhattan Institute, Spring 1992, pp. 27–28.

43. George L. Kelling, "Reclaiming the Subway," *City Journal*, Manhattan Institute, Winter 1991, p. 20.

44. "Victory in the Subways," interview with Police Chief William J. Bratton, *City Journal*, Manhattan Institute, Summer 1992, p. 76.

45. Ibid.

46. Ibid., p. 77.

47. As we mentioned earlier, crime prevention is best accomplished by the family and other community institutions.

48. McPherson, interview with the authors.

49. At times, these norms were racist. As we saw in the systems chapter, rules introduced to prevent individuals from making undesirable choices often have the unintended effect of preventing them from making desirable choices.

50. For a fuller picture of Robinson's story, see James Taranto, "Drug Dealers' War on Housing," *City Journal*, Manhattan Institute, Spring 1992, p. 9–10.

51. William D. Eggers, "City Lights," *Policy Review*, Summer 1993.

52. Marty Collins, interview with the authors, April 1993.

53. Following the example of Portland, Oregon, Milwaukee developed and distributes a landlord training manual. The city also conducts hundreds of training sessions for landlords each year.

54. Edwin Meese III and Bob Carrico, "Taking Back the Streets," *Policy Review*, Fall 1990, p. 26.

55. Charles Francis, interview with the authors, Jan. 1995. The overall crime rate in the Charleston housing projects, which house 7,000 persons, was only 1.2 percent in 1993. This includes 0 homicides, 2 rapes, 5 robberies, 18 burglaries, and 16 aggravated assaults.

56. Judy Butler, interview with the authors, Nov. 1993.

57. Anne Jordan, "Walls that Unite," *Governing*, Oct. 1993, p. 33.

58. Ibid., p. 34.

59. Nicholas Elliot, *Streets Ahead* (London: Adam Smith Institute, 1988), p. 15.

60. Ibid., pp. 17–20.

61. Oscar Newman, *Community of Interest* (New York: Anchor Press/Doubleday, 1981), p. 133.

62. Jordan, "Walls that Unite," p. 32.

63. Ibid.

64. Newman originally advised cutting out Harvard and Rockford, the two worst street areas of Five Oaks, from the street-closure project because he was worried their disease would spread to other parts of the neighborhood. The other mini-neighborhoods would have nothing of it. "Newman said cut out the cancers," said Beverly Quedeweit, who supervised the city's role in the effort. "The community leaders said we will try therapy." Rockford had the second highest decrease in crime amongst all the minineighborhoods after the closures.

65. Five Oaks resident, interview with the authors, April 1994.

66. Jo Anne Means, interview with the authors, April 1994.

67. Beverly Quedeweit, Dayton neighborhood coordinator, interview with the authors, April 1994.

68. Jordan, "Walls that Unite."

69. Bill Lucas, interview with the authors, Nov. 1993.

70. Fred Siegal, "Reclaiming Our Public Spaces," *City Journal*, Manhattan Institute, Spring 1992, p. 38.

71. The $100 million includes $40 million in capital improvements, $50 million allocated to park operations, and $10 million for endowment.

72. Ibid., p. 39.

73. Daniel Biederman, interview with the authors, July 1994.

74. Ibid., August 1994.

75. Ibid.

76. *Private Security Trends, 1970 to 2000: The Hallcrest Report II* (Boston: Butterworth-Heneman, 1990).

Chapter 8: Beyond Welfare

1. Larry Townsend, interview with the authors, Oct. 1994.

2. Strictly speaking, it is not true that if you work harder you make more money. In a free market, labor is subjectively valued. Thus, Frank Sinatra can earn millions for singing a song while a construction worker may put in more effort and earn less money. In general, however, in a system of free exchange people are rewarded in proportion to how much value they give to others. (Frank makes the big bucks because people love to hear him sing.) Other things being equal, people who work hard to satisfy the wants of others will make more than people who are lazy. The more productive you are, the more you will tend to earn.

3. The welfare payments include payments to the six mothers plus two males living in the apartment, Johnny Melton (a brother of five of the mothers), and Gregory Turner (a boyfriend of one of the mothers). It does not include approximately $20,000 in Medicaid benefits received in the preceeding 13 months. See Tom Pelton, "Keystone Kids Neglect Case Unravelling; 75 Misdemeanor Counts Are Dropped," *Chicago Tribune*, April 21, 1994, p. 1, and Susan Kuczka, "Judge Pins Blame on Keystone Moms, Not Poverty," *Chicago Tribune*, Oct. 28, 1994, p. 1. Ms. Kuczka quotes Judge Lynne Kawamoto as saying, "Poverty is not to blame. The government is not to blame . . . Poverty is one thing. Poverty of spirit is another."

4. Kevin Johnson and Patricia Edmonds, "19 kids found amid squalor in Chicago apartment," *USA Today*, Feb. 3, 1994, p. 1.

5. Nancy R. Gibbs, "Murder in Miniature," *Time*, Sept. 19, 1994, p. 54.

6. Scott Fornek, "Young Victims of Their Age; '94 Crime News Put Children in Harsh Spotlight," *Chicago Sun-Times*," Dec. 28, 1994, p. 12. The two brothers, at ages 10 and 11, already had police records.

7. See, for example, Nick Gillespie, "Arrested Development," *Reason*, Dec. 1994, p. 6, and James Q. Wilson, "What To Do About Crime," *Commentary*, Sept. 1994, p. 25.

8. Quoted in Mickey Kaus, *The End of Equality* (New York: Basic Books, 1992), p. 238.

9. Michael Tanner, "Ending Welfare As We Know It," Cato Institute Policy Analysis No. 212 (July 7, 1994) p. 4.

10. Ibid., p. 3.

11. Ibid., p. 1.

12. Charles Murray, "The Coming White Underclass," *Wall Street Journal*, Oct. 29, 1993. Murray does favor "grandfathering" those already on welfare.

13. Ibid.

14. Moreover, when a father is present in the household, teen-age girls get pregnant 50 percent less often than their fatherless counterparts.

15. Irving Kristol, "Life Without Father," *Wall Street Journal*, Nov. 3, 1994.

16. Welfare is not the only factor at work. James Q. Wilson notes that cultural and noneconomic factors clearly affect illegitimacy rates. In Southern California, Mexican-American children in poor families are far more likely than blacks to grow up in a two-parent family and only one-fifth as likely as poor black children to be on welfare. What's more, the illegitimacy rate among blacks is low in a few states with generous welfare payments and high in the Deep South, where welfare payments are relatively low. See James Q. Wilson, "A New Approach to Welfare Reform: Humility," *Wall Street Journal*, Dec. 29, 1994, p. A14.

  Myron Magnet cites the shift in social, sexual, and cultural values that occurred in the 1960s as an important contributing factor. "I'd argue that such pathological, almost hereditary poverty came into being not in spite of, but because of, the cultural shift that began in the Sixties," writes Magnet. "[T]elling the poor they are powerless victims of vast forces over which they have no control relieves them of the sense of personal responsibility and freedom we all need to summon the energy and initiative to change our fate." See Myron Magnet, "Emancipating the Underclass," *Commonsense*, Winter 1994, p. 1. There is little that public policy can do, however, to affect such cultural factors.

17. Kay S. Hymowitz, "The Teen Mommy Track," *City Journal*, Manhattan Institute, Autumn 1994, p. 19.

18. Ibid., p. 24.

19. Ibid., p. 19.

20. Steven Waldman, "Welfare Booby Traps," *Newsweek*, Dec. 12, 1994, p. 35.

21. As noted earlier, Murray does favor allowing those currently on welfare to continue. Writes Murray, "Grandfather everyone now on the system, letting them retain their existing package of benefits under the existing rules. . . . [M]any of the women on welfare are so mired in the habits of dependency and so bereft of job skills that it is unethical for the government now to demand that they pull themselves together. . . ." In addition, any legislation changing the rules should have a grace period. "Nine months and one day is the symbolically correct period." Charles Murray, "What To Do About Welfare," *Commentary*, Dec. 1994, p. 32.

22. William Tucker, "Welfare 'Labs' Test Reform," *Insight*, May 30, 1994, p. 13.

23. Prepared statement of the Hon. Marge Roukema before the House Ways and Means Committee, *Federal News Service*, Jan. 10, 1995.

24. Tucker, "Welfare 'Labs' Test Reform."

25. Eloise Anderson, interview with the authors, Dec. 1994.

26. James Q. Wilson, interview with the authors, Sept. 1994.

27. Sister Connie Driscoll, interview with the authors, Oct. 1994. All subsequent remarks by Sister Connie are from this interview.

28. John H. Fund, "Welfare: Putting People First," *Wall Street Journal*, June 14, 1994.

29. Myron Magnet, interview with the authors, Dec. 1994.

30. Ibid.

31. Allen J. Beck, "Profile of Jail Inmates, 1989," U.S. Dept. of Justice, Office of Justice Programs, 1991, p. 9, cited in Conna Craig, "21 Questions on Foster Care," prepublication mss. (Cambridge, Mass.: Institute for Children and the National Center for Policy Analysis, 1995). This survey of 5,675 inmates in local jails found "an estimated 13.7 percent of the inmates had lived in a foster home, agency, or other institution at some time while they were growing up."

32. Toshio Tatara, "Characteristics of Children in Substitute and Adoptive Care: based on FY 82 to FY 90 data," American Public Welfare Association, Oct. 1993. In Craig, "21 Questions on Foster Care."

33. Ellen Perlman, "The Failure of the Adoption Machine," *Governing*, July 1994, p. 33. For each of the past ten years, more children have entered the system than have left it; in 1989, the number of children entering foster care was 40 percent higher than the number leaving, according to the American Public Welfare Association. The figure of 442,000 represents the number of children in state-run substitute care *at any one time*. Roughly 600,000 children spent all or part of 1994 in "the system."

34. Conna Craig, interview with the authors, Feb. 13, 1995.

35. Judy Jones Jordan, Arkansas IV-D administrator, testimony before the Senate Governmental Affairs Committee, July 20, 1994.

36. Nancy Duff Cambell, testimony before the House Ways and Means Subcommittee on Human Resources, Feb. 6, 1995.

37. Brad J. Franklin, "Delinquent Parents Targeted by DHS Collection Efforts," *Mississippi Business Journal*, Sept. 13, 1993. The task is "currently attempted by approximately 800 state employees."

38. See, for example, John O'Leary, "Private Companies Helping Mothers to Secure Child Support Payments," *Privatization Watch*, May 1992, p. 5; David Haarmayer, "Innovative and Unique Privatization Trend is Emerging in the Field of Child-Support Services," *Privatization Watch* January, 1992 p. 5; and Nadine Dohodas, "Child Support," *Governing*, Oct. 1993 p. 20.

39. Glenn C. Loury, "Ghetto Poverty and the Power of Faith," Center for the American Experiment, Dec. 1993, p. 4.

40. Charles Ballard, interview with the authors, April 1994.

41. Tucker, "Welfare 'Labs' Test Reform," p. 14. In many states, welfare benefits are so high that it's difficult for the potential father without a high-school education to compete with them. In this way, the states edge out the father in his role as "breadwinner." Also see Kristol, "Life Without Father."

42. Marvin Olasky, *The Tragedy of American Compassion* (Washington, D.C.: Regnery Gateway, 1992), p. 21

43. S. Humphrey Gurteen, *A Handbook of Charity Organizations* (published by the author, 1882), pp. 31, 141. In Olasky, *The Tragedy of American Compassion*, p. 75.

44. Ibid, p. 209.

45. "Working on Welfare," *Reason*, April 1994, p. 23.

46. See, for example, Howard Bloom, et al., *The National JTPA Study: Title II-A Impact on Earnings and Employment at 18 Months*, Research and Evaluations Report Series 93-C (Washington, D.C.: U.S. Dept. of Labor, Employment and Training Administration, 1993). Moreover, a 1986 review by the General Accounting Office of 61 job-training programs for the poor in 38 states found that the programs failed to assist recipients in finding jobs or to give them proper education and training.

47. Mickey Kaus, "The Work Ethic State: The Only Way to Break the Culture of Poverty," *New Republic*, July 7, 1986.

48. Tanner, "Ending Welfare As We Know It," p. 3.

49. Ibid., p. 4.

50. William M. Welch, "States Forging Ahead on Welfare Reform," *USA Today*, August 13, 1993, p. 6A.

51. Virginia Ellis, "California's Welfare-To-Work Program Shows Success," *Los Angeles Times*, June 15, 1994, p. A17.

52. Riverside Program Director Larry Townsend believes the program can be replicated and has prepared a guide to help other welfare-to-work programs. But Judith M. Gueron, president of the Manpower Demonstration Research Corp., the group that performed the major study that catapulted Riverside into the national spotlight, testified about her doubts to the Senate Committee on Governmental Affairs on Jan. 25, 1995. "At this time, it is unclear whether Riverside's success can be replicated in diverse communities around the country, particularly in inner-city areas," said Ms. Gueron. "The average JOBS program lags far behind and will have to change considerably to deliver on the program's potential." Ms. Gueron also testified that, "the difference between high-performance and average JOBS programs is not structural. The key is what staff do and how they do it."

53. See, for example, Dayna Straehley and Mitchell Landsberg, "Learning to Open Their Own Doors," *Hemet News*, August 15, 1994. In this piece, the authors conclude that "Riverside may have an edge over other places simply because of the missionary zeal its administrators bring to the program."

54. Larry Townsend, interview with the authors, Oct. 1994.

55. Ibid.

56. Riverside County GAIN handbook, p. 1.

57. According to Judith M. Gueron, president of the Manpower Demonstration Research Corp. "Three years after enrolling in Riverside GAIN, 41 percent of people were still receiving welfare benefits, although some of these were working and receiving reduced grants." Testimony before the Senate Committee on Governmental Affairs, Jan. 25, 1995.

58. Mitchell Landsberg, "Welfare Program With a Message: Get a Job," *Chambersburg Public Opinion*, August 16, 1993, p. 8A.

59. These figures are for all participants in the GAIN programs; the decrease in support for those who do land jobs is much greater.

60. Landsberg, "Welfare Program With a Message." The number of single-parent families that were still on welfare after two years was 47 percent for GAIN participants and 52 percent for non-GAIN participants. These figures are somewhat misleading in that more GAIN participants are at least working in addition to receiving welfare. Larry Townsend notes that a quirk in California law allows GAIN participants to defer their participation by working as little as 15 hours per week, meaning other states could attain higher figures.

61. Ellis, "California's Welfare-To-Work Program Shows Success."

62. Welch, "States forging ahead on welfare reform."

63. Lamar Alexander, "Cut Their Pay and Send Them Home," The Heritage Lectures, The Heritage Foundation, Washington, DC, No. 501, July 27, 1994, p. 2.

64. "Meet the Press," NBC, Nov. 20, 1994.

65. Adding on the earned income tax credit, somebody getting paid the minimum wage who has a few children would be above the poverty line in Oregon, where the minimum wage is $4.75. The employer pays nothing for the labor, contributing just a dollar an hour into an education fund that can be used for higher education by the

participant or his children. Though participation in JOBS Plus is not mandatory, those who refuse to participate will lose more than one-third of the spendable income available to those participating.

66. These include Massachusetts, Virginia, and Wisconsin.

67. "Working on Welfare," *Reason*, April 1994, p. 25.

68. Department of Health and Social Services, State of Wisconsin, "W2-Wisconsin Works," Dec. 1994.

69. Tommy Thompson, interview with the authors, Feb. 1994.

70. Lawrence M. Mead, "The New Paternalism in Action," Wisconsin Policy Research Institute, Jan. 1995, p. 33. Of the 25,921 teens subject to Learnfare, 13 percent faced attendance monitoring, but only 864 (3.4 percent) were sanctioned for poor attendance or dropping out. Learnfare was expanded to include children ages 6 through 12 in four pilot counties in Sept. 1994.

71. Neil H. Shively, "A Message from Wisconsin Governor Tommy Thompson: Just Do It! Welfare Reformed," *Rising Tide*, Republican National Committee, 1994.

72. Gerald Whitburn, interview with the authors, Feb. 1994.

73. Gary Coonan, Wisconsin welfare official, interview with the authors, Feb. 1995. In Pierce and Fond du Lac counties, AFDC caseloads dropped from 989 in March 1994 to 818 in December 1994.

74. Mark Liedl, interview with the authors, Dec. 1994.

75. Peter Overby, "The Michigan Experiment," *Common Cause Magazine*, Spring 1994, p. 14.

76. Andy Little, "Michigan's Private Charities Thrive After Load-Shedding," *Privatization Watch*, Nov. 1992, p. 3.

77. Overby, "The Michigan Experiment."

78. Lawrence W. Reed, "Michigan's Welfare Abolitionist," *Policy Review*, Fall 1993, p. 65. Notes Reed, "Many others who were physically or mentally unable to work are now receiving disability payments and other government services they should have been getting in the first place."

79. John Engler, *Creativity in Organizations*, unpublished draft, 1993. Engler also notes that 500,000 nights of shelter were provided at a cost to the state of less than $10 a night.

80. Sallie Tisdale, "Good Soldiers," *New Republic*, Jan. 3, 1994, p. 22.

81. David Ferrel, "Forcing the Homeless to Help Themselves," *Los Angeles Times*, August 8, 1994. Both quotes and data cited are taken from this article.

82. Ibid.

83. Ibid.

84. Estimates on the precise figure vary. See for example John C. Goodman, Gerald W. Reed, and Peter S. Ferrara, "Why Not Abolish The Welfare State?" National Center for Policy Analysis, Dallas, Tex, Oct. 1994, p. 3 or Tanner, "Ending Welfare As We Know It," p. 4.

85. Robert Rector, "The Facts About America's Poor," The Heritage Foundation, Dec. 23, 1993. The facts cited are all derived from government sources, most notably the Dept. of Housing and Urban Development, Dept. of Commerce, and Bureau of the Census, *American Housing Survey for the United States in 1991*, Current Housing Reports H150/91 (Washington, D.C.: U.S. Govt. Printing Office, April 1993).

86. Fund, "Welfare: Putting People First."

87. Tisdale, "Good Soldiers."

88. Mickey Kaus, "They Blew It," *New Republic*, Dec. 1994, p. 14.

89. Jason DeParle, "GOP Plans to Ax Over 100 Social Programs," *Phoenix Gazette* (from the *New York Times*), Dec. 1994, p. A1.

90. Wilson, "A New Approach to Welfare Reform: Humility."

Chapter 9: Economic Growth from the Bottom Up

1. Dave Barry, "All I Think Is That It's Stupid," interview by Glenn Garvin, *Reason*, Dec. 1994, p. 25.

2. This point is worth elaborating on. Like the song says, "A dollar is a dollar and a dime is dime." Tax dollars are no more powerful at creating jobs than are dollars spent by individuals. If it were not taxed away from you, your money would be spent (thus "creating jobs") or saved/invested (thus making funds available for business, thus "creating jobs"). The only difference is that rather than being spent according to the choice of the individual who earned it, tax dollars get spent by the government, ostensibly on behalf of taxpayers.

In addition, there are collection costs and transfer costs associated with taxation that eat up resources. In other words, the jobs resulting from private spending tend to create more wealth than the jobs resulting from tax spending, because rather than engaging in productive labor individuals spend their time moving dollars around.

The question is: can government really spend your money on you better than you can? Usually not. The debate in economic circles is over the relatively *few* areas where government spending may generate a greater economic return than similar money spent in private industry. One of these areas is basic infrastructure, such as sewers, roads, water plants, and airports. Some economists contend that government spending on basic infrastructure has a job multiplier effect greater than similar spending in the private sector. Why? Because the basic infrastructure allows for productivity enhancements across a whole spectrum of industries and economic activity. However, not all economists agree, and there is substantial disagreement regarding the magnitude of the multiplier.

3. Economic growth results from making better use of existing resources and thus raising people's standard of living. This is achieved by allowing people to specialize in the things they do best and giving them the freedom to innovate (build better mousetraps).

4. When government picks winners and losers, or guides investment and job creation, politics drives investment decisions rather than efficiency and productivity. When government attempts to intervene in individual cases (e.g., targeted tax breaks and abatements and targeted regulatory schemes), it generates uncertainty in the institutional environment in which investment decisions are made. We are grateful to Sam Staley from the Buckeye Center for Public Policy Solutions for his input on this subject.

5. As quoted in Tom Peters, *The Tom Peters Seminar: Crazy Times Call for Crazy Organizations* (New York: Vintage, 1994), p. 55.

6. Ibid., p. 26.

7. Thomas McArdle, "The Untold Philadelphia Story," *Investor's Business Daily*, June 20, 1994, p. 1.

8. Robert P. Inman, "Can Philadelphia Escape Its Fiscal Crisis With Another Tax Increase?," *Business Review* (Federal Reserve Bank of Philadelphia, Sept.-Oct. 1992), p. 17. According to the study, each additional $1 per resident of city revenue would cost that resident about $5 annually due to falling home values if the property tax were used, or $8 annually in missed job opportunities if the wage tax were used, or $8 annually in lower business profits if business taxes were increased.

Numerous other academic studies have similarly demonstrated that tax rates affect the geographical distribution of business activity. Research by economist Timothy Bartik has shown that taxes both impact a company's choice of location and reduce business start-ups of small or new firms. Researchers James and Leslie Papke found that "taxes are a determinant of the geographical distribution of business activity, employment and production facilities . . . differential tax burdens do influence location decisions." A study of 68 cities and suburbs found that for every 10 percent increase in a municipality's property tax rate, the property tax base dropped by 1.5 percent.

9. David Cohen, interview with the authors, Nov. 1994.

10. Larry Light and Julie Tilsner, "Up Front," *Business Week*, Oct. 17, 1994, p. 6.

11. Myron Magnet, "Cruel to Be Kind," *Wall Street Journal*, March 30, 1995, p. A16

12. Stephen Kagan, "New York's Vanishing Supply Side," *City Journal*, Manhattan Institute, Autumn 1992, p. 33.

13. Ibid., p. 35.

14. Jim Powell, "Taxpayers Accelerate Stampede out of New York City: Delaying Fundamental Reforms Allows Business Exodus to Continue," *Economic Perspective*, Citizens for a Sound Economy, Washington, DC, July 3, 1992.

15. U.S. Dept. of Commerce, Bureau of the Census, "City Employment: 1992" (July 1994).

16. Edward Rendell, interview with the authors, Nov. 1994.

17. Barbara Anderson, interview with the authors, June 1994.

18. See, for example, Richard Vedder, "State and Local Economic Development Strategy: A Supply-Side Perspective," Joint Economic Committee, Oct. 1981; Michael Wasylenko and Theresa McGuire, "Jobs and Taxes: The Effect on Business Climate on States' Employment Growth Rates," *National Tax Journal*, Vol. 38, 1985, pp. 497–511; James A. and Leslie E. Papke, "Measuring Differential State-Local Tax Liabilities and Their Implications for Business Investment Location, *National Tax Journal*, Vol. 39, Sept. 1986; p. 357; Victor A. Canto, "The State Competitive Environment: 1987–88 Update," A.B. Laffer Associates, Feb. 1988; Richard Vedder, "Tiebout, Taxes and Economic Growth," *Cato Journal*, Spring/Summer 1990; and Wei Yu, Myles S. Wallace, and Clark Nardinelli, "State Growth Rates: Taxes, Spending and Catching Up," *Public Finance Quarterly*, Jan. 1991.

19. See Richard K. Vedder, "State and Local Taxes and Economic Performance," *Southern Business and Economic Journal*, Winter 1992. The significant variations in performance between the states can partly be explained by factors largely beyond the control of state and local policy makers: different endowments of natural resources and energy, the amount of national defense installations and related defense activity, and disparate quantities of snow and sunshine. One important factor that state policy makers do control is fiscal policies.

20. By reducing the after-tax returns on additional work effort, high levels of taxation cause people to make alterations in consumption, investments, and work effort.

21. Richard K. Vedder, "The Impact of State and Local Taxes on American Eco-

nomic Growth," in *The Crisis in America's State Budgets: A Blueprint for Budget Reform*, American Legislative Exchange Council, 1993, p. 24.

22. Stephen Moore, "Taxing Lessons from the States: Why Much of America is Still in a Recession," Joint Economic Committee, U.S. Congress, Oct. 1993.

23. High personal income taxes lower after-tax incomes, thereby causing people to reduce spending on goods and services. Moreover, they raise the cost of labor because, in order to compensate for the lowering of after-tax income, firms are forced to pay highly skilled professionals more money in high income-tax states. This reduces company profits, discourages business formation, and encourages firms and high-income individuals to shop around for more tax-friendly states.

24. Vedder, "The Impact of State and Local Taxes," p. 19.

25. Pete Du Pont, "An Agenda for the States," The Heritage Lectures, No. 503, The Heritage Foundation, Washington, DC, May 24, 1994.

26. August Cibarish, chief economist, Wisconsin Dept. of Economic Development, interview with the authors, Jan. 1995.

27. Corp. for Enterprise Development, "Bidding for Business: Are Cities and States Selling Themselves Short?" (Washington, D.C.), 1994.

28. Ibid.

29. John Hood, "Ante Freeze: Stop the State Bidding Wars for Big Business," *Policy Review*, Spring 1994, pp. 62–67. Economists differ about the precise value of the package; estimates range anywhere from $250 million to $400 million.

30. Ibid., p. 65. The company's reasoning behind this demand was as follows: because the employees would be mostly in training for the first year they wouldn't really be adding much to production, so Mercedes shouldn't have to pick up the bill.

31. The United Airlines deal cost Indiana taxpayers over $100,000 a job.

32. Bill Styring, "The Ecodevo Gang Doesn't Shoot Straight," *Indiana Policy Review*, April/May 1994, p. 5.

33. See, for example, Thomas R. Plaut and Joseph E. Pluta, "Business Climate, Taxes and Expenditures, and State Industrial Growth in the United States," *Southern Economic Journal*, Vol. 50, 1983, 99–119; and Susan B. Hansen, "The Effects of State Industrial Policies on Economic Growth," paper delivered at the annual meeting of the Midwestern Political Science Association, Washington, D.C., 1984. The literature on the subject that does show states gaining through "job attraction" programs suggests that states only gain by shifting jobs. For the overall economy, these strategies have no net wealth creation effect.

34. These included state bond financing, special tax breaks, job training subsidies, and subsidized land.

35. Margery Marzahn Ambrosius, "The Effectiveness of State Economic Development Policies: A Time-Series Analysis," *Western Political Quarterly*, Vol. 42, No. 3 (Sept. 1989), p. 283.

36. John Rowland, "In Their Own Words," opinion piece, *New York Times*, Oct. 25, 1994.

37. "Labor Blows the Right Whistle," editorial, *Wall Street Journal*, Feb. 3, 1994.

38. Quoted in a brochure published by the Governor's Office of Economic Development, State of South Dakota, 1993.

39. Special Report, *U.S. News and World Report*, Nov. 1993.

40. By moving next door to South Dakota, Luetzow saved enough on taxes to allow him to lower his prices. And money saved on workers' compensation costs freed up 17 percent of the company's payroll.

41. South Dakota's success dispels the notion that only sunbelt states can be successful in attracting new firms. In his book *Job Creation in America* (New York: Free Press, 1988), economist David Birch provides similar evidence that northern states are capable of attracting new businesses and keeping existing firms if they provide the right business climate.

42. Peter Overby, "The Michigan Experiment," *Common Cause Magazine*, Spring 1994, p. 14.

43. Virginia I. Postrel, "Reconstruction," *Reason*, August/Sept. 1992, p. 45.

44. William Fulton and Morris Newman, "The Strange Career of Enterprise Zones," *Governing*, March 1994, p. 33.

45. See, for instance, Rodney Erickson and Susan W. Friedman, "Enterprise Zones: An Evaluation of State Government Policies," a report prepared for the U.S. Dept. of Commerce, April 1989. This report found that while the impact of enterprise zones on providing jobs to zone-area workers varies, most zones do contribute somewhat to economic improvement.

Another major study also found that zones resulted in job creation, but that only 15 percent of these are held by those living in the zone. See Leslie Papke, "Tax Policy and Urban Economic Development: Evidence from an Enterprise Zone Program," Working Paper No. 3945, National Bureau of Economic Research, 1992.

In a study of Ohio's enterprise zones, economist Sam Staley found that an enterprise program never made more than a small, mostly insignificant dent in job creation and economic development. In 1990, Dayton had the largest number of enterprise zone contracts in the state—84. The city was home, however, to over 8,600 establishments that employed over 150,000 employees. Due to the targeted nature of the program, the citywide impact of the enterprise zone was extremely limited. See Sam Staley, "Can Enterprise Zones Revitalize the Central City? An Ohio Case Study," Regional Policy Report No. 1, Urban Policy Research Institute, 1991, p. 14.

46. Philip Kasinitz and Jan Rosenberg, "Why Enterprise Zones Will Not Work," *City Journal*, Manhattan Institute, Autumn 1993, p. 69.

47. Susan Golding, interview with the authors, July 1994.

48. Michael Keeley, Deputy Mayor of Los Angeles, interview with the authors, Dec. 1993.

49. A 1993 survey found that 55 percent of cities with convention centers were planning expansions or new facilities.

50. Lawrence Tabak, "Wild About Convention Centers," *Atlantic Monthly*, April 1994, p. 28.

51. Edwin S. Mills, "Should Governments Own Convention Centers?," Heartland Policy Study No. 33, 1991. Most sports stadiums and arenas also fail to earn back their yearly operating costs. Only one built in the past 30 years has paid back its original investment—and that is the privately owned Dodger Stadium in Los Angeles.

52. Charles Mahtesian, "Escalation in the Convention Center War," *Governing*, July 1994, p. 19.

53. Ibid.

54. Ibid.

55. Keeley, interview with the authors.

56. Policy Economics Group of KPMG Peat Marwick, "The Arts: A Competitive

Advantage for California," executive summary, Oct. 1994, p. 1.

57. Ibid., p. 2.

58. Robert Baade, interview with the authors, Nov. 1994.

59. John Guardiano, "Government Should Leave Convention Center Business to Private Sector, Study Concludes," *Privatization Watch*, April 1991.

60. T. Keating Holland, "Field of Dreams," *Reason*, May 1990, p. 21.

61. Ibid.

62. Ibid.

63. Harry E. Teasley, Jr., is also a board member of the Reason Foundation.

64. Brian Doherty, "The Government as Innkeeper," *Reason*, Dec. 1994, p. 14.

65. Baade, interview with the authors, Nov. 1994.

66. Bill Blaha, "Raging Success; Chicago, Illinois' United Center," *Concrete Products*, Nov. 1994, p. 28.

67. Baade, interview with the authors.

68. Rick Henderson, "Fan Club," *Reason*, March 1995, p. 10.

69. Holland, "Field of Dreams."

70. Mitch Roob, City of Indianapolis, interview with the authors, June 1994.

71. Similarly, a 1992 study by the National Federation for Independent Business (NFIB) Foundation found that the burdens of paperwork and government red tape were the fastest-growing concerns of small business. Its October 1994 survey of members was even more compelling. Approximately 25 percent of NFIB members rate taxes as their number-one problem; regulation was a close second at 21 percent (in 1986, only 10 percent of NFIB members rated regulation as their most important problem). See NFIB, "Small Business Economic Trends," Dec. 1994.

72. David Friedman, "The New Economy Project: Final Report," New Vision Business Council of Southern California, Sept. 16, 1994.

73. Virginia Postrel, "Paternalism Test," *Reason*, Dec. 1994, p. 4.

74. Nancy Hollander, "The More Corrupt the Republic, the More the Laws," *Champion*, Nov. 1992, p. 3. Also see James Bovard, *Lost Rights: The Destruction of American Liberty* (New York: St. Martin's Press, 1994). Bovard's book is a stirring account of all the myriad ways in which the enormous growth in government laws and regulations are reducing our freedoms.

75. Barry, "All I Think Is That It's Stupid," p. 31.

76. Reference is to Stanley Greenberg's election poll for the Democratic Leadership Council (DLC). See, for example, Richard L. Berke, "Moderate Democrats' Poll Warns Clinton of Voter Unrest," *New York Times*, Nov. 18, 1994.

77. Ted Levinson, "Sour Days at the Lemonade Stand," *The Freeman*, Oct. 1994, p. 562.

78. Alexis de Tocqueville, *Democracy in America*, part 2, book 4, chapter 6, "What Sort of Despotism Democratic Nations Have to Fear."

79. "Monique in Tangles," editorial, *Wall Street Journal*, June 18, 1993.

80. Thomas D. Hopkins, "Cost of Regulations: Filling in the Gaps," Regulatory Information Service Center, August 1992. Also see Thomas D. Hopkins, "Cost of Regulation," Rochester Institute of Technology Working Paper, Dec. 1991.

81. Christine Todd Whitman, interview with the authors, August 1994.

82. Peter F. Drucker, *Innovation and Entrepreneurship: Practices and Principles* (New York: Harper & Row, 1985), p. 263.

83. See Peter W. Huber, *Liability: The Legal Revolution and its Consequences*

(New York: Basic Books, 1988), and Peter W. Huber and Robert E. Litan, *The Liability Maze: The Impact of Liability Law on Safety and Innovation* (Washington, D.C.: Brookings Institution, 1991).

84. Virginia Postrel, "Voters to Government: Back Off!" *Los Angeles Times*, Nov. 1, 1994, B7.

85. Cesar Conda, "The Regulatory Tide: High and Rising," *IPI Insights*, Institute for Policy Innovation, August 1994, p. 3.

86. William G. Laffer III and Nancy A. Bord, "George Bush's Hidden Tax: The Explosion in Regulation," Heritage Foundation Backgrounder No. 905, July 10, 1992. Laffer and Bord include indirect costs of regulation, and estimate the total cost of regulation to be between $811 billion and $1,656 trillion a year.

87. Council on California Competitiveness, "California's Jobs and Future," April 23, 1992.

88. Steven Hayward, "West of Eden: California's Economic Fall," *Policy Review*, Summer 1993, p. 44.

89. Ibid.

90. A modest workers' compensation reform bill was passed by the state legislature in 1993.

91. Hayward, "West of Eden," p. 44.

92. Ibid., p. 46.

93. Ibid., p. 45.

94. Golding, interview with the authors.

95. Postrel, "Paternalism Test."

96. Independent Regulatory Review Commission, Commonwealth of Pennsylvania, *1993 Annual Report*, 1993.

97. Richard Sandusky, interview with the authors, Feb. 1995.

98. *The Government Union Critique*, newsletter, Public Service Research Foundation, Nov. 25, 1994, p. 8.

99. Phillip D. Phillips, vice president for development advisory services, Fantus Co., letter to Michael Dolton, Greater Twin Falls [Idaho] Area Chamber of Commerce, June 27, 1986.

100. "Conservative Forum," *Human Events*, May 28, 1988, p. 22. According to Dept. of Labor statistics, 894,700 new manufacturing jobs were created in right-to-work states between 1975 and 1985, compared to 76,300 new manufacturing jobs in nonright-to-work states.

101. Based on figures from Employment and Earnings, U.S. Bureau of Labor Statistics, May 1994, 1988.

102. Gary Glenn, "Right to Work Led to Idaho Resurgence," *Times-News*, Sept. 2, 1991.

103. Catherine Arnst, "Telecom Reform is Becoming a Local Call," *Business Week*, Oct. 17, 1994, p. 178.

104. Robert Michaels, interview with the authors, Nov. 1994.

105. Gregory Millman, "Power Players," *Infrastructure Finance*, Oct./Nov. 1994, p. 15.

106. Steve Goldsmith, "Proposal 72 Would Free the Cabs, Help the City," *Indianapolis Business Journal*, April 18–24, 1994.

107. Tom Rose, interview with the authors, June 1994.

108. Ibid.

109. Stephen Goldsmith, interview with the authors, June 1994.

110. Gerry Lanosa, "Changes Would Spur Taxi Competition," *Indianapolis News*, Feb. 24, 1994.

111. Letter to the Editor, *Indianapolis News*, April 16, 1994.

112. James Chapman, interview with the authors, June 1994.

113. This represents a 120 percent increase in the number of licensed taxi companies in Indianapolis.

114. Rose, interview with the authors, Jan. 1995.

Chapter 10: A Community of Learning

1. At least we *think* Mark Twain said this.

2. Terry Moe, interview with the authors, Oct. 1994.

3. In 1981, Arkansas enacted a law called the Balanced Treatment for Creation-Science and Evolution-Science Act. After a court battle, it was ruled unconstitutional. In 1987, the U.S. Supreme Court ruled a similar Louisiana statute unconstitutional.

4. Milton and Rose D. Friedman, *Free to Choose* (New York: Harcourt Brace Jovanovich, 1990) p. 152. In many states and localities, the maintenance of a "common school" was mandated by law, and while this school generally received some tax money, parents contributed directly for the education of their own children.

5. Of the 146,760 elementary public schools in the United States between 1947 and 1948, 75,096 had a single teacher. U.S. Dept. of Education, *Digest of Education Statistics 1991*.

6. Ibid.

7. See Lance Izumi, "Willie Brown's LAUSD 'Compromise' Compromises Educational Quality," Claremont [Calif.] Institute Briefing 1993-22, April 14, 1993, pp. 6–7. According to Unified Teachers of Los Angeles campaign reports filed with the California Secretary of State, Mr. Horton received $55,000 in cash and in-kind contributions from the union. Other candidates also received tens of thousands of dollars.

8. U.S. Dept. of Education, *Digest of Education Statistics 1991*, p. 17.

9. The Goals 2000 program was initiated under President Bush (as "America 2000"), and enacted into law by President Clinton in 1994 through HR 1804, signed March 31, 1994. "Inclusion of the arts in Goals 2000 and the call for arts education standards reaffirmed the arts as essential to the education of every child," said John Mahlmann of the Music Educators National Conference. Those who admire tough standards should be comforted to know that the new music standards demand that eighth-graders be able to sing "accurately and with good breath control." ("National Art Standards Ready to Go," *State Legislatures*, June 1994, p. 4.)

10. The National Educational Goals Panel, as cited in *State Legislatures*, Feb. 1994, p. 12.

11. Article VII, Section 3, Texas Constitution.

12. Roger Rogalin, vice president of the school division of the Association of American Publishers, interview with the authors, June 17, 1993.

13. Texas State Auditor's Office, "Management Audit of Public Schools II: Controlling Costs Outside the Classroom," Report No. 3–117, May 1993, p. 56.

14. Thomas Paine, *Common Sense*, as quoted in *John Bartlett's Familiar Quotations*, 14th ed. ed. Emily Morrison Beck (Boston: Little Brown, 1968) p. 466.

15. Quote from printed materials distributed at the Marcus Garvey School.

16. Anyim Palmer, interview with authors, Nov. 15, 1994.

17. U.S. Dept. of Education, *Digest of Education Statistics 1993*.

18. U.S. Dept. of Education, "NAEP Reading Report Card for the Nation and the States," Sept. 1993.

19. U.S. Dept. of Education News Release, Sept. 8, 1993, based on the 1992 National Adult Literacy Survey.

20. U.S. Dept. of Education, "National Excellence: A Case for Developing America's Talent." Also see Sally M. Reis, "How Schools are Shortchanging the Gifted," *Technology Review*, April 1994, p. 40.

21. David Firestone, "Overflowing District in New York Holds Classes in Unusual Places," *New York Times*, June 8, 1994, p. 1. The author mistakenly notes an "unmistakable truth: there is barely any room for [students] in the city's public school system and barely any money to fix the problem." Mr. Firestone erroneously attributes the cramped conditions to a lack of resources, rather than to a misuse of existing resources.

22. Sam Dillon, "Teacher Tenure: Rights vs. Discipline," *New York Times*, June 28, 1994, p. 1.

23. In 1993, the average K–12 public school teacher earned $35,334 for 37 weeks of work.

24. U.S. Dept. of Education, *Digest of Education Statistics 1993*.

25. "Report Card on American Education 1993," American Legislative Exchange Council, Sept. 1993.

26. Frank J. Murray, "Justices to Assess Race Issue for Schools; Has Kansas City Judge Overstepped," *Washington Times*, Jan. 9, 1995, p. A1; "The Cash Street Kids," *Economist*, August 28, 1993.

27. "The Cash Street Kids."

28. "A Costly Quest for Racial Balance," *Christian Science Monitor*, Jan. 10, 1995, p. 1. The state claims per-pupil expenditures are $9,412 a year, the district admits to "only" $7,665. See Retha Hill, "School Desegregation Effort Shows High Cost of Change; Missouri Model Offers Lessons for P.G.," *Washington Post*, Jan. 9, 1995, p. A1.

29. "A Costly Quest for Racial Balance." About 1,500 white suburban students have voluntarily transferred into a district of more than 36,000 students.

30. Murray, "Justices to Assess Race Issue for Schools." p. A1. Although overall racial composition has not changed much, there has been an improvement in racial balance. In the 1983–1984 school year, about two of five Kansas City schools were 90 percent or more African-American; by 1993, that figure was down to only about one in five. See L. Anita Richardson, "Desegregating Public Schools," *Preview*, The American Bar Association, Issue 4, Dec. 22, 1994.

31. The implications of this exercise of power are terrifying. Though local voters had consistently rejected levy increases and bond issues, U.S. District Judge Russel G. Clark boosted tax rates from $2.05 to $4.00 per $100 of assessed valuation, and also levied an income-tax surcharge. In his 1987 decision (Jenkins v. Missouri, 77-0420-CV-W-4), Judge Clark wrote: "The court must weigh the constitutional rights of the taxpayers against the constitutional rights of the plaintiff students in this case. The court is of the opinion that the balance is clearly in favor of the students who are helpless without the aid of this court." (See Lynn Byczynski, "Judge Raises Taxes to Pay for School Bias Remedy," *National Law Journal*, Oct. 5, 1987, p. 25.)

In 1990, the U.S. Supreme Court upheld Judge Clark's decision by a 5 to 4 vote. In dissent, Justice Anthony M. Kennedy wrote: "Today's casual embrace of taxation imposed by the unelected, life-tenured Federal judiciary disregards fundamental precepts for the democratic control of public institutions," noting that "the power of taxation is one that the Federal judiciary does not possess." (See Linda Greenhouse, "Court Says Judge May Order Taxes To Alleviate Bias," *New York Times*, April 18, 1990, p. A1.)

32. Richardson, "Desegregating Public Schools."

33. Martha M. Canan, "Court Will Decide if Desegregation Cure Goes Too Far in Missouri Case," *Bond Buyer*, Jan. 12, 1995, p. 1.

34. Court opinions of the Federal District Court and the U.S. Courts of Appeals for the Eighth Circuit have suggested, without explicitly mandating, that the desegregation spending would continue until test scores in standardized achievement tests reached some national norm. In 1995, the state of Missouri asked the Supreme Court to terminate judicial oversight of district schools, arguing that the state had sufficiently remedied past discrimination. The district, anxious to see judicial control continue (and along with it the court-mandated spending), argued that despite the spending the district still had poor test scores, thus demonstrating that the remedy was not complete.

A 1994 report by the Harvard Project on School Desegregation concluded that Judge Clark's good intentions had failed to improve student achievement and had saddled the district with facilities that will be costly to maintain. "The money hasn't been targeted very well, and it hasn't been monitored adequately," says Professor Gary Orfield of Harvard University. (See "A Costly Quest for Racial Balance," *Christian Science Monitor*, Jan. 10, 1995, p. 1.)

35. Lyle Denniston, "Judicial Intervention in Schools Reviewed," *Baltimore Sun*, Jan. 12, 1995, p. 1A.

36. "Pudd'nhead Wilson's New Calendar," *Following the Equator*, 1897.

37. Peter M. Senge, *The Fifth Discipline* (New York: Doubleday Currency, 1990), pp. 42–43. The subsequent statement that "the system creates its own behavior" is adapted from a statement by Donella Meadows, quoted in the same source.

38. Los Angeles Unified School District data sheet, June 1992. Figures are for 1990–1991 school year.

39. Joann Wysocki, interview with the authors, Oct. 1994. Subsequent remarks by Wysocki are from this interview.

40. See especially John E. Chubb and Terry M. Moe, *Politics, Markets, and America's Schools* (Washington, D.C.: Brookings Institution, 1990).

41. Catherine S. Manegold, "41% of School Day is Spent on Academic Subjects, Study Says," *New York Times*, May 5, 1994, p. A13.

42. Moe, interview with the authors.

43. Bret Schundler, remarks at the Pacific Research Institute's Efficiency in Government Awards dinner, Jan. 19, 1994.

44. Bret Schundler, interview with the authors, Dec. 1993.

45. Schundler, speech at the Pacific Research Institute.

46. Bret Schundler, Inaugural Address, January 3, 1993.

47. Schundler, interview with the authors.

48. Dan Parks, "New DPI Structure Unveiled, Norquist Blasts Plan as Out of Touch," *Milwaukee Sentinel*, April 6, 1994, p. 1.

49. Vermont has long had a system of school choice. In towns that do not have their own high school, parents receive tuition vouchers for use at other public or private schools.

50. The MPCP is restricted in several respects. Only students from households

earning less than 1.75 times the poverty line may participate. Participating schools must be private and nonsectarian, with no religious affiliation or training, and MPCP students must make up less than 65 percent of all students in the school. See John F. Witte, et al., "Fourth-Year Report Milwaukee Parental Choice Program" (University of Wisconsin Dept. of Political Science and the Robert LaFollete Institute of Public Affairs, Dec. 1994), p. iii. For a review of national choice programs, see Janet R. Beales, "School Voucher Programs in the United States: Implications and Applications for California," Reason Policy Study No. 172, Jan. 1994, p. 11.

51. Witte, et al., "Fourth-Year Report Milwaukee Parental Choice Program," p. v.

52. Dan Parks, "Mayor Rips Education Bureaucracy," *Milwaukee Sentinel*, Nov. 17, 1993. By preventing parents from choosing church-affiliated schools, the Milwaukee program excludes approximately 80 percent of all private schools. U.S. Dept. of Education, *Digest of Education Statistics 1991*, Table 54, p. 66.

53. Dan Parks, "Religious Schools Eyed for Choice," *Milwaukee Sentinel*, Feb. 17, 1994.

54. Jonathan Kozol, *Savage Inequalities* (New York: Crown, 1991), p. 2–3, 5.

55. David Osborne and Ted Gaebler, *Reinventing Government* (Reading, Mass.: Addison-Wesley, 1992), p. 101.

56. Barbara Boxer with Nicole Boxer, *Strangers in the Senate* (Washington, D.C.: National Press Books, 1993), p. 220.

57. James S. Coleman, et al., *High School Achievement: Public, Catholic, and Private Schools Compared* (New York: Basic Books, 1982), p. 34.

58. Kozol, *Savage Inequalities*, p. 56.

59. Janet R. Beales, "Survey of Education Vouchers and Their Budgetary Impact on California," Reason Foundation Working Paper, August 1992. In this 1992 survey of parents in the Los Angeles Unified School District, the strongest support for vouchers came from those making less than $25,000 a year, nearly 62 percent of whom indicated they would use a $2600 voucher. Among African-American parents, 69 percent said they would use a voucher rather than send their children to the local public school.

60. California, Colorado, and Oregon. People feared choice for several reasons: 1) They thought it would take money away from existing public schools. 2) Many suburban voters believe their schools aren't that bad. 3) Suburban voters feared that choice would lead to an influx of low-income students to their schools.

61. Beales, "School Voucher Programs in the United States," p. ii.

62. Joy Smith, interview by Janet R. Beales, Reason Foundation, March 7, 1994.

63. Janet R. Beales and Maureen Wahl, "Given the Choice: A Study of the PAVE Program and School Choice in Milwaukee," Reason Foundation Policy Study No. 183, Jan. 1995. In reading, over 63 percent of PAVE students scored at or above the National Percentile Standard (NPS) on the Iowa Basics Tests, as opposed to 25 percent of MPS (Milwaukee Public Schools) low-income students. In math, over 60 percent of PAVE students scored at or above the NPS compared to 30 percent of MPS students.

64. "First Year Report: Educational Choice Charitable Trust," Hudson Institute with assistance from Butler University, Nov. 1992, p. 34. In Beales, "School Voucher Programs," p. 5.

65. Beales, "School Voucher Programs," p. 8.

66. Antonio Chavez, interview with Janet R. Beales, Reason Foundation, June 4, 1993.

67. Witte, et al., "Fourth-Year Report Milwaukee Parental Choice Program," p. vi.

68. Tommy Thompson, interview with the authors, Feb. 1994.

69. Myron Lieberman, Charlene Haar, and Leo Troy, *The NEA and the AFT: Teacher Unions in Power and Politics* (Rockport, Mass.: Proactive Publishers, 1994), pp. 2–5. These figures do not account for the spending power of the state affiliates; five state affiliates have budgets in excess of $60 million. See Myron Lieberman, "Teacher Unions: Is the End Near?" Claremont Institute Briefing, Dec. 15, 1994, p. 4. In California, the highest-spending lobby in the state is the California Teachers Association. See Janet R. Beales, "Class Notes," Reason Foundation, July 1994.

70. Milwaukee Teachers' Education Association, "The Sharpener," April 20, 1994.

71. Thompson, interview with the authors.

72. William Weld, interview with the authors, June 1994.

73. The funding varies depending on the municipality in which the charter school is located. Since money flows out of school districts to the charter schools, there is considerable hostility toward the program among existing public schools. Bureaucratic obstacles and lawsuits are likely.

74. Commonwealth of Massachusetts, Executive Office of Education.

75. The schools are the Miami Springs Satellite School at Miami International Airport, the Hidden Valley Satellite School at the Santa Rosa Hewlett-Packard plant, the North Beach Satellite School at Mt. Sinai Medical Center in Dade County, Florida, and a satellite school at Florida Power and Light in Pinellas County, Florida. See Janet R. Beales, "Satellite Schools: The Private Provision of School Infrastructure," Reason Foundation Policy Study No. 153, Jan. 1993.

76. Quoted in Janet R. Beales, "Teacher, Inc.: A Private-Practice Option for Educators," Reason Foundation Policy Study No. 181, Oct. 1994, p. 17.

77. Ibid, p. 5.

78. Ibid.

79. Ibid., p. 16.

80. Franklin Smith, interview with Janet R. Beales, Reason Foundation, April 19, 1994.

81. Kurt Schmoke, interview with the authors, Jan. 1994.

82. Ibid.

83. Moe, interview with the authors.

84. Peter Applebome, "Private Enterprise Enters the Public Schools," *New York Times*, April 8, 1995, p. 10.

85. David Frum, *Dead Right* (New York: Basic Books, 1994), p. 93.

86. The story of the French school revolt is described in Charles L. Glenn, *Choice of Schools in Six Nations* (U.S. Dept. of Education, 1989), pp. 32–34.

87. Douglas Phillips, "The Anatomy of Victory," *Home School Court Report*, the newsletter of the Home School Legal Defense Fund, March/April 1994, p. 4.

88. Brian Robertson, "Is Home Schooling in a Class of Its Own?" *Insight*, Oct. 17, 1994, p. 6. No one knows precisely how many home schoolers there are.

89. There is widespread agreement that home-school children in general demonstrate superior academic achievement. See, for example, *"Home School Court Report,"* the newsletter of the Home School Legal Defense Fund, Dec. 1990.

Chapter 11: Beyond the Beltway

1. Newt Gingrich, "What the Elections Mean to Conservatives," Heritage Foundation Lectures, No. 510, speech to a meeting of the Heritage Foundation's President's Club, Washington, D.C., Nov. 15, 1994, p. 10.

2. Six years in the making, the $33 billion crime bill narrowly passed Congress in 1994, continuing a thirty-year trend of increasing federal involvement in crime control. Dozens of crimes—from credit card stealing to gang membership—became federal offenses. Federal money was earmarked for local cops from Bangor, Maine, to Walnut Creek, California. For good measure, the bill included nearly $10 billion for social programs intended to prevent crime.

The money for the local cops ends in a few years, at which time cities will likely have to come up with the cash themselves for the extra cops hired. Either the federal government continues the money stream forever, or states and localities will eventually be responsible for paying for the expanded programs. Cities that begged for the federal funds may find themselves with an increased fiscal responsibility in the future. "It's more likely to just take a bite out of their [cities'] wallets," claims California Governor Pete Wilson, adding that money from the crime bill "comes with more strings attached than a marionette." See Pete Wilson, "Ending the Mandate Madness: A Contract to Restore State Sovereignty, The Heritage Lectures, No. 509, The Heritage Foundation, Washington, D.C., Nov. 18, 1994, p. 4.

3. Stephen Moore, "Government: America's Number One Growth Industry" (Lewisville, Texas: Institute for Policy Innovation, Feb. 1993), p. 8.

4. Adam Clymer, "G.O.P. Celebrates Its Sweep to Power; Clinton Vows to Find Common Ground," New York Times, Nov. 10, 1994, p. A1.

5. "Clinton: Voters Are Demanding That the Parties Work Together," transcript of press conference, New York Times, Nov. 10, 1994, p. B8.

6. Center for Political Renewal, A Project of the Progress and Freedom Foundation, "The New American Agenda and the 1994 Elections," Nov. 10, 1994. Survey conducted by Lunz Research. An overwhelming majority of those polled said state and local governments, not the federal government, should be responsible for crime, welfare, education, unemployment, and roads and transportation.

7. Wilson, "Ending the Mandate Madness."

8. "Clinton: Voters Are Demanding That the Parties Work Together."

9. Center for Political Renewal, "The New American Agenda."

10. Republican Governors Conference, "The Williamsburg Resolve" (Williamsburg, Va., Nov. 1994), p. 5. Part of the public's anger with government is the inability to sort out who is responsible for what. If a county social service program doesn't work, or if it takes a year to get the required environmental permits to build a microchip factory, who is to blame? The county? The state? Congress? A federal agency? No one knows the answer. To restore the public's trust in their government, accountability and responsiveness—two essential attributes of republican self-government—must be restored.

11. Press conference transcript, U.S. Newswire, Dec. 19, 1994.

12. John Harwood, "Reagan-Era Veterans Are Now Determined To Revive '80s Policies," Wall Street Journal, Jan. 4, 1995, p. A6.

13. Paul Gigot, "Alexander Runs Around, Not Over, 'Waxman State,'" Wall Street Journal, Nov. 25, 1994, p. A8.

14. W. B. Yeats, "The Second Coming." We do not expect that "mere anarchy" will be "loosed upon the world." There is a happy compromise between the iron

control of a central government and anarchy, namely, limited, decentralized government.

15. Quoted in Michael Kelly, "Rip It Up," *New Yorker*, Jan. 23, 1995, p. 34.

16. For a seminal discussion of this subject, see Thomas Sowell, *Knowledge and Decisions* (New York: Basic Books, 1980). Sowell points out that the level at which decision making takes place is crucial, and that there are advantages and disadvantages to either centralizing the decision-making process or placing authority with someone "in the field." Central decision-making authorities must depend on *general* knowledge, but usually have broad access to such information. Local decision makers have access to *specific* knowledge, but often lack "the big picture." As information and communication technology has advanced, it has become easier for local decision makers to gain access to general knowledge, but it is still difficult for central authorities to gain specific knowledge.

An example may illustrate. Federal health officials may have data indicating that, *in general*, 15-day treatments for alcoholics are sufficient. A worker on-site, however, may have firsthand knowledge of a *specific* individual's strong addictive behavior and thus recommend a longer treatment. It is far easier for the on-site worker to access the general information than for the federal government to gain knowledge of every individual's proclivities.

Thanks to fax machines, Internet, and other tools, field workers from Los Angeles, California, to Caribou, Maine, can obtain the most advanced, up-to-the-minute *general* information on a wide variety of subjects. It is much harder for federal officials to predict how a crime, health, or education program will work in Los Angeles or Caribou, because they lack *specific* knowledge of the social and cultural makeup of these very different locales.

Whether central or local decision making is preferable depends on the nature of the decision in question and the nature of the knowledge needed to make advantageous decisions. In general, however, advances in information technology favor a dispersal of decision-making authority.

17. Letter to Charles Hammond, August 18, 1821.

18. Keith Schneider, "A County's Bid for U.S. Land Draws Lawsuit," *New York Times*, March 9, 1995, p. A1. County officials drove a bulldozer past federal officials to repair a road the county claims is rightfully under its control. As the article's title suggests, the federal government has filed suit against Nye County over the disputed land.

19. Wilson, "Ending the Mandate Madness."

20. Tommy Thompson, interview with the authors, Feb. 1994.

21. The Federalist No. 45, at 292.

22. If words have meaning, then the Constitution lists certain powers and functions and prohibits others.

Of course, those activities that are "necessary and proper" to fulfilling a constitutionally authorized activity are expressly consistent with the Constitution. For example, the Constitution authorizes the federal government to wage war, and thereby also grants it the authority to engage in defense-related scientific research, the construction of military hospitals, etc. Similarly, the interstate commerce clause grants the federal government authority to regulate same, and thus federal preemption of states' laws on interstate regulatory issues such as telecommunication and banking are similarly constitutional. The fact that the necessary and proper clause and the interstate commerce clause authorize a wide array of activities not specifically mentioned in the Constitution does not mean that any activity not specifically mentioned is also authorized. Federal art, federal day care, federal puppet shows—it is impossible to stretch the Constitution so as to cover these activities, and attempts to do so tear the Constitution to shreds.

23. Quoted in Nancy E. Roman, "States Take the Tenth—and the Feds—to Court," *Insight*, August 1, 1994, p. 17.

24. The unconstrained expansion of the federal government could not have occurred had the courts fulfilled their intended role as watchdog of the Constitution.

Since the late 1930s, the Supreme Court has increasingly ignored the written Constitution, especially the Tenth Amendment, granting the federal government an ever-greater scope of authority. The implied powers of the necessary and proper clause and the interstate commerce clause have been expanded to a breathtaking extent. "The emasculation of the 10th Amendment adopted to reserve without question to the states their authority in all matters not delegated, first among which is liberty, is the most dramatic constitutional event of our time," writes former Tennessee State Senator Douglas Henry, Jr.

To get around the Tenth Amendment, the due process and equal protection clauses of the Fourteenth Amendment have been used to justify the transfer of authority to the central government. Responding to a Tenth Amendment argument in Garcia v. San Antonio Metropolitan Transit Agency (1985), the U.S. Supreme Court came close to pronouncing the Tenth Amendment null and void: "Any substantial restraint on the exercise of commerce clause powers must ... compensate for failings in the national political process rather than to dictate a 'sacred province of state autonomy.'"

With this ruling, the Supreme Court completed a cycle in which it had gradually thrown out two centuries of Tenth Amendment constitutional understanding. "The Court has done exactly what the Constitution pledged not to do ... make one of the parties to intergovernmental controversy the arbiter of the results," writes constitutional scholar Daniel J. Elazar in Daniel J. Elazar, "Courts, Congress and Centralization," *Journal of State Government*, Vol. 62, No. 1 (Jan./Feb. 1989), Council of State Governments, p. 46.

25. Roger Pilon, "Freedom, Responsibility and the Constitution: On Recovering Our Founding Principles," in *Market Liberalism*, by David Boaz and Edward H. Crane (Washington, D.C.: Cato Institute, 1993), pp. 34–35.

26. Until the 20th century, the Bill of Rights applied only to the legislative powers of the federal government. States had their own constitutions, most of which guarantee similar freedoms. In the 19th century, the equal protection clause of the Fourteenth Amendment was construed to mean that all Americans were protected from violation of their federal constitutional rights. This expansion of federal protection is known as the doctrine of incorporation. We suspect that much of the favorable sentiment associated with an activist federal government stems from the recollection of the civil rights battles of the early 1960s, when states failed to provide equal treatment for their citizens. The federal government did step in to right a wrong. There is a big difference, however, between protecting the rights of individuals against the power of the states and the expansion of government power at the expense of individuals.

27. Gigot, "Alexander Runs Around." Utah also has a constitutional defense council based on the Arizona model.

28. Douglas A. Jeffrey, "Spirit of Rebellion," *National Review West*, August 1, 1994, p. 7.

29. George F. Will, "Tenth Amendment Time," *Newsweek*, Jan. 9, 1995, p. 68.

30. Brian Robertson, "Governor's Mad as Hell, Won't take it Anymore," *Insight*, May 30, 1994, p. 10.

31. Though the writing of the Constitution was clearly a joint effort, Madison is widely viewed as the primary architect of the document that emerged from the Constitutional Convention.

32. The Federalist No. 54.

33. Linda Greenhouse, "Supreme Court Hears Arguments About the Limits of Congressional Power," *New York Times*, Nov. 9, 1994, p. A11.

34. Ibid.

35. Gregory S. Lashutka, "Local Rebellion: How Cities are Rising Up Against Unfunded Federal Mandates," *Commonsense: A Republican Journal of Thought and Opinion*, Vol. 1, No. 3 (Summer 1994), p. 66.

36. "Environmental Legislation: The Increasing Costs of Regulatory Compliance to the City of Columbus, Report of the Environmental Law Review Committee to the Mayor and City Council of the City of Columbus, Ohio," May 1991. The estimate given in the text is the expected cost of mandates during the decade of the 1990s. The total cost of the mandates is over $1 billion over a ten-year period.

37. Columbus was also compelled by the feds to spend $16 million to all but eliminate a chemical called atrazine from its water supply, though even if someone were to drink 3,000 gallons of water a day, that individual would not acquire a toxic dose of the chemical. (That individual would drown.) See Jonathan Adler, "Mandate Mania," *UpDate*, Competitive Enterprise Institute, April 1994, p. 3.

38. Gregory S. Lashutka, testimony before the Senate Committee on Governmental Affairs hearings on federal mandates on state and local governments, Nov. 3, 1993, p. 25.

39. In 1992, Colorado legislators passed a bill that would have instructed a joint budget committee to study the feasibility of the state's opting out of Medicaid and implementing its own Medicaid-style program. Many Colorado lawmakers felt they could operate the system in a more cost-effective way even with the loss of federal funding. They never got to find out; Governor Roy Romer vetoed the bill.

40. The EPA requires cities to remove 30 percent of all organic waste material from their sewage water. "Not the Feds' Business," *Intellectual Ammunition*, Vol. 3, No. 3 (Oct./Nov. 1994), p. 3.

41. G. Tracy Mehan, "The Buck's Passed Here": Unfunded Mandates for State and Local Governments," The Heritage Lectures, No. 467, The Heritage Foundation, Washington, D.C., Sept. 22, 1993.

42. Price Waterhouse has estimated the costs between 1994 and 1998 to be $54 billion.

43. If the money to perform these tasks were supplied, some anti-Beltway "revolutionaries" would be perfectly content to do Washington's bidding.

44. Susan Golding, interview with the authors, July 1994.

45. William Welch, "Governors: States Shouldn't Bear Burden of Balanced Budget Amendment," *USA Today*, Dec. 8, 1994.

46. George Voinovich, "MacNeil/Lehrer News Hour," Jan. 5, 1995.

47. Lamar Alexander, "Cut Their Pay and Send Them Home," The Heritage Lectures, speech at The Heritage Foundation, Washington, D.C., July 27, 1994, p. 5.

48. Before the federal government imposes a mandate (funded or unfunded) on state and local governments, a few important questions should be asked. First, is a

federal regulation needed, or can local policy makers handle the problem better? If yes, do the benefits of the regulation outweigh its costs?

Few domestic issues not already covered require uniform, one-size-fits-all regulations from the federal government. Even many cross-border water and air pollution problems are only regional in nature, not national problems. While there may be some issues that due to their universality should be dealt with through federal mandates—stratospheric pollution, for example—these issues are likely to be quite rare. Careful consideration should be given to local alternatives before imposing a federal regulation.

49. "Reinventing Government by Restoring State Sovereignty," *Intellectual Ammunition*, Vol. 3, No. 3 (Sept./Oct. 1994), p. 3.

50. George Allen, press conference, Richmond, Va., Nov. 14, 1994.

51. Robertson, "Governor's Mad as Hell."

52. Commonwealth of Virginia, "Self-Determination and Federalism," Executive Order Number 37.

53. One judgment from Judge Mueche, for example, overturned an executive order prohibiting inmates from receiving pornographic magazines. In addition, Judge Mueche ordered the state to greatly expand the number of law libraries for prison inmates ("so more prisoners can sue us," says the governor) and threatened to hold Arizona's Corrections Department head in contempt of court if he failed to comply with the orders.

54. Fife Symington, interview with the authors, Dec. 1994.

55. Lamar Alexander, "Cut Their Pay and Send Them Home," p. 4.

56. U.S. Dept. of Commerce, Bureau of the Census, *Statistical Abstract of the United States 1993*, p. 219. The federal government owns 53.4 percent of all these states combined, including 83 percent of Nevada, 68 percent of Alaska, and 62 percent of Idaho. The huge percentage of land owned by the federal government in western states is often a result of conditions placed on these states on their admission to the union. No such conditions were placed on eastern, southern, and most midwestern states.

The Constitution asserts that each new state must be admitted on an equal footing. This means that no limitation or stipulation may be put on any state that did not apply to the original 13 colonies. The doctrine, law for over 150 years, has been upheld every time the Supreme Court has addressed it. See John Howard, "On Appeal: Western Revolt," *The Defender*, Vol. I, No. 5 (Nov. 1994), p. 1. Under the equal footings doctrine, the Los Angeles-based Individual Rights Foundation has filed a lawsuit to establish that all public lands under federal control in the western states properly belong to the states.

57. The federal government has created a number of perverse incentives with regard to western land use. First, timber and mineral interests benefit from nonmarket-rate leases and subsidized federal land improvement. In the case of timber cutting, the federal government pays for all land improvement, but the states—which have no expenses—get most of the royalties for the land's use. This creates an incentive to overuse scarce resources.

A second problem, inherent in public ownership of land generally, is the problem of the tragedy of the commons. With common ownership of land, no one has an incentive to limit his use of the resource. This also results in overuse.

58. Elizabeth Larson, "Grabbing Back the Land," *National Review West*, Dec. 19, 1994, p. 6. For ten years, the feds had dragged their feet on repairing a road in his

county under the control of the U.S. Forest Service. This was deliberate. If the road remained unrepaired for long enough, its use would be permanently banned.

Nye County Commissioner Richard Carver finally decided to repair the road himself but was rebuffed by Forest Service officials who told him he couldn't fix the road unless they gave him a permit. This wasn't how Carver saw the situation. He said he didn't need a federal permit to repair the road. After all, only a few months earlier Nye County officials had declared all federal lands to be under their jurisdiction.

So on a summer day in 1993, in front of 200 spectators, Carver got behind the wheel of a county bulldozer and prepared to go to work. But blocking his way was a U.S. Forest Service official holding a sign that read: "STOP UNAUTHORIZED DISTURBANCE—Dave Young, USFS." A cheering crowd watched on for half an hour while Carver drove the bulldozer slowly down the road and Young walked backwards in front of it, all the while holding the sign above his head. "I will do everything in my power to bring the power of government back to the people," said Carver.

59. Patrick J. Buchanan, "The West Stirs a Rebellion for States' Rights," *Los Angeles Times*, July 22, 1994, p. B7.

60. Ibid.

61. Symington, interview with the authors. The federal government outright owns 42 percent of the land, and another 28 percent is Indian land under federal jurisdiction.

62. Buchanan, "The West Stirs a Rebellion for States' Rights."

63. Have you ever noticed how grandparents and grandchildren get along so well? Perhaps it is because they share a common enemy (the parents). In a similar manner, partisan differences among governors dissolve when they face their common enemy, the federal government. "Republican governors and Democratic governors are totally united to do the right thing," says Democrat Bob Nelson, Governor of Nebraska.

64. Any item receiving the support of the state delegations will become part of the States' Petition; this will be in effect the states' action plan. The governors are confident that it would be unthinkable for Congress not to respond to their formal demands.

65. If the States' Petition includes constitutional amendments, the amendments would require approval by a supermajority of state legislatures to proceed as part of the States' Petition.

66. Virginia Governor Allen has proposed a constitutional amendment with two parts: the states' initiative and the states' veto. The states' initiative would allow states to initiate amendments; if 75 percent of states approved an amendment it would go to Congress, which would need a two-thirds vote to nullify it. The states' veto would allow a three-fourths majority of states to repeal federal laws that unreasonably burden them, unless Congress overrides the states' action with two-thirds vote in both chambers.

67. Symington, interview with the authors.

68. Ibid.

69. Alice Rivlin, *Reviving the American Dream* (Washington, D.C.: Brookings Institution, 1992), p. 17.

70. Richard Berke, "Dole and Gingrich Embrace Before Republican Governors," *New York Times*, Nov. 23, 1994, p. A18.

71. Stephen Goldsmith, interview with the authors, June 1994.

72. William J. Bennett, "A Strategy for Transforming America's Culture: Friendships in the Good," The Heritage Lectures, No. 489, speech at the Heritage Foundation's Annual Board Meeting and Public Policy Seminar, Amelia Island, Florida April 16, 1994. Says Indianapolis Mayor Stephen Goldsmith, "Replacing the Department of Education with inner-city vouchers would assist the poorest families who are being failed most by our public schools."

73. Marlene Cimons, "Administration Sees a Reinvented HUD," *Los Angeles Times*, Dec. 20, 1994, p. A32.

74. New Mexico Congressman Joe Skeen has introduced a bill calling for the federal Bureau of Land Management to repeal its control over western lands.

75. Symington, interview with the authors.

76. Berke, "Dole and Gingrich Embrace."

77. Robertson, "The West Stirs a Rebellion for States' Rights," p. 12.

78. Michael Kranish, "Mayors Lead D.C. Rally for More Urban Aid," *Boston Globe*, May 17, 1992, p. 18. The story noted that "fourteen busloads of Bostonians, including homeless people who said that the city of Boston paid their way, traveled to Washington . . ."

79. Jerry Moskal and Sherry Jacobson, "Marchers Descend on Capital to Save 'Cities . . . Children'," Gannett News Service, May 16, 1992. This article noted that Kim Johnson, a homeless woman from New Haven, Connecticut, had come to Washington by bus.

80. Lawrence J. Kelly, "Why This Mayor Isn't Marching," *Newsday*, May 15, 1992, p. 62.

81. Bret Schundler, speech at the Reason Foundation's "No More Business as Usual" conference, Chicago, May 10, 1994.

82. Quoted in Richard Benedetto, "GOP Leaders Promise Power Shift to States," *USA Today*, Nov. 23, 1994, p. 4A.

83. Berke, "Dole and Gingrich Embrace."

84. Douglas E. Hall, Republican state legislator, in Dan Morgan, "Medicaid Windfall Cuts N.H. Deficit; State Officials Used Loophole While Bloating U.S. Budget," *Washington Post*, Feb. 28, 1993, p. A1.

85. Morgan, "Medicaid Windfall Cuts N.H. Deficit. What New Hampshire did was act rationally if reprehensibly. "Probably it wasn't in the spirit of the law, but it was in the letter," said State Representative Donna P. Systek.

86. "Give us the programs if you want," says Jay Heilor, director of policy for Governor Symington. "But you [the federal government] either have to give us the money you're collecting or say, 'It's your program, you do what you want with it.' In the meantime, stop taxing our citizens so heavily so we have enough capital to absorb these things."

87. Unsigned editorial, In "Beyond the Contract: Setting Priorities," *Wall Street Journal*, Dec. 15, 1994.

88. Education goals set by the state of California, for example, are only marginally preferable to those set by the federal government. Decision-making power should be transferred all the way down to individual schools and parents.

89. Cara Murphy, "Residents Decry Adding Tier to Lot One to Aid Merchants," *Beach Reporter*, Jan. 19, 1995, p. 1.

90. Lisa Mathews, "Pier Height Increase Nixed," *Beach Reporter*, Jan. 19, 1995, p. 17.

91. A $2.5 million parking garage costs each of the roughly 250 million Americans one penny apiece.

92. George Pataki, inaugural address, Albany, NY, January 1, 1995.

93. The prinicples of the new nation were not perfect, the greatest injustice being slavery, am institution clearly at odds with the vision of human equality described in the *Declaration*.

94. Two points are worth noting. The American Revolution was rooted in the philosophy of Locke (and others) who stressed the importance of individual freedom and private property. The French Revolution was rooted in the philosophy of Rousseau (and others) who believed in the primacy of the collective as expressed throu the *volante generale* (general will), and who denigrated private property rights.

In addition to different philosophies, the nations were also guided by disparate experience. In the limited government environment of colonial America, the ability of individuals to cooperate and thrive in the ansence of governemtn was known first hand. The colonists knew first hand the benefits of limited government. France, on the other hand, had experience only with the bureaucratic and extensive royalist regime. They were wedded to the idea of powerful government and hoped—unrealistically—to replace an oppressive powerful government with an enlightened powerful government.

INDEX